Richard Payne Knight (1751–1824) was a distinguished connoisseur and critic who played a very significant role in the cultural life of his day. His outlook on life, inspired by Enlightenment ideas and liberal politics, seemed reasonable to some and scandalous to others, and he was involved in some fierce controversies. In the 1790s he denounced the practice of 'Capability' Brown, who remains Britain's most admired landscape designer. Before that he had written a tract on phallic worship in the Catholic church, and later, despite being the most passionate admirer of all things Greek, he failed to recognise the merits of the Parthenon sculptures when they were brought to England, from which oversight his reputation has never recovered. Nevertheless Knight has serious claims on our attention, not only as someone who was in many ways characteristic of his age, but also because he built himself a remarkable house and established not only a garden but a way of appreciating landscape.

This study traces for the first time the way in which Knight's thought worked across the whole range of his interests, piecing together a coherent philosophical position, based on the sensibly regulated pursuit of pleasure, which, as the nineteenth century advanced, was increasingly out of step with the tenor of the times. The study shows how Knight's ideas mesh together with each other and how, when seen against the background of the culture of the day, landscape and architecture can take on potent and even inflammatory meaning.

Architecture, landscape and liberty

Figure 1. Sir Thomas Lawrence, *Portrait of Richard Payne Knight*, 1794.

Andrew Ballantyne

Architecture, landscape and liberty
Richard Payne Knight and the picturesque

Published by the Press Syndicate of the University of Cambridge
The Pitt Building, Trumpington Street, Cambridge CB2 1RP
40 West 20th Street, New York, NY 10011–4211, USA
10 Stamford Road, Oakleigh, Melborne 3166, Australia

First published 1997

Printed in Great Britain at the University Press, Cambridge
Designed in Quark XPress and Monotype Bulmer

A catalogue record for this book is available from the British Library

Library of Congress cataloguing in publication data

Ballantyne, Andrew.
Architecture, landscape and liberty: Richard Payne Knight
and the picturesque / Andrew Ballantyne.
p. cm.
ISBN 0 521 46200 2 (hardback)
1. Knight, Richard Payne, 1750–1824 – Contributions in aesthetics.
2. Aesthetics, British – 18th century. I. Title.
N7483.K58B36 1997
709′.2–dc20 96-16317 CIP

ISBN 0 521 46200 2 hardback

SE

To Hugh and June Ballantyne

A child in the dark, gripped with fear, comforts himself by singing under his breath. He walks and halts to his song. Lost, he takes shelter, or orients himself with his little song as best he can. The song is like a rough sketch of a calming and stabilizing, calm and stable, centre in the heart of chaos. Perhaps the child skips as he sings, hastens or slows his pace. But the song itself is already a skip: it jumps from chaos to the beginning of order in chaos and is in danger of breaking apart at any moment. There is always sonority in Ariadne's thread. Or the song of Orpheus.

Gilles Deleuze and Felix Guattari, *Mille plateaux* (Paris: Editions de Minuit, 1980), trans. Brian Massumi, *A Thousand Plateaus* (London: Athlone Press, 1987) p. 311

Contents

Illustrations

Preface

This work began in an attempt to understand the way in which Richard Payne Knight (1751–1824) thought about his house, which is represented in most of the essays written about it as a precursor of modernism. Whilst such an approach allows us to look back at the building and be amazed by its 'prophetic' qualities, Knight cannot have thought about it in this way when he designed it, and what I have tried to do is to re-establish the various frames of reference in cultural history which would originally have come into play in generating its meaning. This turned out to be an elaborate but rewarding task. Knight's way of understanding the world has its own intrinsic interest, and because of the wide range of his thought he presents an admirable subject for study in the cultural history of late Georgian England. He not only took an interest in a wide range of material, he also, as happens much more rarely, let his views be known, in his various books, and importantly in their footnotes. This study lets us see how he thought associatively, to reach an understanding of the world which seemed at the time to be falling apart into specialised concerns, leaving most people most of the time to be doomed to live by trusting the judgements of others. Knight's greatest achievement lay in making connections between things, rather than in any one of the various specialisms with which he concerned himself: his ideas when split apart are less remarkable.

Many of the processes which were working in eighteenth-century society are still at work today, and the feeling of fragmentation and disconnectedness which was felt then is seen more than ever as characteristic of the modern age, especially when it is styled 'postmodern'. We have ready access to more information than ever before, but unless we find ways to make connections and find paths through it, it will remain no more than a litter of curiosities, without ever awakening as a vital part of knowledge and of our lives. More than ever we need to be able to fix a cloudy form with an apt image in order to deal with it practically and effectively. The need for well-informed associative thought has never been greater, and the need for inter-disciplinary heroes should never have been more keenly felt.

Many people have, in different ways, helped to shape the ideas here, and I would like to thank them for their support, encouragement and guidance in areas of knowledge which were unfamiliar to me when I set out. My parents head the list, and the book is dedicated to them; the rest of it is incomplete, but certainly includes the owners (who would prefer to remain unnamed) of the various properties and pictures which are discussed; also, the Department of Architecture at the University of Newcastle, and, in alphabetical order, Roger Harper, Gillian Ince, Peter Klein, Claire Lamont, Diana Leitch, Gerard Loughlin, Alison Low, Sophia Preston, William Tavernor and Peter Willis.

Introduction

Richard Payne Knight was well known as a connoisseur during his lifetime, especially between 1794 and about 1816, after which date his wider renown deserted him. He has not been forgotten, but has become a rather marginal figure, who appears in thousands of footnotes because of his involvement with a great many issues and ideas, and particularly on account of his activities as a collector, an architect and a landscape gardener. There have been books about him: Jean-Jacques Mayoux's *Richard Payne Knight et le pittoresque* of 1932 was the first, to be followed by Frank J. Messmann, *Richard Payne Knight: The Twilight of Virtuosity* (1974) and an exhibition and collection of essays edited by Michael Clarke and Nicholas Penny, *The Arrogant Connoisseur: Richard Payne Knight 1751–1824* (1982). He figures significantly in Christopher Hussey's *The Picturesque, Studies in a Point of View* (1927) which revived an interest in Knight's ideas and their influence on painters and architects. He is also important in Walter Hipple's philosophical study *The Beautiful, The Sublime, and The Picturesque in Eighteenth-Century British Aesthetic Theory* (1957), and was one of the central characters in an exhibition held in 1994, which commemorated the bicentenary of the publication of his didactic poem *The Landscape* and produced a book of essays, *The Picturesque Landscape: Visions of Georgian Herefordshire*, edited by Stephen Daniels and Charles Watkins. There have been scholarly essays, most of them about his views on architecture and landscape, some, more recently, about his sexuality;[1] and the late Christopher Hussey, editor of *Country Life*, had intended, with Elisabeth Inglis-Jones, to write a biography. Above all, though, Knight continues to flourish in the footnotes to articles which are not primarily about him, but on which he has a bearing. There is something like poetic justice in this state

1 Nikolaus Pevsner, 'Richard Payne Knight', *The Art Bulletin*, vol. 31 (Rhode Island: 1949), reprinted in *Studies in Art, Architecture and Design*, 2 vols. (London: Thames and Hudson, 1968), vol. I; Christopher Hussey, 'A Regency Prophet of Modernism', *Country Life Annual* (London: Country Life, 1956); Susan Lang, 'Payne Knight and the Idea of Modernity', in *Concerning Architecture: Essays on Architectural Writers and Writing Presented to Nikolaus Pevsner*, ed. John Summerson (Harmondsworth: Penguin, 1968); Alistair Rowan, 'Downton Castle, Herefordshire', in *The Country Seat: Studies in the History of the British Country House Presented to Sir John Summerson*, ed. Howard Colvin and John Harris (Harmondsworth: Allen Lane, 1970); Alessandra Ponte, 'Architecture and Phallocentrism in Richard Payne Knight's Theory', in *Sexuality and Space*, ed. Beatriz Colomina (New York:

of affairs, because Knight's own writings were copiously annotated, to the point that some of them seem to be nothing but footnotes. The rich range of associations in his mind, and the varied scholarly evidence he could adduce in order to draw a conclusion, can lead the reader off at tangents to find, for example, that a poem about the landscape details descriptions of horrific tortures, or that an archaeological record launches into a diatribe against syphilis. The effect can be alarming, and even when, as is usually the case, the footnotes are concerned with more characteristic themes (such as the play of light among trees, or the use of a word in Homer) they can make the works seem diffuse or mis-classified. This is a major problem in dealing with Knight's *œuvre,* as what makes it distinctive and impressive is his ability to move fluently between his different concerns. The need to reconstitute background material in order to make sense of what Knight said makes it necessary to separate ideas into categories which he fused together; and so the various specialised studies of Knight have lost sight of the coherence of his thought and the ideas which most inspired him. The present study is indebted to the various works mentioned above, especially the essays by Nicholas Penny, Peter Funnell, Claudia Stumpf and Michael Clarke collected in *The Arrogant Connoisseur*, but it attempts to piece together the various strands of Knight's thought so that his achievement becomes more clear. The nature of the material, and the need to make associations from one subject to another, has governed the ordering of the text, which ideally would have many tracks through it, to be discovered on repeated readings, the range of associations growing richer with each repetition. The presentation of the material aims to be as methodical as it can be without altogether losing sight of its subject's continual will to digress. The first chapter is introductory and gives a basic orientation in some of the major ideas and the circumstances of Knight's life, and the second examines the theme of philhellenism, which was pervasive in his thought and frequently reappears. Knight's ideas about knowledge, religion and politics are presented in the next three chapters, bringing us to the chapters on taste, landscape design and Knight's own house and garden, which make use of ideas from the earlier chapters as they progress, and so the range of associations and allusions builds up as the text moves on. The structure is determined by the need to invest various terms with meaning, so that once the investment has been made then the meaning can be recalled by allusion. Knight's house and garden now have a place of established significance in architectural history. The house makes a brief appearance in Sir John Summerson's *Architecture in Britain, 1530–1830* (1953), which

Princeton Architectural Press, 1992); G. S. Rousseau, 'The Sorrows of Priapus: Anticlericalism, Homosocial Desire, and Richard Payne Knight', in *Sexual Underworlds of the Enlightenment,* ed. Rousseau and Porter (Manchester University Press, 1987); Giancarlo Carabelli, *In the Image of Priapus* (London: Duckworth, 1996); Ian Jenkins and Kim Sloan, *Vases and Volcanoes: Sir William Hamilton and His Collection* (London: British Museum, 1996).

has been tremendously widely read. The growing interest in the building was reflected in Summerson's two biographies of John Nash,[2] in the second of which Downton Castle's crucial influence on Nash is made clear; and in David Watkin's treatment in his study *The English Vision: the Picturesque in Architecture, Landscape and Garden Design* (1982). Knight, then, is very far from being forgotten, but he is equally far from being generally understood. He has turned from being a writer to a denizen of footnotes, and this book is an attempt to bring him out of their mottled shadows. In those shadows he is fleetingly to be glimpsed almost everywhere, and it can be seen that his influence was a part of the connective tissue of the society in which he lived. Such characters must be understood if we are to appreciate the mechanisms which make a society work, and the society which shaped the taste of persons of quality in late Georgian England has had a lasting influence.

2 *John Nash, Architect to King George IV* (London: George Allen and Unwin, 1935; 2nd edn, 1949); *The Life and Work of John Nash, Architect* (London: George Allen and Unwin, 1980).

1 Setting the scene

Divide and prosper

The basis of prosperity, Adam Smith famously explained, is the division of labour; and he began his analysis of the workings of commercial society by illustrating what he meant with the example of a pin-maker. A workman without special knowledge of the pin-making business, left to his own devices, 'could scarce, perhaps, with his utmost industry, make one pin in a day, and certainly could not make twenty';[1] but in practice the trade was carried on as a series of distinct operations, most of which were carried out by specialists: 'One man draws out the wire, another straightens it, a third cuts it, a fourth points it' and so on.[2] When the various operations had been divided up among ten specialists, Smith said, a small manufactory could produce more than 48,000 pins in a day: he had seen it done. The division of labour increased efficiency in three ways. First because each craftsman was more practised and therefore more expert in his own particular task, second because no time was wasted in moving from one task to another and third because, given the repetition and simplification, machines could be introduced to help.[3] When Smith (1723–90) published this example in 1776, one of his friends, Adam Ferguson (1723–1816), had already applied the same idea more widely in *An Essay on the History of Civil Society* (1767), a work of political theory which overlaps, but remains less well known than, Smith's *Wealth of Nations*. Ferguson said that every artist finds that

> the more he can confine his attention to a particular part of any work, his productions are the more perfect, and grow under his hands in the greater quantities. Every undertaker in manufacture finds, that the more he can subdivide the tasks of his workmen,

1 *An Inquiry into the Nature and Causes of the Wealth of Nations* (1776), ed. Edwin Cannan, 2 vols. (London: Methuen, 1904,) vol. I, p. 6.

2 Ibid.

3 Ibid., p. 7.

> and the more hands he can employ on separate articles, the more are his expences [*sic*] diminished, and his profits increased. The consumer too requires, in every kind of commodity, a workmanship more perfect than hands employed on a variety of subjects can produce; and the progress of commerce is but a continued subdivision of the mechanical arts.[4]

This state of affairs did not apply only to manufacture, but also to thinking itself, which, 'in this age of separations, may become a peculiar craft'.[5] The commercial logic demanded and produced gains in efficiency, but at the loss of a view of the whole and of a unified culture in which members of all parts of a complex modern society could participate. The man of action would specialise in his actions, but speculative leisure for literary conversation or study would be the preserve of others.

> In this scene, matters that have little reference to the active pursuits of mankind, are made subjects of inquiry, and the exercise of sentiment and reason itself becomes a profession. The songs of the bard, the harangues of the statesman and the warrior, the tradition and the story of ancient times, are considered as the models, or the earliest production, of so many arts, which it becomes the object of different professions to copy or to improve. The works of fancy, like the subjects of natural history, are distinguished into classes and species; the rules of every particular kind are distinctly collected; and the library is stored, like the warehouse, with the finished manufacture of different arts, who, with the aids of the grammarian and the critic, aspire, each in his particular way, to instruct the head, or to move the heart.[6]

William Hazlitt (1778–1830), a cultural critic interested in politics, echoed these remarks in 1814 in a way which suggests that the artistic community had paid less attention than it should to Ferguson's analysis:

> There is a certain pedantry, a given division of labour, an almost exclusive attention to some one object, which is necessary in Art, as in all the works of man. Without this, the unavoidable consequence is a gradual dissipation and prostitution of the intellect, which leaves the mind without energy to devote to any pursuit the pains necessary to excel in it, and suspends every purpose in irritable imbecility. But the modern painter is bound not only to run the circle of his own art, but of all others. He must be 'statesman, chemist, fiddler and buffoon'. He must have too

4 Adam Ferguson, *An Essay on the History of Civil Society* (1767), ed. Duncan Forbes (Edinburgh University Press, 1966), p. 181. See also John Barrell, 'Visualising of the Division of Labour: William Pyne's *Microcosm*' in *The Birth of Pandora and the Division of Knowledge* (London: Macmillan, 1992), pp. 89–118.

5 Ferguson, *Civil Society*, p. 183.

6 Ibid., p. 189.

> many accomplishments to excel in his profession. When every one is bound to know every thing, there is no time to do any thing.[7]

The quotations given here span the active life of Richard Payne Knight (1751–1824), who was born into a culture which was fragmenting under the influence of commercial imperatives too strong to be resisted. He accepted what Ferguson and Smith proposed, as quoted here, and inherited one of the first great industrial fortunes, which had been built up on sound commercial practices. This fortune gave Knight the freedom to live the life he chose, in which he attempted to combine active involvement in affairs with studious contemplation. He tried to form a view of the whole, resisting, as far as he could, the fragmentation which the necessary tendency to specialise brings with it; and it was always a danger that he would disappear from view in a cloud of 'irritable imbecility', dissipating his energies among too many accomplishments. That he did not do so is a considerable achievement. It is true enough that he did not achieve a towering eminence in any single field of endeavour, but he did establish himself as a significant presence in a surprising number, and he is an outstandingly valuable subject for the study of cultural history, because he is an unusually accessible member of a small group of men, the dilettanti, who influenced the politely accomplished part of eighteenth-century English society. Knight is accessible to us because he was more diligent than most in publishing his researches into different fields of enquiry, which makes it possible to trace his thought as it moved across from religion into politics and landscape design, into discussions of taste and ancient Greek, into poetry and architecture. Even in a single work Knight's writing digresses in every direction as we advance, and his lengthy footnotes take us off on fresh lines of thought. He cultivated a coherent philosophical viewpoint, which he consistently maintained and developed in his various writings, though it has passed unnoticed because of the division of scholarly labour, which has specialised to a degree which Ferguson might theoretically have conceived, but which would have astonished him as a practical fact of life. We now take it for granted that there should be professionals of thought in every field of endeavour, and professionalism now has such a hold on our various fragmented systems of value that the dilettante has a bad name. In the same way that the French *amateur*, an enthusiast who did things for the love of it, has turned in English into the amateur, who is expected to be more or less inept, so the Italian *dilettante*, who took pleasure in things, has become in English the dilettante who dabbles superficially in whatever

7 'Fine Arts. Whether they are Promoted by Academies and Public Institutions, continued', in Hazlitt, *Complete Works*, ed. P. P. Howe, 21 vols. (London: Dent, 1930–4), vol. XVIII, p. 41n. See also John Barrell, *The Political Theory of Painting from Reynolds to Hazlitt: 'The Body of the Public'* (New Haven: Yale University Press, 1986), p. 331.

takes his fancy, but has no serious insight. Such views are shaped by commercial values, in which the disinterested pursuit of a wide range of knowledge, rather than the sharply focused execution of a well-defined task, seems to lack direction and to be inefficient.

The Society of Dilettanti was founded in the eighteenth century by a group of men who took their pleasures very seriously indeed, pleasures of both a sensual and an intellectual kind. They had ample means, in some cases more than ample and they had all been to Italy on the Grand Tour to civilise them and make them men of the world. This was the society's official condition of membership, but Horace Walpole, Lord Orford (who was not a member of the society) said that the real condition of membership was being drunk.[8] The pages of the society's minute book are splashed with red wine, lending some support to Walpole's view; but the conversation, however well lubricated, could certainly take an intellectual turn, and Knight, in the society's defence when its morality was called into question, described it po-faced as 'a society instituted for the encouragement of liberal art, and of those branches of literature which are peculiarly connected with it'.[9] The society was responsible for the publication of some of the finest works of archaeological scholarship of the day, the most famous of them being Stuart and Revett's account of *The Antiquities of Athens*.[10] That the society's work was conducted without the pressure of deadlines, and to the most exacting standards, can be seen for example in the sumptuous production of *Specimens of Antient Art and Sculpture*, a folio-sized book which was put together by two of the society's members, Knight himself and Charles Townley, and illustrated with extraordinarily fine plates (figure 2). Townley never published anything under his own name, which is surprising given the talents with which he was credited, but his collection of antique sculpture is now in the British Museum. His collection is displayed in a basement, but it was celebrated in its day and when it first arrived at the museum it was the chief attraction. It has been overshadowed, and is shown as displaying a late eighteenth-century collector's taste for the antique, rather than as the superlative examples of classical Greek sculpture which they were taken to be at the time. Townley's collection is now seen to be made up from Hellenistic statues and Roman copies of Greek originals, and has been upstaged by more recent acquisitions of genuinely classical work, principally by the Elgin marbles, the sculptures from the Parthenon, which have a spacious gallery on the museum's main floor. Knight left own his collection of antiquities to the museum, but his means were more modest than Townley's and he collected smaller

8 *The Yale Edition of Horace Walpole's Correspondence*, ed. W. S. Lewis, 48 vols. (New Haven: Yale University Press, 1937–83), vol. XVIII, p. 211, Sir Horace Walpole to Sir Horace Mann, 14 April 1743.

9 *The Progress of Civil Society: A Didactic Poem* (London: 1796), p. xvi.

10 James Stuart and Nicholas Revett, *The Antiquities of Athens*, 4 vols. (London: Society of Dilettanti, vol. I, 1762; II, 1787; III, 1794; IV, 1816).

Figure 2. Townley's *Venus*, from *Specimens of Antient Sculpture*, Society of Dilettanti, folio, 1809. Knight compared the pedimental sculptures from the Parthenon unfavourably with this statue.

objects: coins, bronze statuettes and cameos, along with Old Master drawings. The small objects are dispersed and do not have a striking presence; nevertheless, once alerted, one can find objects from the Payne Knight Bequest regularly on display. The British Museum is now a vast institution which soon exhausts the visitor who thinks of looking all round it, but what is on show to the public at any given time represents only a small part of the museum's holdings: behind secure doors there are study rooms where scholars can examine objects which are not on display, and beyond them there are rooms where objects are kept in store. Knight's bequest is mostly kept out of sight, but it remains important for study, and was very much more important to the museum when the bequest was made, when the institution was much smaller and less well endowed.

By contrast with Townley, Knight published extensively. He was opinionated, and let his views be known on a good many matters, ranging from the authenticity of ancient Greek inscriptions to the need for political reform and the proper way to design gardens. He moved from one subject to another, taking delight in them but nevertheless making serious contributions in some fields of endeavour. His most enduring enthusiasm was Greek scholarship, in which area his work has been entirely superseded, but he had significant influence on the design of landscapes and buildings, which is where his reputation endures most securely. One reason to study Knight is because his range of interests is so well documented. He was a leading light in the Society of Dilettanti, and indeed in that company he could pass as a genius. There were other members, certainly, who were more accomplished in one field or another, and who consequently have more illustrious reputations, but Knight was accomplished across a wider range of polite activities, and could hold forth on a wider variety of topics of common concern. (Who remembers Sir Joshua Reynolds, except for his paintings? What of Sir Joseph Banks's reputation beyond natural history?) Knight's virtuosity has been his downfall, as his many achievements look rather small when seen individually, but come to seem significant when we look more closely and see that they are all the achievements of one man, just as the significance of his collection is easy to miss, even if one is attentive to the labels on the exhibits in the glass cases. Knight's presence is often unarresting, but was much more pervasive than can be guessed by examining in isolation any given sign of his activity. He is an outstanding example of the small class of dilettanti, who were tremendously influential at the end of the eighteenth century. They were well educated, and showed off their learning to one another; they prided themselves on their taste and sense of decorum; and with their substantial means they commissioned work from painters and sculptors. Knight had influence within this group, and the group had a more or less decisive influence on the artistic and cultural world of the day: what they thought mattered to artists looking for commissions for the highest class of painting, to dealers in pictures and antiquities and also to those outside the immediate group who would follow its lead rather than risk a lack of social grace. Knight's views on matters of taste were therefore of some consequence for the artistic circles in London, at least for as long as the other members of the society were convinced that he had a precision of judgement more refined than their own. Knight came by this influence by degrees, as he won the confidence of others, and in the longer term the fact that he once had influence has been overshadowed by the fact that he lost it, and lost it rather suddenly on a public stage, by making the wrong judgement about the Parthenon sculptures, which he compared unfavourably with Townley's collection. His reputation has never recovered. While Knight's judgement was certainly wrong, it was by no means altogether irrational, and it has tended unfairly to obscure a view of Knight's positive attributes, so that we find him being dismissed not so long ago as a 'booby'.[11] There was more to him than that.

The house which Knight designed for himself at Downton has now been recognised as a significant and highly original contribution to the development of architecture in Britain (figure 3). It was a radical departure from the symmetrical porticoed building which had become routine for country seats, and marks a turning-point which saw development through the next hundred years and beyond. Unfortunately for the proper appreciation of Knight, it has been seen most often as a prophetic anticipation of the gothic revival, which took place under Queen Victoria, and which was seen to embody a range of virtues which were anathema to Knight. What he was thinking of when he designed his house was certainly not what a Victorian architect would have seen in it when he looked at it, and made alterations. It is always the case that we bring a body of ideas to bear on a building when we look at it, and the more remote we are from the culture in which the building was produced, the more likely our own interpretation is to differ from that of the designer. In the case of Knight's house there is a way of understanding it as a gothic revival building, which comes readily to mind, but to attribute such an understanding to Knight is anachronistic, and the more we learn about him and his ideas the more clearly we can see that he would not

11 Christopher Hitchens, *The Elgin Marbles* (London: Chatto and Windus, 1987), p. 50.

Figure 3. Downton Castle, from the south-west. The house has been extended and remodelled, principally during the nineteenth century. Compare with figure 33.

have set himself up in a quasi-medieval house. There must be another way of comprehending it, and the desire to piece together a sympathetic way to appreciate the building was the starting-point for the present study. The general point to be made here is that in order to see the significance of buildings we must understand the culture in which they are enmeshed. With Knight it is possible to piece together this culture to an unusual extent, because he committed his views on so many different subjects to print. The purpose of chapters 2 to 6 is to present an overview of Knight's culture so as to be able to examine his ideas about landscape design (chapter 7) and his own house and garden (chapter 8) in an appropriate frame of reference, which significantly changes our appreciation of what they could mean.

Knight's ideas in the various areas which are brought under scrutiny are interesting for a variety of reasons: sometimes because they are eccentric, sometimes because they are characteristic of the age, and sometimes because they seem to be right. Knight's philhellenism, his love for ancient Greece, was his most enduring passion, and can be found in various guises, examination of which begins in chapter 2. Chapter 3 is concerned with Knight's ideas about science, which he supported more in principle than in deed, but about which he was certainly informed (not least by his brother) and which was connected in many an eighteenth-century mind, including Knight's, not only with progress, but also with the rationality of the ancient world before it was overtaken with medieval superstition. Knight also turned to the ancient world in developing his ideas about religion, the subject of chapter 4, which he interpreted as a way of embodying scientific truths in symbolic form, so that forces of nature are turned into gods, nymphs and suchlike. Knight was notorious before Freud for noticing sexual symbolism in ancient artefacts, and he believed it to be the basis of much religious expression, but he was also inclined to notice political symbolism. He sympathised with the revolutionaries in France at a time when most of his class panicked at the thought of them, and he was a Member of Parliament for many years. He did not make speeches at Westminster, but did write about politics in prose and verse, and his political convictions are examined in chapter 5, while chapter 6 covers his ideas about art, and the theory of taste, which we would today call aesthetics. These ideas are closely linked with those about landscape design and architecture, which are covered in chapters 7 and 8.

As a dilettante, Knight's particular achievement was to be able to make connections across his wide range of interests, and so his thought could migrate easily across fields which are now thought of as disparate. This sometimes gives his work a diffuse quality, and he seems always to be digressing rather than sticking to the point. Again this tends to mean that varied sources must be consulted for his views on any given subject to be explained, but the views nevertheless tend to be cogent when they are pieced together, and one of the attractions of Knight's thought is that he did make links between the various aspects of his life. John Locke made the association of ideas the basis of his philosophy, and Knight made it the basis of his aesthetics. The connections which are made in the mind, for whatever reason, logical or irrational, colour our responses to the things we encounter in the world. Knight's mind was unusually well stocked and the connections which he could make were unusually rich, which make his mind fascinating to encounter: his reading of Hellenistic philosophy could lend a moral character to a meal, or a memory of paintings give an air of nostalgia to the setting sun. Such a view of the world is one of the benefits of the culture of the dilettante, a view which is lost when we accept too rigidly the confines of an established discipline, or employ a professional to design the views from our windows.

Reputation

Knight is remembered for his controversies: he disparaged the Elgin marbles, which remain the British Museum's greatest treasure; he attacked the landscape designs of Lancelot ('Capability') Brown, who is still Britain's most revered landscape gardener; he wrote a book about phallic worship in the Christian church, which scandalised his contemporaries. He also designed for himself a strikingly original house which was, indirectly, to change the course of architectural history in Britain, and was a prominent figure in his day: a trustee of the British Museum, a Member of Parliament, a leading light in the Society of Dilettanti, a deputy president of the Society of Antiquaries, a founder of the British Institution who knew the great and the good of the time. The *Dictionary of National Biography*'s 'Epitome' styles him a numismatist, which is a woefully, perhaps satirically, over-simplified description. Christopher Hussey described him as a prophet of modernism,[12] while, according to Sir Nikolaus Pevsner, the modernist architectural historian, he was a 'virtuoso, archaeologist, anthropologist in his way, and bad poet'.[13] His house, Downton Castle in Herefordshire, has always seemed an extraordinary building. Charles Greville, the son of one of Knight's friends, recorded in his diary in 1839 that he

> rode to Downton on Monday, a gimcrack castle, and a bad house, built by Payne Knight, an Epicurean Philosopher, who after building the Castle went and lived in a lodge or cottage in the Park: there he died, not without suspicion of having put an end to himself, which would have been fully conformable with his notions. He was a sensualist in all ways and devoid of religion, but a great and self-educated scholar.[14]

Greville's remarks were well informed, but not always fair to Knight. It was true enough that he left his house in order to live in a cottage on the estate, but it should be said that before making the move he lived in the house for thirty years; and when he did move out it was to make the house available to his younger brother's family. To say that Knight was an Epicurean philosopher, though, shows unusual insight: Knight did make use of the thinking of the ancient Greek philosopher Epicurus (341–271 BC) as a guide in life. As to being devoid of religion, the charge was often levelled against Epicureans from Hellenistic times onwards, but Knight did not consider himself devoid of religion, even though the world at large thought it of him on account of his strongly anti-clerical views. In

12 'A Regency Prophet of Modernism', *Country Life Annual* (London: Country Life, 1956), p. 46.

13 *The Buildings of England, Herefordshire* (Harmondsworth: Penguin, 1963), p. 117.

14 *The Greville Memoirs 1814–1860*, ed. Strachey and Fulford, 8 vol. (London: 1938), vol. IV, p. 182.

his way he was religious, but his religion was closer to being a version of the paganism of ancient Greece than it was to Christianity as it has normally been understood, even though as a Member of Parliament he needed to belong to the Church of England.[15]

Knight is no exception to the rule that we tend to know more about the later than the earlier years in the lives of the famous, because when he was young it was not necessarily clear that he would make a mark, but once his reputation was established then people tended to mention the fact that they had met him to their correspondents. If we look for the formative experiences of his childhood then it is no surprise to find that they are not well documented and records are not likely to be there to be found. In Knight's case there are a few clues to interpret, indicating an unusual and perhaps difficult childhood.

Knight's grandfather, Richard Knight, made one of the first great industrial fortunes: he had been among the wealthiest ironmasters of the early industrial revolution, with forges at Coalbrookdale, Bringewood and elsewhere producing huge quantities of iron.[16] He had married Elizabeth Payne and had four sons and at least one daughter. Three of the sons, Richard, Edward and Ralph, were involved as partners in the family ironworks, while the other, Thomas, the second eldest, took holy orders. In 1745, on the death of the older Richard Knight, his eldest son, Richard, inherited his fortune. He had married Elizabeth Powell, who brought Croft Castle with her, but they had no sons, and their daughter could not inherit the Knight fortune as it was entailed in the male line; so when Richard Knight of Croft died, not long after his father, it passed to the Reverend Thomas Knight, still a bachelor. He rather abruptly married one of his servants (Ursula Nash, a carpenter's daughter) and when their first child, Richard Payne Knight, was born his father was 54 and his mother 37. He was to have a brother, Thomas Andrew (1759–1838) and two sisters, Barbara (1756–75) and Ursula (1760–77). Knight's childhood was not, by his account, a happy one: he was often unwell, and did not remember his parents fondly. His mother was still alive, but presumably unlikely to read long poems, when he wrote:

> neglect my boyish years o'erspread
> Nor early science dawning reason fed:
> Though no preceptor's care, or parent's love,
> To form and raise my infant genius, strove;
> But long, abandon'd in the darksome way,
> Ungovern'd passions led my soul astray;

15 Hence the contorted line of reasoning in Knight, *Progress of Civil Society*, pp. xvii–xviii.

16 Much of the factual material here can be found in Nicholas Penny, 'Richard Payne Knight: a Brief Life' in *The Arrogant Connoisseur: Richard Payne Knight, 1751–1824*, ed. Michael Clarke and Nicholas Penny (Manchester University Press, 1982), (hereafter *Arrogant Connoisseur*), pp. 1–18.

And still where pleasure laid the bait for wealth,
Bought dear experience with the waste of health.[17]

It is unclear what exactly it was that Knight's ungoverned passions led him to, but 'gentlemen jockeys' with lax morals might have been involved in it.[18] The excitement of gambling might have been a pleasurable bait laid for wealth, but it would not have led to the waste of health; and drunkenness might have laid him low from time to time, but it could hardly have become a chronic condition in one so young. There could conceivably have been precocious adventures with prostitutes, apparently before Knight's father's death, which occurred when Knight was 13. Knight had no formal education during his father's lifetime, but remained at home, where Greek and Latin were forbidden to him. It was not until his father died that he began to be able control his destiny and went to a tutor (Mr Blyth at Coleshill in Warwickshire).[19] We have no reports about life in the Reverend Thomas Knight's household, but clearly it was regulated in such a way as to be so unsympathetic to his oldest son that he would be set against him for life. Richard Payne Knight's perpetual association of Christian religion with ignorance must have its roots here, perhaps in his father's refusal to let him learn about pagan Greece. He was supposed to have been kept away from school on account of his ill-health, but from his own account the relation of cause and effect seems to be the other way about: his health was wasted because he was not at school and could therefore be led astray. Somehow at his father's death suddenly he was well enough to go away to be taught, and he generally enjoyed robust good health afterwards.

In February 1772 Knight came of age, and into control of his fortune. He immediately set about building works at Downton,[20] but they had hardly begun when he left the country on a Grand Tour, promising to send a design for the house through the post from France. This year, 1772, was clearly pivotal, the one in which Knight officially became adult, began to establish himself a seat, and then, in order to broaden his horizons, fled from the place where it was going to be. His travels took him through pre-revolutionary France into Italy, especially to the south of Italy, which had been Greek in ancient times. Initially he travelled between 1772 and 1773, but set out again in 1776 for Sicily, a journey of which he kept a journal eventually to be published by Goethe.[21] Many of his attitudes, trenchantly stated, are already evident in this journal, including his anti-clericalism and his tremendous enthusiasm for ancient Hellas.

17 *Progress of Civil Society*, bk. III, lines 489–96. It is worth comparing this with the early life of Lord Byron's fictional hero Childe Harold, which might be autobiographical, but certainly represents a plausible form of ruination for a young man. Knight admired the poem. *Childe Harold's Pilgrimage*, canto I, 2nd stanza:

Sore given to revel and ungodly glee;
Few earthly things found favour in his sight
Save concubines and carnal companie,
And flaunting wassailers of high and low degree.

18 Knight to Lord Aberdeen, undated (1808?) British Library, Additional MSS, (Aberdeen Papers), 43229, fol. 207.

19 Frank J. Messmann, *Richard Payne Knight: The Twilight of Virtuosity* (The Hague: Mouton, 1974), p. 14.

20 Penny, *Arrogant Connoisseur*, p. 4.

21 Johann Wolfgang von Goethe, 'Tagebuch einer Reise nach Sicilien von Henry [*sic*] Knight', in *Philipp Hackert: Biographische Skizze, meist nach dessen eigenen Aufsätzen entworfen, von Goethe* (Tübingen, 1811); Richard Payne Knight, *Expedition Into Sicily*, ed. Claudia Stumpf (London: British Museum Press, 1986), p. 10.

It is not absolutely clear when he returned to settle in England, but it was some time during 1778 or 1779, and he took up parliamentary duties, being returned as Member of Parliament first for Leominster (in 1780) then (from 1784) for Ludlow. He took a house in Whitehall convenient for the Commons, and in 1781 joined the Society of Dilettanti, which was to be an important focus for his social activity, being composed of other gentlemen in comfortable circumstances with similar attitudes and interests. He wrote an essay for the society about phallic worship, *A Discourse on the Worship of Priapus* (1786), his first publication which was received well enough within the society, where it was privately distributed; but when news of it reached the general public it was treated as scandalous, and its notoriety came to dog him for life, to the point that the *Gentleman's Magazine* obituary notice recalled it as his principal accomplishment.[22] After this book, which was to establish Knight's notoriety, came one which laid the foundation for his considerable reputation as a classical scholar: *An Analytical Essay on the Greek Alphabet* (1791). Meanwhile he was also collecting paintings and the antiquities, especially small bronze figures and coins, which were a regular preoccupation and which, along with his collection of Old Master drawings, formed his magnificent bequest to the British Museum.

In 1794 there followed what was on the face of it a completely new departure: a long poem in rhyming couplets, *The Landscape, a Didactic Poem*, which included an attack on the principles of garden design which had been practised by Lancelot ('Capability') Brown (1715–83). By 1794 these principles had been adopted and were being followed by Humphry Repton (1752–1818). In this attack Knight was joined by his friend Uvedale Price (1747–1829) whose *Essay on the Picturesque* was originally intended, at least by Knight, to be bound in the same volume as Knight's poem but was, in the event, published separately, later the same year.[23] Price's estate at Foxley in Herefordshire was very close to the house in which Knight lived as a child, but he seems not to have known him at that stage of his life, when indeed Knight might not have been suitable company for him to keep. In 1821 Price said that he had known Knight 'full fifty years',[24] which would have been since about 1770, by which time Knight would have had some education from his tutor. He was more intellectually able than Price, but Price had been educated at Eton and must have been the more polished. In attacking the current practice of landscape gardeners in 1794, Price and Knight acknowledged each other as partners and, though they had differences, together they promoted an idea of 'nature' which they saw as quite opposed to the gently undulating hills and lawns which had

22 August 1824, p. 185. 'He was chiefly distinguished in a work entitled "An Account of the remains of the worship of Priapus . . .", 1786. This work excited great attention at the time of its appearance, but from the nature of the subject, was not likely to come into general circulation.'

23 *An Essay on the Picturesque* (1794), pp. iv–v.

24 Price to Lord Aberdeen, 22 November 1821 BL (Aberdeen Papers), 43228, fol. 94 R. W. Liscombe, 'Richard Payne Knight: Some Unpublished Correspondence', *The Art Bulletin*, vol. 61 (Rhode Island, 1979), pp. 604–610.

served 'Capability' Brown as a representation of the same principle. The argument generated furious controversy, but Knight's poem sold well, and its success encouraged him to publish another long poem in 1796, this time setting down his ideas about politics in a description of the development of civilisation called *The Progress of Civil Society*.

The progressive ideas which the title suggests, were particularly bound up with the empirical and scientific thinking which characterised the eighteenth-century Enlightenment. Attitudes to this reason-based (as opposed to religion-based) view of the world underwent rapid change after the French Revolution of 1789, which was the most important historical event of Knight's life, with the furthest-reaching consequences. The revolution of 1777 in America had been inspired by similar ideas, and even though it had thrown off British rule, nevertheless the Americans had done so in a manner which sounded principled and high-minded. The case in France was different. There was some initial sympathy when it was thought that a repressive regime had been overthrown, but then when mob rule took over and Louis XVI was guillotined in 1793, and stories about the horrors of the Terror circulated abroad, there was widespread panic in the British ruling class that the news might inspire similar acts on the north side of the Channel, and war with France was declared. Knight's poem set out his ideas about the development of society and its progress, and concluded by hoping for an eventual happy outcome to the French Revolution. It could hardly have been further out of keeping with the prevailing mood among the country's rulers, and it was fortunate for Knight that it did not capture the mood of any more popular audience, because if it had then he would undoubtedly have been tried for sedition.

Knight used to show his collection of paintings and antiquities to visitors, one of whom in 1804 was the poet Samuel Taylor Coleridge (1772–1834) who gave a striking description of Knight's personal appearance:

> He was engaged with a gentleman in looking over his collection. By the by, whether it were that the sight of so many bronzes all at once infected my eye, as by long looking at the setting sun all objects become purple, or whether there really be a likeness, Mr. Knight's own face represented to my fancy that of a living bronze. It is the hardest countenance I ever beheld in a man of rank and letters.[25]

25 Coleridge to Sir George Beaumont Thursday 8 March 1804, in *Memorials of Coleorton*, 2 vols., vol. II, p. 55.

There are two portraits of Knight in his maturity, both by Sir Thomas Lawrence (1769–1830), whose first significant commission on his arrival in London had been from Knight.[26] They seem at first to be very much less flattering than Lawrence's standard line in glamorous portraits of royalty, aristocracy and polite society, but they must have softened and thereby gentrified the appearance of Knight's complexion.

Knight's greatest popular success, *An Analytical Inquiry into the Principles of Taste,* made its first appearance in 1805 and by 1808 had run to a fourth edition. It was an attempt to uncover by philosophical means as much as could legitimately be said on the subject of taste, in particular arguing forcefully against Uvedale Price's theories. It included remarks on a great variety of topics and is a revealing source for Knight's ideas in general, but its method of argument was to pillory and ridicule his opponents' ideas, and a rift with Price developed because he felt hurt personally. They avoided each other for a time, and are not afterwards documented as being in each other's company until 1812.[27]

Knight's career in official politics lasted between 1780 and 1806, and the dates are important landmarks in Knight's life as they indicate the span of what he evidently felt to be his maturity. The decision to stand for Parliament marked an acceptance of adult responsibility, while the decision to relinquish his seat in 1806 was taken in circumstances which correspondingly marked his withdrawal from the world. Charles Townley, a close friend of long-standing, had died in 1804, Knight's relations with Price were strained for some years after 1805, there had been a fire at Downton which was reported early in 1806[28] and in September Charles James Fox, Knight's political mentor, died. After this Knight did not stand for re-election, and by 1808 had made his house over to his brother. He went to live in a very modest house on the estate, Stonebrook Cottage, from where, facetiously overstating the case, he wrote to say that he wanted 'nothing but a long Beard, a skull and a Rosary to be a complete Hermit'.[29] In fact he spent most of his time in London, and worked on scholarly publications both there and at the cottage. His circumstances were more accurately described in the preface to his last published work, an adventure story with an Anglo-Saxon setting and lengthy digressions into metaphysics and politics: *Alfred: a Romance in Rhyme* (1823) has never been highly regarded, but was Knight's longest exercise in versification and he had the good grace to apologise for its quality.[30] He said there that his life was 'spent alternately in the indulgences and dissipations of polished society, and the contemplative tranquillity of studious retirement'.[31] Even after he had withdrawn to the cottage, he continued to dine and entertain at the main house at Downton, and built himself an isolated tower there as another retreat.[32] In London he moved

26 The picture of *Homer Reciting his Verses*, begun in 1788, but not exhibited until 1791. According to William Sandby, *The History of the Royal Academy of Arts from its Foundation in 1768 to the Present Time. With Biographical Notices of All the Members*, 2 vols. (London: 1862), vol. II, p. 24, this was Lawrence's first commission.

27 Knight wrote, 'I saw my brother farmer Price last week at Foxley' on 28 September 1812, which sounds friendly enough, but then Knight was not the injured party. Knight to Lord Aberdeen, BL (Aberdeen Papers), 43230, fol. 147.

28 *Gentleman's Magazine*, January 1806, p. 132.

29 Knight to Lord Aberdeen, 10 October 1809, BL (Aberdeen Papers), 43230, fol. 29.

30 *Alfred: A Romance in Rhyme* (London: 1823), p. v.

31 Ibid., p. xv.

32 One of his nieces wrote: 'In February 1808 we left Elton and went to live at Downton, my Uncle having become tired of the trouble of managing an establishment as a bachelor, and having fitted up a cottage for himself, where he had his books: but he usually dined at the Castle, and received his friends there.' See Messmann, *Richard Payne Knight*, p. 125.

from Whitehall to a larger house, at 3 Soho Square, which he extended with a supposedly fireproof iron-vaulted library and museum to accommodate the paintings, books and antiquities,[33] some of which he had moved from Downton by 1808, as *Feltham's Picture of London* for that year describes him as an established resident of the square:

> Richard Payne Knight is the proprietor of the famous picture of the Cradle by Rembrandt; of a very capital large landscape by Salvator; and of many very capital performances by other great masters. He has also made a very large and admirable selection of antique bronzes, cameos, and intaglios. The collection of bronzes is the most numerous of any private possession of the same kind in London. On application, it is not difficult of access; and Mr. Knight, from having so long resided abroad, is particularly attentive to foreigners.[34]

The Rembrandt has been reattributed, and now hangs in the Rijksmuseum in Amsterdam as of the School of Rembrandt (see figure 16). Knight's life continued to be convivial, and he enjoyed close friendships with Lord Aberdeen, Lady Oxford and Richard Westall, whose paintings he collected and praised immoderately. Meanwhile, he continued to move in a very fashionable circle which included Lord Byron, Richard Brinsley Sheridan, William Wilkins, Sydney Smith, Lady Morgan, Lord Abercorn and others. Having quit the great house at Downton and to some extent freed himself from the country gentleman's duties (which did not much interest him) his scholarly output increased.[35] He contributed to the *Edinburgh Review* (which had been founded in 1802 and came to be an important forum for Whig opinion) and completed the sumptuous folio-sized *Specimens of Antient Sculpture* (1809) which he had begun compiling with Townley, and which included superb engravings of antiquities, preponderantly selected from Townley's marbles and Knight's bronzes. He also, in 1818, published a study of religious symbolism, treating the subject more generally and less scandalously than he had in *The Worship of Priapus*, under the title *An Inquiry into the Symbolical Language of Art and Mythology*. His major task of scholarship during these years, though, was an edition of Homer's epics, the Latin introduction to which he published in draft in 1808, an edition of fifty copies to circulate for scholarly comment, before preparing the final edition which was published as *Carmina Homerica, Ilias et Odyssea* in 1820.

These were Knight's most positive achievements, which attest to an active and thoughtful life, with a devotion to Greek scholarship as its

33 Knight to Samuel Parr, 19 June 1809: 'All my *supellex critica* is now transferred hither, and joined in a spacious library and museum that I have built secure from fire for that purpose, in which I hope to have many entertaining and instructive discussions with you', Messmann, ibid., p. 132. C. R. Cockerell sketched the gallery in 1809, and his sketch is reproduced in *John Soane* (London: Academy Editions, 1983).

34 *Feltham's Picture of London for 1808*, quoted Margaret Goldsmith, *Soho Square* (London: Sampson Low, 1947), p. 145.

35 Knight to Samuel Parr, 19 June 1809: 'Increasing attachment to objects and pursuits of this kind [i.e. scholarship] has so alienated me from the habits and modes of life of a country gentleman, that I have put my brother and his family into possession of Downton', Messmann, *Richard Payne Knight*, p. 132.

abiding enthusiasm. He continued to have a very pleasant life into old age, but his reputation beyond his immediate social circle was permanently damaged by his failure to recognise the Parthenon marbles as classical Greek work, a failure which destabilised his good standing as a philhellene. His part in the controversy which surrounded their acquisition for Britain has been shown in lurid colours, particularly by the artist Benjamin Robert Haydon (1786–1846), who championed them and vilified Knight. Strangely it was Haydon who was completely devastated by the affair, and driven to lunacy and suicide, while Knight's life continued to move between his library and various dinner tables in a very comfortable round.

Knight was obviously opinionated, and it is due to his fondness for letting his views be known that we have such a volume of work from him, but he was not good at repartee.[36] In 1822 it was remarked that he had grown very deaf, which his cousin, the poet and gossip Samuel Rogers (1763–1855) said was because he had so little practice in listening.[37] However Knight could clearly also be a good and generous friend, and those whom he trusted certainly valued his friendship and help. In time the breach with Uvedale Price healed and he, in a letter to Lord Aberdeen, wrote sympathetically about Knight's suffering following an accident at Downton. Knight had been hit by a falling branch which he had been pruning from a tree; a septic wound had swelled on his neck, and for a time it had seemed that he might die, but (Price wrote):

> He is as much a man of bronze as any in his collection, & may go on to a hundred with all his faculties . . . He would have been a great loss both public & private; and I should have felt it very strongly: he is a friend of very old standing, of full fifty years, & I think, like genuine wine, he improves by age: the harshness gone off, & the fulness & flavour remain.[38]

Knight's death is associated with rumours of suicide, which were most elaborately set out by Rogers, who as ever was waspish, imaginative and factually unreliable. There was clearly some tension between the two men, though they socialised together, but Rogers's remarks could draw blood. In 1812 Knight had written to Lord Aberdeen hoping that he might meet up with him that summer in Scotland, when he would be meeting Rogers, and he hoped that Aberdeen might be able to 'mollify the asperity of this atrabilious bard's cynical sarcasms with the milk of human kindness', 'atrabilious' literally meaning 'affected by black bile', which is to say splenetic, or melancholy. If Aberdeen could perhaps dilute the

36 Farington, *Diary*, 27 May 1807. Date references are given for Joseph Farington's diary, 1793–1821, which can be consulted in typescript (28 vols.) at the British Museum Department of Prints and Drawings, and has been published in two editions: K. Garlick, A. Macintyre and K. Cave, eds., 16 vols. (New Haven: Yale University Press, 1978–84); James Greig, ed., 8 vols. (London: Hutchison, 1923–8).

37 P. W. Clayden, *Rogers and his Contemporaries*, 2 vols. (London: 1889), vol. I, p. 345; Thomas Moore, *Memoirs*, ed. John Russell, 8 vols. (London: 1853–6), vol. IV, p. 23 (26 November 1822), quoted Messmann, *Richard Payne Knight*, p. 160.

38 Price to Lord Aberdeen, 22 November 1821 BL (Aberdeen Papers), 43228, fol. 94.

effects of these sarcasms 'in the genial and soothing vehicle of that moral and metaphysical philosophy of which Scotland has been of late so productive, it may make him not only more pleasant to his hosts and fellow traveller, but also to himself; for I suspect the sharp instruments within are employ'd in wounding their case, when not directed externally'.[39] In one of his accounts Rogers said that Knight 'poisoned himself with prussic acid, his nerves destroyed by *women*';[40] but in another even more melodramatic version he described Knight as dying before the poison reached his lips[41] (which might be a poetical allusion to the death of Hamlet) and elsewhere said that Knight's health had been destroyed by his amorous exploits with young men.[42] Some, perhaps most, of this must clearly be fantasy, but Knight did suffer in his last months. After his sickly youth his health was generally very sound (as Price, above, made clear) and if appetite is to be taken as an index then he was certainly in good health when he dined with Lord Aberdeen, the Duke of Argyll, Lord Holland and others, speaking 'as much as the enormous food he devoured would allow him'.[43] It is difficult to imagine him being driven to distraction by personal relationships at this time of his life, as, whoever they might have involved, he seems to have had them very much under control, but he did suffer from uncharacteristic depression, and at the beginning of 1823 he began to think about suicide. 'A night Fever,' he said,

> deprived me of Sleep, and brought an Incapacity of Attention and Dejection of Spirits, I never felt before, and which explain'd to me [something] I could never comprehend before, that Mood of Mind which induces Men to destroy themselves, without being distress'd in Circumstances, disgraced in Character, or tormented with incurable Disease. At the same time my Appetite retain'd its usual Voracity and my Digestion its usual Vigor, and every one said that I look'd well; so that the neighbouring Practitioners could find nothing the Matter with me but a slight intermittent [illegible word]; for which they gave me a Tonic and Bracers; and made me change my Coffee for Port Wine. Dr. Philip . . . discovered a complaint . . . which has been long coming on . . . which would have extended to the Liver and have brought me down in Pain and Misery to the Grave had not its progress been arrested.[44]

Seven months later he called off a dinner and sent Lord Aberdeen a brief despairing note written in a shaky hand, even here noting in a punctiliously epicurean manner that such pleasures as bring suffering in their wake are to be avoided. He explained that he would be able to go round

39 Knight to Lord Aberdeen, 14 May 1812, ibid., 43230, fol. 108.

40 See Elisabeth Inglis-Jones, *Peacocks in Paradise* (London: Faber, 1950), p. 233.

41 Samuel Rogers, *Recollections of the Table-Talk of Samuel Rogers*, ed. Marchand Bishop (London: Richards, 1952), p. 146: 'Payne Knight was seized with a loathing of life, and destroyed himself. He had complaints which were very painful, and his nerves were completely shattered. Shortly before his death, he would come to me of an evening, and tell me how sick he was of existence. He had recourse to the strongest prussic acid; and, I understand, *he was dead before it touched his lips.*'

42 Elisabeth Inglis-Jones, in her manuscript biography of Knight, quoted by G. S. Rousseau, 'The Sorrows of Priapus' in *Sexual Underworlds of the Enlightenment* ed. Rousseau and Roy Porter (Manchester University press, 1987), p. 145, n. 26.

43 *The Journal of the Hon. Henry Edward Fox (afterwards fourth and last Lord Holland) 1818–1830*, ed. the Earl of Ilchester (London: T. Butterworth, 1923), p. 57.

44 Knight to Lord Aberdeen, 4 January 1823 BL (Aberdeen Papers), 43231, fol. 40.

to tell Lord and Lady Holland, the other guests, because his 'locomotive faculties' were not much impaired, but that giving a dinner party would be too great an exertion for him:

> It is true that my spirits are occasionally raised by the excitement of company at dinner parties; but I atone for it the next day, and am become very despondent, in spite of the encouragement of my physician who however forbids me any irritating [i.e. stimulating] exertion. Long life should rather be call'd long death, the greatest of all miseries.[45]

It is easy to see why there were rumours of suicide, and evidently the end was welcome when it came, but there were some remissions along the way. 'When I saw him in the beginning of November [1823], full of blue pills and blue (not to say black) devils,' said one of Samuel Rogers's correspondents, 'I told him that he would, should, and must be himself again. And so he nearly was before I left town.'[46] Despite losing the will to live in his last years, soon after he had finished his work on *Alfred*, his last substantial project, Knight lived to a good age, 73, and the official version of events that he died of 'an apoplectic affection'[47] may well be correct, but he would have defended on principle the idea of suicide as a legitimate act.

The centre of gravity of Knight's varied interests lay in ancient Greece, Hellas, which had been forbidden to him as a child and which he visited as soon as he came of age. It was there that he retreated again, intellectually, after he had shed the duties which were expected of someone of his rank in society. What gives Knight's work such coherence as it has is its devoted loyalty to Hellenic culture, most especially to Homer and Epicurus. When Knight turned his attention to religion he tried to reinstate a version of classical paganism, a deism which he believed had been the religion of Homer. He sought to repopulate the landscape garden with dryads and nymphs, along with rustic labourers, while in politics he sought a return to 'natural' Greek morals. He made a contribution to many areas of life, enjoyed great celebrity for a time, and continues to be remembered for his bequest to the British Museum and for his ideas about designing landscapes and houses, which were to continue to be influential long after his death.

Epicurus' morals

Knight was given to making satirical remarks about marriage and adultery, made his anti-clericalism quite public, and published a book which

45 Knight to Lord Aberdeen, 26 July 1823, ibid., 43231, fol. 87.

46 Clayden, *Rogers,* vol. I, p. 365; letter to Samuel Rogers, 21 January 1824.

47 *Gentleman's Magazine*, August 1824, p. 185.

was reputedly obscene. Certainly to his more pious contemporaries his moral character seemed completely unprincipled, with nothing whatsoever to recommend it; but if we turn to the philosophy of Epicurus then the behaviour can be reconciled with some straightforward guiding principles.

Epicurus (341–271 BC) came from the island of Samos to teach at Athens, where, about 306 BC, he founded a philosophical school, which met in the garden of a house which he bought between Athens and Piraeus.[48] The other important philosophical schools at the time were the Sceptics, or Pyrrhonists, who by this time ran the Academy (the school in the groves of Academus) which Plato had founded; and the Stoics, who took their name from the fact that they had originally met in the Stoa Poikile, at the Athenian Agora, but who by Epicurus' day taught at the Lyceum, another grove outside the city boundaries. There was rivalry among the various schools, which taught different things, the Epicureans being associated principally with their moral theory and their doctrine that the world was composed of atoms. Epicurus believed that life should be regulated in such a way as to ensure the greatest possible degree of happiness. The basis for our knowledge of the world is our sensory apparatus, and if our senses tell us that something is good, then we should believe them and suppose that it is good. Nevertheless, despite seeming in this way to recommend unbridled hedonism as the best basis for life, Epicurus made very moderate and restrained suggestions about proper behaviour. His notion of 'true pleasure' was so very elevated that it closely resembled the more popular conception of self-denial. What distinguishes Epicurus' philosophical hedonism from merely intuitive self-indulgence is the emphasis which was always firmly stressed in the philosophy (but always completely neglected in hostile commentaries from adherents of rival views) that according to Epicurus all violent or excessive pleasure brings suffering in its wake.[49] According to Epicurus, the utmost pleasure is to be had in the simple freedom from bodily pain and mental disorder, and no more than that. Anything which goes beyond this blissful state, even though it might briefly seem to be pleasurable, will bring some sort of suffering which might take time to be felt, whether it be indigestion, anxiety or worse. The appetite was the constant organ of reference, as it showed that the maximum pleasure does not result from the consumption of immoderate quantity. Epicurus tells us that 'the beginning and the root of all good is the pleasure of the stomach; even wisdom and culture must be referred to this';[50] 'it is not the stomach that is insatiable, as is generally said, but the false opinion

48 A. A. Long, *Hellenistic Philosophy* (London: Duckworth, 1986), pp. 14–15.

49 Plato too stressed that pleasures and pains were very closely linked, but unlike Epicurus he thought that the senses were misleading; see *Phaedo*, for example.

50 Cyril Bailey, *The Greek Atomists and Epicurus* (Oxford: Clarendon Press, 1928), pp. 134–5 (Epicurus, *Fragments*, 59).

that the stomach needs an unlimited amount to fill it';[51] and that he was 'thrilled with pleasure in the body' when he lived on bread and water, despising 'luxurious pleasures not for their own sake, but because of the inconveniences that follow them'.[52]

So Epicurus understood pleasure to result from the indulgence of an appetite, but he also argued that pleasure was maximised if the appetite were controlled and therefore moderated so as easily to be satisfied. To have a large appetite is not at all pleasurable if one has no means with which to satisfy it; and the body's balanced state of good health is unbalanced if the appetite is over-indulged. Knight said that 'in intellectual as well as sensual gratifications, the circles of pleasure are expanded only in a simple ratio, and to a limited degree; while those of pain spread in a compound rate of progression; and are only limited in their degree by the limits of our existence'.[53] Intellectual pleasures could, though, be less damaging than alternative means of spending the time employed in pursuing them, and of all desires 'the desire of knowledge is that, of which the gratifications are the most pure and unmixed, as well as the most permanent; and which being, at the same time, the most difficult to cloy or satiate, affords the most certain and ample means of durable and solid happiness'.[54] According to this way of thinking, the most scholarly of activities could diligently be pursued for the sake of maximising the pleasurable activity in one's life. Epicurus' detractors neglected to mention the doctrine of moderation, and portrayed him as advocating gluttony, associating him with the pig.

The adoption of Epicurus as a guide to morality is a symptom of Knight's philhellenism, which is discussed more widely in the next chapter, but it would have been possible to have adopted a mentor no less Hellenic who would have been more straightforwardly compatible with the norms of a Christian society. Plato disapproved of hedonism,[55] but lived before Epicurus and so had nothing to say specifically against Epicureanism, and the Epicureans' principal opponents in antiquity were the Stoics, who based their theory of moral action on the principle of self-denial.[56] Both the Stoics and the Epicureans valued serenity, but the Stoics believed that there could be, and was, divine intervention controlling human affairs (they called it 'Providence') whereas the Epicureans believed in free will.[57] According to the Stoic outlook, the fallible and merely human senses were not to be trusted for guidance, but were to be overcome. A Stoic's goal was to reach a state of complete indifference to bodily well-being so as to be able to sustain the pursuit of virtue even through periods of what to the less philosophical would have

51 Bailey, ibid., pp. 114–15 (Epicurus, *Fragments*, 61).

52 Ibid., pp. 130–1 (Epicurus, *Fragments*, 37).

53 *An Analytical Inquiry Into the Principles of Taste*, 4th edn (London: 1808), p. 464.

54 Ibid., p. 465.

55 See Plato, *Philebus*.

56 Bertrand Russell, *History of Western Philosophy*, 2nd edn (London: Routledge, 1961), p. 260ff, 271, p. 274: 'When the Stoic philosopher is thinking of himself he holds that happiness and all other worldly so-called goods are worthless; he even says that to desire happiness is contrary to nature, meaning that it involves lack of resignation to the will of God.'

57 A. R. Lacey, *A Dictionary of Philosophy* (London: Routledge, 1976), pp. 56, 207.

been acute physical agony. In the 'modern' world Stoicism was taken up by a certain sort of Christian, for example Milton, whose masque for ›w was cast very straightforwardly as a battle between the chaste irtuous, who displayed Stoic virtues, and the lascivious Epicurean us and his followers, who indulged their appetites and turned into als who roamed about the woods. When the polarity between ureans and Stoics was introduced into a Christian context in this then Epicurus, as Sir Walter Charleton had pointed out, became stly known as an 'Atheist, Impious wretch, Secretary of Hell, Enemy Religion'.[58]

These divisions in Hellenistic philosophy were well known to anyone e eighteenth century with a classical education and a general interest ilosophy, not only to a philhellene scholar like Knight. References to abound in eighteenth-century literature, and they were so com- place that they could be made as glancing allusions without the need eavy signalling. For example when Edward Gibbon (1737–94) who, Knight, supported the political activities of Charles James Fox, rked that for his saintly Aunt Hester (with whom he was clearly out mpathy) every meal was an exercise in self-denial, he was claiming he had Stoic tendencies;[59] and when Knight was reported as having t to indulge every appetite as far as possible without causing himself mfort, he was being labelled as a conscientious Epicurean.[60] Knight ght of sexual desire as an appetite to be gratified, or as a flow which d not be stopped; a debt to Epicurus being evident in his referring noral question to his stomach, saying for example that 'there is natu- no impurity or licentiousness in the moderate and regular gratifica- of any natural appetite; the turpitude consisting wholly in the excess rversion'.[61] So Knight was clearly opposed to excessive indulgence; e was also opposed to celibacy, as (comparing desire to flowing) repressed desire gains an undue importance:

> Where 'midst high rocks th'imprison'd waters flow;
> The more confined, the closer pent, the more
> They rush in eddies, and in torrents roar,
> So, to the cell's or convent's shade confined,
> More fiercely rage the torrents of the mind:
> Desires unsated, passions unsubdued,
> In every secret haunt, can still intrude;
> The more we circumscribe their weak domain,
> With more despotic sway the tyrants reign;[62]

Political imagery characteristically crept into the last quoted line: if we fail to acknowledge our desires then we become their slave. Monastic life, in which a virtue is made of celibacy, was for Knight a most thoroughly perverted and unhealthy way of life.

> Here every vice, with which mankind is cursed,
> In sordid selfish Solitude is nursed,
> Here hate and envy rankle in the mind,
> The more malignant, as the more confined;
> While Love unknown leaves every base desire
> To prey in silence with corrosive fire;
> Unsocial Lust usurps Affection's throne,
> And broods o'er pleasures for itself alone;[63]

Knight's theory of desire was that it should be satisfied before it became obsessive and immoderate; the appetite should be controlled, but not altogether denied; and he saw the idea of self-denial as wholly repugnant, unnatural and disgusting. The general impression of the tenor of Knight's life is of a very comfortable, privileged and well-regulated existence. He was motivated by various enthusiasms which led him in different directions, and clearly his conversation could range widely, across different fields of enquiry and in different registers, from abstract philosophy to bodily functions:

> He is more to be congratulated than any other man, on any acquisition, of any sort; being gifted with such extraordinary powers of enjoyment, both intellectual and sensual; from Homer to a haunch of venison; from a drawing of Claude's to a dish of coffee; from Venus de' Medici to Venus de' Meretrici.[64]

Knight saw celibacy as the theoretically desirable state only when it resulted from the appetite being limited, and so he saw no need to condemn himself with any great vigour for his lapses from it; he made sexual symbolism the basis of religion, and has been credited with anticipating Freud on that score.[65] Knight's contemporaries found his moral character highly ambiguous: indulgent and libertine in manner, but prudent in deed. In his writings there is a recurrent call for freedom, and for the abolition of rigid rules, but yet he lived quietly and respectably, if perhaps at times rather secretively. Why the constant railing against rules which did not obviously cramp his style? If Knight, in his highly privileged position in society, felt that he was somehow being crushed, then we very readily, in Freud's wake, look for an undercurrent of sexual

63 Ibid., p. 201.

64 Clayden, *Rogers*, vol. I, p. 365 letter to Samuel Rogers, 21 January 1824.

65 Nikolaus Pevsner, 'Richard Payne Knight', *Studies in Art, Architecture and Design*, 2 vols. (London: Thames and Hudson, 1968), vol. I, p. 114; Christopher Hussey, 'A Regency Prophet of Modernism', p. 48.

repression, perhaps an unconscious one, perhaps quite clearly felt but unvoiced. His life was not punctuated by great deeds on the public stage, but by the publication of books, which sometimes found an audience wider than could have been anticipated. His position in society was close to the heart of the social and political establishment of the day, but his voice was distinctively raised in opposition to its received opinions.

2 Becoming ancient, becoming Greek

First beginnings

Knight's thought was typical of Enlightenment reasoning in the way that he tried to investigate the way things were in his own day by constant reference to the origins of social practices in the far-distant past, a form of reasoning most famously exploited by Jean-Jacques Rousseau (1712–78) in his *Discourses*, where he argued that man's primitive state was his natural and true state, and that any deviancy from that state brought evil with it.[1] Knight did not take up quite this position, but he did try to argue for a change in current practice by saying that it had lost touch with its ancient origins. It is a technique of argument which has had a wide currency in different guises, and there is a long history of traditions growing up or being consciously invented as a way of lending authority or cultural sanction to a practice.[2] In Knight's day Edmund Burke (1729–97) made a very powerful appeal, in the political arena, to traditional 'common-sense' prejudices, as the sedimentation of generations of folk wisdom;[3] but his reason for doing so was to counteract the influence of the arguments of the revolutionaries in France and America who appealed to reason as their guide, and who took some inspiration from Rousseau, amongst others. The appeal to a far-distant, as opposed to an immediate, past brings with it the sanction and authority of tradition, but makes possible change, even radical change, in current practice. This desire for change was Knight's reason for making an appeal to ancient Hellas rather than, like Burke, appealing to the immediate past, or following the previous generation in making appeals to, and finding affinities with, Augustan Rome. For Knight, looking back to ancient Greece involves looking back to the roots of western civilisation, when Socrates was developing patterns of thought which we suppose we would still recognise as academic, when the idea of

1 *Discours sur les sciences et les arts* (Paris: 1750).

2 Eric Hobsbawm, *The Invention of Tradition* (Cambridge University Press, 1983).

3 See chapter 5.

democracy was first mooted and then put into practice and where artistic productions were extraordinarily fine, and were recognised to be so even by the more powerful and practically effective Romans. To look back to Greek culture was to look back to civilisation's first principles, before they had been fossilised into inflexible institutions.

Knight idealised ancient Greek society, and his ideas throughout his life drew on his devotion to Greek culture. His first introduction to it may have been through knowing his father's apparent hostility, but for the sustained involvement which made Knight one of the most respected Greek scholars of his generation more is required than recourse to a Freudian idea of sublimated adolescent 'parricide', which does not fit Knight's circumstances particularly comfortably: first because Knight's father actually did die when Knight was 13, so any practical psychological need to distance himself from his father and establish his own identity can have called for no sublimated act of murder; and secondly, although one might be inclined to see the relationships within the Knight household as having something in common with those of the Butlers as portrayed in *The Way of All Flesh* (in which a severe but well-meaning clergyman alienates his son)[4] the Reverend Thomas Knight does not seem to have been unusually pious, or punctilious in his parish duties, certainly not by the time his children were born. He was Rector of Ribbesford and Bewdley, parishes in Worcestershire, which brought him an income, but he lived in a large house in Herefordshire, Wormsley Grange, some 30 miles away. Knight said little about his childhood, but when he mentioned it he did not describe it as having been coloured by the fanatical religiosity which he very readily condemned when he did come across it; rather he felt that he had been neglected, and it is quite possible that he would have experienced his father's death as a continuation and intensification of this parental neglect. Whatever the personal feelings involved, from the moment of the father's death we see Knight moving, presumably of his own volition, rapidly towards the classical world: initially by studying its languages, then by visiting its remains. By 1794 he had come to see ancient Greek society as absolutely perfect.

> The state of society in Greece was such that it afforded the artist the advantages of savage, joined to those of civilized life; and in the games and public exercises, exhibited the most perfect models of strength and agility in men of high rank and liberal education, whose elevation of mind gave a dignity of expression to every act and gesture of their bodies.[5]

4 Samuel Butler, *The Way of All Flesh* (London: 1903). Butler was born in 1835.

5 Richard Payne Knight, *The Landscape: A Didactic Poem*, 2nd edn (London: 1795), p. 4n. Compare with the opening chapter of Johann Joachim Winckelmann, *Gedanken über die Nachahmung der greichischen Werke in der Mahlerey und Bildhauer-Kunst* (Dresden: 1755) trans. by Henry Fuseli, *Reflections on the Painting and Sculpture of the Greeks with Instructions for the Connoisseur, and an Essay on Grace in Works of Art* (London: 1765).

Knight did not go to university, which, given his later involvement with scholarship, might have been expected, and which the excuse of his poor health hardly seems to explain, given that his alternative was the Grand Tour, which had risks of its own, whatever benefits the Mediterranean climate might have been supposed to bring. In the event his specifically Hellenic studies were more readily pursued in Italy than in Oxford, as at this time they were relatively undeveloped. Roman remains were more plentiful and better preserved, as well as being more easily reached; but the ancient prestige of Greek culture, evident from the Latin literature, made knowledge of it highly desirable. Knight may not have set out initially with Greek interests foremost in his mind: his interest could have taken root on his first visit, to be developed in earnest on his second. He can have had little information about Greece and Greek art at his disposal, and most of it would have been inaccurate by today's standards, now that with the passage of time so much more attention has been given to the material.

The unsettled political climate on mainland Greece made it a place which all but the most adventurous avoided. The indigenous Orthodox Greek-speaking population lived under Islamic Turkish rule, which was disputed around some important ports by Catholic Venetians. Early travellers in Greece had included the Marquis de Nointel, who was there to promote the interests of France as Louis XIV's ambassador, and had thought the Parthenon frieze worthy of a place in the Sun King's collections,[6] and went so far as to take away some statuary, which was later dispersed in France. Also, in 1674 he commissioned one of his attendant artists to record the Parthenon in a set of 400 drawings,[7] which remains an invaluable record on account of the disastrous bombardment of 1687, when a Venetian mortar hit the Turkish arms being stored there, causing a terrible explosion. Others visited Athens, among them Jacob Spon and the Reverend George Wheler, who had seen these drawings at Constantinople, where they met Nointel in 1675 before going on to Greece. They both published accounts of their travels, which were the first to combine a knowledge of the classical sources such as Pausanias (a Roman who had travelled in Greece and wrote a guide book in the second century) and familiarity with the remains themselves.[8] Nevertheless the problems which beset travelling scholars in search of the antique in Greece itself were daunting, and continued to be so throughout the eighteenth century. They included difficulties in dealing with the Turkish authorities which were understandably great, because the Acropolis was in active military use, and the political situation was

6 Nointel quoted by le compte Léon de Laborde, *Athènes aux xve, xvie et xviie siècles* (Paris: 1854), vol. I, pp. 124–5, quoted by David Constantine, *Early Greek Travellers and the Hellenic Ideal* (Cambridge University Press, 1984), p. 12: 'ils méritteroient d'estre placés dans les cabinets ou galleries de Sa Majesté'.

7 The drawings, by an anonymous draughtsman (for a long time wrongly thought to be Jacques Carrey) are in the *Bibliothèque Nationale* in Paris. Constantine, *Early Greek Travellers,* pp. 14–15. The drawings are reproduced (attributed to Carrey) by Fani-Maria Tsigakou, *The Rediscovery of Greece: Travellers and Painters of the Romantic Era* (London: Thames and Hudson, 1981), p. 15.

8 Jacob Spon, *Voyage d'Italie, de Dalmatie, de Grèce et du Levant*, 5 vols. (Lyon: vols. I–III, 1678; Amsterdam, vols. IV–V, 1679); Sir George Wheler, *A Journey into Greece* (London: 1682).

volatile with the threat of attack by Venetians or Russians, or, in 1770, by the oppressed Greeks themselves. Added to this were the fears of capture by pirates at sea and attack by brigands on land, which were real enough to deter all but the most intrepid, so that despite sustained interest for decades it remained possible for James Stuart and Nicholas Revett, sent to Greece by the Society of Dilettanti, to cause a sensation among those interested in archaeological matters by publishing in 1762 accurate drawings of the remains of ancient buildings in Athens. There would eventually be four volumes of their records, but at the time of Knight's travels only the first had been printed so the project was still current, and continued to be so even after Knight had returned and himself joined the society.[9]

Knight also knew the work of the great Winckelmann (1717–68) who had been writing about Greek sculpture with a fervent, inspirational and sometimes erotically charged (more specifically: homoerotically charged)[10] passion, through which he established throughout Europe an idea of Greek beauty which had a new urgency, poignancy and spirituality. His vision was compelling, and inspired Knight very much more than he acknowledged in his writings. In detail Winckelmann's work was in some respects faulty, despite his prodigious scholarship, mainly because he was working in Rome, not in Greece, and his observations were largely based on Hellenistic sculptures, or Roman copies rather than Greek originals of the fifth century BC. He never faced the perils of travel to Greece, even in 1768 actually deciding against going there to investigate the possibility of making excavations at Olympia (where he was confident of finding the fine statues of victorious athletes which Pausanias had described) in favour of returning to visit his native Germany, which should have been a safer decision, but which led him to an arbitrary and unedifying death at the hands of a stranger in Trieste.[11] Much later, Knight was himself contemplating the possibility of excavating at Olympia, but still thought it inadvisable to go ahead:

> I should like extremely to be a partner in an Olympian Adventure under the auspices of [Sir William] Gell, if we could be sure of proper protection from *any* Government: but in the present state of Europe [i.e. in 1809] there is none that can give it; for if Napoleone is successful on the Danube, the Turkish Empire is parceled out and disposed of, so that the Peloponnesus will be in his possession before we can get a spade put into the Banks of the Alpheus. I think therefore that it will be prudent to wait the Event of the present

9 James Stuart and Nicholas Revett, *The Antiquities of Athens*, 4 vols. (London: Society of Dilettanti, vol. I, 1762; vol. II, 1787; vol. III, 1794; vol. IV, 1816).

10 Johann Joachim Winckelmann, *Abhandlung von der Fähigkeit der Empfindung des Schönen in der Kunst, und dem Unterrichte in Derselben* (Dresden: 1763), trans. Susan Powell, 'Essay on the Beautiful in Art', in *Winckelmann: Writings on Art*, ed. David Irwin (London: Phaidon, 1979), p. 92: 'since human beauty has to be expressed in a general concept, I have observed that those who are only aware of beauty in the female sex and are hardly or not at all affected by beauty in *our* sex, have little innate feeling for beauty in art in a general and vital sense. The same people have an inadequate response to the art of the Greeks, since their greatest beauties are more of our sex than the other.'

11 David Constantine, *Early Greek Travellers*, pp. 104–27; Alex Potts, *Flesh and the Ideal: Winckelmann and the Origins of Art History* (New Haven: Yale University Press, 1994).

> contest; which, if successful, may procure us many Advantages, and if not, will preclude all Attempts. A very few months must now decide it. There cannot be a better person than Gell for such an undertaking, as he will unite the Activity of an Agent to the Zeal of a friend and the principles of a Gentleman: but unless the constituted Authorities of the Country are favourable, ponderous objects cannot be rescued even should they be discovered, and all that are discovered probably will be ponderous.[12]

Sicily

Knight's early expedition to Sicily of 1777, then, combined the scholarly excitement involved in the recording of Greek remains with the prudent decision to remain on Italian soil. The prudence however was relative, as the number of patients in Neapolitan hospitals with knife-wounds made him aware.[13] He was not the first traveller to have visited the ancient sites at Agrigento, Paestum, Segesta and Selinus, but there were no good archaeological records of them, and the journal which he kept was evidently intended for publication, accompanied by illustrations made by Charles Gore (1729–1807) and Philip Hackert (1737–1807). Another artist, John Robert Cozens (1752–97) went with Knight from London but for some reason they parted company at Naples and Cozens did not reach Sicily; however, they met up again at Rome on Knight's return journey, and Cozens reworked some of the other artists' images, and Knight was later (in 1797) to help to raise money to support Cozens after he had suffered a nervous collapse, so this curious desertion from the Sicilian adventure was evidently forgiven him.[14] Back in England, as late as 1782, some of the pictures were modified under Knight's guidance by Thomas Hearne (1744–1817), but the project did not reach fruition, because publication was pre-empted by the appearance of works which covered very similar material.[15]

Despite the fact that Knight did not visit modern Greece he did have contact with authentic Greek monuments, and he was very impressed by them. He described seeing the archaic temples at Paestum, noting that 'When one examines the Parts near, they appear rude, massive and heavy; but seen at a proper distance, the general effect is grand, simple and even elegant. The rudeness appears then an artful negligence, and the heaviness a just and noble Stability.'[16] Knight's drawing room at Downton has a Doric fireplace, its columns modelled specifically on those at Paestum, but without their ruggedness, a much higher degree of

12 Knight to Lord Aberdeen, 15 July 1809, British Library, Additional MSS (Aberdeen Papers), 43230 fol. 8.

13 *Expedition Into Sicily*, ed. Claudia Stumpf (London: British Museum Press, 1986), p. 62: 'In the Hospital [at Girgenti] there was not a single Patient, that had been stabbed, while in the kingdom of Naples, every Hospital and Infirmary is full of them.'

14 Frank J. Messmann, *Richard Payne Knight: The Twilight of Virtuosity* (The Hague: Mouton, 1974), p. 100.

15 Claudia Stumpf, ed., in Knight, *Sicily*, p. 15. The rival works were by the Abbé de Saint-Non, *Voyage Pittoresque ou description des Royaumes de Naples et de la Sicile* (Paris: 1781–6) and Ignazio Paterno, Principe di Biscari, *Viaggio per tutte le antichità della Sicilia* (Naples: 1781). Knight described meeting the Prince of Biscari and mentioned that he was 'publishing a large work upon the Antiquities of Catania, which from the Drawings I saw, promises much, *Sicily*, p. 55. Also see J. Houel, *Voyage pittoresque des Isles de Sicile, de Malte et de Lipari* (Paris: 1784–7).

16 *Sicily*, p. 28.

finish being appropriate to their tamed domestic setting. Knight also introduced some caves into the Teme Gorge, his garden at Downton, which have antecedents in those he saw in Sicily, which ranged in character from the domestic to the sublime:

> A Cave in the Rock supplied us with a Kitchen, and, had it not been for our impatience to see Sicily, we could have passed our time agreeably enough *nunc veterum libris, nunc somno et inertibus horis* [now with books of the ancients, now with sleep and idle hours].[17]

> In one of these Caverns is a Manufactory of Saltpetre, which heightens its natural gloominess. The Smoke of the furnace, the dim light of the fire, and black visages of the People made it look like some enchanted Scene of a Romance.[18]

In the general remarks with which Knight concluded his account, and with which he peppered it along the way, he prefigured many of the concerns which would find more elaborate treatment elsewhere in his work. He was, for example, already observant of various picturesque (or *pictoresque*)[19] effects, noticing that 'The infinite variety of tints were all harmonised together by that pearly hue, which is peculiar to this delicious climate. (This Tint very particularly marks Claude Lorraine's Coloring.)'[20] Knight's attention was regularly caught by things which were very appealing to the eye but which were in some other way deplorable, a category of objects which was significant in his aesthetic analyses; and this pearly hue would reappear in 1794 in a different guise:

> The beautiful pearly hue of the air in Italy, so happily imitated in the pictures of Claude, arises in great measure from the putrid vapours, which in summer and autumn infect all the low parts of the southern provinces. To sleep in these vapours is almost certain death, especially to a foreigner. I remember an Englishman of rank in Sicily, who treated it as a prejudice, and in spite of every argument and persuasion that could be used to the contrary, passed a night in a fisherman's hut, on the borders of the lake of Lentini; but he waked in a putrid fever, and survived only thirty-six hours.[21]

This passage, more appropriate to the traveller's journal than to the poem in which it actually appeared, gives an idea of some of the unexpected perils of travel; others were more predictable, such as finding that

17 Ibid., p. 30; the Latin is a quotation: Horace, *Satires*, ed. Loeb (London: 1926), II, VI, 61.

18 *Sicily*, p. 55.

19 This form of the word (used at pp. 31, 43, 52) is closer to *pittoresco*, from which Knight construed his argument for the meaning of the word 'picturesque'; see chapter 6.

20 *Sicily*, p. 55.

21 *The Landscape: A Didactic Poem*, 2nd edn (London: 1795), p. 84n.

although Lipari looked wonderful from a distance, on closer inspection it was all 'filth and misery'.[22] The conditions of life and the general character of the modern Sicilians came in for a good deal of criticism, despite Knight's appreciation of their warmth and friendliness to strangers, but he said that 'however amiable and commendable their intention may be, it rather incommodes than assists a Stranger, for attention and civility become tiresome and impertinent, when those who show it have neither wit to amuse, nor knowledge to instruct'.[23] He found them credulous and of low moral calibre, and worst of all they set themselves against the very influences which could have improved their lot:

> This fear of innovation keeps the Sicilians in a State of the most profound ignorance. Arts & Sciences of every kind are despised & unknown, & even the common implements of husbandry are in a very imperfect state. Their Corn is trod out by Oxen, and ground by Hand, there not being a single flour Mill in the whole Island. There was a Windmill lately built at Girgenti, but the prejudices of the People were such, that they would not use the flour, so it was pulled down.[24]

He blamed the church for this state of affairs, for encouraging unquestioning belief rather than enquiry, and saw a clear link between the people's deplorable lack of intellectual development, their conditions of life, and their standard of taste.

> Their Houses are poor and ill-built, almost all the wealth of the Country belonging to the Church. The Archbishop alone has an Income of near 20 000. £ Sterling p^{r}. [*sic*] annum, which is a constant drain for the Country, for he never resides there. His Palace is large, but in a very bad taste.[25]

> The City [of Catania] is almost intirely new, the Streets regular & spacious, but the houses built in a bad taste, and a great part of them only half-finished.[26]

This miserable state of affairs contrasted with the astounding accomplishments of ancient times: a trope familiar enough in the reports of travellers who set out in search of the antique. The standard of taste, said Knight, declined from perfection under the Hellenes to admit the use of 'barbarous mosaics' under the rule of the 'Greek Emperors',[27] who were the Christian emperors of late Roman antiquity, and the Byzantine era, who ruled from Constantinople until 1453. The only sign of progress

22 *Sicily*, p. 31.

23 Ibid., pp. 46–7.

24 Ibid., p. 61.

25 Ibid., p. 46.

26 Ibid., p. 54.

27 Ibid., p. 38.

was at the palace of the Prince of Biscari, an enlightened individual and a collector of antiquities, who lived in a 'great irregular building, the ancient part of it in the barbarous taste of the Sicilians, charged with monstrous figures, and unnatural ornaments, but the part, which he has built himself is simple, regular & elegant'.[28]

By contrast with the modern scene, where decorous good taste was exceptional, the ancient pagan civilisation of Sicily had produced endless perfections and wonders. Knight's favourite pieces of statuary were two brass rams,

> somewhat larger than the life, and of the most exquisite Sculpture. It is astonishing what an Air of dignity & grandeur the Artist has given to so humble an Animal, & yet preserved the exactitude of a portrait. The finishing is in that bold masterly Stile, which is peculiar to the best ages of Greece. – Even in the turn of the Horns there is Grace & elegance, & the Wool tho' seemingly neglected has all the softness & lightness of Nature. Upon the whole these Bronzes are equal if not superior to any thing I have seen at Rome, Portici, or Florence, & may be ranked among the few genuine Works that exist of the fine Greek Artists.[29]

The fact that ancient buildings of such a scale and such a degree of refinement could have been produced showed Knight what could be achieved in a society where the people were free. Such a small population would never have been coerced into such prodigious quantities of work as were entailed in the greater monuments, still less have managed to develop so refined a mode of expression. Selinus, he said, had been hardly more than a trading company, but yet the ruins there were immensely impressive:

> While one views them, one cannot but reflect how inestimable is the blessing of Liberty, that enabled so small a State as Selinus, whose dominions extended but a few miles to perform what the mighty Lords of the Earth have scarcely equalled.[30]

His visits to the ruins of ancient buildings led him to ponder the achievements of past civilisations and their regimes of political and moral order, in a wistful and rather melancholy mood, but the natural scenery brought out a more heightened emotional state, evidenced here by the journey up Mount Etna, and the view looking down.

> The Night was clear, and just light enough to show the general forms of the objects, but nothing distinct, – there was an universal

28 Ibid., p. 54.

29 Ibid., p. 38.

30 Ibid., p. 42.

> Silence, except when interrupted at intervals by the Noise of the Mountain, which was loud and solemn, like the breaking of the Sea in a Storm. The Crater was distinguishable by a red gloomy light piercing thro' the vast volumes of Smoke, that rolled from it. – The whole together formed the most tremendous Scene I ever saw & which perhaps is not to be equalled any where else in the world.[31]

> I felt myself elevated above humanity, & looked with Contempt upon the mighty objects of Ambition under me. The Scenes where so many numerous fleets and Armies have fought for Universal Empire, seemed no more than a Spot.[32]

So we find Knight experiencing an oceanic and sublime feeling when facing the natural scenery, without doubt inspired by Winckelmann, who had made the same connection between political freedom and Greek art, for example in saying that

> The same freedom that was the mother of great occurrences, changes of regime, and emulation among the Greeks, planted as it were at the moment of its birth the seeds of a noble and sublime way of thinking; and just as the sight of the unbounded surface of the sea and the beating of the majestic waves on the cliffs of the shore expands our outlook, and makes the mind indifferent to any lowly considerations, so in the sight of such great occasions and men it was impossible to think ignobly.[33]

Knight was appreciative of and amazed by the achievements of the ancient Hellenic inhabitants of Sicily, but he contrasted these great achievements with the current state of the peasantry, and the 'Ecclesiasticks' who influenced them too much. Characteristically he traced the execrable taste which prevailed in modern times back to the time that Christianity had begun to guide the Sicilians' ideas, being influenced here by Edward Gibbon, who attributed the decline and fall of the Roman Empire largely to its adoption of Christianity. Knight's ideas about religion are discussed in chapter 4, but in outline he believed that the ancient Greeks, particularly Homer, had a thoroughly good religion which was taken over by Christians and made into a systematic way of thinking which inhibited, if it did not entirely prevent, worthwhile human achievement. The political and religious freedom which the ancients had enjoyed were no longer prevalent in Sicily and Greece, the one oppressed by religion, the other by the Turks, and these deplorable

31 Ibid., p. 56.

32 Ibid., p. 56.

33 Winckelmann, *Geschichte* (Vienna: 1776), p. 234, trans. Potts in *Flesh and the Ideal*, p. 54.

Figure 4. Stonebrook Cottage. The building has been extensively remodelled since Knight's day, but the location in woodland remains.

conditions of life he saw as productive of a bad aesthetic sense, along with general poverty.

Stonebrook Cottage

The Hellenic ideal guided Knight much later in his life when setting up house at Stonebrook Cottage in his retirement (1808–9) where he could escape from public duty and the expectations of polite society (figure 4). The Greek influence is not immediately apparent, because very similar behaviour could have been prompted by quite different ideas as it was, for example, when William Wordsworth (1770–1850) and his sister moved to Dove Cottage at Grasmere in 1799. Knight took care to exercise by walking several miles a day, and enjoyed being close to the trees and streams of the ancient forest. 'I am enjoying [October] to the utmost in the retirement of my cottage,' he said, writing to Lord Aberdeen in 1809, still pleased with the novelty of his situation, '*nunc veterum libris, nunc somno et inertibus horis.*' This quotation from Horace apparently came readily to Knight's pen,[34] but here it seems apposite, particularly if restored to its context in Horace, as it is in his rural home, with books, leisure and simple food that Horace expects to be able to forget life's cares. Knight was living as close to nature as he could imagine, being absorbed into the landscape, in a small house of plain design with absolutely no distinguishing features; 'It is a mere sulky with only one sitting room of 16 feet square and a bedroom over it, situated in a little dell, with a little stream, little rocks, and everything little about it.'[35] Knight made his situation sound altogether very appealing and Lord Aberdeen seems to have replied that he too should set himself up in a modest cottage remote from the world, because in his next letter Knight said: 'It is too soon for *you* to think of a sulky – when a man enters his 60th year, as I am about to do, he has a right to live for himself; but before, he ought to live for society. The dregs of life then left are not worth bestowing; and it is all that can be hoped that one may not become tiresome to ones self as well as to others.'[36] The cottage itself was very simple indeed. Knight, calling it a 'hut', went on to explain

> The building is of common masonry quite plain without any affectation either of rudeness or finish or any way differing from a common cottage of grey stone, except that the projecting window in the sitting room, and that in the bedroom over it are of the same material as the walls, and not of wood. In the architrave of the former I have inscribed the following line ΚΑΛΛΙΣΤΟΝ ΕΝΘΑ ΚΤΗΜΑΤΩΝ ΣΧΟΛΗ ΤΥΧΟΙ: which I have made out of a maxim of Plato's σχολη καλλιστον κτηματων; with what success critics may decide. It expresses my meaning very exactly.[37]

Knight in a subsequent letter made it clear that he intended σχολη to mean 'leisure' (rather than 'idleness') and the Plato becomes 'leisure is the best of possessions', meaning presumably that it is most valuable to have time for philosophical contemplation. Knight's adaptation suggests that the best of properties is that in which leisure is to be found, and expresses a wish that it would be found here.[38] This motto is the clearest clue in the building's fabric to indicate what was going on in Knight's

34 See above at footnote 17.

35 Knight to Lord Aberdeen, 10 October 1809, BL (Aberdeen Papers), 43230 fol. 29.

36 Knight to Lord Aberdeen, undated, but late October or early November 1809, BL (Aberdeen Papers), 43230 fol. 47.

37 Ibid.

38 I would like to thank Professor Robert Cook, Professor T. V. Buttrey, Professor Niall Rudd and Mr Maurice Whitby for their translations from Knight's Greek; also the members of the Hellenic Society of Aesthetics with whom it was discussed.

Figure 5. Sir Thomas Lawrence, *Homer Reciting his Verses*, 1790.

mind, and its exact interpretation is not especially important. What mattered most about it was that it was in Greek.

The major project on which Knight was engaged whilst he was in the cottage was the preparation of an edition of Homer, and he immersed himself thoroughly in the culture of ancient Greece. He imagined Homeric society to have been very close to nature, and had commissioned from the young Thomas Lawrence a painting, *Homer Reciting his Verses,* showing the blind poet speaking in the open air, in countryside which looks more English than Greek, with an audience among trees in various states of undress (figure 5). Knight's friends saw him as having adopted the outlook of an ancient, and even the ardently philhellene Lord Aberdeen found Knight's stance a bit extreme. 'I have no particular wish,' he said, 'to bear such a close resemblance to the sturdy hero of Homer as may be discovered in our friend Knight.'[39] The deliberateness

39 Lord Aberdeen to Uvedale Price, 23 September 1816, BL (Aberdeen Papers), 43228 fol. 61.

of the decision to live in a very small cottage is thrown into sharp relief when we see that he kept the most sophisticated company when he was at his other house in Soho Square, London. The Hon. Henry Edward Fox (later Lord Holland: Charles James Fox's nephew, who had been orphaned and so brought up by his uncles) remarked: 'I dined at Payne Knight's, and met Lord Aberdeen, Lord Morpeth, Mr Wm Bankes, Mr Combe, Cimietelli. Something was talked of as a recent invention by Knight, "quite latterly, quite modern". "When about?" asked somebody. "Oh! lately, since Croesus; Homer knew nothing of it," answered the Pagan.'[40] So we can see Knight the Pagan in the company of the cultural elite of his day, affecting to adopt the viewpoint of an ancient Greek, here in jest, but elsewhere with more serious purpose. This renunciation of worldly pleasures, however, was not the result of a new-found saintliness but was a refinement of pleasures, and was based on thinking from Greek sources. For example, we find the ancient Athenian Thucydides, setting the scene for his account of the Peloponnesian War, explaining that

> It was the Spartans who first began to dress simply and in accordance with our modern taste, with the rich leading a life that was as much as possible like the life of the ordinary people. They, too, were the first to play games naked, to take off their clothes openly, and to rub themselves down with olive oil after their exercise. In ancient times even at the Olympic Games the athletes used to wear coverings for their loins, and indeed this practice was still in existence not very many years ago. Even today many foreigners, especially in Asia, wear these loincloths for boxing matches and wrestling bouts.[41]

Knight's generation did not wear the powdered wigs which its fathers had worn, so one can imagine him identifying with the new style of dress in Hellas which led the old men of Athens to be the only ones left wearing their hair tied up in a knot at the back, fastened with a pin of golden grass-hoppers,[42] and similarly he took up a cottage which had formerly been rented out to one of his humble tenants. He was not so completely unadorned as Thucydides' athletes, but he was living as simply as decorum allowed. A certain neoclassicising tendency in Rousseau's work is brought out in his parallel assertion that the honest man, *l'homme de bien*, 'is an athlete who chooses to fight naked. He despises all these vile ornaments which impede the use of his powers, most of which were only invented so as to hide some deformity.'[43] Knight made it clear that even if some people thought it improper to display nudity

40 Entry for Tuesday 26 March 1822. *The Journal of the Hon. Henry Edward Fox (afterwards fourth and last Lord Holland) 1818–1830*, ed. the Earl of Ilchester (London: T. Butterworth, 1923), p. 106.

41 Thucydides (*c.* 460–*c.*400BC), *History of the Peloponnesian War*, trans. Rex Warner, introduction by M. I. Finley (Harmondsworth: Penguin, 1972), p. 38.

42 Ibid.

43 'L'homme de bien est un athlète qui se plaît à combattre nud: Il méprise tous ces vils ornemens qui gêneroient l'usage de ses forces, et dont la plus part n'ont été inventés que pour cacher quelque difformité', Jean-Jacques Rousseau, *Discours sur les arts et les sciences*, in *Œuvres complètes*, 3 vols. (Paris: Bibliothèque de la Pléiade, 1964), vol. III, p. 8.

> the artist must exhibit the genuine man, as formed originally by his Creator, undisguised by any adscitious trappings of ornament or concealment; and if such exhibitions excite any improper associations, it will only be in those whose minds are more habituated to such associations, than to any of a purer kind; – vice-hunters, who still delight in the pursuit of what they are no longer able to retain or enjoy; and eagerly follow the scent or the shadow, when the substance has escaped them; – who are continually prying every where in quest of their game, and equally ready to worry whatever their prurient and morbid imaginations invest with its semblance.[44]

The only genuine men in the ancient world, by this criterion, according to Thucydides, would have been the Greeks; and comparably neo-classical noble savages are to be found in *The Landscape,* where Knight said:

> It has been frequently observed by travellers, that the attitudes of savages are in general graceful and spirited; and the great artist who now so worthily fills the President's chair in the Royal Academy [Benjamin West], assured me, that when he first saw the Apollo of the Belvidere, he was extremely struck with its resemblance to some of the Mohawk warriors whom he had seen in America. The case is, that the Mohawks act immediately from the impulse of their minds, and know no acquired restraints or affected habits.[45]

West painted an ideal Mohawk figure in his depiction of the death of General Wolfe, a work which Knight admired (figure 6).[46] The comparison, using Knight's own circumstantial detail, had in fact been made earlier, by Winckelmann: 'Behold the swift Indian outstripping in pursuit the hart: how briskly his juices circulate! how flexible, how elastic his nerves and muscles! how easy his whole frame! Thus *Homer* draws his heroes.'[47] The type of man in the modern world who seemed most closely to resemble the type heroically idealised in Greek sculpture was to be found living in conditions which were remote from the constraints of civilisation as Knight knew it, and increasingly the retreat to the countryside came to be a way for Knight to escape polite society. He thought of September and October as being his months for business at Downton, but would prolong his stay at Stonebrook Cottage until the first fall of snow began to restrict the paths he could take on his walks.[48]

44 [Richard Payne Knight], 'Review of *The Life of Sir Joshua Reynolds, Knight, late President of the Royal Academy, &c.*, by James Northcote', *The Edinburgh Review*, Vol. XXIII (Edinburgh: 1814), pp. 263–92; pp. 291–2.

45 *The Landscape*, p. 3n.

46 See page 171.

47 Winckelmann, *Gedanken*, trans. Fuseli, p. 6.

48 Knight to Lord Aberdeen, 14 May 1812, and November 1812, BL (Aberdeen Papers), 43230 fols. 72 and 88.

Figure 6. Benjamin West, *Death of General Wolfe*.

He pitied those who missed the exquisite effects of early morning and late evening sunshine through being 'pent up in a bed or a dining room' or 'treading through turnip fields in search of partridges', but, he added,

> I have probably brought my mental sanity into some question among my more discreet and social neighbours; and their doubts might perhaps have been consolidated into firm belief by my having been heard of wandering through the bye Roads alone in the night, and sleeping at Hedge Alehouses . . . I hear that some pious matrons of the Wilberforcian sect have concluded me to be possest of the Devil, and were not the antient Rite of Exorcism held by them to be Popish Heathenish and abominable, I might perhaps stand a chance of having some salt water thrown in my face the next time I apprehend them. If Lady Oxford had not been with you[, then you, Lord Aberdeen] and [Sir William] Gell would probably have pass'd for the Doctor and Apothecary from whose custody I had escaped.[49]

49 Ibid., 3 September 1810; 43230 fol. 72.

The 'Wilberforcian Sect' was the Clapham Sect of evangelical Christians, with which William Wilberforce (1759–18), MP for Yorkshire, was particularly associated. They were trying, with notable success, to reinvigorate Christianity in England, not merely as a matter of church attendance but in a much more muscular form, as is made clear by the title of Wilberforce's book: *A Practical View of the Prevailing Religious System of Professed Christians in the Higher and Middle Classes of this Country Contrasted with Real Christianity* (1797). As part of this mission the Sect promoted the code of respectability which we now think of as characteristically Victorian, and with which Knight was profoundly out of sympathy. In response Knight immersed himself ever more completely in pagan culture and aestheticised his whole manner of living, trying to reclaim the grace and freedom of a savage society without losing touch with the benefits of civilisation, moving between the 'indulgences and dissipations of polished society, and the contemplative tranquillity of studious retirement',[50] between the fashionable company of Soho Square and his books of the ancients in the cottage, where he was preparing his edition of Homer. This was exactly the kind of regime which he portrayed ancient Hellas as having offered, and he was endeavouring to make England offer it too, even if it meant behaving oddly. He felt that he had reached a time of life when he could live for himself and need not worry about society's opinion of him. As he grew old his behaviour became increasingly eccentric, because he was not adopting patterns of behaviour drawn from the society of those around him, but so far as he was able was thinking by using concepts adapted from his knowledge of ancient Greece. Knight saw every artefact as expressive of the culture's values, and admired even the most commonplace relics:

> O happy days, when art, to nature true,
> No tricks of dress, or whims of fashion knew!
> Ere forms fantastical, or prim grimace,
> Had dared usurp the honour'd name of grace;
> When taste was sense, embellish'd and refined
> By fancy's charms, and reason's force combined;
> Which through each rank of life its influence spread,
> From the king's palace to the peasant's shed;
> And gently moulded to its soft control
> Each power of sympathy that moves the soul.[51]

The ancient Greeks were in a state of grace and in Knight's eyes could do no wrong:

50 Knight, *Alfred; A Romance in Rhyme* (London: 1823), p. xv.

51 *The Landscape*, pp. 55–7, bk. II, lines 336–45.

> The uniform principle of grace and elegance which prevails in all the works of Greece and her colonies, through such a vast variety of states, differing in climate, manners, laws, and governments, has been observed by antiquaries as one of the most extraordinary phaenomena in the history of man. The beautiful, and yet varied forms of the earthen funereal vases, which are called Etruscan, though principally of Greek manufacture, have been fully and happily illustrated in the publications of my learned friend, Sir William Hamilton; and it may be further observed, that the same systematic elegance was preserved in works of a still humbler class.[52]

Knight here shows some independence from Winckelmann, who said that 'The superiority which art acquired among the Greeks is to be ascribed partly to the influence of climate, partly to their constitution and government, and the habits of thinking which originated therefrom.'[53] Knight here stresses that the constitutions and governments and climates varied from one city-state to another (the attitudes of the Athenians were quite different from those of the Spartans; and the climate of Thrace quite different from that of Agrigento), but the same spirit of freedom and grace prevailed throughout, and influenced small works as much as the great. He emphasised this point by reference to a small jug from his collection, a simple utensil 'of that plain and cheap kind, which could only have been meant for the common use of the common people. With us, such articles, even when of more precious materials, and more expensively decorated, are made without any attention to symmetry and proportion, or harmony of parts ... But in the little specimen of ancient manufacture here given, all is harmony and unison.'[54] (figure 7).

The conditions of life in ancient Greece were varied, but in all important respects they were ideal; and consequently every thought, every gesture and every artefact, even the most commonplace little brass jug, would unaffectedly and harmoniously fall into place in the general scheme of things. The enthusiasm is clear enough, as is the unwillingness to notice anything which detracts from the idea of general perfection, such as the curious forward tilt which the jug would have when placed on a flat surface. Again, despite the minor cavils about the variety to be found in climates and constitutions, the idea as Knight expressed it is a development from Winckelmann, who similarly described the Greeks' state of grace, and supposed that the same spirit was pervasive, through from their bodies to even their most commonplace artefacts.

52 Ibid., p. 56n.

53 Winckelmann, *Geschichte der Kunst des Alterthums* (Dresden: 1774), trans. G. H. Lodge, *The History of Ancient Art*, 2 vols. (London: 1881), vol. 1, p. 286.

54 *The Landscape*, p. 56n.

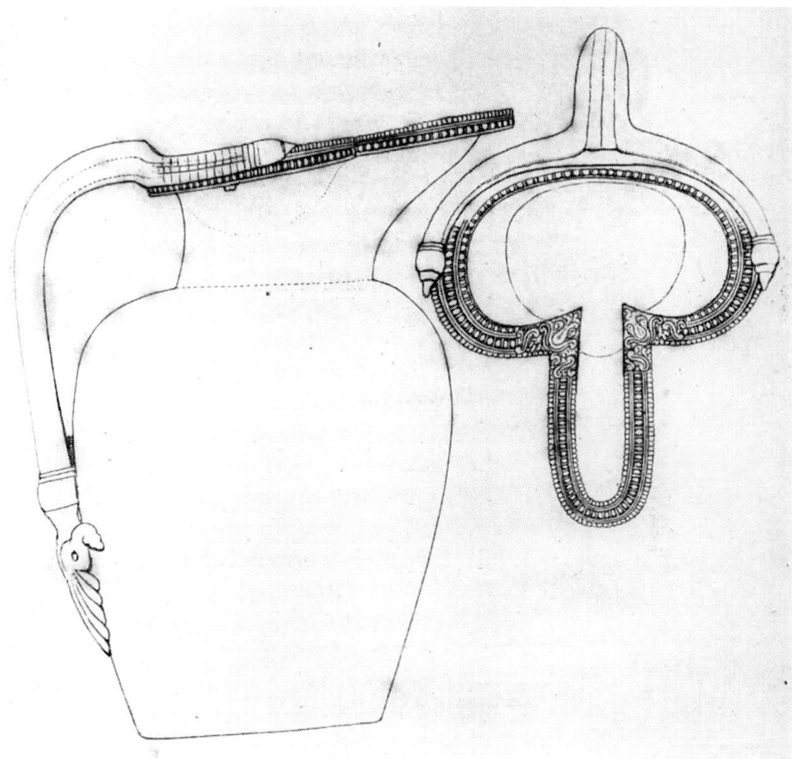

Figure 7. A small Greek jug. Plate from *The Landscape*, 1794.

Among beautiful youths the artist found the cause of beauty in unity, variety, and harmony. For the forms of a beautiful body are determined by lines the centre of which is constantly changing, and which, if continued, would never describe circles . . . This diversity was sought after by the Greeks in works of all kinds; and their discernment of its beauty led them to introduce the same system even into the form of their utensils and vases . . . The greater unity there is in the junction of the forms, and in the flowing of one out of another, so much the greater is the beauty of the whole.[55]

Sculptures from the Parthenon

Given this extreme attentiveness and sensitivity to the nuances to be detected even in civilisation's most common-place works, Knight's reaction to the Parthenon marbles when Lord Elgin brought them to London was bizarre. Not only was he apparently quite unmoved by them, and argued that they were not tremendously good, but he at first supposed that they were not Greek at all. His involvement with the Elgin marbles

55 Winckelmann, *Geschichte*, vol. I, pp. 312–13.

was catastrophic, and needs to be considered in some detail. He mistakenly thought them to be second-century work and was thus shown to be fallible in his judgement, but that this should have had so lasting an impact is surprising, since other critics have made mistakes without such long-term consequences, but it was a spectacular oversight: this prominent devotee of all things Greek failed to respond appropriately when he came into contact with the most important Greek treasures, and so his judgement in all lesser things was called into question. We are still being told that Knight is 'best remembered as something akin to a figure in a Bateman cartoon with the caption "The Man who did not like the Elgin Marbles"';[56] or that 'if he is remembered today, it is chiefly as the connoisseur who refused to see the merit of the Elgin Marbles . . . Knight stubbornly persisted in stigmatising them as second-century restoration work long after the government, to his disgust, had bought them and lodged them in the British Museum';[57] and William St Clair, in his important study of the marbles' progress from the Parthenon to the British Museum, tells us that Knight 'is now remembered only for his disparagement of the Elgin Marbles'.[58] Even such sympathetic attention as Knight has had in recent years has not yet overcome the reputation which has been wished upon him by those who have studied the marbles and known them, with the benefit of hindsight, to be self-evidently of the most outstanding merit. It would follow therefore that Knight in condemning the marbles would have been unaccountably blind to their quality. Yet if we turn to the report made by the Select Committee which recommended that the marbles should be bought for the nation, we find Knight saying not only that he thought the purchase *should* be made, but also that Elgin deserved to be paid more than the statues' market value.[59] Knight's reputation does not, it cannot, result from an interpretation of the evidence.

The principal responsibility for this state of affairs must lie with Benjamin Robert Haydon (1786–1846), the artist who saw himself as the marbles' champion. His antipathy to Knight cannot be exaggerated: seeing himself as pious, he thought of Knight as a daemonic fiend, and while some of Knight's neighbours in Herefordshire might have concurred with Haydon, nevertheless in London it was Haydon's friends who had doubts about his sanity, not Knight's.[60] Haydon, rhetorically, in his diary, warned Knight that

> the fame of the marbles will encrease with our knowledge and treble with time. Remember that when all thy works are sunk into

56 Martin Royalton-Kisch, 'Scholar and Connoisseur', *The Times Higher Educational Supplement*, 5 March 1982.

57 Grevel Lindop, 'The Property of a Gentleman', *The Times Literary Supplement*, 19 February 1982.

58 William St. Clair, *Lord Elgin and the Marbles* (London: 1967), pp. 173–4.

59 *Report of the Select Committee of the House of Commons on the Earl of Elgin's Collection of Sculptured Marbles* [hereafter *Report*], 1816, p. 43.

60 Farington, *Diary*, 7 May 1810.

> oblivion, Priapus & all, thou will be only recollected by thy presumption in disbelieving their beauty. Thy name shall be mentioned by posterity in conjunction with these immortal works, but it shall be with contempt, with sneers of indignation. I cannot speak of such a cold blooded being without having my frame shake & my lips become pale.[61]

Haydon wrote this out as a way of cursing Knight, who was well beyond the range of Haydon's vocal invective, but because he wrote it in his diary it seems to have been read as if it were history, or at least as an uncannily accurate prophecy, and has been reported as fact even when the evidence flatly contradicts it. In the field of classical antiquities it may be true to say that this is how Knight is remembered, but even there his benefaction to the British Museum is not exactly forgotten, and elsewhere, for example in architectural history or landscape studies, he has remained a figure of some significance. It is, however, true to say that Knight did not feel any great enthusiasm for the major statues which Elgin had brought back with him, which is very extraordinary in so ardent a philhellene. Perhaps Knight himself was convinced that genuinely classical Greek works should have struck him forcefully and immediately as great; and since they did not do so, he could, as a connoisseur, have concluded that they must not have been genuine. Haydon on the other hand had no doubts whatsoever about the marbles' quality and authenticity. Fired with enthusiasm, he was convinced that the marbles would set the whole world alight, or at least the world of historical painting. 'Here was I,' he said without false modesty,

> the most prominent historical student, perfectly comprehending the hint at the skin by knowing well what was underneath it! Oh, how I thanked God that I was prepared to understand all this! . . . I felt as if a divine truth had blazed inwardly upon my mind and I knew that they would at last rouse the art of Europe from its slumber in the darkness. I do not say this *now*, when all the world acknowledges it, but I said it *then, when no one would believe me*.[62]

Haydon was the first artist to be given permission to study the marbles and he set to work with enthusiasm, tending to stress their naturalistic aspects (figures 8 and 9). His drawings were good, but the first of his paintings to feel the influence of the Parthenon sculpture was his *Assassination of Dentatus*, which he was convinced was a work of genius (figure 10). From the beginning there were those who doubted this judge-

61 *Diary*, ed. Willard Bissel Pope, 5 vols. (Cambridge, Mass.: Harvard University Press, 1960–3) vol.1, p. 442, 13 May 1815.

62 *Autobiography and Memoirs*, ed. Tom Taylor, 2 vols. (London: Peter Davis, 1926), vol. 1, p. 67.

Figure 8. Sculpted figure of Dionysus from the east pediment of the Parthenon, In Knight's day this figure was usually taken to represent Theseus.

ment, and they included Knight, who, as a founder and trustee of the British Institution, was someone whose good opinion could have done much to help Haydon's career.

The British Institution was founded as a complement to the Royal Academy. Whereas the Academy was composed of artists, who set its agenda and established its values, the British Institution was set up by patrons. Their aim was to encourage a higher style of painting than the portraits which seemed to be monopolising the Academy. Portraits could be lucrative, but as works of art they did not rival the Old Masters, because they did not engage the intellect and the imagination to the same degree. In particular the British Institution encouraged 'history painting' (which could include mythological subjects) by setting up exhibitions and awarding prizes. Had its directors taken Haydon to be the genius he thought he was, then it would have been ideally suited to the gifts he thought he had. He felt that Knight in particular undervalued him and caused his genius to go unrecognised; or rather, as we shall see, when Haydon let his feelings be known unreservedly he felt that Knight was out to destroy him, stalking him in a mad vendetta.

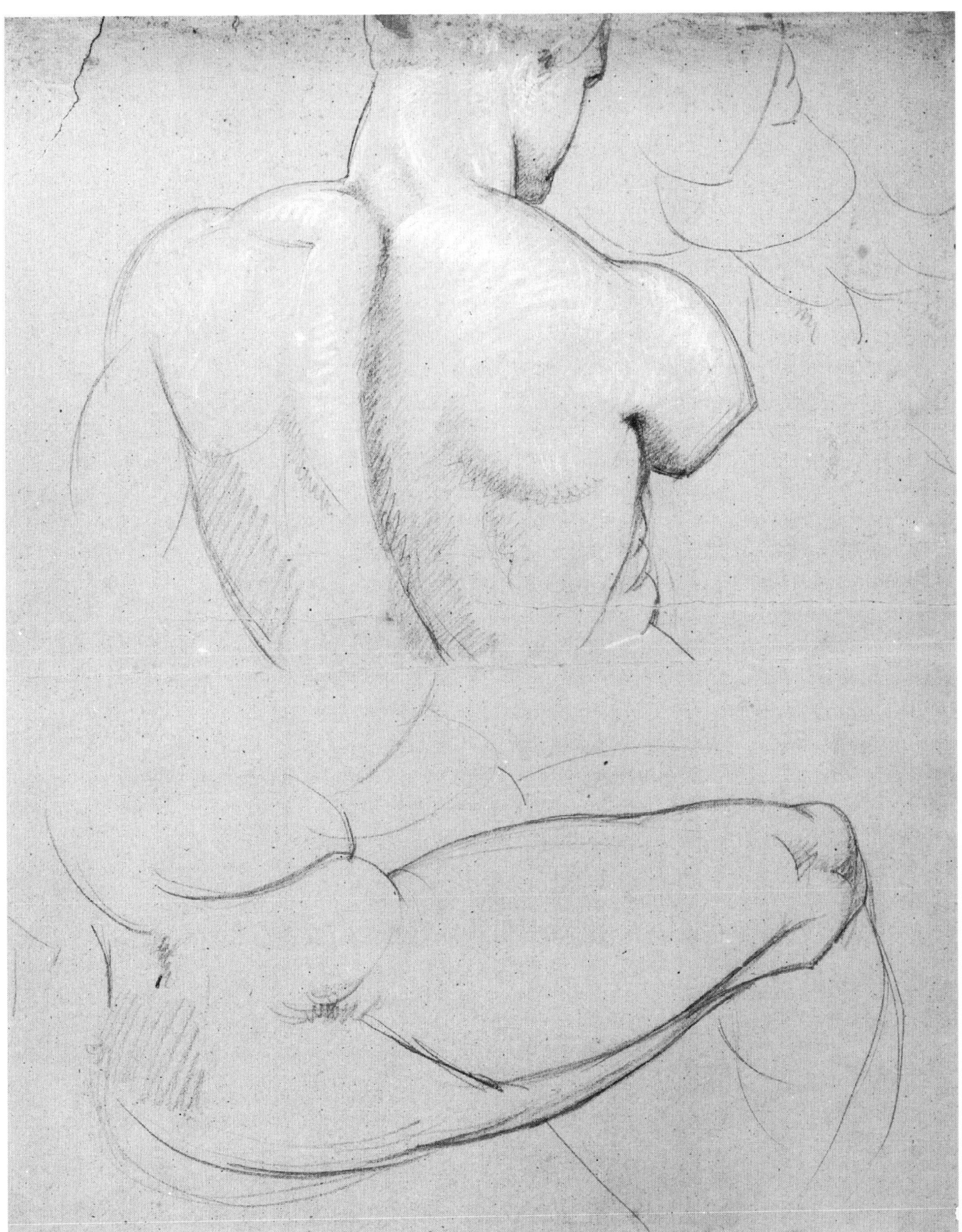

Figure 9. Benjamin Robert Haydon, drawing from the 'Theseus'.

Figure 10. Benjamin Robert Haydon, *The Assassination of Dentatus*. Engraved print, from Haydon's canvas, with improved clarity in the figures.

Haydon did not claim, in the quotation given above, that Knight was uniquely blind to the sculptures' merits, but that on the contrary only he, Haydon, could see them. Knight was not making a very extraordinary claim when he supposed that Phidias did not carve every part of the Parthenon's sculpture himself, though, as might be expected, when writing to Lord Aberdeen he expressed himself trenchantly:

> The preserved Fragments of the Frieze are interesting; but I do not think the workers of them deserve any better Title than common *Stone-hewers* of the age of Phidias; and doubt not of your

> being of the same opinion, when you come to compare them with some of the great Artists of that Age in the Townlian collection. The difference is as great as between an Altarpiece of Titian and a pannel [*sic*] by Rebecca.[63]

'Rebecca' here is Biagio Rebecca, who painted decorations for the ceilings and walls of the grander houses built by Knight's contemporaries, including a near neighbour, Thomas Harley, the Earl of Oxford's brother, at Berrington, which was under construction at the same time and in the same county as Knight's own house. Knight's point was that the Parthenon sculptures were not pure statuary to be treated as independent works of fine art, but were architectural ornament, which is not approached with the same level of critical expectation: they could be serviceably decorative, and even worthy of high praise as ornament without ever reaching exalted heights of artistic endeavour. Knight found that the Elgin marbles left him unmoved; so how could they be genuinely Greek? He did not invent the idea that they were Roman copies, the idea was widespread, but he could have known better.[64] Over-confident of his position, at a dinner with Lord Elgin in 1806, soon after the statues had arrived in London, he made an irretrievable gaffe, calling out (according to Haydon) in a loud voice, 'You have lost your labour, my Lord Elgin; your marbles are overrated; they are not Greek, they are Roman of the time of Hadrian.'[65]

At this time Haydon had yet to see the marbles, and it is not clear whether or not Knight had done so. Haydon said that if 'Payne Knight had no foundation but historical evidence for such an opinion, his evidence was shallow indeed, and if it proceeded from his knowledge as a connoisseur, the perfection of the works he wishes to traduce at once proved that his judgement, taste, and feeling, were utterly beneath notice.'[66] Unsure whether Knight had seen the marbles, Haydon did not know whether to attack his slipshod scholarship or his faulty taste, and so he attacked both, just to make sure. It would have been more to the point to condemn Knight's crass insensitivity in trying to humiliate Elgin after the financial ruin the sculpture had already brought him. He had only recently been released from a French prison, and had there been any sort of fellow feeling then Knight would have said nothing, and would have had more room for manoeuvre when more evidence came to light. Clearly Knight did not like Elgin, and after that dinner the feeling was mutual.

Charles Townley had died in 1804, his marble statuary found its way

63 Knight to Lord Aberdeen, undated [1807?], BL (Aberdeen Papers), 43229 fol. 237.

64 *Sicily*, introduction by Claudia Stumpf, ed., p. 19.

65 Farington, *Diary*, 30 March 1808.

66 Ibid., 3 June 1808.

to the British Museum and in 1812, before the acquisition of the Elgin marbles had finally been made, Knight was appointed as the Townley family trustee. He would have liked Townley's marbles to have kept their pride of place in the museum, rather than see them cede it to Elgin's. Despite having landed absolutely the most spectacular catch of marble statuary, Elgin was not a connoisseur, and there must have been something galling about his upstaging much worthier collectors. The British Museum's trustees bought at auction another classical Greek work at just the time, in 1815, when a Select Committee of the House of Commons was convened to enquire into the acquisition of the Elgin marbles. It was the frieze from the Temple of Apollo at Bassae, and Knight was enthusiastic about it. While the enthusiasm was certainly deserved, it could nevertheless have been the more forthcoming if Knight saw in it a way of stealing Elgin's thunder. Knight enjoyed Lord Byron's invectives against Elgin, no doubt being dazzled by Byron, as so many people were, but what he really relished about the verses was not their arguments, but rather the fact that their barbs were directed against Elgin. 'Rogers and his companion,' he remarked,

> may come fresh whetted from the society of another atrabilious Bard, Lord Byron, who has brought over with him and publish'd a most powerful and splendid poem in which he has pour'd out an abundant quantity of bile against Scotland, more particularly directed against Lord Elgin. It has probably reached Ireland before this time, having made a great impression here, though not more than it deserves; for I really think it on the whole, tho' very unequal, the work of the greatest vigour both of conception and expression that has appeared since Milton. I did not however discover, in the little I have experienced of his conversation, any of the energy or asperity of his writings, though much of the melancholy . . . He has since printed, though not published, another brilliant invective against the spoliation of Athens; but after what he has publish'd he may write or say any thing.[67]

Knight refers here to *Childe Harold's Pilgrimage* (especially the second canto, stanzas XI–XV) and *The Curse of Minerva*, both of which damned Lord Elgin for making a more barbarous desecration of Athena's temple than any had dared before.

> But most the modern Pict's ignoble boast,
> To rive what Goth, and Turk, and Time hath spared:

67 Knight to Lord Aberdeen, 14 May [1812?], BL (Aberdeen Papers), 43230 fol. 108.

Cold as the crags upon his native coast,
His mind as barren and his heart as hard,
Is he whose head conceived, whose hand prepared,
Aught to displace Athena's poor remains:[68]

In a curious reversal of Thucydides' argument that Attica's barren ground had brought Athens long-term benefits, the soil of Scotland is seen to have had a less wholesome effect on Lord Elgin:

And well I know within that bastard land
Hath Wisdom's goddess [Athena] never held command;
A barren soil, where Nature's germs, confined
To stern sterility, can stint the mind;
Whose thistle well betrays the niggard earth,
Emblem of all to whom the land gives birth;
Each genial influence nurtured to resist;
A land of meanness, sophistry, and mist.[69]

It is not at all clear that what Knight relished in these poems was Byron's argument that Elgin should not have brought away the statuary: on the contrary, as we shall see, he adduced no such argument against its acquisition for the British Museum, along with the Bassae frieze and much else besides. Nor would he have found the anti-Scottish sentiments particularly apt, as he contributed to the *Edinburgh Review* and read Scottish philosophers, and admired some of the Scottish scenery as 'among the finest that I have ever seen'.[70] What he enjoyed was the personal abuse heaped on Elgin, along with the poems' (admittedly variable) level of craftsmanship. Knight never said that the statuary should have been left at the Parthenon, though, given his finely tuned responses to landscapes we can be certain that had he visited Athens he would have responded rapturously to the building in its setting: he would have had to revise a great many of his ideas had he done so.

Nevertheless there is no reason to be particularly surprised by Knight's inability to appreciate the marbles' qualities: it does not show an absolutely unaccountable blindness to their aesthetic merits, as has been supposed.[71] Like Winckelmann, Knight supposed the greatest statuary must have dated from the great age of Athens, the fifth century BC, but in fact the statuary for which he had the strongest liking was rather later, being Hellenistic work. Like Winckelmann, Knight mistook Hellenistic statues for classical ones, and thought that he admired fifth-century work when in fact he admired something later. This mistake

68 Lord Byron, *Childe Harold's Pilgrimage*, canto 2, 12th stanza, lines 1–6.

69 Lord Byron, *The Curse of Minerva*, written Athens, Capuchin Convent, 17 March 1811, from Knight's letter clearly circulating unpublished in 1812. This particular extract is a parody of Gray's fragment *On Education and Government*: see chapter 7, p. 199.

70 Knight to Aberdeen, 15 August 1812, BL (Aberdeen Papers), 43230 fol. 133.

71 Nikolaus Pevsner, 'Richard Payne Knight', *The Art Bulletin*, vol. 31 (1949), reprinted in *Studies in Art, Architecture and Design*, 2 vols. (London: Thames and Hudson, 1968), vol, I, p. 115ff.

was widespread at the time and propagated by Winckelmann. Knight was of the opinion that Townley's marbles were excellent, and this was the normal view: they represented established taste; and he could see that Elgin's statues were different from Townley's, and therefore thought Elgin's statues less than excellent. This does not amount to blindness but on the contrary shows Knight to have been observant; it was because Elgin's statuary did not belong within the accepted canon of taste that Knight found them suspect as Greek work; and it is for exactly the same reason that Haydon found them invigorating. Had the statues belonged securely within the accepted canon then Knight might have accepted them the more readily as being genuine, but it would have been absolutely impossible for them to have 'awakened the art of Europe from its slumber'. They could only do that because they challenged the established point of view, of which Knight was the most prominent representative, and there is no need to attribute to Knight any great propensity for evil and malice. The statues did not conform to Knight's idea of what they should have been, so he inclined to the view – which was already circulating, and traceable back to Spon – that they were Hadrianic. He was wrong, but his taste is not shown thereby to be remarkably deranged: Winckelmann's tact would certainly have saved him from this blunder, but had he hastily pronounced on the statues' merits, consulting only his taste as a connoisseur, then he could easily have made the same mistake. Knight had the taste of an older rather than a younger generation; which is just what he might have expected, given his argument that tastes were given to change.[72] It is understandable that Knight's old-fashioned taste, seen through the medium of Haydon's paranoia, turned Knight into a monster and a devil; but it is very much more surprising that this version of events continues to be reported.

Now that the Parthenon marbles are accepted as absolutely canonic, and Townley's bequest is consigned to something rather like oblivion, it is difficult to recapture a state of mind in which they seemed to be challenging to aesthetic values; but surprisingly few were enthusiastic about them when they first arrived. Nollekens the sculptor, who was certainly not immune to a sculpture's aesthetic appeal, 'did not find anything fine about them'.[73] They were seen as 'a mass of ruins',[74] and even Sir George Beaumont (who had treated Haydon with sympathy and more indulgence than he deserved) suggested in a well-meaning way 'that the mutilated fragments brought from Athens by Lord Elgin should be restored as at present, they excite rather disgust than pleasure in the minds of

72 *An Analytical Inquiry Into the Principles of Taste*, 4th edn (London: 1808), pp. 475f.

73 Farington, *Diary*, 6 June 1807.

74 Ibid., 30 March 1808.

people in general, to see parts of limbs, & bodys, stumps of arms &c'.[75] Haydon, however, reserved an especially fevered hatred for two individuals among the many who were initially unimpressed by the statues: Knight and the painter Henry Fuseli. He harboured dark, not to say deranged, thoughts about them both:

> The Engines in Fuzeli's mind are Blasphemy, lechery, and blood . . . Fuzeli was engendered by some hellish monster, on the dead body of a speckled hag, some hideous form, whose passions were excited & whose lechery was fired at commingling with fiery rapture in the pulpy squashiness of a decaying corpse . . . To be sure never were two higher compliments paid to the Elgin Marbles than to have such minds deny them as Knight's and Fuzeli's, the one teeming with Priapism & the other with hell.[76]

And Haydon, again in his diary, not in person, addressed Knight, saying 'You have hung on me during my career with the malignity of a demon: you have sneered at my views & endeavoured to blast their success.'[77] This was because Knight found Haydon's work 'bombastical', and said so. Posterity has sided with Knight, whose dislike of Haydon's work was simply that and not a malevolently nursed grudge. It is possible to think that Haydon might have been a misunderstood genius when one reads his diaries, but not when one sees his paintings. Haydon even complained when Knight would not attack him personally, but only condemn the principles for which he stood.[78] Knight was of course being characteristically high-handed, but it was Haydon, feeding on his resentment, who cultivated the grudge and unstopped the vitriol. Knight dismissed much better artists than Haydon with airy nonchalance, but devastating effect: he memorably brushed aside the ceiling of the Sistine Chapel as 'vast and turgid'.[79] Haydon, who saw the matter in personal terms, vented his emotions by making an elaborate record in his diary of Knight's death 'in extreme agony' on 27 May 1815, anticipating the event by some nine years.[80]

In 1816 a Select Committee set up by Parliament began to enquire whether Elgin's statues should be bought for the nation, and, if so, then at what price. Since the marbles' arrival opinion had shifted, and everyone (including Knight) agreed that they should be purchased for the nation, although the artists who were asked were generally very much more enthusiastic than the connoisseurs. Haydon was not asked for his views, but they were well known. Knight presented his views in a reasonable and moderate way. He said that he knew nothing in high-relief so

75 Ibid., 3 June 1808.

76 *Diary*, vol. I, p. 489.

77 Ibid., p. 442.

78 Ibid., p. 398.

79 Knight, *Principles of Taste*, p. 308.

80 *Diary*, vol. I, p. 448.

fine as the metopes, and that he thought the frieze first-class work, but still he could not bring himself to find exalted merit in the pedimental sculptures.[81] On the other hand he did think that they would influence British art for the good and would 'become a very valuable acquisition for the importation of which Lord Elgin is entitled to the gratitude of his Country'.[82] So Knight was in full agreement with Haydon and all the witnesses called by the committee in saying that the government should buy the sculptures. Far from being disgusted by the government's decision he actually lent his support and recommended the purchase. The limit of his crime against Haydon's taste at this stage was to say that only some and not all of the sculptures were the best he had ever seen.

Knight has also been condemned for suggesting that the sculptures' market value was the insultingly low sum of £25,000, which was lower than the prices suggested by the other two witnesses to suggest a valuation. Lord Aberdeen, another trustee of the British Museum, suggested £35,000 as appropriate; and Elgin's secretary, the connoisseur who advised him at Athens, William Hamilton (not to be confused with *Sir* William Hamilton) suggested £60,000, which was surely as optimistic as he dared to make it. Not one of them approached the £137,000 which Elgin said he expended in order to bring the sculptures to London,[83] but the Select Committee's terms of reference did not allow it to consider compensating Elgin, only to reimburse him for the works' market value. This may have been ungenerous and philistine, but it is the sort of decision which governments make, and it cannot be blamed on Knight.

Townley's collection had been acquired by the nation for £20,000,[84] and Knight arrived at his figure by making comparisons with it. He noted that Townley had paid £700 each for his *Discobolus* and his large *Venus* (see figure 2) and went on to suggest that £1,500 would be an appropriate price for Elgin's principal statues. This was quite extraordinarily generous in view of the fact that he thought each of Townley's pieces to be 'worth more than any two in Elgin's collection, and is a thousand per cent better in preservation'.[85] Hamilton's estimate of £4,000 each looks exorbitant when compared with the prices for Townley's figures, which, it must be remembered, were thought also to be Greek, some of them the work of celebrated ancient artists (such as the sculpture of two boys, one almost complete, the other virtually missing, fighting over a game of knucklebones, which Winckelmann himself had identified as a work by Polykleitos, which Pliny mentioned as being in the Palace of Titus).[86] The quality and authority of Townley's collection was not yet doubted, fantastical though some of the attributions now appear. Lord Aberdeen

81 *Report*, p. 7.

82 Ibid., p. 7.

83 Ibid., pp. 7–8.

84 B. F. Cook, *The Townley Marbles* (London: British Museum Press, 1985), p. 59.

85 *Report*, p. 29.

86 Cook, *Townley Marbles*, pp. 10–11.

said that Townley's marbles 'may be considered in some respects more valuable',[87] but he did not attach prices to individual items, while his friend the architect William Wilkins unhesitatingly preferred Townley's *Venus* to anything in Elgin's collection.[88]

The great differences between Knight's and Hamilton's estimates arose, however, not through their differing valuations of the principal figures but because of the stress which Knight placed on the sculptures' finished surface, which he maintained greatly affected a work's expressive power. Whereas parts of Townley's statues were missing, the surviving parts' surface was intact and restorations could be made (for example the arms of the *Venus* are substantially restored). In Elgin's statues, by contrast, the surface was weathered and worn away, as can be seen in Herakles' pitted face, which belongs to the only human head in the whole collection to have survived among the major figures. Knight first published his views about the importance of the finish (which he seems to have owed to Winckelmann) in 1794, more than twenty years before the hearing, so there is no question of his inventing this as a spurious excuse for denigrating the marbles;[89] but it led him in assessing the value of the frieze (which he thought first-rate) to see thirty-five of the pieces as 'completely ruined' and virtually worthless, whereas Hamilton thought that he would be able to sell them for £400 *each*.[90] This astonishing discrepancy, accounting for £14,000 of the difference between the estimates, is overwhelmingly the greatest, and there is no reason to suppose that Knight's estimates were maliciously low; indeed his valuation of the collection of coins which was part of the hoard was actually £200 higher than Hamilton's.[91]

The Select Committee decided to recommend that Elgin be paid £35,000, which his friends of course thought unjust, but there had never been any question of compensating him fully for his pains. Parliament may well have asked the committee to consider the wrong question in asking it to determine the sculptures' market value, but it gave a responsible answer to the question it had been asked. From the moment the committee's remit was agreed Elgin was bound to lose money, and Knight did not begrudge him the committee's award, as he concluded his evidence by saying, 'I think my Lord Elgin, in bringing them away, is entitled to the gratitude of the Country; because otherwise they would have been all broken by the Turks, or carried away piece-meal. I think therefore the Government ought to make him a remuneration beyond the amount of my estimate';[92] which is exactly what it did, so Knight can hardly have disapproved or been disgusted by the decision. Had Knight

87 *Report*, p. 48.

88 Ibid., p. 46.

89 The *Laocoon* is the finest of all the statues which have received their last finish from the chisel, and here, in particular, an observant eye can discover with what masterly address and skilful boldness the chisel has been managed, in order not to impair, by polishing, the effect of those traits which most evince the knowledge of the artist. Though the outer skin of this statue when compared with a smooth and polished surface appears somewhat rough, rough as a soft velvet contrasted with a lustrous satin, yet it is, as it were, like the skin of the ancient Greeks, which had neither been relaxed by the constant use of warm baths, – as was the case with the Romans after the introduction among them of effeminate habits, – nor rubbed smooth by a scraper, but on which lay a healthy moisture, resembling the first appearance of down upon the chin.

Winckelmann, *Geschichte*, trans. G. H. Lodge, vol. II, p. 58. Compare with Knight, *The Landscape*, p. 8n.

90 *Report*, pp. 29, 40.

91 Ibid., pp. 29, 40.

92 Ibid., p. 43.

not made his casually humiliating remark at dinner then his earlier position would have been his own affair and his evidence to the committee would have been taken at face value. He changed his mind about the statues' worth, but so did many others, as is hardly surprising since they were initially very badly displayed as well as being quite different from the established taste. The reason that Elgin lost heavily was that the Select Committee was asked to consider only the market value of the statuary, the blame for which decision can hardly be pinned to Knight, who in saying that he thought Elgin should be remunerated beyond his estimate was, in effect, saying that the wrong question had indeed been asked. That the connoisseurs who gave evidence were markedly less enthusiastic about the sculptures than were the artists is to some extent explicable, because artists might be expected to see the creative potential in an antique sculpture long before a critic, but Knight knew the other connoisseurs through the British Institution and the Society of Dilettanti, and would have influenced them in the formation of their views. Also we should not lose sight of the fact that behind his statesman-like mask, Knight gleefully thought that Byron's squibs insulting Elgin were the best thing since Milton.

Damocles

Knight in his retirement relished his life as a private citizen and was not too worried about his public reputation. His reputation as an authority on ancient Greek matters was completely undermined by his slip, as William Hazlitt charitably called it, about the marbles.

> The Catalogue-writer carries his bear-garden notions . . . into the Fine Arts, and would set about destroying Dutch or Italian pictures as he would Dutch shipping or Italian liberty. He goes up to the Rembrandts with the same swaggering Jack-tar airs as he would to a battery of nine-pounders, and snaps his fingers at Raphael as he would at the French. Yet he talks big about the Elgin Marbles, because Mr. Payne Knight has made a slip on that subject; though to be consistent he ought to be for pounding them in a mortar.[93]

In 1811, by when Knight's remarks had circulated, but the matter had not been resolved by the meeting of the committee, he bought a painting from Richard Westall which depicted *The Sword of Damocles* (figure 11) in which Damocles, flatteringly envious of his king's position, is allowed

93 William Hazlitt, *Complete Works*, ed. P. P. Howe, 21 vols. (London: Dent, 1930–4), vol. IV, p. 143.

Figure 11. Richard Westall, *The Sword of Damocles*, 1811.

to sit in his throne, only to find, when he is sitting there, that a sword comes into view, hanging over him, supported by a single hair. Westall used the picture as a vehicle to depict not only the two central protagonists, the king looking magisterial, Damocles looking apprehensively at the sword, but also some servant girls in Grecian costumes and some scheming courtiers looking on from the shadows, together with objects of antiquarian interest such as a term of Bacchus, an ornately carved stone throne, a bronze standard lamp and various ornamented Greek vessels. It is an exhibition of Greek furnishings and costumes, but it is also a political image, showing that the splendid trappings of high office are undercut by the insecurity which goes with them. It could be read as an image of the precarious state of Knight's public celebrity at the time he bought it. He was still at the height of his fame, but not at all securely. He had already made the remark which would skewer his public persona, but the thread had yet to snap. He must, at some level, have known that the game was up.

Progress and retreat

It will be clear from Knight's virtual idolatry of the ancient Greeks that he felt their achievements in the general arrangement of life could not be bettered. He thought that their morality and taste were ideal, and had been corrupted by the pernicious influence of Christianity. In order to make progress in bringing about a satisfactory life then it would be necessary to reclaim as much as possible of the ancient state of affairs, and this he sought to do in his own life. There was a possibility of making improvements and progressing from the present state of affairs, but it would entail recapturing long-lost elements of a very much earlier state of society. In one reading this could be seen as reactionary, but in fact because it was an attempt not to retrieve a recent and remembered past, but a long-lost past, it was so very reactionary as to overturn completely the current state of affairs and therefore look revolutionary. This is not to say that in all respects the ancient Greeks had the last word. We shall see in the next chapter and elsewhere that against this conviction that the Greeks' values were the best, Knight was also convinced that there could be advances in knowledge and in the arts. Nevertheless he believed that the best ancient Greek work would never be bettered, and that it was the result of the artists living freely in well-regulated society, so that not only their artefacts, but also their movements, along with every gesture of an educated man, would be harmonious and graceful. In making these connections, Knight aestheticised the whole of the ancient Greeks' way of life, and also, working along the same line of thought but in the opposite direction, he politicised their art.

3 Atoms and analysis

Division of knowledge

Epicurus' moral teaching meant that he was vigorously attacked by many thinkers, and as we have seen his ideas about morals could easily be mistaken for a licence to abandon altogether any sense of ethical behaviour. Generally, but with exceptions, Epicurus was condemned for his ideas about religion from his own time onwards; on the other hand his scientific ideas, which were easily dismissed in antiquity, acquired tremendous prestige from the seventeenth century onwards. Knight, taking his cue from Enlightenment thinkers of the previous generation, enthusiastically endorsed both sides of Epicurus' teaching. He was well acquainted with scientific ideas, though unlike his brother, who was a member of the Royal Society, he was not a fully-fledged scientist, nor was he a diligent amateur in this field, as was Sir William Hamilton, who studied volcanoes, and on whom Knight drew in his account of his visit to Mount Etna.[1] He was, however, an intelligent and well-informed layman with philosophical interests, and, particularly in the *Analytical Inquiry into the Principles of Taste,* he showed some familiarity with scientific theory as well as drawing on medical and zoological cases for his examples. Knight seems to have been on good terms with his brother and in conversation he would have been able to keep abreast of topical information. In addition, both brothers knew Sir Joseph Banks (1743–1820) who enjoyed some celebrity because he had accompanied Captain Cook on his antipodean travels: Thomas Andrew Knight knew him as a fellow scientist, as the president of the Royal Society, and as a learned and sympathetic correspondent,[2] while Richard Payne Knight knew quite a different side of him, seeing him as the secretary of the Society of Dilettanti and latterly as a neighbour in Soho Square.[3] Not

1 Richard Payne Knight, *Expedition into Sicily*, ed. Claudia Stumpf (London: British Museum Press, 1986), pp. 55–7, and note 116, p. 78.

2 Some of Banks's letters to Thomas Andrew Knight are among the Downton Castle Papers at the Herefordshire County Record Office, Hereford.

3 Banks acted as secretary between 1778 and 1797; Lionel Cust, *History of the Society of Dilettanti* (London: Macmillan, 1898). From 1808 Knight lived at 3 Soho Square, while Banks lived at no. 32 (seven doors away): *Richard Payne Knight 1751–1824 The Arrogant Connoisseur*, eds. Michael Clarke and Nicholas Penny (Manchester University Press, 1982), pp. 7–8.

only practical scientific achievements but also the theory of science have developed greatly since the eighteenth century, and for Knight to try to be what we would call 'scientific' would have entailed him trying to do something rather different from what might be recognised as 'scientific' today, though having said that it is quite possible for practical scientists to work well away from the philosophical battleground which the theory of science has become.[4] Further to complicate matters, the word 'science' had not, in the eighteenth century, acquired the meaning that generally attaches to it today. In a general way in Knight's day 'science' meant learning or knowledge, whereas in the twentieth century it has come to mean learning or knowledge which has about it at least the appearance of a particular discipline. Knight would have used the term 'natural philosophy' to refer to what we would today want to call 'science'.

Plato in the fourth century BC had divided knowledge into three categories: natural philosophy, moral philosophy and rational philosophy; natural philosophy being speculation about the world, while moral philosophy was speculation about how one should act, and rational philosophy (or logic) was concerned with the separation of truth from falsehood and was used in the pursuit of knowledge in the other two disciplines. This division of knowledge was systematically set down in the *Organon* by Aristotle of Stagira (384–322 BC) who studied at Plato's Academy for twenty years before Plato's death, and whose philosophy therefore had much in common with Plato's, but with a rather less mystical outlook. The 'Neoplatonist' Saint Augustine of Hippo (AD 354–430) drew particularly on Plato's ideas in formulating his own, which were important in generating a framework for Christian thought, and the old division of the sciences was perpetuated.[5] And Aristotle became tremendously important to medieval Christians, who found his idea of the soul and his moral philosophy had much in common with their own, and his physics, his natural philosophy, came to be accepted as authoritative by the church. This state of affairs was not effectively challenged until the early seventeenth century with the work of Francis Bacon (1561–1626), whose *Novum Organum* of 1620 was explicitly designed to supersede Aristotle's *Organon*. For Bacon the most important division in philosophy was that made between a 'natural philosophy' which took its authority from observation of the world, and 'divine philosophy' which ultimately took its authority from God through divine revelation. Before Bacon if such a division were made at all then it was not thought to be particularly helpful and certainly did not assume much importance: divine

4 A. F. Chalmers, *What is this Thing called Science?* (Milton Keynes: Open University Press, 1978); *Criticism and the Growth of Knowledge*, ed. Imre Lakatos and Alan Musgrave (Cambridge University Press, 1970).

5 Saint Augustine of Hippo, *Concerning the City of God against the Pagans*, trans. Henry Bettenson (Harmondsworth: Penguin, 1972), bk. VIII, chapter 4: 'Plato the chief disciple of Socrates. His division of philosophy into three parts', pp. 303–4; bk. VIII, chapter 5: 'Theological questions are to be discussed with the Platonists rather than with any other philosophers, whose opinions must be counted inferior,' pp. 304–7.

certainties were to be valued more highly than the fallible products of human observation and reason. This, at least, was the Enlightenment version of events.

In the twentieth century the word 'science' refers to knowledge which is part of Bacon's natural philosophy; but in the eighteenth century John Locke, for example, could use 'science' in a technical way to mean *well-founded* or *certain knowledge,* saying that he supposed that natural philosophy could *never* be scientific: observations from the world could never lead to absolute certainty, whereas the truths of religion were absolute: 'how soever human industry may advance useful and experimental philosophy in physical things, *scientifical* will still be out of our reach'.[6] By contrast a twentieth-century philosopher who conspicuously invoked divine intervention in making explanations would be thought unscientific. Knight's sympathies lay very firmly with the proponents of natural philosophy, and he set himself up in trenchant opposition to those for whom divine philosophy was more important. This is made very clear in the Sicilian journal, where, for example, we find Knight at his most heated, and most pained, when describing the behaviour of people guided by religious belief. Knight felt that religion had been subverted into superstition and ignorance and that it prevailed 'among the Sicilians to an incredible degree':

> all inquiry or improvement of every kind is checked. Men, who gain vast emoluments of the blind belief of a few incomprehensible Mysteries, are naturally jealous of every thing, that can tend to dissipate the cloud of darkness which protects them. Weak as human reason is, it would be sufficient in its lowest state to penetrate the thin veil of Priestcraft, if People only dared think . . . The Ecclesiasticks in Sicily, as everywhere else, are perfectly sensible of this, & therefore oppose every thing, that can possibly imploy the mind.[7]

In Catania Knight had made a note of a story that the populace had been faced with certain destruction by streams of lava from an eruption of Mount Etna in 1699, but

> instead of making Walls to avert its fury . . . brought out St. Agatha's veil, & a whole Legion of Saints, each of whom, the Priests assured them, was sufficient to perform much greater Miracles. The consequence of this was, as usual. – A great part of the City was destroyed, its Port filled up and the Inhabitants

6 John Locke, *An Essay Concerning Human Understanding* (London: 1690), bk. IV, chapter 3, section 26.

7 *Sicily*, p. 61.

> ruined; but the Saints remained in greater credit, than ever, the People readily believing, that the Calamity arose from their own want of faith and not from any fault in their heavenly Guardians.[8]

Knight (drawing his images from the Roman Epicurean poet Lucretius, of whom more will be said in due course) saw religion as a species of blindness associated with images of dark clouds and obscurity – an absence of light – standing in direct and complete opposition to the exercise of reason.[9] Where Knight was concerned this point of view was neither absolutely commonplace nor remarkably original. It shows him to have been in tune with the values of the Enlightenment, with such intellectuals as Voltaire, Diderot and David Hume.[10] Knight's phrase 'if People only dared think' refers to Horace's *Sapere Aude!* (Dare to know!) which Immanuel Kant (1724–1804) cited as the *dictum* of Enlightenment.[11]

The Enlightenment's values and prejudices were supported by a view of history which divided the past from the origin of the world into four epochs: two ages of superstition and two ages of enlightenment, – two ages of faith which stood in contrast to two ages of reason. The first age of reason began with the dawn of Greek civilisation and ended with the fall of the Roman Empire. The second age of reason began with the 'revival of letters', the Renaissance, which means re-birth, specifically the re-birth of ancient reason. This second age was seen in the eighteenth century to last until the present; and Knight thought of himself as belonging to it. Before the first age of reason there had been the first age of the world, called 'primeval', which included human development up to and including the priest-ridden culture of ancient Egypt;[12] and between the two ages of reason, one ancient, one modern, there was another age (called 'medieval', the *middle age*) which was likewise in the grip of superstition. It is scarcely possible to exaggerate the horror which Enlightenment *philosophes* expressed when they considered the medieval period; for example Joseph Addison (1672–1719), an admirer of Locke, wrote of that era as a time of darkness and superstition 'when pious Frauds were made use of to amuse mankind, and frighten them into a Sense of their Duty. Our Forefathers looked upon Nature with more Reverence and Horrour, before the World was enlightened by Learning and Philosophy, and loved to astonish themselves with the Apprehensions of Witchcraft, Prodigies, Charms and Enchantments.'[13] Knight's feelings about the Church could well have influenced his decision not to go to university. Edward Gibbon thought of the fourteen months he spent at Magdalen College Oxford as the most completely wasted fourteen months of his entire life:

8 Ibid., p. 53.

9 E.g. Lucretius, *De Rerum Natura*, bk. I, lines 62ff.

10 For the importance of Lucretius to Enlightenment thought see Peter Gay, *The Enlightenment: An Interpretation*, 2 vols. (New York: Knopf, 1966 and 1969).

11 Horace, *Epistles*, bk. I, no. 2, line 40; Loeb edn trans. H. Rushton Fairclough (London: Heinemann, 1970), pp. 264, 265; Immanuel Kant 'Was ist Aufklärung?' (Berlin: 1784), trans. A. F. M. Willich, 'What is Enlightening?', in *Essays and Treatises on Moral, Political, and Various Philosophical Subjects*, 2 vols. (1798 and 1799), vol.I; repr. *The Age of Enlightenment*, ed. S. Eliot and B. Stern, 2 vols. (London: 1979), vol. II, p. 250 (where the quotation from Horace is mistakenly said to be from the *Epodes*).

12 Gay, *Enlightenment*, vol. I, pp. 34–6.

13 Joseph Addison, *The Spectator*, no. 419, 1 July 1712, ed. Gregory Smith, 4 vols. (London: Dent, 1907, rev. 1945), vol. III, p. 301.

> The schools of Oxford and Cambridge were founded in a dark age of false and barbarous science; and they are still tainted with the vices of their origin. Their primitive discipline was adapted to the education of priests and monks; and the government still remains in the hands of the clergy, an order of men whose manners are remote from the present world, and whose eyes are dazzled by the light of philosophy.[14]

Knight wholeheartedly subscribed to this view of history and inevitably it coloured his perception. To twentieth-century sensibilities these notions seem to be at best gross caricatures, any possible basis in fact having been overtaken by ignorance and misunderstanding, but it was because Knight shared this kind of hostility to superstition that he would in the first place have been drawn to the poetry of Lucretius, and thereby to Epicurean thought. The sympathy for scientific inquiry and the hostility to superstition were attitudes which went hand in hand, particularly after the ideas of Isaac Newton (1642–1727) had found general acceptance in the scientific community. Both Newton's ideas and Epicurus' depended heavily on the idea of the atom.

Atoms

The atom was an ancient Greek idea which was promoted by Leucippus and Democritus in the fifth century BC, but it was taken up in the second half of the fourth century BC by Epicurus, who none the less claimed to be completely self-taught. He went so far as to deny that Leucippus had ever existed, and nicknamed Democritus 'Lerocritus', which means 'nonsense'; his pupils, though, were prepared to acknowledge the influence.[15] Epicurus claimed that nothing is created out of the non-existent, that all matter is composed of atoms and that between the atoms there is empty space, which extends infinitely in all directions; he said that atoms are in a constant state of flux, that there is an infinite number of atoms and of sizes and shapes of atoms.[16] This theory of matter was the basis of Epicurus' thought, and from it he developed a comprehensive philosophy which could cover every aspect of life: he wrote more than 300 books in which he set it down, including 37 books on nature and others on such varied subjects as disease and music, love and death,[17] but they are all lost. Only a few fragments of this vast outpouring survive, most of them in the biography of Epicurus written by Diogenes Laertius in the early third century.[18] The text of primary importance for anyone who has taken an interest in Epicurean ideas since the Renaissance has therefore been the

14 Edward Gibbon, *Memoirs of my Life*, ed. Betty Radice (Harmondsworth: Penguin, 1984), pp. 76–7.

15 Cyril Bailey, *The Greek Atomists and Epicurus* (Oxford: Clarendon Press, 1928), p. 226.

16 Ibid., pp. 275–338.

17 Cyril Bailey, *Epicurus: the Extant Remains* (Oxford: Clarendon Press, 1926), pp. 158–9 (Diogenes Laertius, *Life of Epicurus*).

18 These fragments are gathered in Bailey, ibid.

long didactic poem *De Rerum Natura* (On the Nature of Things) by Lucretius (*c.*100–c.55 BC), whom Knight believed to have been the greatest poet to have used the Latin language.[19] *De Rerum Natura*, the poet's only surviving work, set out Epicurus' teaching with spirited vehemence, ranging over a great many ideas in the poem, but striking its most characteristic note when attacking religion. Voltaire said of one line in the poem, '*tantum religio potuit suadere malorum*' (such evil deeds could religion prompt), that it deserved to last as long as the world.[20]

Epicurus taught that all matter, including the human soul, was composed of atoms, and from this he deduced that when the body died the soul was dispersed and that there was only oblivion after death – 'Death means nothing to us' – [21] and consequently there was nothing to be gained in making preparations for an afterlife, nor anything to be feared in hell. Officially at least Epicurus taught that the gods did exist, but he supposed that they lived in the depths of infinite space and could not affect anything on earth. Often non-Epicureans could see no point in believing in such gods, and so the Epicureans were frequently supposed to be atheists.[22] As for the gods of popular religion, Epicurus taught that they were illusory and that the real cause of such effects as were visible in the world was not the gods but his atoms. Epicurus' physics (particularly in Lucretius' polemical formulation) were designed to combat the idea that there was divine intervention in the everyday running of the world, and the result of this thinking was that pleasure found its way to the heart of Epicurean philosophy, the aim of which came to be to describe how best to find happiness in the world. The argument ran that because the soul was made of atoms and dispersed at death, there could be no life after death, and that therefore one should aim to maximise the benefits in life. The atoms which constituted matter were capable of recombining in different ways, through collisions and interactions, and the world was seen to have evolved through a sequence of these random events, not to have been created by supernatural means. We can see these theories finding their way into Knight's observations of natural scenery on Sicily, where he was shown a cave in which strata of marble were separated with strata of what he believed to be human bones, petrified, and which were presumably some sort of fossils:

> To offer any Conjectures, how these bones came here, would be useless, as the great revolutions, which this globe has evidently undergone, have their causes too remote for our Comprehension. We can only conclude, that Matter, endued with Motion, governed by the Laws of physical necessity, must, during the course of

19 *The Progress of Civil Society: A Didactic Poem* (London: 1796), p. v.

20 Lucretius, *De Rerum Natura*, bk. I, line 101m, trans. Cyril Bailey (Oxford: Clarendon Press, 1947), p. 181. For Voltaire, see George Depue Hadzsits, *Lucretius and His Influence* (New York: Cooper Square, 1963).

21 Bailey, *Epicurus*, pp. 94–5 (Epicurus, *Principal Doctrines*, II).

22 Cicero, *De Natura Deorum*, trans. H. C. P. McGregor, *The Nature of the Gods* (Harmondsworth: Penguin, 1972), p. 120: 'Posidonius argued . . . that Epicurus did not believe the gods existed at all and what he said about them was said merely to avoid the odium of atheism.'

> infinite time, have undergone every possible transmutation. In these infinite changes it must have been in disorder as well as order, which perhaps regularly spring from each other.[23]

In 312 Constantine made Christianity the official religion of the Roman Empire, and its influence grew. Aristotle's physics came to be accepted by the church on theological, not experimental, grounds;[24] but Aristotle's gods, the old Greek gods, became demons and devils along with the gods of all other cultures. Thus we find, after a thousand years of unsympathetic reinterpretation, that Jupiter the heavenly father was transmogrified into the foul creature at the heart of Dante's *Inferno*.[25] Lucretius was useful to the earliest Christians because his tirades against religion were directed against the old gods, but once the new religion had become established *De Rerum Natura* did more harm than good, and it was actively suppressed.[26]

Through the Middle Ages, while the church dominated all intellectual activity, Aristotle's ideas were used extensively, as were those of Plato; but there was no scope for making use of the ideas of Epicurus which were couched in a language that was self-evidently seditious. During this period the truths of religion were unshakeable: if there were a discrepancy between Aristotle's description of the world and one's own impression of it then it was one's own frail human senses that were at fault, not the authoritative word. The concern of an investigator who might be recognised as a 'natural philosopher' was always subservient to the demands of divine philosophy, and so the philosopher's purpose was to show how the word of God was made manifest in the world. The natural world was seen as a system of signs to be decoded, or a text to be interpreted;[27] so that, for example, since there was known to be a similarity between the nature of light and God's word, optics were studied in the hope that learning more about light would reveal more about God's word.[28]

The Renaissance saw the development of a wider and more critical interest in classical texts, and also, in the newly powerful mercantile class, an unscholarly cult of practical effectiveness; but ideas taken from ancient sources were assimilated into a broadly Christian framework of belief. Epicureanism (having been destroyed) was not an immediate danger, and Christian writers can be found making some limited use of Epicurean ideas. For example Erasmus of Rotterdam (1466–1536) turned the Epicurean pleasure principle into an argument for Christianity by insisting that only the Christian could be truly happy;[29] and the inhabitants of Thomas More's *Utopia* (*c*.1477–1535) had much the same attitude to life; they were engaged in the pursuit of pleasure, but only

23 *Sicily*, p. 30.

24 Robert Hugh Kargon, introduction to Walter Charleton, *Physiologia Epicuro-Gassendo-Charletoniana* (London: 1654) (repr. New York: Johnson Reprint Corporation, 1966); Kargon, *Atomism in England from Hariot to Newton* (Oxford University Press, 1966), gives further background from this standpoint.

25 Dante Alighieri, *Inferno*, canto 34.

26 Ronald Latham, entry for 'Lucretius' in *Encyclopedia of Philosophy*, ed. Paul Edwards, 8 vols. (New York: Macmillan, 1967), vol. V, p. 101b.

27 Michel Foucault, *Les Mots et les choses* (Paris: Gallimard, 1966), trans. Alan Sheridan, *The Order of Things: An Archaeology of the Human Sciences* (London: Tavistock, 1970).

28 David C. Lindberg, *Roger Bacon's Philosophy of Nature*, a critical edition of *De multiplicatione specierum* and *De speculis comburentibus* (Oxford: Clarendon Press, 1983), pp. xxxv–xlii.

29 Erasmus, 'Epicureus' in *The Colloquies of Erasmus*, trans. C. R. Thompson (Chicago University Press, 1965), pp. 535ff.

'virtuous' pleasure.[30] Michel de Montaigne (1533–92) often quoted Lucretius in his celebrated *Essays*, while evidently remaining a sincere Christian. He divided mankind into two classes, a saintly elect and ordinary people; and he thought it quite proper for the saintly to abandon the body, to live for the sake of the soul alone, even though among ordinary folk this would be madness. He advised that these ordinary people, among whom he included himself, should learn to keep their bodies and souls comfortable,[31] and found (in John Florio's translation) that virtue was 'a pleasant and buxom quality'.[32]

There were occasional, but repeated, attempts to revive Epicurean ideas about the physical constitution of matter through the Middle Ages, which were suppressed because the atom was too dangerous an idea: it brought with it arguments for the soul's mortality and, consequently, Epicurean morals and atheism. For example William of Conches (*c.*1080–1154) tried to propose an atomic theory of matter, but he was charged with granting too much to reason and too little to faith.[33] It is not in the least surprising that the Church stood in opposition to these developments as Lucretius made it perfectly plain that the main advantage of the atom was that it was an effective means to 'cure' religious faith; so the Church by its own lights was acting very reasonably in suppressing the doctrine.

The major breakthrough in the rehabilitation of the atom is credited to Pierre Gassend (1592–1655), a priest who worked at the same time as Descartes. He saw the atom as a useful idea and therefore set about purging it of its reputation for immorality by suggesting that, although atoms acted according to mechanical principles, they were nevertheless under the conscious guidance of God.[34] Gassend's attempt was not immediately successful, but he had embarked upon a monumental undertaking and had established a foundation on which others could build. One of his friends was Thomas Hobbes (1588–1679), whose reputation in the twentieth century rests principally on his contributions to political thought, but who would seem to have been the central figure in the dissemination of Epicurean ideas in England.[35] His *Leviathan* (1651) could be understood as a resolution of Epicurean ideas into a political theory, since the self-interest which was the basis of Hobbes's thought was a version of the pursuit of happiness and the aversion from pain.[36] *Leviathan* was not popular with the clergy (bishops in the House of Lords thought that Hobbes should be burnt on its account)[37] and he did nothing to court their goodwill. He discussed religion under the heading 'Of the Kingdome of darknesse,' and found some remarkable similarities

30 Edward Surtz, *The Praise of Pleasure: Philosophy, Education and Communism in More's Utopia* (Cambridge, Mass.: Harvard University Press, 1957), chapters 4–7, particularly chapter 4, 'The Fortunes of Epicurus in Utopia'.

31 M. A. Screech, *Montaigne and Melancholy* (London: Duckworth, 1983), p. 97.

32 Michel Eyquem de Montaigne, 'Upon some verses in Virgil' in *Essays*, trans. John Florio, ed. L. C. Harmer, 3 vols. (London: Dent, 1910), vol. III, p. 67.

33 John L. Kraus, *John Locke: Empiricist, Atomist, Conceptualist and Agnostic* (New York: Philosophical Library, 1968), p. 37.

34 *Ibid., pp.* 37ff.; Kargon, *Atomism in England*; Howard Jones, *Pierre Gassendi 1592–1655: An Intellectual Biography* (Nieuwkoop: B. De Graaf, 1981).

35 David Hume, *An Enquiry Concerning the Principles of Morals*, in *Philosophical Works,* eds. T. H. Green and T. H. Grose, 4 vols. (1886), vol. IV, p. 267: 'Probity and honour were no strangers to EPICURUS and his sect . . . And among the modern, HOBBES and LOCKE, who maintained the selfish system of morals, lived irreproachable lives; though the former lay not under any restraint of religion, which might supply the defects of his philosophy . . . An EPICUREAN or a HOBBIST readily allows, that there is

between the church and 'the Kingdome of Fayries'.[38] One of Hobbes's English friends was Walter Charleton (1620–1707) who, remarkably, acted not only as physician to Charles I, but also (after the Restoration) to Charles II.[39] He wrote about a great many things including wine-making and Stonehenge, and published three books which had a bearing on the fate of the atom: *The Darknes of Atheism Refuted by the Light of Nature: a physico-theologiall Treatise* (1652); *Physiologia Epicuro-Gassendo-Charletoniana* (1654); and *Epicurus's Morals* (1656).

In the first of these books Charleton promoted the atom while taking care to dissociate it (and himself) from opinions which could be labelled heretical; for example he did not suggest that the soul was mortal, neither did he argue that motion was inherent in matter (the church taught that God had set things in motion at the creation).[40] Indeed he turned the atom into a defender of faith by arguing that he found it inconceivable that a world made of atoms could have evolved without the guidance of a designer.[41] The second book, the *Physiologia*, explained on its title page that the hypothesis (which is to say the conjecture) of atoms was founded by Epicurus, repaired by Gassend and augmented by Charleton;[42] so there is no doubt that Charleton's atoms were genealogically descended from those to be found in Epicurus and Lucretius, even though Charleton had modified their moral character so as to make them available to seventeenth-century physicists. Charleton's survey of Epicurean morals which followed was evidently aimed to further the efforts of the earlier two publications by showing that Epicurus' morals were at heart not really very different from Christian morals, which should have had the effect of reducing the level of panic that might be felt on seeing Epicurus' name. According to Charleton's reading the principal virtues of Epicureanism were prudence, temperance, fortitude and justice:

> It is not perpetual Feastings and Drinkings; it is not the love of, and Familiarity with beautiful boys and women; it is not the Delicacies of rare Fishes, sweet meats, rich Wines, nor any other Dainties of the table, that can make a Happy life: But it is Reason, with sobriety, and consequently a serene Mind; investigating the Causes, why this Object is to be Elected, and that to be Rejected; and chasing away those vain superstitions and deluding opinions, which would occasion very great disquiet in the mind.[43]

This is not the philosophy of the depraved monster one would have expected had Epicurus lived up to his reputation; and if Epicurus' morals were not entirely wicked then maybe his atoms, suitably purged,

such a thing as friendship in the world.' Hume's judgement that Hobbes lived an irreproachable life was not universal.

36 Thomas Hobbes, *Leviathan; or the Matter, Forme and Power of a Commonwealth Ecclesiastical and Civil* (1651).

37 John Aubrey, *Brief Lives*, ed. Andrew Clark, 2 vols. (Oxford: Clarendon Press, 1898), vol. I, p. 339.

38 Hobbes, *Leviathan*, part IV, chapter 47.

39 Kargon, introduction to Charleton's *Physiologia*, pp. xv, xvi.

40 Kargon, *Atomism*, p. 85.

41 Ibid., pp. 85–6.

42 *Physiologia*.

43 *Epicurus's Morals* (1656), p. 23.

could be allowed a place in the world of ideas. It is in part because of Charleton's advocacy and exposition of ideas and his interpretation of atoms with respect to morals that Isaac Newton (1642–1727) was free to think as he did. Newton also read Charleton's *Physiologia*, so there was direct influence as well as the less certain influence felt through the climate of intellectual opinion.[44]

By the end of Newton's life, and increasingly as his reputation was popularised by the likes of Voltaire, he was seen as one of the two great heroes of the new learning, the other being Francis Bacon.[45] Newton was seen as having realised the potential of the experimental science, natural philosophy, which had been established by Bacon; and Aristotle's physics looked very old-fashioned. Charleton's friend the poet John Dryden (1631–1700) wrote an *Epistle* to the doctor which first appeared prefacing Charleton's book about Stonehenge. It began:

> The longest Tyranny that ever sway'd,
> Was that wherein our Ancestors betray'd
> Their free-born *Reason* to the *Stagirite*,
> And made his Torch their universal Light.

'The Stagirite' here is Aristotle, who came from Stagira. Dryden continued:

> Among th'*Assertors* of free Reason's claim,
> Th'*English* are not the least in Worth or Fame.
> The World to *Bacon* does not onely owe
> Its *present* Knowledge, but its *future* too.[46]

Charleton's achievements were portrayed as belonging in this exalted frame of reference: a philosophical battle fought for high stakes across millennia. The eventual victor was undoubtedly Newton, who could scarcely have been praised more highly than in the famous couplet by Alexander Pope (1688–1744) which was written to be set above the crossing arch at the threshold of the choir at Westminster Abbey:

> Nature, and Nature's Laws lay hid in Night.
> God said, *Let Newton be!* and All was *Light*.[47]

But Newton's ideas were not immediately acceptable to everyone. Gassend and Charleton had attempted to dissolve the links which Epicurus had made between physics and morals, but those of a pious disposition were still inclined to think of the new physics as a threat to morality. Untypically the philosopher David Hume (1711–76) in

44 Kargon, *Atomism*, chapter 11.

45 E.g. Gay, *Enlightenment*, vol. I, pp. 11–12: 'The propagandists of the Enlightenment were French, but its patron saints and pioneers were British: Bacon, Newton and Locke had such splendid reputations on the Continent that they quite overshadowed the revolutionary ideas of a Descartes or a Fontenelle'; see also Voltaire's *Letters on England* in *The Complete Works of Voltaire*, vol. CXVIII: *Correspondence and Related Documents*, ed. Theodore Besterman (Banbury, Oxfordshire: The Voltaire Foundation, 1974), letters 14–16.

46 John Dryden, 'Epistle: To My Honored Friend, Dr Charleton'. The poem first appeared prefacing Charleton's *Chorea Gigantum; or, the Most Famous Antiquity of Great-Britain, Vulgarly Called Stone-Heng, Standing on Salisbury Plain, Restored to the Danes* (1662). The book repudiated Inigo Jones's idea that Stonehenge had been built as a temple by the Romans. In *The Works of John Dryden*, ed. Hooker and Swedenberg, 19 vols. (Berkeley: University of California Press, 1956–79), vol. I, pp. 43ff.

47 Alexander Pope, *Poems*, ed. N. Ault and J. Butt, 11 vols. (London: Methuen, 1954), vol. VI, p. 317: 'Epitaph, Intended for SIR ISAAC NEWTON in Westminster Abbey.'

Edinburgh faced a very different problem, finding Newton's ideas plausible enough, but entertaining doubts about Christian morality. His *Enquiry Concerning the Principles of Morals* made a new connection between science and morality; instead of taking a theoretical proposition which was undoubtedly true and developing it into a set of inferences about the physical world, he worked in the opposite direction and attempted to treat moral problems in the same way as physical problems, as a part of natural philosophy.[48] He set out to derive a set of moral principles by observing people's behaviour and by the application of reason to his observations; and Knight too, most likely under Hume's influence, derived his theory of morals in this way, declaring that 'in morals, as well as physics, there is no effect without an adequate cause'.[49] Now whereas Charleton's study of Epicurus' morals had attempted to conciliate by showing that they were very much like Christian morals, Hume did not follow this strategy, which would, after all, have entailed allowing that Christian morals were reasonable. His system of ethics 'founded on fact and observation' led him to conclude that

> as every quality is useful or agreeable to ourselves or others is, in common life, allowed to be a part of personal merit; so no other will ever be received, where men judge of things by their natural, unprejudiced reason, without the delusive glosses of superstition and false religion. Celibacy, fasting, penance, mortification, self-denial, humility, silence, solitude, and the whole train of monkish virtues; for whatever reason are they rejected by men of sense, but because they serve no manner of purpose; neither qualify him for the entertainment of company, nor increase his power of self-enjoyment? We observe, on the contrary, that they cross all these desirable ends; stupefy the understanding and harden the heart, obscure the fancy and sour the temper. We justly, therefore, transfer them to the opposite column, and place them in the catalogue of vices; nor has any superstition force sufficient among men of the world, to pervert entirely these natural sentiments. A gloomy, hair-brained enthusiast, after his death, may have a place in the calendar; but will scarcely ever be admitted, when alive, into intimacy and society, except by those who are as delirious and dismal as himself.[50]

While it is clear here that Hume was taking the pleasure principle as the basis for a discussion of morality, it is perhaps less clear how it could be that both he and Charleton were drawing on the same source:

48 *Morals*, in *Philosophical Works*, ed. Green and Grose, vol. IV, p. 174: 'we can only expect success, by following the experimental method, and deducing general maxims from a comparison of particular instances'.

49 *A Discourse on the Worship of Priapus, and its Connexion with the Mystic Theology of the Antients* (London: 1786), p. 24.

50 Hume, *Morals* in *Philosophical Works,* ed. Green and Grose, vol. IV, pp. 247–8.

Epicurus's Morals had made no mention of celibacy and self-denial being vices. The problem is solved however if we turn to Epicurus himself, who said,

> You tell me that the stimulus of the flesh makes you too prone to the pleasures of love. Provided that you do not break the laws or good customs and do not distress any of your neighbours or do harm to your body or squander your pittance, you may indulge your inclination as you please. Yet it is impossible not to come up against one or other of these barriers: for the pleasures of love never profited a man and he is lucky if they do him no harm.[51]

Epicurus presented abstinence as the surest route to pleasure, and Charleton stressed the abstinence whilst Hume stressed the pleasure. We have already seen how sympathetic this form of thinking was to Knight, who did not quite scandalise his neighbours, but left them thinking that he was more or less insane. Epicurus expected that the principles of his followers would not be those of society at large, and he advised them to follow the law of the land and to avoid causing scandal. He did this not because the established law or the morality of the public at large were necessarily correct, but only because one would be more likely to find peace of mind if one co-operated in these matters: Epicurus did not ask for martyrs. Knight of course did not act according to conventional ideas, but, at least so far as the world beyond his front door was concerned, he did keep within the law, even to the point of observing Christian custom when legislation obliged him to do so.[52] To a committed Christian his position will inevitably seem hypocritical, but an Epicurean would see it as no more than prudently defensive. Epicurus advised:

> Let us sacrifice piously and rightly where it is customary, and let us do all things rightly according to the laws not troubling ourselves with common beliefs in what concerns the noblest and holiest of beings. Further let us be free of any charge in regard to their opinion. For thus can one live in conformity with nature.[53]

In Epicurus' opinion, then, a show of conventional piety was advisable, providing always that it remained unclouded by superstitious belief. We find that despite Knight's clear and vigorously expressed dislike of Christianity he claimed nevertheless to uphold the values of the Church of England;[54] and it is safe to assume that he did so without the slightest sincerity. It was necessary that he should be seen, at least technically, to endorse these values because he was a Member of Parliament,

51 Bailey, *Epicurus*, pp. 114–15 (Epicurus, *Fragments*, 51).

52 *The Progress of Civil Society*, p. xviii.

53 Bailey, *Epicurus*, pp. 134–5 (Epicurus, *Fragments*, 57).

54 *Alfred; A Romance in Rhyme* (London: 1823), p. vii.

and membership of the Church of England was required for all MPs in order to show that they were loyal to the king, who was head of the church as well as head of state. As the law stood at that time, had Knight converted to Roman Catholicism (which of course he would have had no inclination to do) then the priest who received him into the church would theoretically have faced a charge of high treason and the penalty of death; though in practice sentences were milder. Gibbon tells us that it was usual for the priest in such a position merely to be sentenced to imprisonment for life, and for the convert to sacrifice his estates to the crown.[55] Knight of course did not feel drawn towards Catholicism, but he did think the law unfair (his friend Charles Townley was a Roman Catholic, but not a convert) and as a Member of Parliament he might have been able to help bring about change, for example by supporting the bill moved by Charles James Fox which (had it not been successfully opposed) would have disestablished the Church of England.[56]

The case for Knight's Epicureanism is overwhelming, but the same cannot be said of Hume, who is a far more elusive character, and whose writing ducks and weaves as a defence against those who would condemn the drift of the arguments. He did not acknowledge that Epicurus had any connection with his own principles of morals, which he said were drawn from observation of the world around him; but in the *Enquiry Concerning Human Understanding* Hume found that the argument advanced in favour of Epicureanism was unanswerable. He did not endorse the philosophy in his own person in the text, but advanced its case through the opinions of a 'friend', an *alter ego* who confounded 'Hume', who could find no objections to what the 'friend' said, much as (so we are led to understand) he would have liked to have done so.[57] As a philosopher Hume defended the position that there could never be certain knowledge, which made him a Cynic, or Pyrrhonist, not an Epicurean (who would have held that Epicurus taught the truth); but then neither was Hume's 'friend' a classical Epicurean as the philosophy he undertook to defend was a mixture of Epicurean and sceptical Academic ideas. Hume does not allow us to say definitely that this was his own view, though it may well have been, but this Academic Epicureanism was certainly close to Knight's, and Knight would have found his own views sympathetically reflected when he read Hume. Hume saw himself as continuing Academic endeavour as it had been formulated by Cicero, being critical of everything and affirming nothing,[58] but the state of knowledge had changed since Cicero's day. When Cicero sided with the Stoics in *De Natura Deorum* he did so not because he

55 Gibbon, *Memoirs*, p. 86.

56 Fox's bill was successfully opposed by Edmund Burke: *Dictionary of National Biography*, vol. XX, p. 105b.

57 David Hume, *An Enquiry Concerning Human Understanding*, section XI: 'Of a Particular Providence and of a Future State' in *Philosophical Works*, ed. Green and Grose, vol. IV, pp. 109ff.

58 Cicero, *De Natura Deorum*, p. 73.

found the Stoics' assertions demonstrably correct, but because he supposed that their respect for the gods was good for political stability and public morality.[59] The Epicureans' ideas offered no such practical advantages, but their greatest weakness for Cicero lay in the fact that they were totally dependent on the idea of the atom, and Cicero could not believe that such a thing as an atom could exist.[60] The religion which Cicero supported was Roman paganism, which Hume found preferable in various ways to Christianity,[61] and the Epicureans' doctrine of atoms had changed from being implausible into the most compelling reason for listening to what they had to say.

Analysis

Francis Bacon put up a show of religious orthodoxy which is surprising when compared with his actual behaviour.[62] He believed that there were two distinct species of knowledge, one earthly, one divine, and he particularly stressed the fact that they were independent of one another, and could both in some way be true: that the findings of natural philosophy were true even when they did not agree with the findings of divine philosophy. Indeed he went even further than this, and argued that the triumph of faith was greatest when to the unaided reason a religious dogma appeared the most absurd, because if reason suggested one thing and divine teaching another then there was a real need for faith in order to reconcile the two; whereas when the teachings of religion and reason coincided there was no need for faith.[63] In other words faith, which was strongly encouraged by the church, was necessary only when the church taught things which the everyday senses knew not to be true. Bacon was certainly sympathetic to Epicurean ideas, but he took care to shield himself from attack by the conventionally pious, so that although he could describe Epicurus as a heretic,[64] he could say none the less that Epicurus 'doth most demonstrate religion' even though he was usually considered an atheist, which seems rather to suggest that Bacon was inclined to go along with the heresy.[65] He also made use of the atom, though not in his published writings, before it had been purged of its atheistic taints. He realised that though attractive as an idea, the atom should be subject to the same scepticism as other hypotheses, and he therefore abandoned it for more basic considerations; the works in which he used the atom were, however, published after his death and became influential.[66] Knight made frequent reference to Bacon in his footnotes, and presumably saw him as a fellow Epicurean.[67]

59 Ibid., p. 70.

60 Ibid., p. 95.

61 Hume, *The Natural History of Religion* (1757) in *Philosophical Works*, ed. Green and Grose, vol. IV, pp. 309 ff.

62 Aubrey, *Brief Lives*, vol. I, pp. 70 ff.

63 Bertrand Russell, *History of Western Philosophy*, 2nd edn (London: Routledge, 1961), p. 527.

64 *The Advancement of Learning* (1605), ed. Arthur Johnston (Oxford: Clarendon Press, 1974), p. 174.

65 'Of Atheism' in *Essays* (1625), ed. Spedding, Ellis and Heath (London: Dent, 1915), p. 49.

66 Kargon, *Atomism*, pp. 52, 53.

67 Bacon was the Viscount St Albans, and Knight cited his name in footnotes in the form 'Verulam', Verulamium being the Roman name for St Albans.

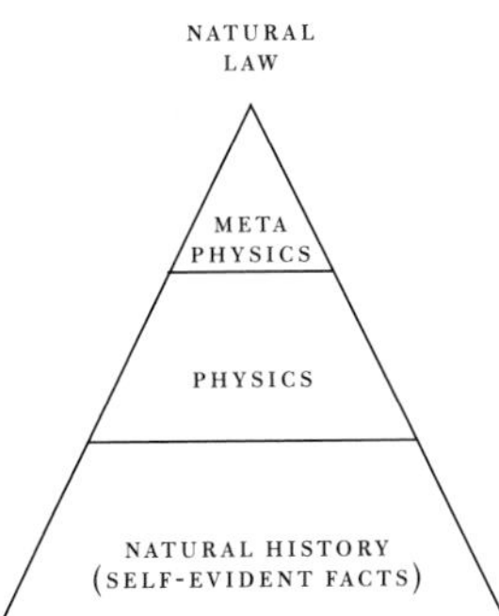

Figure 12. Pyramid of knowledge, according to Bacon.

Once Bacon had made the division of knowledge into natural philosophy and divine philosophy, he put the divine philosophy safely on one side 'inclosed and bounded by itself' and said nothing more about it.[68] He was concerned only with natural philosophy, which he argued did not challenge theology at all because it was entirely separate from its concerns,[69] and therefore in theory he could not be attacked by the church because his concerns and the church's concerns at no time overlapped.

Bacon divided natural philosophy into two: on the one hand there was the 'inquisition of causes' and on the other the 'production of effects'; one was speculative, the other operative, which can roughly be translated into a more modern vocabulary to say that he was making a distinction between primary research and technological application. He further divided the speculative research into two, into physics and metaphysics, which could cause confusion because in the twentieth century metaphysics is definitively unscientific,[70] but that was not the case for Bacon: his physics and metaphysics both drew on facts, on observation of the world and on descriptions (which he called 'natural history'). Physics, he said, was a description of variable causes whereas metaphysics was a description of constant causes. Summarising, he said that 'knowledges are as pyramides, whereof history is the basis. So of natural philosophy, the basis is physic; the stage next the vertical point is metaphysic. As for the vertical point, *opus quod operatur Deus a principio usque ad finem* [the work which God worketh from beginning to end], the summary law of nature, we cannot know whether man's inquiry can attain unto it.'[71] He was using words to describe a diagram: each layer in the pyramid is made up of generalisations from the layer below, the lowest layer of all being made up of self-evident facts. The knowledge in the higher layers is knowledge of a higher order, the generalisations helping to 'abridge the infinity of individual experience' and thereby 'to remedy the complaint of *vita brevis, ars longa*' [life is short and art is long];[72] but the authority of the knowledge in question lies always in the lowest layer: the generalisations can only be correct when they agree with the self-evident facts of experience (figure 12).

This view of science stands in direct contrast to that of the scholastic tradition of the church, which took general principles (revealed by God, or by respected authorities such as Aristotle) as its starting-point and made elaborations from there. If observed facts did not correspond with the theoretical deductions then the fallibility of the human senses was demonstrated, along with the frailty of human reason. The principles were always correct, and what one made of them was not always to be

68 Bacon, *Advancement of Learning*, p. 90.

69 Bacon, 'We do not presume . . . by the contemplation of nature to attain to the mysteries of God'; quoted by A. Quinton, *Francis Bacon* (Oxford University Press, 1980), p. 22.

70 Karl Popper, *Conjectures and Refutations*, 4th edn (London: Routledge, 1972), pp. 253 ff.

71 Bacon, *Advancement of Learning*, p. 93.

72 Ibid., p. 92.

trusted. Of this procedure Hume said that 'The other scientific method, where a general abstract principle is first established, and is afterwards branched out into a variety of inferences and conclusions, may be more perfect in itself, but suits less the imperfection of human nature, and is likely to be a common source of illusion and mistake.'[73] He supported the ideas of Bacon and Newton, which look to be theoretically unsophisticated now that for example we no longer have self-evident facts;[74] but Bacon's theory of science, in slightly modified forms, was current (if not absolutely universal) in the scientific community throughout the eighteenth and nineteenth centuries. In Hume's day, and Knight's, the great triumph of scientific knowledge was the discovery in the previous century of Newton's 'laws', which seemed universal and to underlie everything; but the status of these discoveries remained a vexed question. Newton's laws of motion were published as *Philosophiae naturalis principia mathematica* (*The Mathematical Principles of Natural Philosophy*, usually called the *Principia*) which began by making the boldly counter-intuitive assertion that 'Every body preserves in its state of rest, or of uniform motion in a right line, unless it is compelled to change that state by forces impress'd thereon.'[75] Newton's ideas were hotly disputed, notably by John Hutchinson, who published a 'refutation' (*Moses's Principia of the Invisible Parts of Matter; of Motion; of Visible forms; and their Dissolutions, and Reformation*, 1724) which started its reasoning from the 'indisputable' axiom that 'In the beginning God created the Heavens and the Earth';[76] and he developed his reasoning from there, reminding us of the source of Newton's ideas, saying that 'our Philosophers have taken or mistaken most of their Maxims from *Lucretius* . . . He . . . (as the perverted *Jews*, and all the *Heathens*) allows a God, but supposes him in another System, and that he concerns himself not with this,'[77] Newton himself did claim that 'the system of Epicurus and Lucretius is true' in so far as it claimed that matter was composed of small hard impenetrable atoms endowed with motion and inertia.[78] Edmund Halley as early as 1693 claimed that '*Epicurean* and *Atomical* Philosphers . . . at present obtain in the world',[79] but nevertheless it was Hutchinson's physics, not Newton's, that Gibbon found taught at Oxford when he was there in 1752.[80]

Before Newton the status of the atom had been very dubious. The title page of Charleton's *Physiologia* prudently described the contents as a 'Fabrick of Science Natural upon the Hypothesis of Atoms'; which is to say that it was a construction of fallible human knowledge resting on a foundation of unwarrantable conjecture. It laid claim only to the status of

73 Hume, *Morals* in *Philosophical Works,* ed. Green and Grose, vol. IV, p. 174.

74 This theory of science is called 'naïve inductivism' by A. F. Chalmers, *What is this Thing Called Science?*, p. 1. 'There are no facts, only interpretations' has become the *dictum* of postmodernity, but it is to be found in Friedrich Nietzsche, *The Will to Power*, trans. Walter Kaufmann and R. J. Hollingdale (New York: Vintage, 1967), no. 481, p. 267.

75 Isaac Newton, *Philosophiae naturalis principia mathematica* (1687), trans. Andrew Motte, *The Mathematical Principles of Natural Philosophy* (London: 1729), p. 19.

76 John Hutchinson, *Moses's Principia* (London: 1724), p. 2, quoting Genesis, 1:1.

77 Hutchinson, *Moses's Principia*, pp. 539, 540.

78 Newton quoted by Kargon, *Atomism,* p. 131.

79 Edmund Halley, quoted ibid.

80 Gibbon, *Memoirs*, p. 80.

fiction, a status which was, at least among scientists, seen as inappropriate after Newton's treatment of the ideas. The churchmen did not immediately concede the ground: Bishop Berkeley (1685–1753) argued that Newton's ideas could not possibly be taken as a true description of anything real, but agreed that they might be useful tools in the prediction of appearances, an idea which Hume (here according to Thomas Reid, 1710–96) took a step further: 'as the Bishop undid the whole material world, [Hume], upon the same grounds, undoes the world of the spirits, and leaves nothing in nature but ideas and impressions, without any subject on which they may be impressed'.[81] Hume himself said that

> 'Tis impossible upon any system to defend either our understanding or our senses; and we but expose them farther when we endeavour to justify them in that manner. As the sceptical doubt arises naturally from a profound and intense reflection on those subjects, it always encreases, the farther we carry on our reflections, whether in opposition or conformity to it. Carelessness and in-attention alone can afford us any remedy. For this reason I rely entirely upon them.[82]

Richard Payne Knight's philosophical position was somewhat different because he was less rigorously sceptical; instead of relying like Hume entirely on carelessness and inattention, he relied instead on his understanding and the evidence of his senses, which in practice amounted to much the same thing. Again in this philosophical sense he can be said to have been a sensualist. He agreed with Hume in seeing that this was incompatible with any system, and in Knight's own vocabulary the term 'systematic' was abusive: 'system' was a 'radical vice' and he approvingly quoted Jonathan Swift's lines:

> All Philosophers, who find
> Some favourite system to their mind,
> In every point to make it fit,
> Will force all nature to submit.[83]

For Knight, 'system' carried overtones of Aristotelian scholasticism taking its authority from the top of the pyramid, whereas genuine knowledge, as he saw it, should take its authority from observed facts. When Knight investigated a matter he approached it analytically, aiming to begin with self-evidently observable facts and to move from them to make useful generalisations, after Bacon's model. This intent was declared in the titles *An Analytical Inquiry into the Principles of Taste* (which is dis-

81 Thomas Reid, *An Inquiry into the Human Mind on the Principles of Common Sense* (1764) in *Thomas Reid's Inquiry and Essays*, ed. Ronald E. Beanblossom and Keith Lehrer (Indianapolis: Hackett, 1983), p. 8.

82 *Treatise of Human Nature*, in *Philosophical Works*, ed. Green and Grose, vol. I, p. 505.

83 Jonathan Swift, 'Cadenus and Vanessa', lines 722–5, in *The Poems of Jonathan Swift*, ed. Harold Williams, 3 vols. (Oxford: Clarendon Press, 1958), vol. II, p. 709; Knight, *An Analytical Inquiry Into the Principles of Taste*, 4th edn (London: 1808), p. 382.

cussed in chapter 6) and *An Analytical Essay on the Greek Alphabet,* and is evident in the fragmentary quality of his observations which crept into the footnotes of his poems and which made up the substance of his discourses on ancient mythology. The essay on the Greek alphabet was a scholarly triumph because it involved the detection of wholesale fraud on the part of a French scholar, the abbé Michel Fourmont (1690–1746), who had gathered ancient inscriptions in Greece and supplemented his discoveries with forgeries, which were universally accepted as genuine and given very respectable academic publication after his death.[84] Knight's method in the study, though, involved the painstaking study of the ancient Greek letter forms with a view particularly to discovering how to pronounce the sounds which they denoted. The method of study, then, by breaking the object of study, the Greek language, into its smallest possible components, aimed certainly to be analytical and perhaps in a sense 'atomic' in its outlook. It could conceivably have been motivated by a concern, which is evident in Lucretius, to find a link between the letters in words and the substance of the world. According to Epicurean linguistic theory words were first formed by uttering sounds which in some way corresponded with the objects of attention. The sounds were later codified and conventionalised into the languages which we know, but at their origin there was supposed to be a direct link between the object and the sound.[85] One is reminded of Rousseau's idea (in *Essai sur l'origine des langues*) that language developed out of song, and might wonder if perhaps Knight's concern with the atomic components of language, its phonemes as represented by letters, might have been inspired by a desire eventually to reconstruct this primal language, the language of Homer being the oldest which could at that time be understood.

In the field of science, or natural philosophy, progress was possible in a quite different way from in moral and cultural matters. According to Bacon's theory, meticulous observations should have laid down a firm foundation of reliable information from which, with careful thought and inspired insight, general principles could be inferred. As principles became better understood they could be used more effectively and surely in order to produce reliable results. The Knight family was very conscious of the benefits to be had from technical advances, and Knight himself was keen to support technical progress, which became one of the great causes of the age as the power and riches unleashed in the industrial revolution made England ever wealthier. So in Knight's mind there was a clear division between the ancient Greek ideal of living close to nature, in which progress was possible only in so far as it led back towards the

84 See Messmann, *Richard Payne Knight*, pp. 54–8.

85 J. M. Snyder, *Puns and Poetry in Lucretius' De Rerum Natura* (Amsterdam: 1980).

ancient condition, and the technical means by which this manner of living could be brought about, which might be very new indeed and which could become ever more effective. Progress was desirable in the means, but the ends were to be found well established in ancient times, and it was necessary not to invent them but to re-establish them.

Picturesque atoms

A good example of an attempt to find general principles from a mass of observations is to be found in Uvedale Price's attempt to establish his principles of the picturesque, which are utterly misguided at a theoretical level, as Knight took pains to point out at considerable length in *An Analytical Inquiry into the Principles of Taste.* We can see Price trying to adopt scientific ways of thinking, but misunderstanding the principles involved. He followed the painter William Hogarth (1697–1764) and the politician Edmund Burke in supposing that beauty was inherent in beautiful things. He seems in fact to have believed that there were *atoms* of beauty in beautiful things and that Lucretius had described them. Knight, on the other hand, followed Hume in supposing that beauty lay in the mind of the beholder, and thought that the attempt to isolate particular objects as being inherently beautiful or picturesque was completely wrong-headed.[86] The avowed genealogy of Price's conception of the picturesque begins with Hogarth's *Analysis of Beauty* of 1753, which Burke took up and refined, adding a second aesthetic category, the sublime, which Price endorsed, but further refined the system by adding a third category, the picturesque.

Hogarth's subtitle declared his analysis to have been 'Written with a view of fixing the fluctuating IDEAS of TASTE'. He isolated a 'line of beauty': a graceful serpentine curve which he believed to be characteristic in all beautiful objects and images (figure 13). Where Hogarth's influence was felt, the serpentine curve was understood to be beautiful in itself and if a beholder could not see the beauty in the line then it was because of some bluntness of the senses. For the idea to be plausible we need to see that the cultural climate in which Hogarth's thought took shape was influenced decisively by Plato and Newton. Hogarth's suggestion of an 'essence' of beauty made sense because of the form of questioning pursued by Socrates in Plato's dialogues, which produces the illusion that there is such an essence to be found, since the interlocutors who give more concrete answers are shown to have given inadequate replies.[87] Ironically Price's lasting influence was effective precisely in so

86 See chapter 6.

87 The 'essentialist' fallacy, countered for example in the form of argument used by Gilles Deleuze against Plato in *Nietzsche et la Philosophie* (Paris: 1962), translated by Hugh Tomlinson, *Nietzsche and Philosophy* (London: Athlone, 1983), pp.75–6.

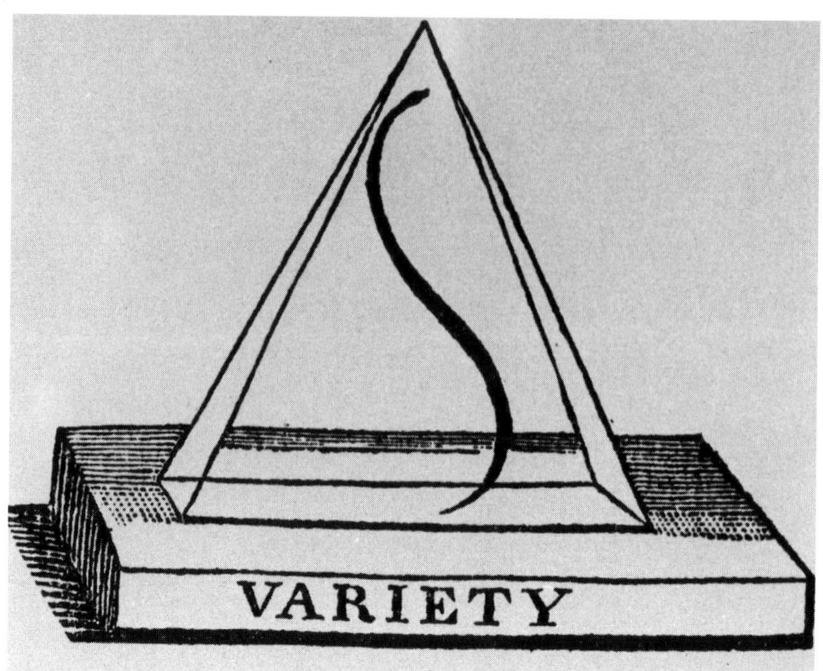

Figure 13. Hogarth's line of beauty. Frontispiece from *The Analysis of Beauty*.

far as he escaped giving abstract answers about the 'essential' picturesque: his iteration of concrete examples, embodied in the particular and the contingent, actually communicated his vision and taste, and did so very effectively. It was possible for others, including Knight, to endorse Price's taste and his practical recipes for the production of picturesqueness whilst repudiating completely the theory which he thought underpinned his enterprise. Hogarth would have felt Newton's influence through his reputation rather than familiarity with particular works. Hogarth's proposal, had it been tenable, would have made compositional success in painting absolutely routine, reducing it to a simple readily understood principle, no more complex than the mathematical principles with which Newton had summarised the working of the universe. Hogarth's system was taken up by Burke who, as a young man, published *A Philosophical Enquiry into the Origin of our Ideas of the Sublime and Beautiful* (1757), in which he extended the scope of Hogarth's work by grafting on to it a second set of qualities, derived from Longinus' ancient dissection of the sublime. Broadly speaking Burke saw objects as sublime when they were impressive and awesome, and as beautiful when they were charming and attractive.[88] Artists found his observations helpful and made use of them, and Kant used these divisions in his *Critique of Judgement* (1790), though allied to a different aesthetic theory. Burke's thinking clearly depended on Hogarth's example, but Burke was not scrupulous in acknowledging his sources, and in the first edition the debt went unremarked; in the second (1759) he admitted not influence but common ground.

> It gives me no small pleasure to find that I can strengthen my theory in this point, by the opinion of the very ingenious Mr. Hogarth; whose idea of the line of beauty I take in general to be extremely just . . . But I must add . . . that, so far as I could observe of nature, though the varied line is that alone in which complete beauty is found, yet there is no particular line which is always found in the most completely beautiful in preference to all other lines. At least I never could observe it. [89]

This minor shortcoming did not lead Burke to sweep away the whole system in favour of the Edinburgh school of relativism which Knight supported. Burke could not doubt that beauty was a real thing; he thought it 'too affecting not to depend upon some physical qualities . . . we must conclude that beauty is, for the greater part, some quality in bodies, acting mechanically upon the human mind by the intervention of the senses'.[90] Aristotle had held that 'colour, sound, and smell, as well as extension, figure and hardness, are . . . different forms of matter';[91] and Burke clearly supposed that beauty and sublimity were material in a comparable way. He concluded that smooth polished beauty and rough sublimity were 'ideas of a very different nature, one being founded on pain, the other on pleasure'.[92]

Burke's analysis seems to draw on a description of different types of atom, made by Lucretius, a correspondence of ideas which was noticed by one of Price's contemporaries, Dugald Stewart (1753–1828), who was the most distinguished Scottish philosopher of his day – said to be (after the death of his mentor Thomas Reid in 1796) 'the only writer of recognised authority upon philosophical topics in the island'.[93] There is, then, every reason for giving weight to his noting that 'In this part of his theory, Mr. Burke has very closely followed Lucretius';[94] the passage in question ran:

> take the case of liquids like honey and milk
> Which leave a pleasant sensation upon the tongue

88 Edmund Burke, *A Philosophical Enquiry into the Origin of our Ideas of the Sublime and Beautiful* (London: 1757); page refs. are to the Boulton edn (London: 1958).

89 Ibid., pp. 115–16.

90 Ibid., p. 112.

91 The quotation referring to Aristotle is from a Scottish source contemporary with the debate under discussion: Reid, *Inquiry*, in *Inquiry and Essays*, ed. Beaublossom and Lehrer, p. 59.

92 Burke, *Sublime and Beautiful*, Boulton edn, p. 124.

93 *Dictionary of National Biography*, vol. XVIII, p. 1170b. Archibald Alison dedicated his association-based essays on aesthetics to Stewart.

94 Dugald Stewart, *Philosophical Essays*, 3rd edn (Edinburgh: 1818), p. 290n.

In contrast with the bitter flavour of wormwood
Or centaury, whose flavour puckers the mouth;
You can easily see that smooth and rounded elements
Must form the things agreeable to the taste
While things which are bitter and rough upon the palate
Are composed of hooked and implicated elements
And because of that have to cut their way through the senses
Breaking open the organs to find a way in.[95]

In Lucretius, then, we find smooth atoms with the attributes which Burke found characteristic of beauty, and correspondingly sublime rough atoms. Stewart remarked that 'the continuation of the passage is not less curious';[96] and indeed it is not. The continuation however bears on Price's introduction of the third category, the picturesque, into the system.

Above all it was the Reverend William Gilpin (1724–1804) who focused attention on the picturesque with books about his 'picturesque tours', published from 1782. He defined the term 'picturesque' as 'expressive of that peculiar kind of beauty, which is agreeable in a picture',[97] and this he found to be uneven and irregular, having contrasts of light and shade.[98] This definition satisfied neither Knight nor Price, who examined the word etymologically and found 'picturesque' to mean *after the manner of painters*, from the Italian *pittoresco*.[99] However, when Knight tried to elaborate the meaning of the word he considered the actions of the mind, whereas Price tried to focus on the 'picturesque' objects themselves.

Knight argued that the word '*pittoresco*' would not have developed had not painters 'adopted some distinct manner of imitating nature, appropriate to their own art . . . since, unless painters had some peculiar manner, such epithet could mark no peculiar discrimination, nor have any distinct meaning'.[100] He credited Giorgione with the invention of this style, and Titian with its perfection,[101] and it was, he said, soon after their work became known that the word '*pittoresco*' made its first appearance. According to his definition, an object would properly be called 'picturesque' if it called to mind the work of painters.

Price disagreed, being unable to accept Knight's subjectivity. Not only did he agree with what Burke had to say about the beautiful and the sublime, he was prepared to go further and include a third, equally distinct, aesthetic category: the picturesque. Whereas Gilpin could write of 'picturesque beauty' Price found this a confusion of terms: properly defined the beautiful and the picturesque were as separate from one another as were the beautiful and the sublime.[102] We have seen how

95 Lucretius, *De Rerum Natura*, bk. II, lines 398–407, trans. C. H. Sisson, *The Poem on Nature* (Manchester: Carcanet, 1976), pp. 54–5.

96 Stewart, *Essays*, p. 290n.

97 *An Essay upon Prints* (London, 1768), p. x. Quoted by Carl Paul Barbier, *William Gilpin: His Drawings, Teaching, and Theory of the Picturesque* (Oxford: Clarendon Press, 1963), pp. 98ff.

98 Barbier, ibid., pp. 102–3.

99 Knight, *Principles of Taste*, p. 148; Uvedale Price, *Essays on the Picturesque*, 3 vols. (London: 1810), vol. I, p. 44.

100 *Principles of Taste*, p. 151.

101 Ibid., p. 150.

102 *Essays*, vol. I, chapter 3, p. 37ff.

Burke thought of beauty and sublimity in terms of atoms, and even if in Burke's case one continues to entertain a lingering doubt it must surely be dispelled when we turn to Price. The continuation of Dugald Stewart's quotation from Lucretius ran:

> every sort of sight which pleases the senses
> Has been created out of some smooth elements
> While on the other hand things which look unpleasant
> Will always contain some elements which are rough.
>
> There are also elements neither entirely smooth
> Nor yet, so to speak, entirely covered with prickles
> But rather with some slight protuberances
> Which tickle the senses rather than actually hurt them; [103]

Price evidently recognised in this third group the qualities which Gilpin had found characteristic in the picturesque, but whereas Gilpin had seen the picturesque as a type of beauty, Price addressed himself in his *Essay on the Picturesque* to the task of separating these qualities from each other and from the sublime. Beauty, clearly enough, was composed of smooth round atoms which were sensed as pleasure, and sublimity of hooked and implicated atoms which acted as pain, causing horripilation (so much could be learned from a parallel reading of Burke and Lucretius), so Price's third quality, picturesqueness, should work in the same way as tickling. That this was indeed what he thought is most clearly shown in his analysis of different types of music, in which

> we no more scruple to call one of Handel's choruses sublime, than Corelli's famous *pastorale* beautiful. But should any person simply, and without qualifying expressions, call a capricious movement of Scarlatti or Haydn *picturesque*, he would, with great reason, be laughed at, for it is not a term applied to sounds; yet such a movement, from its sudden, unexpected, and abrupt transitions, – from a certain playful wildness of character and appearance of irregularity, is no less analogous to similar scenery in nature, than the concerto or the chorus, to what is grand or beautiful to the eye. [104]

At first sight this is a puzzling passage: why should Price want to argue that music is in a sense picturesque? Given Knight's definition of the idea it does not make sense at all, since no music puts one in mind of the manner of great landscape painters, but if we remember Lucretius then Price's argument seems straightforward: he was imagining a

103 Lucretius, *De Rerum Natura,* bk. II, lines 422–9; trans. Sisson, *Poem on Nature,* p. 55.

104 *Essays*, vol. I, pp. 45–6.

Scarlatti sonata, played at the harpsichord, 'tickling' the sense of hearing just as the sight of a picturesque object 'tickled' the sense of sight. It is plausible enough to make a connection between a scherzo and tickling, and between harmonious sounds and smoothness, but the connection between a Handel chorus and the sublime is more difficult, since we are asked to accept that the sublime is made of those hooked and implicated atoms which tear their way through the senses. Even given that for Price Handel's music was modern, surely he could not have thought it so very abrasive? There is evidence, however, which shows a congruence more complete than could reasonably be expected: Knight made the identical connection in arguing against Price's assertions. Discussing sounds, Lucretius had said:

> Things which are disagreeable to the senses,
> And things agreeable, are made up of different shapes:
> You should not imagine that, say, the screech of a saw
> Is made of elements of the same smooth texture
> As those which make up the most musical sounds
> Which can be evoked by strings plucked by skilled fingers.[105]

If Price was comparing Corelli's music with the smooth atoms in Lucretius, then equally he was comparing the sound of a screeching saw to the sound of a Handel chorus; and, unlikely as it might seem, a screeching saw was the very thing with which Knight compared Handel's music. He did not think that Handel's choruses were sublime, because he did not think that *any* music could be sublime, any more than it could be picturesque:

> The filing of a saw, or any other harsh and discordant sound of that kind, though not loud, will create a very uneasy and even painful sensation in the human organs, which we commonly call *setting the teeth on edge* ... Extremely loud and jarring sounds, such as those of kettle-drums or artillery, will extend through the whole body; as I very sensibly felt at the performance of some of Handel's choruses in Westminster Abbey: but, as they were in harmony, the sensation was not at all unpleasant. On the contrary, if I could conceive any sensation to be sublime, I should admit this to be so: but the sentiment of sublimity belongs to the affections of the mind, and not to organic sensation.[106]

Price was elaborating ideas set out by Burke, seeing the connection which Burke had made between beauty, sublimity and Lucretius' atoms.

105 Lucretius, *De Rerum Natura,* bk. II, lines 408–13; trans. Sisson, *Poem on Nature*, p. 55.

106 *Principles of Taste*, p. 46.

Not only did Price anticipate Dugald Stewart in noticing this, he also made creative use of the perception; unfortunately his thinking belonged to literary dilettantism, not to science as he perhaps imagined it did, and we can now see all too easily that Price was elaborating a false premiss. A genealogical network can be traced to show the relations between the picturesque and its wider culture. The example of Newton's penetrating principles was dazzlingly attractive, too powerful to be overlooked. Hogarth would have been to art what Newton is to science, if only his discovery had been more sustainedly fruitful. Burke and Price, however, in extending Hogarth's system, did not so much conduct experimental research on empirical evidence as assimilate ideas from literary sources; so their working methods had more of the scholastic about them than of the scientific. Burke's idea of the sublime came from Longinus, Price's picturesque from Gilpin; they both drew directly on Lucretius, another part of whose influence they felt indirectly through Newton.

In Knight's intellectual landscape natural philosophy was based on self-evident facts, from which principles might be inferred. The most powerful of them were those which Newton had discovered, which presented a model to which those working in other disciplines might aspire. Advances in understanding the natural world had been made in opposition to the church, whose teaching worked on quite different principles, but in the eighteenth century there had been great progress in natural philosophy and in its application to the practical world. Newton's principles had proved to be very useful in dealing with the world, and they were bound up with an idea of atoms which had been adapted from the teachings of Epicurus. The Epicurean atoms were in turn bound up with a system of morals, which was quite different from that promoted by the church. The analytical thinking which Knight employed so far as he was able was, in his culture, strongly associated with the moral thinking which he employed in the conduct of his life. It need not be the case that the physics were related to the morals in a strictly logical way: Epicurus would have said that they were, and Newton would strenuously have insisted that they were not. The associations were strong in a cultural sense because the ideas had grown up together in the ancient world. Knight was impressed by scientific and technological achievements, but not by Christian morality, and he restored the link which had been made firmly in the ancient world, but which practical experimenters had endeavoured to weaken, or to ignore. The atom was once again an agent against superstition.

4 Symbolical paganism

Religion without superstition

Despite Knight's anti-clerical stance, his mind was not devoid of all religion; on the contrary, it was something of a preoccupation: he published a study of ancient religion early in his career, in his *Discourse on the Worship of Priapus, and its connexion with the Mystic Theology of the Antients* (1786); a late book, *The Symbolical Language of Ancient Art and Mythology* (1818), was devoted to the subject, and religion recurred as a theme in most of his work. An antipathy towards the church (and conventional Christianity in general) is apparent from the first writings we have from him in the Sicilian journal, where he denounced the superstition he found among the populace, but the ancient Greeks' religious ideas held some considerable attraction. Knight made use of references to classical gods in his poems in a way that was completely conventional in the eighteenth century, but his study of ancient religion was much more thorough and general than that of any of the more celebrated poets of his age, more thorough indeed than that of most scholars, and so these works have been republished.[1] While he pursued his study of the ancient Greeks' religion as a scholarly enquiry, he adopted some ideas from it into his personal religious belief, and in so far as he did, he could be said quite properly to have been a pagan. His idea of religion, though, sought to avoid the pitfalls of 'superstition', which could trap the pagan as easily as the Christian, and he made a clear distinction between the superstitious creed of the 'ignorant vulgar' of ancient Greece and the more philosophical view which he and his readers were to take.

Knight understood the Greek myths to be a symbolic language, in which important truths could be conveyed, and he saw it as a forebear of written language. Language had passed through four stages in its

1 His *A Discourse on the Worship of Priapus, and its Connexion with the Mystic Theology of the Antients* (London: 1786) had a sequel, written by Thomas Wright (1810–77) published by the Society of Dilettanti, and distributed among the members. It was published without a date on the title page: Thomas Wright, *The Worship of the Generative Powers During the Middle Ages of Western Europe*. Knight's and Wright's works were reprinted jointly as *A History of Phallic Worship* (New York: Dorset Press, 1992). Richard Payne Knight, *The Symbolical Language of Ancient Art and Mythology, An Inquiry* (London: 1818) was republished in nine consecutive issues of *The Classical Journal* 1821–3 (Peter Funnell, 'The Symbolic Language of Antiquity', in *The Arrogant Connoisseur*, ed. Michael Clarke and Nicholas Penny (Manchester University Press, 1982), p. 63) and as a book edited by Alexander Wilder

development: the first stage involved the 'simple representation' of objects and events (whatever that might mean); the second used metaphor ('some particular characteristic quality of the individual was employed to express a general quality or abstract idea; as a horse for swiftness, a dog for vigilance, or a hare for fecundity'); the third stage developed conventional signs, such as Chinese characters, to refer to ideas; and the fourth used conventional signs to represent vocal modulations, in a phonetic alphabet. As Knight understood it, the second of these stages in the development of language had been used 'to convey or conceal the dogmas of religion', not only those of the ancient Greeks, but those of all other cultures in which religion had operated.

> The remote antiquity of this mode of conveying knowledge by symbols, and its long-established appropriation to religious subjects, had given it a character of sanctity unknown to any other mode of writing; and it seems to have been a very generally received opinion, among the more discreet Heathens, that divine truth was better adapted to the weakness of human intellect, when veiled under symbols, and wrapped in fable and enigma, than when exhibited in the undisguised simplicity of genuine wisdom or pure philosophy.[2]

The implication is that it would be better, at least for those with developed intellects, to be able to unwrap the divine truths from their fables and enigmas and express them directly in philosophical language. That indeed was the burden of Knight's books on ancient religion, but the first of them chose to unveil a part of ancient worship which in eighteenth-century England generally seemed very simply scandalous and obscene. *The Worship of Priapus*, despite the fact that it was privately printed for the Society of Dilettanti in a small edition, brought Knight more attention than any other of his works, most of it unwelcome. It can never have been widely read, but its reputation was sufficient to establish Knight's name, and to link it to a reputation for wickedness. It is not the pornographic work which it has sometimes been taken to be, but a study of sexual symbolism in religion in which Knight set out his ideas not only about phallic worship, but also about religion in general, remarkably including Indian as well as pagan and Christian symbols. The fact that it saw the light of day at all is remarkable, given the period in which it was published, and in order to understand how it could have seemed to be a desirable undertaking for a young scholar we need to know something of the milieu in which it developed.

in 1835, republished in 1876 and 1894. References are to the 1876 edn, published in New York.

2 Knight, *Symbolical Language*, p. 6. (section 11).

The Society of Dilettanti, which printed the discourse, and which was its intended audience, was not composed of a representative cross-section of English society, but was a convivial dining club for gentlemen who had made the Grand Tour: a select, moneyed, all-male group, with some worldly sophistication and exposure to Italian culture and morals. Among these men there was a general interest in archaeology, and already when Knight joined them, in 1781, Stuart and Revett's scholarly expedition to Greece had been funded, followed by another into Asia Minor which resulted in the publication of *Ionian Antiquities*.[3] The society, however, had been founded primarily for the sake of sociability rather than the advancement of learning; and conviviality, if not drunkenness, was certainly a condition for membership.[4]

Charles James Fox and Uvedale Price were already well-established members when Knight joined. They had been at Eton and toured Europe together and Fox had joined the society in 1769 on his return, introducing Price soon after. Among the other members were Sir Joseph Banks and Sir William Hamilton, who was British Ambassador to the Court of Naples, and Knight used Naples as a base from which to visit Sicily, during one of Hamilton's visits to London. Knight was to become very prominent in the society, and over the years various friends and relatives were elected to its ranks, including among them his cousins Thomas Johnes (1783), Edward Knight of Wolverley (1786) and Samuel Rogers (1805); and among his friends Charles Townley (1786), Clayton Mordaunt Cracherode (1787), Edward Winnington (1788), Lord Abercorn (1791) and Lord Aberdeen (1805).[5]

On 17 July 1781 Hamilton sent a letter to the society describing how he had found at Isernia, in a remote region of Naples, peasants who were practising pagan rites of phallic worship as part of a Christian ceremony. His letter was published as the first part of a book, the bulk of which was given over to Knight's commentary on the practice. Hamilton said that at the feast of the Holy Martyrs Cosmas and Damian wax phalluses were presented at the altar, and he sent back some of the votive offerings as evidence to corroborate his story (they are now in the British Museum).[6] He saw this rite as evidence that the Roman Catholic Church was riddled with superstition, and Knight agreed with him:

> It is curious, in looking back through the annals of superstition, so degrading to the pride of man, to trace the progress of the human mind in different ages, climates, and circumstances, uniformly acting upon the same principles, and to the same ends. The sketch

3 R. Chandler, N. Revett, W. Pars, *Ionian Antiquities* (London: Society of Dilettanti, 1769).

4 See p. 7.

5 Lionel Cust, *History of the Society of Dilettanti*, ed. Colvin (London: Society of Dilettanti 1898) gives a complete list of members of the society from its inception, pp. 239ff.

6 Funnell, in *Arrogant Connoisseur*, ed. Clarke and Penny, p. 50.

> here given of the corruptions of the religion of Greece, is an exact counterpart of the history of the corruptions of Christianity, which began in the pure theism of the eclectic Jews, and by the help of inspirations, emanations, and canonizations, expanded itself, by degrees, to the vast and unwieldy system which now fills the creed of what is commonly called the Catholic Church.[7]

Knight accepted Hamilton's thesis that the phallic worship at Isernia was a relic of ancient paganism, interpreting the ceremony as an expression of devotion to the god Priapus, the personification of male fertility. The best accredited source for his ideas was Pierre François Hugues, who called himself (without any known justification) the Baron d'Hancarville.[8] In Naples he had been Hamilton's protégé, which doubtless accounts for the complete congruence between Hamilton's and Knight's views on this matter. D'Harcarville then came over to England where he lived with, and was kept by, Charles Townley. Knight may well have met him in Naples, and had certainly met him by 1782, when Townley was bemoaning to Knight the expense involved in maintaining d'Hancarville's profligate bohemianism, but both Townley and Knight were persuaded that he was a genius, despite the fact that he was known on the continent as a fraud.[9] D'Hancarville, who had previously charmed both Sir William Hamilton and Winckelmann, now dazzled Townley and Knight. Townley found his disquisitions on ancient art 'more rational and more satisfactory than all I had found in the absurd books of Antiquaries';[10] and Knight helped by subsidising his work on pagan religion, which promised 'to be such an Acquisition to all lovers of Ancient Arts and History that he must at all events be enabled to complete it'.[11]

D'Hancarville believed that once, long ago, there had been a single religion which had spread throughout the world, which had been monotheistic in its original state, but had been corrupted into the many religions now evident in the world. He had studied coins, sculptures, vases and other decorated artefacts from the ancient world, supposed that the decorations were symbolic, and, supported by his vast erudition, he maintained that the image at the root of all religion was the sexual union of male and female.[12] The act of conception, the primal act of creation, was sometimes directly represented in sexual imagery (which was to be found in Greece, Rome, Asia and India) and sometimes indirectly represented through the use of symbols. He managed, by very elaborate argument, to infer that the first representation of the

7 *Priapus*, pp. 207–8.

8 Funnell, in *Arrogant Connoisseur*, ed. Clarke and Penny, p. 52. Francis Haskell, 'The Baron D'Hancarville: an Adventurer and Art Historian in Eighteenth-Century Europe', *Past and Present in Art and Taste* (New Haven: Yale University Press, 1987).

9 G. S. Rousseau, 'The Sorrows of Priapus', in *Sexual Underworlds of the Enlightenment* ed. Rousseau and Roy Porter (Manchester University Press, 1987), p. 115.

10 Charles Townley to Richard Payne Knight (undated), Townley family archive, British Museum; quoted G. S. Rousseau, *Sexual Underworlds of the Enlightenment,* p.115.

11 Knight to Townley (undated), Townley archive, quoted Rousseau, ibid., p.115.

12 Funnell, in *Arrogant Connoisseur*, ed. Clarke and Penny, pp. 52–3. Pierre François Hugues [Baron d'Hancarville], *Recherches sur l'Origine et les Progres des arts de la Grece*, 3 vols. (London: 1785).

Figure 14. The Bull and Egg, from D'Hancarville's *Recherches sur l'Origine, l'Esprit et les Progrès des Arts,* 1785.

creation of the universe took the form of a bull skewering on its horns an egg which represented the universe in its chaotic uncreated state (figure 14).[13] D'Hancarville found that this image had been worshipped in Japan, and saw a connection between it and the bull-worshipping cults of the ancient Mediterranean; and he took this to explain, for example, why so many coins, round like eggs, should have depicted bulls.[14] Not everybody found these ideas intuitively plausible: John Pinkerton, for example, in his *Essay on Medals* thought that bulls on coins indicated the place of manufacture, and no more than that;[15] and some of the images which had not been encoded in abstruse symbols could, with some plausibility, have been thought pornographic rather than religious in content. However far-fetched d'Hancarville's ideas may seem to us (and they certainly seemed far-fetched to most of Knight's contemporaries), there is no need to doubt his sincerity in putting forward his system, as it is no more absurd than, for example, Jacob Bryant's monumental work *A New System – or, an analysis of Ancient Mythology* in three huge volumes (1774–6), which sought through close and elaborate argument to persuade the reader that Egyptian priests had, after the biblical flood, migrated to many parts of the world, where they became known as Druids. Druids, though, were the particular province of William Stukeley, who had written about

13 Funnell, in *Arrogant Connoisseur*, ed. Clarke and Penny, p. 53.

14 Hugues, *Recherches,* vol. I, pp. 67ff. quoted by Funnell in ibid.

15 *An Essay On Medals*, 2 vols. (1789), vol. I, p. xxvi, quoted by Funnell, *Arrogant Connoisseur*, p. 55.

Stonehenge and Avebury, claiming them for the Druids, and in his *Palaeographia sacra* he included a dedication to Augusta, Princess of Wales, on whom he had bestowed the title 'Archdruidess of Kew'.[16] Stukeley made hay with the evidence at his disposal, 'not pretending to a stiff scholastic proof of everything I say, which would be odious and irksome to the reader, as well as myself'.[17] The lack of stiffness could bring startling results, such as his conclusion that Christianity had been the first religion of the world.[18] D'Hancarville's ideas belong in this category of eighteenth-century study which attempted to give general principles to a vast and obscure field of knowledge, which in retrospect look naively and radically under-informed in their very basis. Studies such as these show very clearly why specialism and division of intellectual labour are necessary. The vastness and obscurity of the material to be considered made it attractive to obsessive interpreters with a visionary idea and a conviction that, with industry, everything would fall into place around it. They have their definitive fictional form in George Eliot's description of the labour of the Reverend Mr Casaubon in *Middlemarch*. His delusional great work, a *Key to All Mythologies*, had exactly the same scope as d'Hancarville's work, and there is a precision of irony in that his preoccupation with the work was his perpetual excuse for the sexlessness of his marriage, if the key to all mythologies is seen to be, as d'Hancarville said it was, sex itself.[19] While d'Hancarville was obsessive, he was hardly more so than Freud was to be at a much later date, and Knight seems to have been completely convinced, despite expressing some minor reservations as to detail. D'Hancarville's ideas were not properly compatible with any of the religions whose derivation he sought to explain, as each of them preferred to trace its origins back to a divine source of wisdom rather than to an earlier culture; but his outlook is quite compatible with an Epicurean position, which would see all religions equally as developments from human ignorance.

According to Epicurus the world developed from chance collisions of atoms which fell in a constant stream through infinite space. The world, he said, was not created through an act of intelligence, but gradually evolved as the result of the forces which were naturally inherent in things. He explained that in his own day there were many occurrences which men had insufficient knowledge to understand: they saw lightning, waterspouts, earthquakes and floods, for example, and because they did not understand them, they attributed them to the actions of tremendously powerful beings, gods.

16 *Palaeographia Sacra: or, Discourses on Sacred Subjects* (London: 1763).

17 *Stonehenge: a Temple Restored to the British Druids* (London: 1740), preface.

18 Ibid., contents page.

19 George Eliot, *Middlemarch* (1871–2). The action of the novel was set earlier, before 1832.

There are other phenomena men perceive in the universe
Which often cause their minds acute suspense
And make them cringe before the fear of the gods,
Pressing themselves to the ground, because ignorance
Of the causes forces them to attribute everything
To the power of the gods, who, they suppose, are in charge.[20]

Gods here are seen as the personifications of natural forces, and therefore the primitive religion was the worship of nature. Knight favoured d'Hancarville's description of this original nature worship as a monotheistic religion, but there is much common ground with David Hume's claim that the original religion was polytheistic. Hume claimed that religion arose in precisely the same way, but whereas d'Hancarville saw his many symbols as representations of a single god, Hume saw the symbols as many gods representing aspects of a single force, nature, which was of course d'Hancarville's single god.[21] Lucretius, moreover, began *De Rerum Natura* with a dedication to nature, personified in this case as Venus, the female fertility symbol and a counterpart to Priapus:

everything under the stars
– The sea that carries ships as well as the earth that bears crops –
Is full of you: every living thing is conceived
By your methods and so comes into the daylight.
The winds elude you and the sky is apt to be cloudless
When your month comes, and under your feet the earth
Sends up her lovely flowers, and the sea's surfaces
Glitter placidly as the light gleams from the sky.
As soon as the face of spring puts in an appearance
And the fertilising wind blows in from the west
The birds of the air are the first to notice your coming
And your effluence strikes at their very hearts;
The wild cattle jump about in their pastures,
They plunge and swim over the rivers, delight has taken them.[22]

So Lucretius not only described the popular gods as symbols, he also put the fertility principle at their head; and we find a corresponding interpretation in Thomas Hobbes's work, where we find both religion and superstition defined as '*Feare* of power invisible, feigned by the mind, or imagined from tales'.[23] There is no mention of any benefit to be derived from religious belief, only the characteristically Epicurean equation of religion with fear. According to him, the difference between superstition

20 Lucretius, *De Rerum Natura*, bk. IV, lines 51–5, trans. C. H. Sisson, *The Poem on Nature* (Manchester: Carcanet, 1976), p. 178.

21 David Hume, *The Natural History of Religion* (1757) in *Philosophical Works*, ed. T. H. Green and T. H. Grose, 4 vols. (1886), vol. IV, pp. 307 ff.

22 Bk. I, lines 2–16, trans. Sisson, *Poem on Nature*, p. 15.

23 Thomas Hobbes, *Leviathan, or The Matter, Forme, & Power of a Common-Wealth Ecclesiasticall and Civill* (1651) part 1, chapter 6, ed. C. B. Macpherson (Harmondsworth: Penguin, 1968), p. 124.

and religion lay not in their truth-content, but in their social acceptability. When the fear is admissible in public it is called 'religion'; 'And when the power imagined, is truly such as we imagine, it is called TRUE RELIGION.'[24] Hobbes imagined that Christianity gradually replaced the old religions; and that a household already equipped with effigies of gods would not have troubled to replace the actual artefacts. They would have continued to worship through the old images as before, giving them new names 'upon the pretence of doing it in the honour of *Christ*', so that one might find 'an Image of the *Virgin Mary*, and of her *Sonne* our Saviour, which before was called the image of *Venus* and *Cupid*; and so of a *Jupiter* make a *Barnabas*, and of *Mercury* a *Paul*, and the like'.[25] Hobbes imagined that not only the images of the gods, but also the ceremonies used in worship, were absorbed into the teachings and practices of the new church:

> The Heathens had also their *Aqua Lustralis*, that is to say, *Holy Water*. The Church of Rome imitates them also in their *Holy Dayes*. They had their *Bacchanalia*; and we have our *Wakes*, answering to them: They their *Saturnalia*, and we our *Carnevalls*, and Shrove-tuesdays liberty of servants: They their Procession of *Priapus*; we our fetching in, erection, and dancing about *May-poles*; and Dancing is one kind of worship.[26]

It is clear that although in eighteenth-century England the notion that Christianity had absorbed ideas from paganism was unconventional, it was by no means confined to Knight's immediate circle, nor was it new.[27] The use to which Knight put the idea, though, took an extreme form which, had it been his intention to circulate the book widely, would have seemed calculated to outrage the general public. Whereas Hume had linked the proliferation of saints in the Roman Church with the polytheism of the ancients, and Hobbes had linked Christ with Cupid or Eros (as another personification of the same principle: love) Knight identified Christ with Priapus, and continued to do so later in life, explaining that

> The Greeks changed, as usual, the personified attribute into a distinct deity called Priapus, whose universality was, however, acknowledged to the latest periods of heathenism. In this universal character, he is celebrated by the Greek poets under the title of Love or Attraction, the first principle of animation; the father of gods and men; and the regulator and disposer of all things.[28]

24 Ibid.

25 Ibid., p. 678.

26 Ibid., p. 681.

27 Peter Gay, *The Enlightenment: An Interpretation*, 2 vols. (New York: Knopf, 1966 and 1969), vol. I: *The Rise of Modern Paganism*.

28 *Symbolical Language*, pp. 12–13, sections 23–4.

Priapus embodies a principle which would seem to be altogether more carnal than Christian love is generally taken to be; but the interpretation is innocuous compared with Knight's statement in 1786 that the Christian cross had earlier been a fertility symbol sacred to Priapus, 'a lucky coincidence of ideas which, without doubt, facilitated the reception of it among the faithful';[29] the remark being made as a casual aside, without giving a particular example, which might have made the point persuasive. The rhetoric of persuasion which Knight used most readily in this essay involved portraying religion as a *natural* evolution from natural acts and understandable fears, which were shaped by psychological forces into systems of superstition. He aimed to be found plausible by portraying his ideas (his adaptation of d'Hancarville's ideas) as lying in an understanding of human nature: just as d'Hancarville himself had claimed that his theory had its basis in nature's laws.[30] When Knight wrote about religion he intended to investigate religious principles in a scientific manner, treating religion as subject to the same rules as natural philosophy, trying to find generalisations which could be, in Bacon's term, a 'physics' of religion. Just as Newton's generalisations about matter were intended to apply to the merest speck of dust as well as to the largest planet, so Knight's generalisations about religion were intended to apply to all religions at all times. His field of study would today be called anthropology, sociology or religious studies, not theology. In this he was not uniquely influenced by d'Hancarville, but by the general tenor in Enlightenment thought, which attacked established Christianity and favoured deism, a belief in a god or gods who, like those of the Epicureans, could not directly intervene in events. Voltaire, for example, had, like d'Hancarville, thought of his religion as being the original religion of the world, the religion of Adam, Seth and Noah;[31] but Enlightenment deists, like Voltaire, were often supposed to be atheists. Knight's general theoretical ideas in *The Worship of Priapus* were mostly anticipated in David Hume's *The Natural History of Religion*; which (when Hume had decided to publish it, in 1757) his publisher was warned tried 'to establish *naturalism*, a species of atheism, instead of religion'.[32] In the work Hume tried to defend himself by making use of a series of subterfuges which depend for their effectiveness on the prejudices of a hostile Christian audience. His principal protection was provided by Bacon, Hume arguing that he was not making a challenge to any sort of religious belief, that *The Natural History of Religion* was in no sense a theological work, but a study in natural history. It was not addressing questions about the truth or falsity of the content of any reli-

29 Knight, *Priapus*, p. 48.

30 Hugues, *Recherches*, vol. I, p. xix.

31 Arthur O. Lovejoy, 'The Parallel of Deism and Classicism,' *Essays in the History of Ideas* (Baltimore: Johns Hopkins University Press, 1948), p. 87.

32 Hume, in *Philosophical Works*, ed. Green and Grose, vol. III, p. 61.

gious teaching, but only looking at the question 'concerning the origin of religion in human nature',[33] which was quite distinct; so he argued that the truth of Christianity need not detain us, because of course we all know that Christianity is true, and that was not the point under discussion. In the light of other things which Hume said it is impossible that he could have believed this assertion, but how could any Christian object to it? He claimed in short that his study belonged not to divine philosophy but to natural philosophy; it happened that divine philosophy was the subject of the enquiry, that was all.

The impulse to understand religion in terms of simple general laws derived from the example of science, and led to the origins of religion being sought because at its origin religion would have been at its simplest, just as the origins of language, of architecture and of social organisation were discussed at the time. Primitive peoples were in close contact with nature and could therefore be expected to be in tune with natural principles, and if the primary attributes of these things could be understood, then they could be separated from their later accretions and reformed. Primitive people in the early stages of civilisation did not need to understand 'natural law' as the extremely abstract body of knowledge proposed by Bacon, because they would instinctively act in accordance with its practical dictates: they were still in a state of grace. The word 'nature' could thus mean a great many different things, from instinctive (in human behaviour) to highly developed ('natural law' probably being beyond the reach of human understanding),[34] which goes some way towards explaining how flexible and useful the term was in eighteenth-century rhetoric. That Knight should have appealed to nature to support his ideas was not at all surprising, since the appeal was being made all the time by his contemporaries, and being made in support of completely opposed ideas. However, for what it is worth, Epicurus too felt that nature should be respected, not least human nature, warning that 'If on each occasion instead of referring your actions to the end of nature, you turn to some other nearer standard when you are making a choice or an avoidance, your actions will not be consistent with your principles',[35] and 'We must not violate nature, but obey her; and we shall obey her only if we fulfil the necessary desires and also the physical, if they bring no harm to us, but sternly reject the harmful.'[36]

According to Knight the primal natural religion was subverted along two principal routes, one leading to the monotheism of Jews and Christians, the other to the polytheism of classical antiquity and elsewhere;[37] and he regarded polytheism as the preferable alternative, as it

33 Hume, *Works*, vol. IV, p. 309.

34 Lovejoy, *Essays*, p. 80; see also Lovejoy, 'Nature as Aesthetic Norm' in *Essays*, pp. 69 ff.

35 Cyril Bailey, *Epicurus: the Extant Remains* (Oxford: Clarendon Press, 1926), pp. 100, 101 and 108, 109 (Epicurus: Principal Doctrines, XXV and XXI).

36 Ibid., pp. 100–1 and 108–9 (Epicurus: Principal Doctrines, XXV and XXI).

37 Frank J. Messmann, *Richard Payne Knight: The Twilight of Virtuosity* (The Hague: Mouton, 1974), p. 49.

avoided 'two of the greatest curses that ever afflicted the human race, dogmatical theology, and its consequent, religious persecution'.[38] Hume had developed this argument, though he expressed it more guardedly than Knight, stopping short of saying that classical polytheism was in general better than Christianity, only that it was better in a single respect: it did not entail religious persecution. In fact Hume presented a good many more such 'single respects', and no arguments in favour of Christianity, the absolute correctness of which had, of course, been taken for granted at the opening of the work.[39] The argument ran as follows: monotheism 'furnishes designing men with a pretence for representing their adversaries as profane, and the objects of divine as well as human vengeance'; whereas, by contrast, 'The Romans commonly adopted the gods of the conquered people; and never disputed the attributes of those local and national deities, in whose territories they resided.'[40] Hume tells us that if the Romans were besieging a town they would try to persuade the gods protecting it to defect to their own side by offering them better sacrifices than the townsfolk.[41] What of the persecution of the early Christians by the Romans? The Romans would have raised no objection to the new god and would presumably, in Hume's reading, have been happy to have accepted Him alongside the others, had the Christians agreed to it; but the Christians would not make sacrifices to the old gods, and there was a close link between the state and religion (some emperors being gods) so their refusal was interpreted as political disloyalty, a legitimate matter for punishment by the state.

Hume (in common with Epicurus, Hobbes and Knight) saw the origin of religion in '*unknown causes* which become the constant object of our hope and fear';[42] and the unknown causes were turned into gods by the same process of identification by which 'we find human faces in the moon, armies in the clouds; and by a natural propensity, if not corrected by experience and reflection, ascribe malice or good-will to every thing'.[43] Sometimes, though, the 'mere poetical or imaginary personage' may have been taken 'into the creed of the ignorant vulgar'[44] and then (in Knight's words) 'the characteristic properties of animals and plants were not only regarded as representation, but as actual emanations of the divine Power, consubstantial with his own essence'.[45]

38 *Priapus*, p. 60.

39 Hume, *Natural History of Religion*, in *Works*, vol. IV, p. 309.

40 Ibid., p. 337.

41 Ibid., p. 336n.

42 Ibid., p. 316.

43 Ibid., p. 317.

44 Ibid.

45 *Priapus*, p. 50.

A system of emanations

According to Knight's understanding of the matter, religious superstition was founded on ignorance: it involved imagining that natural occurrences are the work of an intelligent hand, and that appeals might be made to the intelligence to sway the actions of the hand. He saw superstition beginning to operate at the threshold which separated knowledge from ignorance, and as operating most effectively when there was ignorance all round. He maintained this stance throughout his life, and it is evident right from the Sicilian journal through to *Alfred*, published the year before his death. Within his frame of reference a true, unsuperstitious, religion was possible, but would be legitimate only when it was seen as a source of symbols which could be used to dramatise and describe knowledge, and was totally misconceived when it was seen as an explanation of events which was finally and absolutely true. In *Alfred* various points are clarified, Knight describing the 'supernatural agency' of the poem as a 'system of emanations' which is

> the most pleasing and poetical, and not the least reasonable and authenticated, of the different modifications of Christianity, which have, in different ages and nations, been more or less generally received, and the only one entirely compatible with the now generally received system of the universe. It still forms the fundamental principles of the religions of a large majority of the human race, whom it were most impious to suppose that a just and merciful God hath created to damn eternally; and though not now acknowledged by any established sect of Christians, was extremely prevalent during the third and fourth centuries, as far as the writings of the learned and laborious Origen were circulated; that is, through all the Greek and Oriental churches. That it hath not been extended further, and continued longer, is most devoutly to be regretted, it being not only the most pleasing and poetical mode of faith, but the most charitable, mild, and moral; inasmuch as that it excludes that horrible article, which accuses an omnipotent and omniscient God, to whose intellectual view all causes and consequences, through the boundless duration of time and extent of space, must be equally present, of peopling the world, which he had made, with generations on generations – millions of millions [*sic*] of his creatures, called into a short and precarious being here, to suffer endless torments hereafter; for an act of their common progenitor, which none of them could in any degree share, impede, or oppose; and of which all were, therefore, as entirely innocent as the child born yesterday is of the crime of his father who was hanged last year.[46]

46 *Alfred; A Romance in Rhyme* (London: 1823), pp. vii–viii.

That Knight should be trying to pass off his 'system of emanations' as a modification of Christianity is extraordinary and is only to be explained on account of Knight living in a Christian country. It was a very serious modification indeed, eliminating such traditional elements as original sin, damnation and redemption; elements which have been seen by others more respected by the church as essential to the faith. Society, however, demanded that he declare himself some sort of Christian; and he declared himself to be a Christian of a very unusual cast: the last theologian of whom he could approve being Origen, who was born in or about 185, and whose work was declared heretical under Justinian in 543,[47] so that Knight's so-called 'modification of Christianity' was not 'acknowledged by any established sect of Christians' at all, and had not been for some considerable time. In fact Knight's metaphysics in the poem owed rather more to Plato (on whom Origen drew) and much more to Epicurus than to any later metaphysicians, though there were elements drawn from more recent scientific thought, which of course overlapped with the ideas drawn from Epicurus.

Knight claimed that his ideas were compatible with the generally received system of the universe, the system described by Newton: following the principle already described whereby natural forces were turned into gods, Knight made his belief in the primacy of nature into a religion by using a specialised vocabulary of divinity when he spoke of things which he did not, and did not claim to, understand. In fact Newton himself can be found doing something very similar at the end of the *Principia*. In the course of that work he described with great precision the effects of the force of gravity, but then at the end he stopped to ask: what is this gravity? He had to admit that he did not know:

> And now we might add something concerning a certain most subtle Spirit, which pervades and lies in all gross bodies; by the force and action of which Spirit, the particles of bodies mutually attract one another at near distances, and cohere, if contiguous; and electric bodies operate to greater distances, as well repelling as attracting the neighbouring corpuscles; and light is emitted, reflected, refracted, inflected, and heats bodies; and all sensation is excited, and members of animal bodies move at the command of the will, namely by the vibrations of this Spirit, mutually propagated along the solid filaments of the nerves, from the outward organs of sense to the brain, and from the brain to the muscles. But these are things that cannot be explain'd in a few

47 Henri Crouzel, *Origène* (Paris: Pierre Zech, 1985), trans. A. S. Worrall, *Origen* (Edinburgh: T. & T. Clark, 1989), pp. xi–xii.

> words, nor are we furnish'd with that sufficiency of experiments which is required to an accurate determination and demonstration of the laws by which this electric and elastic spirit operates.[48]

Newton used the language of mathematical demonstration for most of his book, but when he reached the boundary of what he could say in those terms he resorted to a metaphysical vocabulary and began speaking of spirits. This 'most subtle Spirit' gravity could happily be personified as Venus, who represented a principle of attraction (and coincidentally Dante tells us that it is Divine Love, *l'amor divino*, which holds the stars on their course).[49] On the other hand one could substitute the male equivalent, Priapus, Cupid or Eros. Such an association of ideas may sound over-elaborate, but it is both simpler than and essentially similar to a remarkable speculation which Francis Bacon made in *De Sapientia Veterum* (*The Wisdom of the Ancients*) in which work as a whole he argued that the pagan myths were symbolic representations of moral, political and scientific teachings. Of particular interest here is his explanation that the god of love (Cupid–Eros–Priapus) should be understood as a personification of the atom:

> They say that *Love* is the ancientest of all the Gods, and of all things els except *Chaos*, which they hould to bee a cotemporary with it. Now as touching *Chaos*, that by the ancients was never dignified with divine honour, or with the title of a God. And as for *Love*, they absolutely bring him in without a father, onely some are of the opinion that hee came out of an Egge which was laid by *Nox*, and that on *Chaos* hee begot the Gods and all things els.
>
> This fable tends and looks to the Cradle of *Nature*, *Love* seeming to be the appetite or desire of the first matter, or (to speake more plaine) the naturall motion of the *Atome*, which is that ancient and onely power that formes and fashions all things out of Matter, of which there is no Parent, that is to say, no cause, seeing every cause is as parent to its effect. Of this power or vertue there can bee no cause in Nature.[50]

So it was love, or attraction, that brought the first things out of chaos, represented by the egg of night (Nox). Remembering Bacon and the Epicurean atoms which fell endlessly through infinite space, in infinite numbers, until (perhaps by attraction) one of them swerved and set in motion the chain of events which made the world and everything in it come into being, we can turn to a passage in which Knight described his 'emanations':

48 Isaac Newton, *The Mathematical Principles of Natural Philosophy*, trans. Andrew Motte, 2 vols. (1729), vol. II, p. 393.

49 Dante, *Inferno*, canto I, line 39; trans. John D. Sinclair (London: Bodley Head, 1939), p. 25.

50 Francis Bacon, *De Sapienta Veterum* (1609), trans. Arthur Gorges, *The Wisedome of the Ancients* (1619), pp. 77–8.

henceforth learn, that though through boundless space
Unnumber'd spirits from Heaven their lineage trace
Though endless emanations ever flow,
Yet all alike in different modes fulfil
Their Great Creator's universal will;
And acts as predisposed by general laws,
To one great end, from one efficient cause.[51]

The boundless space is Epicurean, and Newtonian, and the unnumbered spirits which act by predisposed laws seem to be atoms. Epicurus taught that the soul was composed of unusually fine atoms, which seem to have constituted the mind, and to have left the body when it died.[52] These atoms of mind when they were in the body would make it live, but when they were separated from it their role was less clear, since they would be separated from any sensory apparatus and so incapable of receiving new stimulation, or of communicating. Knight explained that when the mind was separated from the individual's body, it returns to the universal soul, which is an aggregated universal mind, Knight's deity. He described it in *The Worship of Priapus*, with help from Virgil:

They say that a spirit fills earth and sky and sea;
That man and his fellow-creatures, the wild and the tame,
Take from it the delicate stuff of their life.
There is no dying, they believe, when a body fails;
But, released, the life leaps lightly away to its place
In the depth of heaven, a brightness pointing the stars.[53]

The continuity is to be found in a universal life force, from which the souls of the new-born are constituted and to which they return. Knight's commentary on the above passage ran:

> The Etherial Spirit is here described as expanding itself through the universe, and giving life and motion to the inhabitants of earth, water and air, by a participation of his own essence, each particle of which is returned to its native source, at the dissolution of the body which it animated. Hence not only men but also animals, and even vegetables, were supposed to be impregnated with some particles of the divine nature infused into them, from which their various qualities and dispositions, as well as their powers of propagation, were supposed to be derived.[54]

The 'Etherial Spirit' is explicitly said to be composed of particles, and to be separable from the body. If we now turn to Charleton's

51 *Alfred*, p. 37.

52 A. A. Long, *Hellenistic Philosophy* (London: Duckworth, 1974), pp. 50–3.

53 Virgil, *Georgics*, bk. IV, lines 222–7, trans. Robert Wells (Manchester: Carcanet, 1982), p. 85. Quoted in the original Latin by Knight, *Priapus*, p. 49.

54 Knight, *Priapus*, p. 50.

Epicurus's Morals we find it said in the preface that 'We have our soules derived from the universall divine minde; And again, when they affirmed, that our Soules were taken from Heaven, and to return thither again after their emancipation from the body: All of which the Prince of Poets elegantly insinuateth in these Verses.'[55] And here Charleton cited the above-quoted passage from Virgil, word for word the same as Knight's (both Charleton and Knight giving it in its original Latin). The similarity of outlook is made still clearer as Charleton continues:

> you shall not finde one among the Pagans that is not (more or lesse) tainted with that so common Errour, of the refusion of all mens souls after death, into the Anima Mundi, or genrall Soul of the Universe, which is upon consequence, That they cease to exist per se, or to be what they were before, so soon as it is separated from the body.[56]

Given the identical quotation from Virgil being used to make an identical point, and given the fact that Knight appears to have organised his life in accordance with the principles set out in *Epicurus's Morals*, it does not seem unreasonable to suppose that Knight was familiar with the work, even though, again, he did not overtly acknowledge it. Knight repeatedly used the idea of the universal soul, not only in *The Worship of Priapus* and *Alfred*, but also in the *Monody on the Death of Charles James Fox* and *The Progress of Civil Society*. In the *Monody* he imagined the soul leaving the body through the pores of the skin, and his friend's soul mingling with the souls of Timoleon, Solon and George Washington.[57] The idea, prevalent among the pagans, had become part of his own personal system of belief.

In *Alfred*, Knight drew also on Platonic ideas, using them in conjunction with those mentioned above. Plato in the *Timaeus* imagined that there were as many souls as there were stars and that each soul had its ideal resting-place on a star in heaven. There is a description of the gods' being instructed by the Father of the Universe to imitate his creation by making living beings from a fusion of physical and divine elements (which is completely in accord with Knight's descriptions and the idea of the universal soul). The bodily elements were derived from the earth, the living mind from heaven:

> Then, ah! ye blooming nymphs and tender swains
> Shun transient pleasures bought with lasting pains:
> Ere love becomes of power supreme possest,
> Expel the lurking tyrant from your breast:

55 Walter Charleton, *Epicurus's Morals* (1656) preface (unnumbered pages).

56 Ibid. (unnumbered pages).

57 *A Monody on the Death of the Right Honourable Charles James Fox* (London: 1806–7), pp. 12–13.

For know that, did no force those hearts divide
The sated passion would itself subside.
It sprang from earth, while prudence came from heaven.[58]

The morality here again is Epicurean, laying stress on lasting pleasures as against immediate ones (the most lasting pleasure being peace of mind), but where we might have supposed that the elements of matter and of mind might have arrived from similar sources, they are different. Epicurus and Lucretius did not make this distinction, but Plato did, and so did Origen, who read the opening chapters of Genesis (where two accounts of the creation follow one another) as a double creation, the first spiritual, the second material. In the first, spiritual, creation man was made in God's image, and only in the second was he given bodily form.[59] Going back to Plato: in the *Timaeus* there then follows a passage which describes reincarnation, which seems to be at odds with Knight's description of the universal soul, but he nevertheless made use of it in *Alfred*, though he put the speech in the mouth of a mystic sage, and since it does not recur in Knight it does not seem to represent his personal belief. Plato had said that 'anyone who lived well for his appointed time would return home to his native star and live an appropriately happy life; but anyone who failed to do so would be changed into a woman at second birth. And if he still did not refrain from wrong, he would be changed into some animal suitable to his particular kind of wrongdoing.'[60] Knight elaborated this idea at some considerable length, presumably because he found the idea pleasing and poetical rather than because he would have wanted to defend it in any rigorous way:

And thus corrupted, in some baser sphere,
[It] Atones for all it did, or suffer'd here.
Some ribb'd in ice, in torpid anguish lie
Some toss'd in tempests round the horizon fly;
Others, in gulfs of subterraneous fire,
Purge off each sinful stain of foul desire,
Or, doom'd to transmigration, lost remain
From age to age, in servitude and pain;
Till call'd again in human forms to try,
If life renew'd new virtues can supply.
"Ferocious tyrants, thirsting still for blood,
To tigers turn'd, destroy mankind for food.[61]

A long list follows: greedy statesmen become wolves and foxes; humble drudges become beasts of burden; gluttons and drunkards become swine;

58 *Alfred*, pp. 27–8.

59 Crouzel, trans. Worrall, *Origen*, p. 94.

60 Plato, *Timaeus*, trans. Desmond Lee, 1965, rev. edn 1977 (Harmondsworth: Penguin, 1977), p. 58.

61 Knight, *Alfred*, p. 42.

obdurate knaves, stubborn fools, martyrs and persecutors all become mules.[62] This is clearly fanciful and not to be taken too seriously, but there is a quite different tone about passages which treat of the universal mind:

> Alone th'Eternal Universal Mind
> Knows why to each his office is assign'd;
> To His all perfect intellect alone
> The purpose of each act is fully known;
> By Him, but not by us, is understood
> What partial ills are universal good;
> What means incomprehensible may tend
> Best to fulfill each necessary end.
> He, through the boundless void of time and space,
> Assigns to each his period and his place;
> Through worlds on worlds, his ministers attend,
> Direct their progress, and assign their end.
> In forms organic, elements condense,
> And vital order through the whole dispense;
> Bid generations from each other grow,
> And life from death still renovated flow;
> Yet, through each change of species, shape, and name,
> Preserve primordial substances the same;
> Obedient to the plastic power that guides
> Each flux and reflux of th'eternal tides;
> And, flowing still from one unvarying cause,
> Though various agents, acts by various laws.[63]

The atoms here appear as 'ministers' of the Great Creator, as 'elements' and as 'primordial substances' ('primordia' – literally *first-beginnings* – being the name Lucretius used in Latin for Epicurus' ατομοι, 'atomoi' – literally *indivisibles* – which found their own way into English). The plastic power that guides the flux and reflux of the eternal tides is of course the attractive spirit gravity; and Knight portrays this potent combination of gravity, attraction and love as literally making the world go round, with groups of primordial substances or forces holding the orbs of heaven in place:

> And worlds unnumber'd round their centres roll;
> Attraction's chains from globe to globe extend,
> Direct their progress, and their orbits bend;
> Teach every planet its due course to run
>
> ...

62 Ibid., p. 43.

63 Ibid., p. 38.

> Others direct the waters where to flow,
> And teach the winds from various points to blow;
> Raise the full tides the moon's bright orb to meet,
> Or bid them refluent in their shores retreat.[64]

There are many different types of primordial substances and forces acting between them; others pervade the earth, adorn the surface of the earth, reign over different states and kingdoms, and guide the passions and affections.[65] Knight's elemental substances included mind or soul as well as more conventional matter, and he thought that the matter of the body could influence the matter (the spirits) of the mind:

> Imperfect spirits, who in part obey,
> The frail and turbid passions which they sway:
> For though thus sprung from God's all-perfect mind
> And first by Wisdom to their tasks assign'd;
> Immerged in matter's dross, from strains impure,
> Not e'en celestials can remain secure;
> Toss'd in the troubles of this world, they find
> Some earthly passions warp th'etherial mind
>
> ...
>
> For man, like them, his vital spirit draws,
> From one Supreme and Universal Cause;
> Like theirs, his reasoning soul from heaven descends,
> And upward still, when freed from matter, tends
>
> ...
>
> In pain and sorrow it begins and ends,
> Through pain and sorrow to oblivion tends;
> While transient intervals of bliss sustain
> The links renew'd, that still prolong the chain: –
> Great Nature's chain, which through all worlds extends,
> And plastic mind with pliant matter blends;
> Immortal both, the matter and the mind,
> Though both alike in mortal forms combined.
> Through everlasting time and boundless space,
> Their endless circuits, transmigrations trace;
> While still through all, one universal Cause
> Extends immutable its equal laws;
> And worlds unnumber'd still those laws obey,
> Here rise renew'd, there perish in decay;
> While revolution's changes but maintain

64 Ibid., pp. 39.

65 Ibid., pp. 40–1.

The general unity of order's reign;
And varied but in colour, form, and name,
Th'eternal substance ever is the same.[66]

The transmigrations here apply equally to matter and mind, and Knight argued that just as indestructible atoms of matter could be recombined from one body into another, so could indestructible elements of mind. In between their release from one body and their recombination into another, the mind-atoms dispersed into a general atomic flux, which Knight called the universal mind, which he described as all-knowing, but with which it was impossible to communicate. He did not argue for personal survival in an afterlife (as has been claimed) but on the contrary said that everything tends to oblivion, through pain and sorrow. What he was claiming here was that the 'elements' (the *primordia*, or atoms) of mind are indestructible and will last to the end of time, but they can be redistributed from one personal mind to another, in exactly the same way as the atoms in a body survive and can be recombined into new things, even though the corpse decays, all mind and all matter being subject to this discipline:

This throne of Nature – this all-teeming earth,
Which heirs to heaven supplies from mortal birth,
Shall, sunk into a torpid mass, decay,
Or shiver'd into atoms, pass away,
Through boundless space to wander unconfined,
Till new attractions to new centres bind

. . .

Whate'er hath a beginning still must tend,
By its inherent nature, to its end;
Must still to new created forms supply,
Eternal matter for mortality:
Alone the source from which creation flows,
No change, nor end, as no beginning knows.[67]

When freed again bright emanations rise,
And each again its native virtue tries.[68]

Both Knight's morals and his metaphysics were derived from classical sources, the 'system of Emanations' being prevalent in the ancient world and even in early Christian metaphysics; but they were mostly pagan, and where they were not distinctly pagan they were heretical. They certainly went far beyond the conventional paganism which would

66 Ibid., pp. 41, 42, 44.

67 Ibid., pp. 44, 45.

68 Ibid., p. 43.

have given a poetically classical gloss to the literary productions of a Georgian gentleman. Knight's view of religion was that it ought to convey ideas about the world in symbolic guise; it should be subservient to natural philosophy, what is known about the world, dressing the mysteries at the edge of knowledge in pleasing and poetical garb as a way of enacting and thereby in some way engaging with the mysteries of the universe. 'All religious subjects,' he said,

> being beyond the reach of sense or reason, are always embraced with violence and heat. Men think they know because they strongly feel; and are firmly convinced, because strongly agitated. Hence proceed that haste and violence with which devout persons of all religions condemn the rites and doctrines of others, and the furious zeal and bigotry with which they maintain their own; while perhaps, if both were equally well understood, both would be found to have the same meaning, and only to differ in the mode of conveying it.[69]

And of the phallic worship at Isernia, he said 'than which nothing can be more monstrous and indecent if considered in its plain and obvious meaning, or as a part of Christian worship; but which will be found to be a very natural symbol of a very natural and philosophical system of religion, if considered according to its original use and intention'.[70] Despite this protestation, the philosophical principles of *The Worship of Priapus* remain arcane, while the 'plain and obvious' meaning was all too immediate and memorable. Knight must have been aware of this, and some of the illustrations do nothing to help the gravity of his argument: for example following the perfectly serious and persuasive passage from Virgil above (see p. 100), explaining how the universal soul spreads through the world, we are referred to the image which closes the text, which may, just possibly, show symbolically what Knight suggested it did, but which directly and obviously shows a satyr engaged in intimate relations with a goat. This seems like mischief, and it would not be surprising to find the book instantly condemned as 'monstrous and indecent', but, to begin with, that was not what happened. Initially the book circulated only within the closed circle of Knight's friends in the Society of Dilettanti.

The reception of Priapus

The milieu into which *The Worship of Priapus* was introduced was, as has been mentioned, far from being typical of British society in general.

69 *Priapus*, p. 23.

70 Ibid., p. 24.

The book was produced specifically for the Society of Dilettanti's members, and they were not shocked by it. The society's minute book, which, referring to Knight's book as the *Priapeia*, records that

> Mr. Windham on the part of the Committee of publication reported that the Priapeia ordered by the Society to be printed is finished and ready for delivery. Ordered, motion made by Ld. Bessborough, Father of the society, That the Thanks of this Society be given to R. P. Knight Esq[re.] for the able & elegant manner in which he has investigated the interesting and deficult subject of this valuable work & that they be delivered to him at the next meeting he shall attend by the arch-master of his deputy appointed by the Society, dressed in his Crimson Taffety Robe & other insignia of his office.[71]

This passage shows something of the society's character, politely and appreciatively (and with some ceremony) accepting as 'able and elegant' this work which, in society at large, could have been calculated to scandalise. The whiff of scandal was not alien to the society: the 'crimson taffety robe' was one of a series of outfits designed by one of its founders, Francis Dashwood, Baron le Despencer (1708–67), best known now for his orgies and so-called 'devil-worship' at Medmenham Abbey (the Hell-Fire Club).[72] Knight was fully aware that *The Worship of Priapus* would not be suitable for general circulation, and told Joseph Banks (who oversaw the printing) that 'it will be impossible to make the work fit for any but very prophane persons';[73] so it was arranged that the work's distribution should be carefully controlled, and as a security measure it was agreed:

> That the Copies be lodg'd in the custody of the Secretary & one of them deliverd to each member of the Society, & that except these he do not on any Pretence whatever part with any other copy without an order made at a regular meeting. That each member be allowd once & no more to move the Society recommending by name a Friend to whom he wishes the Society to present a copy.[74]

Copies were presented to the Prince of Wales and, understandably, to d'Hancarville; also, a little later, to Lord Orford, Horace Walpole, who had allowed one of his sculptures to be engraved as an illustration.[75] Among these 'very prophane persons' and within the society the publication caused no upset, but was most decorously received, officially and ceremonially by 'Mr. Wilbraham as Deputy Arch-Master Dressd in all

71 Minutes of the Society of Dilettanti (MS) 3 March 1787, quoted in Cust, *Dilettanti*, ed. Colvin, pp. 122–3.

72 In 1790 Knight was implicated, along with the Duke of Norfolk and the Earl of Sandwich, in the disappearance of the presidential toga. Knight was summoned to a meeting in order to account for his conduct, but he did not go, sending along a letter the following day:

> Dear sir,
>
> I received your official letter yesterday just as I was sitting down to a good dinner with a keen Appetite; a situation so critical, that I am persuaded you will excuse my sending a verbal Answer.
>
> As for the robe I have never seen it since I had the Honour of dining with the Society . . . (Knight to the Society of Dilettanti, 3 May 1790, Correspondence File (Society of Dilettanti, MS). The background is given in Cust, *Dilettanti*, pp. 26–7.)

An Epicurean reference to the primacy of the stomach, followed by a denial which could have been disingenuous, as he did supply the society with a replacement robe, but a Greek chlamys, rather than a Roman toga.

73 Knight to Sir Joseph Banks, 18 June 1785, quoted Funnell, in *Arrogant Connoisseur*, ed. Clarke and Penny, p. 58.

74 Minutes of the Society of Dilettanti (MS) 3 March 1787.

the insignia of office [who] returned the Thanks of the Society to R. P. Knight Esqur. for his able work of the Priapeia.'[76]

The work was introduced to a wider public by Thomas Mathias (*c.*1754–1835) in *The Pursuits of Literature*, which appeared anonymously and went through sixteen editions from 1794. It upheld decently philistine values in the face of the threat, which was then felt, that the British populace would riot, following the example of the French revolutionaries, who had guillotined their king in 1793, and were terrorising one another. Britain had declared war on them, and feelings were running high: in Britain the revolutionaries' reputation as propagated in the press included atheism and general immorality, both of which seemed to Mathias to be amply evident in *The Worship of Priapus*. He said that a friend of his

> would *insist* upon my perusing a long disquisition in quarto, on the Worship of Priapus (printed in 1786) with numerous and most disgusting plates . . . all the ordure and filth, all the antique pictures, and all the representations of generative organs, in their most odious and degraded protrusion, have been raked together and *copulated* (no other idea seems to be in the mind of the author) and *copulated* I say, with a new species of blasphemy.[77]

Knight replied that his work was no more obscene than a medical textbook, and he regretted that Mathias's friend who *insisted* upon his reading the book did not also enable him to understand it.[78] Mathias's denunciation was curiously self-defeating, because while it spoke of his outraged piety, its practical effect was to bring to public attention a publication which Knight had taken some pains to keep obscure. It was designed for the eyes and minds of the country's rulers, not the fractious populace, and had no seditious intent, because it was not at any time seen by its author or publisher as an instrument with which to rouse a rabble. It was entirely on account of Mathias's denunciation in his best-seller that what should have been Knight's most secret publication was turned into his 'chief distinction' in the eyes of a wider public, though the book itself remained unseen.

The reception of *The Worship of Priapus* shows very clearly how the attitudes in one social group can generate a completely different culture from those in another. The book remained the identical artefact, but its readers responded in completely different ways. Mathias became librarian at Buckingham Palace in 1812 and eventually retired to Naples, from where the wax effigies, which he found so offensive, had originally come.

75 Funnell, *Arrogant Connoisseur*, p. 58.

76 Minutes of the Society of Dilettanti (MS) 1 April 1787.

77 Thomas Mathias, *The Pursuits of Literature, A Satirical Poem in Four Dialogues*, 3rd edn (London: 1797), p. 20n.

78 *The Progress of Civil Society: A Didactic Poem* (1796), p. xix.

He was no more part of the mob than was Knight, but he evidently feared it, and saw the promotion of piety among the common people as a way to maintain good order; but it is unlikely that drawing their attention to the existence of Knight's book was an effective means to that end.

Knight was not devoid of religion, despite his reputation, and despite his anti-clericalism. He devoted much time and thought to the development of his ideas on the subject, and returned to it repeatedly throughout his life, clarifying and elaborating his ideas rather than changing them. His sublime image of the universal mind, all-knowing, but unknowable, was his image of God; inspiring everything and animating it, but without any capacity directly to influence the course of events. This is very readily reconciled with the role which Epicurus gave to the gods, and with the metaphysical thinking of Enlightenment thinkers such as Voltaire and Thomas Jefferson, who were certainly not atheists, but neither did they hold conventionally Christian ideas, and are conveniently called deists. This thinking puts Knight in the mainstream of a line of Enlightenment thought, but late in the day, at a time when piety was being seen as increasingly necessary, and the power of people like Knight's Wilberforcian neighbours was on the increase.

The arcane and inspiring universal mind might have been Knight's most powerful religious vision, but it was very abstract and could find expression in the world only by way of symbols. Knight's interpretation of symbols could be tremendously elaborate, and could admittedly be unconvincing, even facetious at times in *The Worship of Priapus*. He was determined at all times to be free from the taint of superstition, and in his determination he banished most of the attitudes and beliefs which have been associated with piety; but nevertheless there is in his work a serious search for unsuperstitious religion, and a genuine respect for symptoms of the numinous, when he found them.

5 Civil society

Social links

At Westminster Knight voted with Charles James Fox, whom he described as 'Heaven's model of a man' such as is found on earth no more than once in a thousand years,[1] but Knight's ideas about heaven were unconventional, and his estimate of Fox was not universal. Fox was cited as 'one of the most notable examples of intellectual perversion we have ever known',[2] and his social life scandalised the followers of William Pitt ('the Younger', 1759–1806), who was prime minister virtually throughout Fox's political career. Fox was deeply rooted in Knight's social circle, having made his Grand Tour as a young man with Uvedale Price (with whom he had been at school) and they went to see Voltaire together.[3] Fox's career was marked by his espousal of great causes which did not achieve their goals under his own immediate guidance; for example he was inspirational in the movement to abolish slavery, but the slave trade was not made illegal in Britain until 1807, after his death. Knight bemoaned the continuing failure of this cause in the *Monody* which he wrote to mourn Fox.

> Millions shall cry, while gall'd by slavery's chain:
> This had we shunn'd, had FOX not spoke in vain.[4]

When Knight spoke in this poem of Fox's 'godlike mind'[5] he was not simply lapsing into hyperbole, but was referring to the fifth book of *De Rerum Natura*, where Lucretius rhapsodised Epicurus in the same way.[6] The major edition of this work to be prepared during the second half of the eighteenth century was Gilbert Wakefield's (1756–1801), which was dedicated to Fox. Wakefield's radical views, sympathetic to France,

1 Richard Payne Knight, *A Monody on the Death of the Right Honourable Charles James Fox* (1806/7), p. 6.

2 W. Combe, *Letter from a Country Gentleman to a Member of Parliament, on the Present State of Public Affairs* (London: 1789), pp. 23–4.

3 There is a description of Price's early relationship with Fox in a letter from Price to E. H. Barber, 24 March 1827, in *Reminiscences and Table-Talk of Samuel Rogers*, ed. G. H. Powell (London: Brimley Johnson, 1903), pp. 44–6; see also *The Complete Works of Voltaire*, vol. CVIII: *Correspondence and Related Documents*, ed. Theodore Besterman (Banbury, Oxfordshire: The Voltaire Foundation, 1974), p. 40n.

4 *Monody*, p. 4.

5 Ibid., p. 4.

6 Bk. V, lines 1ff.

similar to Fox's but unguardedly expressed,[7] brought him to prison after he had been convicted of seditious libel in 1799; and while gaoled he and Fox corresponded, discussing prison conditions and the pronunciation of Greek in roughly equal proportions, Knight being respectfully mentioned.[8]

Knight's poem *The Progress of Civil Society* (1796) is as close as he came to writing a political treatise. It tells us something about his politics, and shows his attitude to laws and regulations in general. We find in it the mixture of views to be expected in one of Fox's supporters, who made up a diminishing minority in Parliament and who were thought by both the Tories, and by Edmund Burke's supporters among the moderate Whigs, to be inciting sedition and revolution. Knight was not at all an original political thinker, clearly following Fox's lead, allying himself with those who took a principled stand on the moral high ground, but never finding himself in a position of real power. His only official parliamentary appointments were to committees which advised on matters of taste, selecting artists to be commissioned for monuments at St Paul's Cathedral, and a war memorial;[9] and of course he was asked to advise the Select Committee which enquired about the acquisition of the Elgin marbles. So he was always close to, but never at, the heart of the establishment; he seems always to have been allied with the opposition, and never showed any sign of political ambition; never, for example, making a speech at Westminster.

The Progress of Civil Society was a description of mankind bound and linked in various metaphorical chains, which calls to mind Rousseau's rousing opening to *Contrat Social*: 'Man is born free, and everywhere he is in chains.'[10] Knight was well aware that readers would link his ideas with Rousseau, and took care to warn against it, giving as one of his reasons for printing the poem that he might 'contribute to wean men's affections from those splendid paradoxes and pompous absurdities, by which several late writers, particularly Rousseau, have contributed to captivate the ignorant and unwary'.[11] The model for the poem was stated unambiguously at the opening of the preface:

> The learned reader will perceive, that the general design of the work is taken from the latter part of the fifth book of Lucretius, beginning with verse 923; and that I have also borrowed many particular passages, which I should have given at the bottom of the page, did I not rather wish that the whole page should be read in its proper order, as a text, upon which I have written a

7 In Gilbert Wakefield, *A Reply to Some Parts of the Bishop of Llandaff's Address to the People of Great Britain* (London: 1798).

8 Gilbert Wakefield and Charles James Fox, *Correspondence of the late Gilbert Wakefield B.A. with the Right Honourable Charles James Fox in the years 1796–1801* (London: 1813).

9 Joseph Farington, *Diary*, 1 April 1802; Knight to Lord Aberdeen, 16 Jan. 1816 British Library, Additional MSS (Aberdeen Papers), 43230, fol. 311. See Nicholas Penny, 'Richard Payne Knight: a Brief Life' in *The Arrogant Connoisseur*, ed. Michael Clarke and Nicholas Penny (Manchester University Press, 1982), pp. 12 and 14.

10 Jean-Jacques Rousseau, *Du Contrat Social; ou Principes du Droit Politique* (1762) in *Œuvres Complètes*, 3 vols. (Paris: Bibliothèque de la Pléiade, 1964), vol. III, p. 351: 'L'homme est né libre, et partout il est dans les fers.' Quoted as trans. G. D. H. Cole (London: Dent, 1913), p. 5.

11 *The Progress of Civil Society: A Didactic Poem* (London: 1796), p. xxii.

> commentary, as nearly in the same style and manner, as my poor abilities, and the inferior language which I employ, will allow; for that style and manner I consider as perfect. Lucretius is, in my opinion, the great poet of the Latin language.[12]

The influence of Lucretius was pervasive, as Knight acknowledged, and is evident even in the passage quoted immediately above: Lucretius had found it necessary to coin new Latin words in order to explain Epicurean ideas to his Roman audience, and Knight was paraphrasing Lucretius' complaints about his own Latin when it was compared with the Greek of Epicurus.[13] The overall shape of Knight's poem was also taken from *De Rerum Natura*, being both long and didactic, and also by being divided into six books, to which Knight gave the following titles: I. Of Hunting; II. Of Pasturage; III. Of Agriculture; IV. Of Arts, Manufactures and Commerce; V. Of Climate and Soil; VI. Of Government and Conquest. The first four books describe how society developed from primeval beginnings into a civilised state which could support the refinements of an urban life, and this part of the poem is wholeheartedly optimistic, one improvement following another. The fifth book breaks the sequence, by showing instead how civilisation can develop in different ways according to the climate and soil in which it grows. The sixth shows how civilisation can become oppressive, and ends with a description of the French Revolution, in which (by Knight's account) oppression was overthrown. This gives the poem a fairly optimistic conclusion, fierce hope being sustained despite the Revolution's bloody wake, but it was a conclusion which (to say the least) missed the mood of the moment.

The poem begins in a state of uncertainty by suggesting Epicurean atoms as a possible, but not a certain, starting-point for the development of the world:

> Whether primordial motion sprang to life
> From the wild war of elemental strife;
> In central chains, the mass inert confined
> And sublimated matter into mind?
> (I, 1–4)

This was one possible starting-point for the world, taking the view that mind somehow developed from inert matter. Knight could not be sure of it as a historical fact, and he went on to consider others, such as the possibility that the universal mind had shaped it:

12 Ibid., p. iii.

13 *De Rerum Natura*, bk. V, lines 1 ff.

Or, whether one great all-pervading soul
Moves in each part, and animates the whole;
Unnumber'd worlds to one great centre draws;
And governs all by pre-established laws?
(I, 5–8)[14]

Then there is the question of free will: is everything pre-determined and guided by the deity? Or is it only the limits of the possible that are fixed, with freedom to act within those limits? Knight, again, raised the question without attempting to answer it.

Whether in fate's eternal fetters bound,
Mechanic nature goes her endless round;
Or, ever varying, acts but to fulfil
The sovereign mandates of almighty will?
(I, 9–12)

The opening of the poem is full of hesitancy and doubt, falling short of making any positive assertions. We have already seen that with the publication of *The Worship of Priapus* Knight had angered Thomas Mathias,[15] and Knight's responses to these first broadsides were published in the preface to *The Progress of Civil Society*, which did nothing to calm Mathias. Further angered, he responded again, at some length, in the third edition of *The Pursuits of Literature*:

> Mr. K. is very fond of beginning all his books *with doubt*, like a true philosopher; he always uses the words '*whether* this, or *whether* that – or *whether* the other,' – is the case; never deciding, as Mr. Hume kindly used to do. But *whether* Mr. K. understands himself, even in the very beginning of his poem, may be a doubt; but *whether* his readers understand him, is no doubt at all.[16]

This misses the point altogether, since Knight's doubtful and mysterious opening was not attempting to explain anything, but on the contrary to say that there was uncertainty about the beginning of life and matter. This lack of a clear starting-point is a condition we face when we make enquiries into origins, at least if we do so as natural historians, but the uncertainty as to the origins does not make it impossible to discuss what comes after. Knight's argument was not premissed on the acceptance of any particular theory of the origin of life but, significantly, he did not include the biblical account of the creation, which was the only one

14 'Universal mind', see chapter 4, pp. 101–5.

15 See chapter 4, p. 108.

16 Thomas Mathias, *The Pursuits of Literature*, 3rd edn (London: 1797), p. 177n.

which Mathias would have thought necessary, and he opened with the Epicurean view, which described the origin of life without the intervention of any gods. Knight's obscurities and uncertainties all led to one certain conclusion, that life did in fact at some point begin. The passage has a parallel in book III *De Rerum Natura* in which Lucretius set out many arguments, each of them reaching the same conclusion (that the soul is mortal). It did not matter to Lucretius which of the arguments the reader found convincing, but it was important that at least one of them be accepted because the rest of the work was heavily dependent upon that conclusion. Knight's conclusion by contrast was, for once, uncontroversial: life did at some point begin, and Knight's argument needs us to accept only that. Perhaps the opening not only describes but also takes on some of the characteristics of the primal sludge out of which life emerged, but Mathias exaggerated its obscurity and the main part of the poem was concerned with the emergent life, not the constituents of the sludge. *Whether* this, or *whether* that, or *whether* the other was the case

> Let learned folly seek, or foolish pride;
> Rash in presumptuous ignorance decide.
> Let us less visionary themes pursue,
> And try to show what mortal eyes may view;
> (I, 13–16)

So Knight announced that he would not be speculating about the creation of the world, which was beyond the capacity of human sense, but would be confining his treatment to the realms of natural philosophy. That intent may seem sensibly limited and uncontentious, but *The Worship of Priapus* had given Knight a reputation which led some of his readers to read between the lines all too clearly. Knight had weighed his words carefully, and on the basis of them could have argued evasively, but for his arguments to have been entertained his good faith would have to have been established, whereas in fact he had established exactly the contrary. The passage above so incensed the Reverend William Mason (1724–97) that he wrote to Horace Walpole to say that 'The extract, which I have before me, contains only six lines of his last production, taken from the very first page, which contains so much rash scepticism, if not worse, plainly contending that, in his opinion, none but *learned fools* would *decide* that there was a *God*, that it moved my indignation'.[17] To which Walpole sympathetically replied that he was 'offended and disgusted by Mr. Knight's insolent and self-conceited poem; considering the height he dares to carry his impious attack, it might be sufficient to

17 *The Yale Edition of Horace Walpole's Correspondence*, ed. W .S. Lewis, 48 vols. (New Haven: Yale University Press, 1937–83,) vol. XXIX, p. 334, William Mason to Horace Walpole, 15 March 1796.

lump all the rest of his impertinent sallies in one mass of censure as trifling peccadillos'.[18]

Knight at his own valuation was not making any scandalous assertions at all, simply saying that there were various ideas about origins and not enough evidence to decide between them; and he would have argued that Mason's reaction was philosophically unjustifiable. As a matter of eighteenth-century common sense, however, it is clear enough that Knight's poem was highly provocative in neglecting to give prominence to a Christian theory of origins, and in entertaining doubts at a time when Parliament was preoccupied with sedition, and when religious doubt was linked with the outrages being perpetrated in revolutionary France. Given Knight's thoroughly justified reputation for harbouring anti-Christian sentiments, and his hostility (which will become clear)[19] to everything that Mason held dear, the reaction is not surprising in type, though its vehemence may startle. On the face of it, though, Knight's carefully chosen words said that he would be addressing the matter in the poem as a natural philosopher (a scientist) and that he would not be addressing questions which lay beyond the scope of natural philosophy in its current state. His programme, he declared, was to

> Trace out the slender social links that bind,
> In order's chains, the chaos of mankind
> (I, 17–18)

The chains in Knight's imagery can be analysed into three principal groups: first, references to the Great Chain of Being; secondly oppressive chains, which should be cast off; and thirdly beneficial chains which acted for the general good. Each of these groups will be discussed in turn below.

The Great Chain of Being, and despotic chains

The classic Great Chain of Being began as a metaphor in Plato, reached its fullest elaboration in the Elizabethan age, and was widely used as a metaphorical reference in the eighteenth century.[20] According to the Elizabethan system the Great Chain stretched from God in Heaven down to inert matter, and each of its links represented a gradation between these two extremes. From the rocks at the bottom there was a gradual ascent through plants and animals to man, the beings in the chain having more awareness and greater ability as they ascended. The lowest form of life was represented by the oyster, hardly animate, which makes

18 Ibid., p. 338, Horace Walpole to William Mason, 22 March 1796.

19 In chapter 7.

20 Arthur Lovejoy, *The Great Chain of Being* (Cambridge, Mass.: Harvard University Press, 1936).

an appearance in *Progress of Civil Society* as the creature 'Fix'd on rocks', lying in 'vital torpor' (line 32). There was an ascent through the gradually differentiated species of animals to the lion (or sometimes the elephant), the King of the Beasts; and then there was man, in a class by himself, who of all corporeal creatures was the only one to have a spiritual nature. But mankind did not stand at the head of the chain: symmetry demanded that for each rank in the earthly sphere there be another in the spiritual zone. Humans were therefore the middle link in the chain: above them there were the angels, and at the top there was God.

Knight did not make use of the Great Chain in this form, but adapted it to his own world-view. He accepted the classical model as it applied to the corporeal world, but, dispensing with the usual symmetry, so far as individuals were concerned he saw man as the topmost link in the chain. Instead of supposing that there were invisible beings who were more developed than mankind, and placing them higher up the chain, Knight supposed that they were less developed. His ministering spirits (as we saw in chapter 4) were the atoms, which were located at a level below the rocks. Beyond the atoms, from which everything was made, there was nature, the unknown cause of things. This might at first seem to be, as Mason said, an uncommonly arrogant view of the world, with man as the culmination of all things, but it is necessary also to appreciate that Knight supposed a completely different power-structure in the universe from that assumed by the Elizabethans. In their chain the power in the universe was vested in God, and it was one's duty to obey Him; whereas in Knight's chain the power is vested in nature, and it is nature that must be obeyed. All questions therefore were to be referred to natural law, which is exactly what Epicurus would have advised.[21] So far as government is concerned, then, this leaves us with the question as to what is human nature, which is a question addressed to philosophers, not theologians. It was a question which Montaigne attempted to answer in his *Essais*, to which Walter Charleton and Thomas Hobbes gave seventeenth-century answers, and which became a central concern in the eighteenth century. Hume's *Treatise on Human Nature* was symptomatic; as were the *Lettres Persanes* (1721) of Baron Montesquieu, Charles-Louis de Secondat (1689–1755). These fictional letters, supposedly written by and to Persians travelling in Europe, shed light on the matter by examining a familiar culture through unfamiliar eyes, showing how what seemed 'natural' in one culture looked highly artificial to someone brought up in another, though in Montesquieu's truly great book *De l'ésprit des lois* (*The Spirit of Laws*, 1748) he clearly supposed his own analysis to be

21 See chapter 4, p. 95.

objective, and somehow in this sense outside of culture. Montesquieu's political analysis inspired virtually every Enlightenment thinker, and had influenced Knight from an early age, as is clear from his Sicilian journal,[22] and he drew on him again in the fifth book of *The Progress of Civil Society*, in assuming a relation between the climate, the soil and the government of a country.[23] Knight might have thought, perhaps legitimately, Montesquieu to be declaring an allegiance to *De Rerum Natura* in saying that he did not draw his principles from his prejudices but from 'the nature of things'.[24]

Montesquieu set out an analysis of three different types of society: democracy, monarchy and despotism,[25] and found that each of them was driven by a different principle. Democracy was dependent on virtue, on a concern on the part of the individual for the good of the state as a whole. Monarchy depended on honour, which in Montesquieu's usage seems to mean 'social prestige', or snobbery: the offer of the Prince's arm being enough to persuade people to act for the good of the state. Despotism, by contrast, was driven by the principle of fear, through the strength of its laws.[26] In Knight's view, inspired by Lucretius, organised religion was also driven by fear, particularly the fear of death, but also fear of eternal punishment after death, and the fear of divine retribution for misdemeanour, and he consequently made a link between religious superstition and repressive government, which led him to conclude that the Church of England should be disestablished. The law could never inculcate a genuine religious sensibility, but 'the various edicts ... by which ... princes had bestowed privileges or inflicted penalties on particular systems of faith, or forms of worship, had only served *to convict their subjects of worshipping the purple rather than God*, the only effect which such laws ever had, or ever will have'.[27] This point of view stood in flat contradiction to the position which Edmund Burke had taken, seeing a state religion as 'the basis of civil society'.[28] The prominence of priests in the ancient Egyptian state was a reason for Knight to condemn the pyramids as works of art.

Egypt's sons, in frigid method bound,
Still onward move their dull mechanic round

...

Drawl'd on through life, as mystic priestcraft taught;
And, only as directed, moved and thought; –
Through ages toil'd vast fabrics to produce,
Alike devoid of ornament or use;

22 'This love of false brilliancy, from which none of the moderns [i.e. modern Sicilians] are totally free, has been attributed by the Northern Nations to the heat of the climate, & this Opinion having been supported by Montesquieu has become rather general'. Richard Payne Knight: *Expedition into Sicily*, ed. Claudia Stumpf (London: British Museum Press, 1986), p. 65.

23 Montesquieu, *De l'ésprit des lois* (Geneva: 1748), bks. XIV–XIX.

24 Montesquieu, *L'Esprit des lois*, in *Œuvres Complètes*, ed. Roger Caillois, Bibliothèque de le Pléiade, 2 vols. (Paris: Gallimard, 1966), vol. II, p. 229: 'Je n'ai point tiré mes principes de mes préjugés, mais de la nature des choses'; trans. Anne M. Cohler, Basia Carolyn Miller, Harold Samuel Stone, *The Spirit of Laws* (Cambridge University Press, 1989), p. xliii.

25 Montesquieu, *L'Esprit des lois*, bks. II and III.

26 Ibid., bk. III, chapter 3, para. 1.

27 Knight, *Civil Society*, p. xvi. Knight citing the consular oration of Themistius to the Emperor Jovian.

28 Edmund Burke, *Reflections on the Revolution in France* (1790), in *The Works and Correspondence of the Right Honourable Edmund Burke*, 8 vols. (London: 1852), ed. C. W. Fitzwilliam and Richard Bourke, vol. IV, p. 224.

Enormous piles, where labour, wealth, and waste;
Strove to supply the want of sense and taste;
Where barbarous strength perpetuated shame,
And sumptuous folly damn'd to endless fame.
Hence rose the pyramids, whose senseless pride
Served but some tyrant's loathed remains to hide;
And the vast labyrinth its chambers spread,
Useless to all; – the living or the dead;
In sculptured granite, monstrous figures grew,
And shapes unknown to nature, rose to view;
The mystic symbols of a gloomy creed
Which priests employ'd the gaping crowd to lead;
Which art, obedient to the rules they taught,
With patient, dull, mechanic labour wrought; –
Feeble, yet harsh – without correctness dry,
And still, though formal, void of symmetry.
(IV, 417–19, 425–44)

Ancient Egypt, then, was enchained in various pernicious ways, bound to method and rule, in the grip of tyranny and priests. Winckelmann had made similar observations about the lack of freedom in Egyptian art, saying that 'their artists were not permitted to deviate from the ancient style; for their laws allowed no further scope to the mind than mere imitation of their forefathers, and prohibited all innovations',[29] but without attributing this to the influence of their priests. So far as Knight was concerned, ancient Egypt's works of art were monstrous and unnatural; also, incidentally, ostentatious and without utility, criticisms which we will find Knight aiming at other targets. The most pernicious state of mind of all was that in which oppression was actually welcomed by the oppressed, an idea which Knight might have connected with Epicurus' teaching that one should renounce appetite so far as possible, to avoid being enslaved by it. Certainly Knight spoke of the pursuit of power, luxury, fashion and religion in these terms, using the imagery of chains: 'The chains, themselves imposed, the victors wore' (VI, line 46); 'In sordid luxury the soul enchain'd' (line 67); 'fashion's magic chains' (line 209):

Press'd by the hand of power, we freedom crave,
Ourselves beneath worse tyrants to enslave; –
Heaven hears the prayer, by ignorance address'd
And Damns whole nations at their own request.

29 Winckelmann, *History of Ancient Art* (1764), in *Winckelmann, Writings on Art*, ed. David Irwin (London: Phaidon, 1972), p. 109.

> Yet let not willing slavery hug its chain,
> Nor boast the blessings of a despot's reign.
> (VI, 687–92)

Beneficial chains

Another group of chains to be considered is that where the effects of the chains are wholly beneficial, prominent among them the 'gilded chains of commerce'. Knight took his economics very straightforwardly from Adam Smith (1723–90) whose immensely influential book *An Inquiry into the Nature and Causes of the Wealth of Nations* has already been mentioned.[30] In his essay 'On the Natural Progress of Opulence' Smith wrote:

> That order of things which necessity imposes in general . . . is promoted by the natural inclinations of man . . . But though this natural order of things must have taken place in some degree in every . . . society, it has, in all the modern states of Europe, been, in many respects, entirely inverted . . . The manners and customs which the nature of their original government introduced, and which remained after that government was greatly altered, necessarily forced them into this unnatural and retrograde order.[31]

A natural state of affairs had been obscured by more recent developments, and reform would involve the removal of late accretions: the pattern of description is identical to Knight's argument that Christianity had imposed an unnatural and retrograde order on human nature. The usual appeal to 'nature' as the final arbiter is again being made, but the two most important models of 'human nature' in the eighteenth century were completely contradictory. They had been put forward by Rousseau and Hobbes, the former seeing mankind as naturally good, the latter as naturally bad. Diderot characterised their differences, saying that

> The philosophy of Monsieur Rousseau of Geneva is almost the inverse of that of Hobbes. The one thinks man naturally good, and the other thinks him wicked. For the philosopher of Geneva the state of nature is a state of peace; for the philosopher of Malmesbury it is a state of war. If you follow Hobbes, you are convinced that laws and the formation of society have made men better, while if you follow Monsieur Rousseau, you believe instead that they have depraved him. One was born in the midst of tumults and factions; the other lived in civilised society, and among men of

30 Chapter 1, pp. 4–5.

31 Adam Smith, 'On the Natural Progress of Opulence', in *An Inquiry into the Nature and Causes of the Wealth of Nations* (1776), ed. Edwin Cannan, 2 vols. (London: Methuen, 1904), vol. I, bk. III, chapter 1.

learning. Different times, different circumstances, different philosophies.[32]

The first four books of *The Progress of Civil Society* describe the development of society from earliest times until it reached the perfection to be found in classical Greece. We have seen how Knight followed Winckelmann in connecting the Greeks' personal freedom in ancient times with the quality of the achievements of their states.[33] Lady Morgan (*c.*1776–1859), best remembered as the author of *The Wild Irish Girl* (1806), used the same idea to account for the superiority of the ancient over the modern Greeks. In her youth she moved in Knight's set, frequenting Bentley Priory, Lord Abercorn's household, where Knight was a regular guest. In 1809, when they were both moving in this circle and when Knight's influence was at its height, she said that 'the Greeks are only *debased* because they are no longer *free*',[34] and in doing so reflected the current received wisdom of the Bentley Priory set, responding to the philhellenic mood of her friends. The remark appeared in the preface to *Woman; or, Ida of Athens* (1809) the subject of the which, she said, had been suggested to her by William Gell.[35]

From the time of ancient Greek perfection onward, Knight described further developments which tended to bring about the 'unnatural and retrograde order' of the present. It is here that Knight's views are most clearly to be distinguished from Rousseau's, though they were less extreme than Hobbes's. Both Knight and Rousseau made an appeal to nature, and both felt nostalgia for a time long passed, probably in both cases fused with fond memories of an earlier time in their own lives, but while they both agreed that nature should be the guiding principle, Knight could not accept that 'the arts and sciences owe their birth to our vices' and that therefore no good can come of them, as Rousseau maintained.[36] On the contrary, Knight saw the arts and sciences as good things, provided that they did not work against nature. As described by Hobbes, Montesquieu and Smith, civilisation is an evolutionary and 'natural' process which is beneficial to all so long as it is not subverted. Knight saw the Greek city-state as the culmination of that development. Even when the motives which inspired an act were selfish, in an ideally constructed society the act redounds to the society's benefit. Such at least was Smith's theory of commerce, which Knight adopted, saying that

> the soft intercourse of commerce ran,
> From state to state, and spread from clan to clan;

32 Denis Diderot, from the entry for 'Hobbisme', vol. VIII of the *Encyclopédie* (Paris: 1765), collected in Denis Diderot, *Political Writings*, trans. John Hope Mason and Robert Wokler (Cambridge University Press, 1992), p. 27.

33 Chapter 2, pp. 43–5.

34 Lady Morgan, *Woman; or, Ida of Athens,* 4 vols. (1809), vol. I, pp. 2–3.

35 See Lionel Stevenson's biography of Morgan, *The Wild Irish Girl* (London: Chapman and Hall, 1936), p. 108.

36 E.g. in Rousseau, *Discours sur les sciences et les arts,* in *Oeuvres Complètes,* ed. B. Gagnebin and M. Raymond, 4 vols. (Paris: Gallimard, 1959–69), vol. III, pp. 1–57.

Each link of social union tighter drew,
And rose in vigour as it wider grew

. . .

the bold merchant

. . .

Though selfish avarice was his only guide,
Around him liberal plenty pour'd its tide;
Each path of life, with gayer pleasure strew'd,
And bade the springs of evil flow with good

. . .

For though each object of pursuit be vain,
The means employ'd are universal gain.
(IV, 71–4, 77, 83–6, 127–8)

Knight also gave an account of the division of labour, describing how

industry still works with more effect
Where different classes different works select;
And each to one peculiar task confined,
Lets no extraneous thoughts distract his mind.
Thus, too, while each can only parts produce,
Which other hands arrange and join for use,
Mutual desires and wants the whole pervade,
And rank to rank unite, and trade to trade.
(IV, 249–56)

Self-interest could, then, benefit the whole community in economic matters, and here again there was no conflict between personal desire and communal good, just as in the moral schemata of Epicurus, Hobbes and Hume. The 'natural' self-interest was seen to generate civilisation, which was seen by all except Rousseau to be a good thing. Knight was targeted by the *Anti-Jacobin,* a periodical founded in the heat of the anxieties about the French Revolution, which promoted staunchly anti-liberal views. It associated Knight's politics with anarchy, with Thomas Paine (1737–1809) and William Godwin (1756–1836).

Tom Paine was the author of *The Rights of Man* (part I, 1791) which was a response to Burke's *Reflections on the Revolution in France* (1790), but he was famous before that on account of his involvement in the American Revolution, and his pamphlet, *Common Sense* (1776). The first part of *The Rights of Man*, which was priced at 3 shillings in the first edition, sixpence in the second, to bring it within reach of a popular audience, had sold more than 50,000 copies in 1791, more than Burke's *Reflections*.[37] He was found guilty of sedition in 1792, but escaped to France. Godwin's sentiments were much the same as Paine's, and might have been tried on the same charges, but his book *An Enquiry Concerning Political Justice and its Influence on Morals and Happiness* (1793) had a more academic tone and, at a cost of 36 shillings, was beyond the means of the rabble he was charged with rousing, and so he was not prosecuted.[38] To some extent, and not only in the *Anti-Jacobin*, 'democracy' and 'anarchy' were interchangeable terms: Hobbes, for example, explained that a 'popular' government would be described as a democracy by those who supported it and as an anarchy by those who did not; just as a 'tyranny' was a 'monarchy' which was facing criticism.[39]

At one level Knight would have favoured democracy because it would have seemed to him to have been scientific, since its structure was that which Bacon described for natural philosophy.[40] As natural law takes its authority, in Bacon's analysis, from the facts which it seeks to summarise in its generalisation, so should civil law take its authority from those whom it seeks to regulate: a representative government should, in effect, be a summary of popular opinion just as natural law should be a summary of facts. The individual in a society could be seen to correspond with an atom in a material body, and an atom will never act against its nature, its inclinations. Hobbes took some such view of the body politic, and the title page of *Leviathan* shows an image of the state as a corporate body made up of many atomic individuals, given coherence by the monarch who was its head. There was a more immediate connection between atoms and democratic insurrection in the rebellion which had been necessary to establish the doctrine of atoms in the face of the church's opposition; so we find Hobbes's friend Edmund Waller (1606–87) making a connection between democratic organisation and atoms:

> Lucretius with a stork-like fate
> Born and translated in a state
> Comes to proclaim in English verse
> No Monarch rules the Universe.
> But chance and Atomes make this All
> In order Democratical
> Without design, or Fate, or Force.[41]

It was quite usual for eighteenth-century political thinkers to consider themselves scientific in their approach. Adam Smith's pupil and

37 Marilyn Butler, *Burke, Paine, Godwin, and the Revolution Controversy* (Cambridge University Press, 1984), p. 108.

38 Ibid., p. 150.

39 Thomas Hobbes, *Leviathan* (London: 1651), ed. C. B. Macpherson (Harmondsworth: Penguin, 1968), p. 699.

40 See chapter 3, p. 75.

41 Waller, quoted by Robert Hugh Kargon, *Atomism in England from Hariot to Newton* (Oxford University Press, 1966), p. 92.

friend John Millar went so far as to say that 'the great Montesquieu pointed out the road . . . He was the Lord Bacon in this branch of philosophy, Dr. Smith is the Newton'.[42] Despite Knight feeling the need to recognise personal freedoms, and a general sympathy for democracy, he did not think of it as a practical possibility for the government of a country. According to Montesquieu's analysis a democracy was driven by virtue, and in order for it to work the individual would need to appreciate and respond to the needs of the state, rather than trusting to more immediately personal inclinations. Knight, following Montesquieu, felt that it was practically necessary to introduce a monarch into the system so as to make it run on the principle of honour, snobbery being a more dependable force in society than a call to be virtuous. It was also necessary, though, to limit the monarch's power to prevent the state from developing into a despotic tyranny, and so that the monarch should be able to act only in accordance with the general wishes of the people. The model for such a system, and one which was singled out for the highest praise by Montesquieu, was the British constitution, in which each of three legislative bodies (the sovereign and two Houses of Parliament) acted as a check on the other two on any occasion when they did not share a general will.[43] Knight's (which is to say Fox's) supposed radicalism went only so far as to say that the monarch should generally act in accordance with the will of Parliament, this fortunate state of affairs being described in his poem:

> Yet happy Britain! – with proportion'd weights,
> Guard the just balance of thy three estates;
> For in that balance only canst thou find
> Order and rule with liberty combined:
> Man's feeble virtue can't itself maintain,
> Unless some curb each bold excess restrain:
> Whence, still, dominion, in one centre placed,
> By foul injustice ever is disgraced; –
> Kings or Conventions – they are still the same –
> Despots, that differ only in a name.
> Let then severe reciprocal control
> Poize every part, and regulate the whole;
> (VI, 567–78)[44]

And in a footnote to this passage Knight endorsed the political system in the United States of America,[45] which was, under the influence of

42 Peter Gay, *The Enlightenment: An Interpretation*, 2 vols. (New York: Knopf, 1966 and 1969), vol. I, p. 333.

43 Montesquieu, *L'Esprit des lois*, bk. XI, chapter 6.

44 The similarity with Fox's analysis is shown, for example, in a speech delivered to the House of Commons on 11 May 1791, advising on the reform of the government in Canada: 'First he [Fox] laid it down as a principle never to be departed from that every part of the British dominions ought to possess a government in the constitution of which monarchy, aristocracy, and democracy were mutually blended and united; nor could any government be a fit one for British subjects to live under, which did not contain its due weight of aristocracy, because that he considered to be the proper poise of the constitution, the balance that equalised and meliorated the powers of the two other extreme branches, and gave stability and firmness to the whole.' *Speeches of the Right Honourable Charles James Fox in the House of Commons*, 6 vols. (London: 1815), vol. IV, ed. J. Wright, p. 228.

45 Knight, *Civil Society*, p. 150n.

Montesquieu's ideas, deliberately structured so as to bring to its citizens the same benefits as the British administration. In America the President and the two parliamentary houses were elected, but the intent was to design a system with enough checks and balances in it for any individual within the system to be corrupt without the effects being harmful to the state as a whole. It was Knight's hope that there would be similar reforms in France in the wake of the Revolution, a hope that was fairly widely shared before the excesses of the Terror caused most, but not Fox or Knight, to abandon it. Knight himself had been in France before the Revolution and had heard about some of the cruelties of the *ancien régime*, which were enough to convince him that the monarchy had become despotic. His footnotes mention 'a committee of surgeons sitting to invent tortures',[46] and include an extended and detailed account of the sufferings of Bury Desrues and his widow, which begins by explaining how

> Bury Desrues, a man of liberal education, was in the year 1777, condemned at Paris, for poisoning Madame Le Motte, to be broke on the wheel, and then burned alive. By the strength of his own constitution and the skill of the executioner, he was enabled to retain his senses, and sensibility, through every stage of this dreadful punishment; so that when placed upon the pile, amidst the flames that were rising to consume his mangled limbs, he solemnly and emphatically declared his innocence.[47]

Knight, sympathising with the French people, saw the Revolution as a liberation from tyrannical power, whereas in England during the 1790s it was more usual in Britain to see it as a complete breakdown in the rule of law. Knight's poem ended with a description of the bloodshed of the Reign of Terror (in a passage again modelled on Lucretius, who concluded *De Rerum Natura* with a vivid description of the annihilation of the population of Athens by plague), events which caused a widespread fear that the British people might themselves revolt. Uvedale Price, jittery, wrote a pamphlet on the protection of rural property,[48] but Knight felt that the circumstances in England and France were not directly comparable, that the French situation was only the most immediate result of throwing-off despotic rule, and he was optimistic about France's long-term future.[49] In a previous poem, *The Landscape*, he had similarly concluded with the Revolution in France, attempting to put it in perspective with a note drawing such comparison as could be made with ancient Greece:

46 Ibid., p. 148n.

47 Ibid., p. 146n.

48 Uvedale Price, *Thoughts on the Defence of Property. Addressed to the County of Hereford* (Hereford: 1797).

49 Knight's position on the matter was exactly that of Fox: see Fox, *Speeches*, vol. IV, p. 53: 'The scenes of bloodshed and cruelty which had been acted in France no man can have heard of without lamenting; but still, when the severe tyranny under which the people had so long groaned was considered, the excesses which they had committed, in their endeavour to shake off the yoke of despotism, might ... be spoken of with some degree of compassion; and he was persuaded that, unsettled as their present state appeared, it would be preferable to their former condition, and that ultimately it would be for the advantage of this country that France had regained her freedom.'

> The expulsion of the higher orders of society by the lower frequently happened in the little republics of Greece; but those revolutions were upon too small a scale to afford any analogies, by which we may judge of the present great convulsion. In one important point only there appears a strong resemblance. It was not, as Thucydides observes, either the most numerous or most able party that prevailed, but invariably the most weak and stupid; which, conscious of its inability to contend openly for superiority, proceeded immediately to murders and proscriptions, and oppressed their adversaries before they were prepared to resist.[50]

It was because he continued to express his view that the revolution would ultimately be beneficial, even after revolutionary France had declared itself at war with Britain in 1793, that Knight was seen in some quarters to favour dangerously radical political policies; yet the position which Knight set out was not at all revolutionary so far as Britain was concerned, as he simply took the view that some other countries would do well to be governed in the same way as Britain. That this should have been seen as supporting anarchy is, on the face of it, quite incredible, and serves more reliably as an index of panic on the part of Knight's critics than it does of Knight's views. The fact that the nations were at war at the time explains the panic, since Knight saw the enemy with more sympathy than suited the nation's mood; but, he concluded:

> Yet let not willing slavery hug its chain,
> Nor boast the blessings of a despot's reign;
> For e'en the fever, which the body shakes,
> Oft, the numb'd seeds of vital vigour, wakes;
> Purges the dregs of vice inert away;
> And raises virtue sinking to decay.
> Did only gentle gales o'er ocean blow,
> The mass, unmoved, would dull and putrid grow;
> Foul exhalations, from its gulphs, would spread,
> And o'er the earth their vapoury poisons shed;
> But the same hurricane, which lifts the waves
> To whelm whole navies in untimely graves,
> Clears the putrescent waters of the deep,
> And rouzes nature from her morbid sleep.
> (VI, 691–704)

50 *The Landscape: A Didactic Poem*, 2nd edn (London: 1795), p. 93n.

The politics of affection

Turning from political interactions on the national scale to interpersonal politics on the domestic scale, we find that in Knight's scheme of things marriage occupied a middle place between the oppressive and the unequivocally beneficial chains. Knight did not set out to condemn marriage 'from which I derive all the blessings and benefits of Civil Society; but merely . . . its indissolubility'.[51] He thought that the institution of marriage was no bad thing in itself, but that it had become systematised and made subject to rules which might not follow nature ('fix'd by laws, and limited by rules, / Affection stagnates and love's fervour cools' – book III, lines 150–1); whereas by contrast when the contract was only 'natural', and not legally binding, no unfortunate consequences followed:

> While mutual wishes form love's only vows,
> By mutual interests nursed, the union grows;
> Respectful fear its rising power maintains,
> And both preserve, when each may break, its chains.
> (III, 156–9)

The feelings which find expression in these lines were grounded not only in Knight's philosophy, but also in the personal circumstances of his friends, and they had some significance in Westminster politics. If we turn first to the philosophers whom Knight consulted then we find a surprising consensus against marriage. Epicurus did not teach that it was a bad thing, but did say that it should not be undertaken out of a sense of duty;[52] while Lucretius taught that romantic love was misguided (which is not an injunction against marriage as such).[53] Francis Bacon described a wife and children as 'impediments to great enterprises either of virtue or mischief' and said that 'the best works, and of greatest merit to the public, have proceeded from unmarried or childless men';[54] but yet he married. As a courtier of the unmarried Queen Elizabeth it might have been politic to pronounce some benefits in an unmarried state, and indeed Bacon did not marry until after James had taken the throne, though Aubrey reports that Bacon was a pederast,[55] which equally could have been politic at James's court. David Hume wrote an essay on marriage, but it was merely playful and gave away nothing of his feelings on the matter, though he did not marry.[56] Knight himself, of course, was not constrained by marriage vows, but in his circle even heterosexual relationships could be very much more complex than those vows envisaged.

51 Knight, *Civil Society*, p. 55n.

52 Walter Charleton, *Epicurus's Morals* (London: 1656), pp. 55 ff, chapter 9: 'Of Prudence Domestick', p. 54 (the page numbers here are transposed, so that p. 54 follows p. 55): 'it is far below the part of a Wise man, willingly to put himself upon Chance, to undergo the hazard, and engage himself in that condition, from whence, in case he should afterward repent, he cannot withdraw himself'.

53 Lucretius, bk. IV, *De Rerum Natura,* lines 1058 ff.

54 Francis Bacon, 'Of Marriage and the Single Life', in *Essays* (London: Dent, 1972), p. 22.

55 John Aubrey, *Brief Lives*, ed. Andrew Clark, 2 vols. (Oxford: Clarendon Press, 1898), vol. I, p. 71.

56 David Hume, 'Of Love and Marriage', in *Philosophical Works,* ed. T. H. Green and T. H. Grose, 4 vols. (London: 1886), vol. IV, pp. 383 ff.

Lady Morgan, who met Knight at Lord Abercorn's, was to remark with reference to Nathaniel Hawthorne's *Scarlet Letter* (1850) that 'The story is perfectly monstrous. I cannot understand making a lady who has committed some peccadillo, wear a great scarlet patch upon her chest. Why, if we were all obliged to wear scarlet patches in consequence of our peccadillos, we could never venture out of doors, and there would soon be an end to all society.'[57]

Jane Elizabeth Scott, the daughter of a Hampshire vicar, had married Knight's neighbour Edward Harley, fifth Earl of Oxford, in 1794.[58] As Lady Oxford, her numerous affairs were public knowledge to the extent that her children were known as 'the Harleian Miscellany' on account of their varied parentage.[59] Wordsworth hinted disapprovingly of a certain picturesque irregularity in Uvedale Price's marriage;[60] Sir William Hamilton's second marriage furnished the age with the most notorious example of the straining of marriage vows in his wife's liaison with Lord Nelson; and we find Knight's cousin, the Reverend Samuel Johnes Knight reputedly performing a wedding service of doubtful legitimacy (because it was carried out without the king's permission) between the Prince of Wales and the Roman Catholic widow Mrs. Fitzherbert.[61] Knight's circle was obviously far from puritanical in such matters, and he would not have caused any great outrage amongst his friends by giving voice to these views, but in the tense political atmosphere of the 1790s Burke had taken the opposing view. He saw increased divorce rates in France as symptomatic of the revolutionaries' absolute moral bankruptcy, saying that

> The practice of divorce, though in some countries permitted, has been discouraged in all . . . [The French revolutionaries'] law of divorce, like all their laws, had not for its object the relief of domestic uneasiness, but the total corruption of all morals, the total disconnexion of social life . . . With the Jacobins of France vague intercourse is without reproach; marriage is reduced to the vilest concubinage; children are encouraged to cut the throats of their parents; mothers are taught that tenderness is no part of their character, and, to demonstrate their attachment to their party, that they ought to make no scruple to rake with their bloody hands in the bowels of those who came from their own.
>
> To all this let us join the practice of cannibalism.[62]

Whilst, again, this sounds more like blind panic than reasoned argument, it shows that divorce was a contentious issue, and was highly

57 W. J. Fitzpatrick, *The Friends, Foes and Adventures of Lady Morgan* (Dublin: 1859), pp. 130–1.

58 *The Italian Journal of Samuel Rogers*, ed. J. R. Hale (London: Faber, 1961), p. 249n.

59 The Earl of Oxford's family name was Harley. The 'Harleian Miscellany' was more properly the name given to a collection of manuscripts from the ancient family archives, now at the British Museum.

60 In *Memorials of Coleorton*, ed. William Knight, 2 vols. (Edinburgh: 1887), vol. II, p. 134.

61 Revd Charles J. Robinson, *Castles of Herefordshire* (Hereford: 1869), p. 37. Johnes was not the only suspect, nor the likeliest.

62 Edmund Burke, 'Three Letters addressed to a Member of the Present Parliament, on the Proposals for Peace with the Regicide Directory of France, 1796', in *Works and Correspondence*, ed. Fitzwilliam and Bourke,

charged with political overtones, so that even though it occupied only a few lines of Knight's poem it was seized upon by satirists. The *Anti-Jacobin* published a parody called *The Progress of Man* (by one 'Mr. Higgins of St. Mary-Axe') which claimed to be 'a didactic poem in forty cantos', but actually brought to the light of day the merest fragment, extracts from two of the cantos, one of them devoted entirely to the subject of marriage:

> ON MARRIAGE
> Marriage being indissoluble, the cause of its being so often unhappy. – Nature's Laws not consulted in this point.– Civilised Nations mistaken. – Otaheite. – Happiness of the Natives thereof. – Visited by Capt. Cook, in his Majesty's ship Endeavour – Mast, Rigging, Sea-sickness, Prow, Poop, Mess-room. – Surgeon's mate . . . Dissolubility of Marriage recommended – Illustrated by a game at Cards – Whist – Cribbage – Partners changed – Why not the same in Marriage? – Illustrated by a River – love free.[63]

When this reputed opposition to the institution of marriage was joined with Knight's other reputation from *The Worship of Priapus* and his public position as a Member of Parliament, he began to look like a threat to morality. Rumours circulated, and although we do not find him suspected of advocating murder and cannibalism we do find him reported as 'philandering Lady Oxford down the Wye',[64] and suspected of being responsible for the corruption of her morals which led to her scandalous behaviour. Lady Holland said that Knight had 'corrupted [Lady Oxford's] mind by filling her head with vain conceits, and teaching her to exclaim against institutions, especially that of marriage, to which she says she has been a helpless victim'.[65] Lady Holland's own earlier career had involved marriage at the age of 15 and various affairs and a divorce in her mid-twenties, before she was happily married to Lord Holland; she was not a puritanically severe judge.[66] Uvedale Price was completely indulgent, and apparently absolved Knight, saying that to have behaved in the manner expected by society, a woman with Lady Oxford's charms would have needed to have 'either a strong head or a cold heart', and that in fact she had neither.[67] In fairness to Knight it should be repeated that he advocated divorce only when marriage had become a burden to those involved in the contract. If both parties were happy to be bound together then marriage could only be a good thing; the criterion for judgement here, as elsewhere, was whether the chain, the legal bond, acted in accordance with nature or in opposition to it.

vol. V, pp. 302–3.

63 *Poetry of the Anti-Jacobin* (London: 1890 edition), p. 134. The verse was originally published anonymously but was apparently the work of G. Canning, J. Hookham Frère, G. Ellis, and W. Gifford.

64 Price to Sir George Beaumont, 16 August 1801, quoted Penny, *Arrogant Connoisseur*, ed. Clarke and Penny, p. 15.

65 *The Journal of Elizabeth, Lady Holland (1791–1811)*, ed. the Earl of Ilchester, 2 vols. (London: Longmans, 1908), vol. II, pp. 136–7.

66 Stanley Ayling, *Fox: the Life of Charles James Fox* (London: John Murray, 1989), pp. 187–91.

67 Uvedale Price to Samuel Rogers, December 1824, quoted by James Greig: Joseph Farington, *Diary*, ed. James Grieg, 8 vols. (London:

When natural inclinations were subjected to rigid rules, then the results could be repressive; the bonds of affection, when institutionalised, could turn into a prisoner's chains, and in Knight's circle, if Lady Morgan is to be believed, the enforcement of a firm line on adultery would have destroyed, not preserved, the social links which made the parties at Bentley Priory so enjoyable.

Taking liberties

Although Knight's published remarks caused public scandal, they were statesmanlike in comparison with what he said to his friends. Part of his attraction to Mediterranean culture was presumably to the atmosphere of sexual freedom which he found there. The Grand Tour was, of course, an educational matter, offering contact with important cultural, artistic and archaeological works, as well as introducing the tourist to foreign manners and ways and thereby acquiring some social polish. The tourists left England as callow youths and returned as men of the world, having been a long way from home, and an unofficial part of the education was certainly erotic and sentimental. English morals and prejudices had been left behind, and here the young men had no inescapable responsibilities; and whilst perhaps any foreign environment at all might have been found liberating, Italy was very much more relaxed than any other country in Europe in so far as sexual morality was concerned, as even an Italian native, Casanova, remarked.[68] Knight in his Sicilian journal departed from his preoccupation with antiquities to note with apparent approval the lax morals to be found at Palermo, finding the assemblies there more agreeable than those at Rome and Naples because manners were more relaxed and the men and women were not so formally coupled for the evening:[69]

> Before going to the Assemblies they meet upon the Quay, which is a kind of Mill. During the summer they pass the evening in walking about there & have Music, refreshments etc. The Ladies have lately found it convenient to introduce a very singular regulation, which is that all torches are extinguished before the carriages come upon the Quay, to prevent any disagreeable discoveries, for it seems that some Men here are still so unreasonable, to expect fidelity from their Wives. These expectations indeed, are generally vain, for the Constitutions of the Sicilians are too warm, to resist opportunity, which is never wanting here . . . During the month of May they have a fair in the

68 In this regard to Casanova's eye Protestant England and Catholic France and Spain were all intolerant when compared with Italy. See Randolph Trumbach, 'Sodomitical Subcultures, Sodomitical Roles, and the Gender Revolution of the Eighteenth Century: The Recent Historiography' in *'Tis Nature's Fault: Unauthorized Sexual Behavior during the Enlightenment*, ed. R. Maccubbin (Cambridge University Press, 1987), p. 113.

69 *Sicily*, ed. Stumpf, p. 36.

> Piazza del Domo, which . . . opens about sunset, & continues till Midnight. The whole town assemble here and are all upon an equality – Princes and Coblers, Princesses & Milleners are upon the same footing, and mix undistinguished in the Crowd. It may be imagined that such excellent conveniency for pleasure & debauchery are not neglected by People so lively as the Sicilians.[70]

The remark about the unfaithfulness of married women is characteristic, here written when Knight was a young man, but repeated years later, when he was in his sixties, in correspondence with Lord Aberdeen. 'The Countess,' he said, presumably meaning Lady Oxford,

> has been amusing the neighbouring Notables by having your noble Country man with his Boy by the pseudo Duchess to compare I suppose the produce by different Classes. All this would be very well if there were only a Husband in the Case: for putting Horns upon the head of that Animal is only fulfilling the purpose of his Creator by adding one Attribute more: but . . . it is quite too patriarchal for the nineteenth Century.[71]

The socially acceptable degree of licence narrowed during Knight's life-time. He found marriage an unattractive proposition for himself, and thought of ancient Greek society as having been free from unnatural constraints, a view coloured by his experiences in travel and by his reading. He felt that some part of him was in danger of being crushed by the decorum required in eighteenth-century England, though when one sees his friends' behaviour the demands do not seem to have been exacting. It is possible, as Samuel Rogers suggested, that his inclinations were not exclusively heterosexual:[72] the link between philhellenism and homosexuality has been present from Winckelmann onwards.[73] The philosopher Jeremy Bentham in Knight's day wrote (but did not publish) some 300 manuscript pages on the history of 'paederasty', saying that 'In ancient Greece everybody practised it: nobody was ashamed of it',[74] but he was not prepared to publish these views, he explained, because 'To other subjects it is expected that you should sit down cool: but on this subject if you let it be seen that you have not sat down in a rage you have betrayed yourself at once.'[75] On account of homosexuality William Beckford fled to France and Italy, before returning to live in spectacular isolation at Fonthill, determinedly out-ostracising the society which ostracised him; Sir William Gell more happily set up house in Naples with the Hon Keppel Craven; and Winckelmann lived in a restrained way without scandal in Germany, but felt that his life only properly began

70 Ibid., pp. 36–7.

71 Knight to Lord Aberdeen, 28 September 1812, British Library (Aberdeen Papers), 43230 fols. 148–9. The Scottish Duke was probably the Duke of Hamilton, with whom Knight stayed when he visited Scotland.

72 In Elisabeth Inglis-Jones, in her manuscript biography of Knight, quoted by G. S. Rousseau, 'The Sorrows of Priapus' in *Sexual Underworlds of the Enlightenment* ed. G. S. Rousseau and Roy Porter (Manchester University press, 1987), p. 145, n. 26.

73 Linda Dowling, *Hellenism and Homosexuality in Victorian Oxford* (Ithaca: Cornell University Press, 1994). The standard work on ancient Greek homosexuality is K. J. Dover, *Greek Homosexuality* (London: Duckworth, 1978). 'Homosexuality' as a term, and therefore to some degree as a concept, was alien to eighteenth-century and to ancient thought, because the term was coined only at the end of the nineteenth century.

74 Louis Crompton, 'Jeremy Bentham's Essay on "Paederasty"', *Journal of Homosexuality*, vol. 3 (1978), pp. 383–405 and vol. 4 (1978), pp. 91–107, quoted by Rictor Norton, *Mother Clap's Molly House: the Gay Subculture in England, 1700–1830* (London: GMP, 1992), p. 120.

75 Norton, ibid., p. 122.

when he moved to Rome, at the age of 38. We cannot now say whether the lack of evidence of Knight's sentimental attachments stems from their absence or his secrecy, but they do not seem to have taken up much of his time. There were rumours of affairs but they did not originate from well-informed sources. Uvedale Price remarked that Lady Oxford 'was full of affectionate kindness to those she loved whether as friends or as lovers';[76] and from the direct glimpses we have of Knight's relationship with her, it seems to have had the pattern of a steady friendship, not the briefer intensity of her passionate affairs. Knight can be found treating her very sympathetically during the summer of 1799, far too sympathetically so far as Lady Holland was concerned; but yet Lady Holland nowhere suggests that Knight was attempting a seduction or was himself predatory: she disapproved of his conduct only because he was doing nothing to break the spell of Lady Oxford's infatuation with Sir Francis Burdett:

> Ly. O. has lost her vivacity and beauty. She is in a deplorable state of spirits, proceeding, I fancy, from an enthusiastic, romantic admiration of Sr Francis's ideal perfections. She fancies herself a victim of sensibility, and is really so drooping that I should scarcely be surprised if she perished from imagining grief. Mr. Knight encourages her in these *bursts* of sensibility; he compares her tears to April showers that sprinkle and revive the freshness of the violet.[77]

Lady Holland felt that Knight was bad for Lady Oxford's mind, but made no accusation that he had designs on her body.[78] Again, it is unlikely that Lady Oxford would have invited both Knight and Burdett to Holland House on 11 March 1801 had they both been her lovers, and here too we find Lady Holland bewailing Burdett's depredations along with Knight's ideas about morality, saying that Burdett had corrupted Lady Oxford's mind.[79] If Knight and Lady Oxford visited the Wye together in the summer of 1801, given the mores of their circle and the fact that they both, in different ways, had rather scandalous reputations, then Price may quite inaccurately have assumed that they were philandering,[80] without feeling the need for any firm evidence to confirm it (or that any harm was being done). When Lady Oxford visited Paris in 1802, her regular appearances paired with Arthur O'Connor, an Irishman 'banished for acknowledged treason',[81] were more obviously scandalous; and her name was linked with Lord Byron's, though again their reputations would have made the rumour irresistible, whether or not it had sub-

76 Price to Samuel Rogers, 26 December 1824, in P. W. Clayden, *Rogers and His Contemporaries*, 2 vols. (London: 1889), vol. I, p. 398.

77 *The Journal of Elizabeth, Lady Holland*, ed. Earl of Ilchester,vol. II, p. 8; 26 August 1799.

78 George Rousseau has surmised that Knight did not feel comfortable with women except for the explicit purpose of sexual gratification, but Lady Oxford would seem to have been an exception. *Sexual Underworlds of the Enlightenment*, ed. Rousseau and Porter, p. 111.

79 *The Journal of Elizabeth, Lady Holland,* vol. II, p. 136; 11 March 1801.

80 Price to Sir George Beaumont, 16 August 1801, quoted Penny, *Arrogant Connoisseur*, p.15.

81 Farington, *Diary*, 27 September 1802.

stance. Whenever the observation of Lady Oxford in Knight's company is direct, and we are less reliant on an intermediary's summary interpretation, the evidence is always ambivalent. Lady Morgan, for example, left an account of how she found Lady Oxford and Knight together at a party at Bentley Priory,

> one of the most agreeable I ever was at in my life. I spent the evening, seated on the second flight of stairs, between Lady C[aroline] L[amb] and Monk Lewis. The beautiful Lady Oxford sat a few steps above us, the Aspasia of the Pericles who lay at her feet, wooing in Greek, in spite of Johnson's denunciation against learning in love; while Payne Knight looked on, with 'eyes malign, askance'. [82]

This is highly ambiguous. Knight's sidelong glances might have expressed jealousy, Lady Oxford's attention being turned away from him; or envy, because she had the young man's attention. Coleridge hinted that Knight might have treated him better when Knight showed him round his collection, had Coleridge been better looking.[83] Knight in his will left an allowance to 'Caroline Elizabeth Gregory commonly called Ford, as a reward for the affectionate kindness and sincerity with which she has always behaved towards me',[84] which can be taken to indicate that she was his mistress, but might simply have meant that she had been kind and sincere. According to Elisabeth Inglis-Jones's interpretation of Samuel Rogers, Knight ruined his health by his 'amorous habits' and paid Elizabeth Gregory £3 a week to be a permanent standby and camouflage for his young male friends.[85] Uvedale Price evidently construed that a mistress had died of consumption in 1794,[86] but he might have reached this conclusion from some calculatedly evasive remark on Knight's part, or even a straightforward lie. Knight's moral code would not have precluded homosexuality, for which the ancient Greeks had a place. Moreover, according to Knight's theory, it would have seemed healthier to act on any desires he might have had, rather than to deny them: to satisfy a moderate appetite before it became an intense craving. In Knight's circle there would have been no scandal had he kept a mistress; indeed, it would have been expected of him, and Rogers's remarks show that Knight could have kept a mistress as a means of preserving his repectability. Rogers may have been wrong to impute subterfuge on Knight's part, but he shows us a milieu in which minor misdemeanours could screen more serious transgressions from view. The clearest idea of Knight's intimate activities is given by a letter written soon after he had

82 Lady Morgan, *The Book of the Boudoir*, 2 vols. (1829), vol. I, p. 173.

83 Coleridge to Sir George Beaumont, 8 March 1804, in *Memorials of Coleorton*, ed. William Knight, vol. II, p. 56: 'in *words* he [Knight] was extremely civil . . . [but] In tones, looks, and manners he was *embarrassing*, and this I was willing to consider as the effect of my own *unbellerophontic* countenance and mein.' Bellerophontes is mentioned in the *Iliad*, one of Knight's treasured Homeric texts, where it is said that the gods granted him 'beauty and desirable manhood', which caused him trouble when he did not return the affectionate attentions of Anteia, who turned vengeful. He fled from the Xanthian women when they made sexual advances. Homer, *Iliad*, trans. Richard Lattimore (University of Chicago Press, 1951), bk. VI, lines 155 ff. Robert Graves, *The Greek Myths*, 2 vols. (Harmondsworth: Penguin, 1960), vol. I, pp. 253–4.

84 Knight's will is preserved amongst the Downton Castle Papers at Herefordshire County Records Office; quoted Penny, *Arrogant Connoisseur*, p. 16. Caroline Elizabeth Gregory's name was introduced when the will was amended on 22 October 1821, 'inserted in the place of that of a Person now no more'.

85 (Quoted by Rousseau, *Sexual Underworlds of the Enlightenment*, p. 145, n. 26.) Rogers is credited as the source, but Elizabeth

moved from the great house at Downton into Stonebrook Cottage, when he told Lord Aberdeen that he should

> not imagine that I am in any danger of becoming lovesick in my cottage – I am either too old or too young; and, were it not so, am so bristled over with Greek that Cupid might as well point his arrows at a porcupine. Indeed I believe that Love, such as poets and novel writers have imagined and described never frequented any cottages but those ideal ones of their building. At least my experience, which has been very long and extensive, never found any in them, but of a sort which was to be bought ready made. Of this I get enough to keep my thoughts at home, (and a little now sufficing) in a very secret and comfortable way – not of course without some suspicions, but without any glaring scandal. The rustics are not nice [i.e. scrupulous], so that a small endearment gets a husband a cloak [which] is wanting. I have however been fortunate in Borrels [i.e. rustics]; and since the army has been put into barracks and no soldiers have been quartered at Ludlow the greatiss Evil has never visited us. Before, the arrival of a regiment always spread contagion round, and poor Cupid was again put under the tuition of Mercury; who in the interpolated tale of the Odyssey expresses the most eager desire to share with Mars in the favours of his mother as he has since done most abundantly.[87]

Here we find a characteristically Epicurean expression of concern for moderation and the neighbours, which moves into Homeric coding.[88] The term 'venereal' is derived from the name Venus, and the metal mercury was used in the medical treatment of syphilis. When this aside is put with Knight's statement about his early ill health one might wonder whether the influence of the gentlemen jockeys led the boy to contract a venereal disease from a village girl who had been with soldiers. In his Sicilian journal Knight had made reference to venereal disease giving rise to various symptoms of illness, which were the same symptoms as were variously given in describing Knight's own ill health: 'that dreadful [disease], which pollutes generation in its source, & which for some time threatened the destruction of the human Race. The disorders, which that has produced in weakening the Constitutions, & deranging the nerves are certainly very great.'[89] To whom would it seem that syphilis 'threatened the destruction of the human Race'? The remark is emphatic, even taken out of its original context, an account of an archaeological tour, in which it is so intrusive that it seems heartfelt. It leaves one wondering,

Gregory's name and the sum of money come from Knight's will.

86 Price to Sir George Beaumont, 28 November 1794; quoted Penny, *Arrogant Connoisseur*, p. 15.

87 Knight to Lord Aberdeen, 28 November 1809, BL (Aberdeen Papers), 43230, fol. 58.

88 The specific allusion is to Homer, *Odyssey*, bk. VIII, line 342. Knight's scholarly endeavour was to distinguish the various hands which he thought were at work in the Homeric texts, an enterprise which is now generally thought to be misguided, but which was the work pursued in many distinguished German academic careers during the nineteenth century. Knight was ahead of the field, but in what is now thought to have been the wrong direction.

89 *Sicily*, p. 65.

inconclusively, whether a bout of syphilis, which could have given Knight recurrent problems, was perhaps visited on him at a tender age, when his 'ungoverned passions' led him to buy pleasure for the price of his health. It would have been a harsh lesson, but would very logically have led to his adoption of Epicurean morals, which particularly stressed the evils which followed from an over-indulgence in pleasures, and would reasonably have led him to favour undogmatic celibacy in practice.

Freedom and regulation

In general Knight did not trust firm rules and exact definitions: a tendency which, in a law-maker, could well give the appearance of supporting some kind of anarchy. Knight would rather have trusted instinct than intellect as a guide, and he made it clear that he felt his own instincts were being reined in:

> But still, as more society's refined,
> Each native impulse less affects the mind;
> Instinct to intellect is slowly brought,
> And vague perception methodized to thought
> (I, 243–6)

One of the many faults he found with Christianity was its attempt to be consistent and systematic, where pagan religion had been less rigorous and therefore more liberal.

> Religion's lights, when loose and undefined,
> Expand the heart, and elevate the mind;
> Brighten the fancy, and the spirits raise,
> Exalt the artist's touch, and poet's lays
> . . .
> But in dogmatic definitions bound,
> They only serve to puzzle and confound,
> To awe the timid, and the weak enslave,
> And make the fool subservient to the knave:
> Reason itself becomes a useless tool,
> When bent by force, and modified by rule.
> (IV, 456–9, 466–71)

There will be more to say about the dulling effects of rules in due course; suffice it to repeat that in ancient Greece Knight believed there to have been an ideal relation between nature and culture, which remained undistorted by regulations and systems.

By no dull methods cramp'd, or rules confined,
Each effort bore the impression of the mind; –
Warm from the fancy, that conceived it, flow'd,
And, stamp'd with nature's genuine image, glow'd.
Alike the poet sung and sculptor wrought, –
Each sound breathed sentiment, each figure thought;
Beauty and grace, and easy motion shone,
In forms of ductile brass or fragile stone,
And each expressive feature learn'd to impart,
Back to the eye, the impressions of the heart.
(IV, 403–12)

The climate of opinion at the time of the poem's appearance meant that it was not fairly reviewed. An anonymous visitor to Downton, who reported his visit in the *Gentleman's Magazine* in 1797, remarked that 'The *Progress of Civil Society* if not a work of the highest merit, is yet far above most of the poems of the present day. The Reviewers had given such unfair extracts from this book, that I was foolish enough to suffer my curiosity about it to subside. I have since been very angry with myself for it.'[90] After the hostile reception and consequent lack of interest in the poem (no second edition was published) Knight published no more poetry until the shorter *Monody of the Death of Charles James Fox*, which was his farewell to politics as well as to a friend.

Knight eulogised freedom in virtually all his works, and he clearly opposed any political regime in which institutional power became tyrannical by resorting to force or the fear of force. Nevertheless at a practical level there were limits to his liberality, and he authorised the use of force against troublesome colliers working for his estate, though even then he did not fall into the state of panic that led to the deaths of rioters at Manchester (the Peterloo Massacre) which he remarked upon, critical of those in authority.[91] Knight was not altogether at ease with the state of society in England, as is shown by his attachment to his vision of ancient Greece, fused with nostalgia for southern Italy, and perhaps his youth. In ancient times the Greeks had belonged to civilised states but still enjoyed an unaffected contact with nature,[92] and Knight felt that it was legitimate to overthrow any laws which had intervened to warp this relation, at whatever level; so the French revolutionaries were broadly justified in their acts (but not in their riotous excesses) and it would have been proper to reform the divorce law for the sake of human feelings. In time Knight was to detest the despotic power which Napoleon came to per-

90 Anon., *Gentleman's Magazine*, June 1797, p. 474.

91 Knight to Lord Aberdeen, 9 October 1819, BL (Aberdeen Papers), 43230, fols. 332–4.

92 *The Landscape*, p. 4n.

sonify,[93] but he felt some attraction to America, where the rhetoric of freedom flourished, along with vast open spaces and just government. It was even possible to find among the native Americans living models of the ancient Greeks' uncorrupted vigour.[94] Perhaps not very seriously, Knight entertained the idea of moving there, apparently regretting that he had left it too late in life to make the move without disturbing the many friendships he had formed:

> Though equal beauties grace Atlantic streams,
> And waves as clear reflect more genial beams;
> Though, deep-embower'd, each limpid current flows,
> And richer foliage o'er its margins grows;
> Yet, no bright visions to the soul it brings; –
> No Muses drink at Apalachian [*sic*] springs
>
> . . .
>
> In early youth, the exile doom'd to roam,
> Where'er he goes, still finds, or makes a home;
> His habits moulds, and his affections bends
> To meet each change of life, and change of friends
>
> . . .
>
> But when, in life's decline, and health's decay,
> Unfeeling power condemns the wretch to stray;
> He tears, while feebly struggling to depart,
> The strings, which time hath wound about his heart;
> And finds, when of his early friends bereft,
> No gleam of hope, or ray of comfort left.
> (VI, 640–5, 652–5, 660–5)

Knight, though he had travelled, was no hardy pioneer, and even had he not been loath to break individual attachments, he might have realised how unlikely he was to have found others there with his antiquarian interests. One can see, though, why he would be attracted, as the revolution there had been carried out without the spectacular bloodshed that had been seen in France, and the Declaration of Independence had enshrined such an Epicurean sentiment as the pursuit of happiness. Its author, Thomas Jefferson (1743–1826), was privately to call himself an Epicurean, admonishing his correspondent against laziness, which he was evidently indulging in Epicurus' name:

> As you say of yourself, I too am an Epicurean. I consider the genuine (not the imputed) doctrines of Epicurus as containing

93 *Alfred; a Romance in Rhyme* (London: 1823), p. 343.

94 Knight, *The Landscape*, p. 3n. See chapter 2, p. 41.

> everything rational in moral philosophy which Greece and Rome have left us . . . I take the liberty of observing that you are not a true disciple of our master Epicurus, in indulging the indolence to which you say you are yielding. One of his canons, you know, was 'that indulgence which presents a greater pleasure, or produces a greater pain, is to be avoided'. Your love of repose will lead, in its progress, to a suspension of healthy exercise, a relaxation of mind, an indifference to everything around you, and finally to a debility of body, and hebetude of mind, the farthest of all things from the happiness that the well-regulated indulgences of Epicurus ensure; fortitude, you know, is one of his cardinal virtues.[95]

This shows how it is possible to reconcile Epicureanism with a Protestant work ethic. Knight did not emigrate, never even visited America, but his basic conception of the governed individual's native freedom, which should not be infringed, is close to the idea of human rights as expounded by the likes of Tom Paine (in *The Rights of Man)*; William Godwin (in his *Enquiry Concerning Political Justice);* and his wife, Mary Wollstonecraft (1759–97, in *A Vindication of the Rights of Women*, 1792). Although there was some attempt to associate Knight with Paine and the Godwins in the public imagination,[96] they did not subscribe to the ideal of a balance between the 'three estates' and it would have been dangerous for him to have supported them in public, even if he had agreed with them. Fox loathed Paine's *Rights of Man*, and when accused of being a democrat, strenuously denied it.[97] For Knight, progress in the political arena would be measured against the standard of 'nature', which would mean the state of society in ancient Greece, and any unnatural and retrograde order which had been overlaid, constraining natural vitality, should be stripped away. The authority for laws and regulations would be found in the things which the laws and regulations governed, as with scientific laws. There was a role for a monarch because, human nature being what it was, a sovereign would be able to influence people who were not inclined to be virtuous for virtue's own sake; but there was no question of any divine rights, as the monarch and the two Houses of Parliament should have powers sufficient to keep each other in check. Knight's ideal society would be one in which unwarped human nature, formed by the influence of genial social links, and exemplified in the high-minded classical Greek athlete, would happily obey civil laws, and feel absolutely unconstrained because the laws would be manifestly reasonable, flexible, just and in complete accord with human nature.

95 Thomas Jefferson to William Short, 31 October 1819; in *The Portable Thomas Jefferson*, ed. M. D. Peterson (New York: Viking, 1975), pp. 564–6.

96 See chapter 7, p. 226.

97 John W. Derry, *Charles James Fox* (London: Batsford, 1972), p. 311.

6 Principles of taste

Divisive views

In the preface which Knight added to the second edition of *The Landscape* in 1795, he had made it clear that he did not share Price's theoretical views about beauty (and more particularly the picturesque) and had tried briefly and politely to explain the basis of their disagreement. Price took up the matter in 1801, when he published *A Dialogue of the Picturesque,* which involved three characters: one of whom was supposed to be setting out Knight's views, another Price's while the third acted as an articulate audience. This was problematic as Price did not understand Knight's point of view, and he obviously felt himself to be on thoroughly unsafe ground because the theoretical explanations given by Knight's character (called 'Mr Howard') made use almost exclusively of the words which Knight himself had used in the preface to *The Landscape*. This was not good for the dialogue as art, because the phraseology which Knight had employed was very evidently not conversational, and this clumsiness was compounded into calumny by the linking passages which Price inserted, in which 'Mr. Howard' expounded his conviction that the words 'beautiful' and 'picturesque' had the same meaning. Knight had not done this: he had said that there was no hard line of division between the categories of the beautiful and the picturesque, which is not to state that they are the same thing (any more than stating that black and white must be identical, because one can turn into the other through modulated shades of grey). Knight likened Price's methods to those of the Spanish Inquisition, and seeing that he would not easily explain his views to Price set about writing a general analysis of the issues involved, which appeared in 1805 as *An Analytical Inquiry*

Into the Principles of Taste; this was to be Knight's most sustained consideration of what we would call aesthetics.

It seems to have been Price's intention in the *Dialogue* to present fairly the rival theories to stand against one another as alternative views, without necessarily arguing for one rather than another, but Knight took his purpose to have been to overturn Knight's ideas, and so his response was robustly argued, aiming to scotch Price's ideas once and for all, and Price was offended by it. He had shown the manuscript of his dialogue to Knight and invited comments before publication; he then would be able to make any minor adjustments as might be necessary so as not to misrepresent him.[1] Knight, who must have felt that minor changes would not be enough to correct the dialogue's wrongheadedness, did not suggest any changes, and published his enquiry (his own inquisition) without conferring with Price about it. Price, wounded, took umbrage, and felt publicly humiliated, but did not concede that Knight's views were in any way to be considered as more correct than his own. Nevertheless Knight certainly had the better of the argument. His philosophical ideas were not original, but, he argued, this was all the more reason for them to be right, because he would not have made use of an idea unless it were appropriate; whereas Price, on the other hand, having invented his own idea, would be prepared, out of 'parental fondness' for it, to defend it whether or not it was reasonable to do so,[2] thereby contriving to present his lack of originality as a positive virtue. If Knight had simply been unoriginally correct then his book would have had nothing to recommend it; in fact it sold very well. There are probably two reasons for this. The first is that his sources were not well known to the reading public in London in 1805–8 when the book went through its four editions. The second is that his argument was presented through the use of colourful examples, which frequently employed ridicule, and which are entertaining: it was a literary scrap, conducted in the public gaze.

The argument

Knight began his book with a consideration of the diversity of taste, from one culture to another, and even from one individual to another, concluding this section with a quotation from Hume:

> 'Beauty,' says Mr. Hume, 'is no quality in things themselves: it exists merely in the mind, which contemplates them, and each mind perceives a different beauty. One person may even perceive deformity where another is sensible of beauty; and every

1 Uvedale Price, *Essays on the Picturesque*, 3 vols. (London: 1810), vol. III, p. 398–9.

2 Richard Payne Knight, *An Analytical Inquiry into the Principles of Taste*, preface to 2nd edn (London: 1805).

> individual ought to acquiesce in his own sentiment, without pretending to regulate those of others. To seek the real beauty or real deformity is as fruitless an inquiry, as to pretend to ascertain the real sweet or real bitter. According to the disposition of the organs the same object may be both sweet and bitter; and the proverb has justly determined it to be fruitless to dispute concerning tastes. It is very natural, and even quite necessary, to extend this axiom to mental as well as bodily taste; and thus common sense, which is often at variance with philosophy, especially with the sceptical kind, is found, in one instance at least, to agree in pronouncing the same decision.'[3]

Hume's essay borrowed its title from a lost book by Epicurus, for whom the standard of judgement was nature.[4] Although quoted approvingly, Knight did not agree with Hume's analogy with bodily taste, saying that 'To every sound and uncorrupted palate, sugar is sweet, and gall bitter',[5] and his greater philosophical debt was to Hume's friend Thomas Reid (1710–96). Knight's *Inquiry* was modelled, to some degree, on Reid's *An Inquiry into the Human Mind on the Principles of Common Sense* (1764), which endeavoured to overcome Hume's scepticism by resorting to 'common sense'; but Reid had developed his 'common sense' philosophy very directly in response to Hume, and therefore had much in common with him. Reid's philosophy stands in the British Empiricist tradition, which developed from Locke, through Berkeley and Hume, and Knight saw them as a group, with Reid as the most recent representative of the line.[6] Indeed this was how Reid portrayed himself in the dedication of his own book, where he explained that his views had been formulated after reading Hume's *Treatise of Human Nature* (1739) before which he had followed Berkeley's thinking.[7] Knight accepted Reid's account of the working of the human mind and based his analysis of taste upon it.

An Analytical Inquiry into the Principles of Taste was conducted in the manner of a scientific inquiry, which is what Knight took 'analytical' to mean: dividing up the object of his enquiry into its simplest, supposedly self-evident components. On first acquaintance the book seems to be highly anecdotal and to amount to being hardly more than a collection of the profuse footnotes which Knight included as annotations to his poems. The structure of the book is not arbitrary, however. After the introduction, in which the tone was set by Hume, the book is divided up into three parts. The first of them deals with sensory perception, the

3 'Of the Standard of Taste', quoted by Knight, *Principles of Taste*, p. 16. Reference here, and hereafter, to 4th edn (London: 1808) unless stated otherwise.

4 The book was mention by Cicero, *De Natura Deorum*, bk. I, line 43; Loeb edn, trans. H. Rackham (London: Heinemann, 1939), p. 45.

5 Knight, *Principles of Taste*, p. 17.

6 Ibid., p. 36n.

7 Ronald E. Beanblossom, introduction to Thomas Reid, *An Inquiry into the Human Mind on the Principles of Common Sense* (Edinburgh: 1764), ed. Lehrer and Beanblossom (Indianapolis: Bobbs-Merrill, 1975), p. xi.

second with the association of ideas and the third with the emotions. The distinction which had the utmost importance for Knight's aesthetic theory, and for his demolition of Price's views, was that to be made between, on one hand, the stimuli picked up through the senses, and on the other, what the mind subsequently made of these stimuli. Reid had said that 'All the systems of philosophers about our senses have split upon this rock, of not distinguishing properly sensations which can have no existence but when they are felt, from the things suggested by them.'[8] Knight made this distinction between sensory perceptions and associated ideas (which give rise to emotions) the central concern of his enquiry, the rock against which other theories, especially Price's, could be dashed to pieces. Repeatedly through the text Knight's colourful examples are related back to this central concern, which generated the structure of the work. The argument is in effect that beauty is an emotion (a mental state); and in the same way that if no fear is felt then an object cannot be said to be frightening, so if no beauty is felt then the object cannot be said to be beautiful, at least so far as the particular observer is concerned. Beauty, as Hume said, is not in objects but in minds. Reid credited Epicurus with having made a comparable distinction between the primary and secondary characteristics of objects, unlike Aristotle who had not.[9]

The first part of Knight's enquiry was therefore, like Reid's, concerned with the senses, the source of the information which was under consideration. Kant too, who like Reid was responding to Hume's scepticism, made criticism of the senses his starting-point, and he was an important influence on Romantic theory through Coleridge, but we can be confident that he did not directly influence Knight who made no direct reference to Kant, but remarked that 'in Germany . . . nonsense seems to have become the order of the day'.[10]

According to Reid's 'common sense' view the only way of overcoming scepticism (which has its own internal contradictions) is to base our understanding on the evidence of the senses; and Knight's argument proceeded as if the senses gave access to the 'self-evident' facts which were the proper basis of an analytical enquiry. Stimuli, or 'irritations' as Knight called them, acted on the nerves so as to start a train of ideas. Knight contended that although the senses could to some extent feel pain and pleasure, emotion could only be felt as the result of the association of ideas in the mind, the association of ideas being caused by the trains of thought which were set in motion by the initial stimuli. So we move through the three sections of the book: 'Of Sensation', 'Of the Association of Ideas' and 'Of the Passions'.

8 Reid, *Inquiry into the Human Mind,* p. 59. Knight accepted Reid's description of the mechanism of the sense of sight; Reid allowed a special importance to painters. See Peter Funnell, 'Visible Appearances', in *The Arrogant Connoisseur*, ed. Michael Clarke and Nicholas Penny (Manchester University Press, 1982), p. 87.

9 *Inquiry into the Human Mind,* p. 59.

10 Knight, *Principles of Taste*, p. 399.

Knight's opening exposition of the working of the senses is dull and makes no claims which should startle a twentieth-century reader. Off-putting though it is, it is how it should be, since the beginning of an 'analytical enquiry' should present us with the self-evident premisses on which subsequent deductions are to be founded. The tone is given by the following passage, about the working of the eye:

> Sight, as well as hearing, is produced by immediate contact of the exciting cause with the organ; which exciting cause is the light reflected, from the objects seen, upon the retina of the eye; the pictures upon which, by some impressions or irritations upon optic nerves, the modes of which must be for ever unknown to us, are conveyed to the mind, and produce the sense of vision, the most valuable of all our senses.[11]

It would be a mistake to look for originality in such a passage as this, and Knight particularly referred the reader to 'Newton's theory of Light and Colours' and 'Dr. Reid's Essay on the Mind, where a very clear and full explanation of the theory of vision is given'.[12] The 'irritation' of the senses stimulated the mind, via the nerves, and the mind would take these impressions and associate them with others. It would normally do this in ways which were productive of 'common sense', but the associations of ideas could be downright erratic, as in the case of insanity or drunkenness. We are liable to associate ideas in our own characteristic ways, which means that our

> dispositions are melancholy or gay; and if either be carried to such an excess as to break the natural connection, or derange the natural order of them, the effect is lunacy . . . Intoxication is a temporary lunacy arising from a similar derangement in the trains of ideas, caused by irritation, produced in the stomach by wine or other intoxicating liquors or drugs, extending itself to the brain . . . Similar effects of excessive and irregular action also take place in dreams, which equally proceed from the irritations of the stomach being extended to the brain . . . As the irritations of the stomach, in cases of intoxication, disorder the mind through the medium of the brain; so do all violent irritations of the mind, such as those of excessive grief, anxiety, or vexation, disorder the stomach through the same medium.[13]

The well-being of the stomach and the well-being of the mind were ideas which, in Knight's mind, were firmly associated. Traditionally, a

11 Ibid., p. 57.

12 Ibid., pp. 57 n and 58 n.

13 Ibid., pp. 137–8.

connection was made between insanity, drunkenness, fasting and religious ecstasy;[14] and though Knight did not make the last connection in the passage cited here it has relevance to his behaviour. Montaigne pointed out that the stern Stoics, who felt that the mind should endeavour to overcome the weaknesses of the body, advised 'an occasional excess in wine, even to intoxication'.[15] The hedonistic Epicureans preached abstinence, and Knight favoured sobriety: he would drink coffee after meals while his guests continued with wine.[16] He did not value the transported states of mystics and enthusiasts, but put his faith in his senses and therefore wanted them to be trustworthy.

Knight's theory of the beautiful, and the picturesque, developed from his theory of perception. According to his understanding of optics and the eye, the sense of sight could respond to only two stimuli: colour and light. Anything else perceived by looking was the result of the action of the mind and the association of ideas. Therefore Knight argued that any pleasure to be felt by the sense of sight in itself in looking at an object must derive from the light and colour which are all that the eye is mechanically equipped to perceive. This was his most effective argument against Price. The eye in itself cannot react to beauty or picturesqueness as such because it is not physically equipped to be stimulated by them: if we are to have pleasure of any sort directly from our eyes then it can involve nothing but light and colour, and any other sort of pleasure we might have from looking at things must derive not solely from the eye, but must involve the intervention of the mind.

There was a special place for paintings in Knight's thought, because he supposed that artists were the people who were most skilled in gratifying the visual sense. Their vocation was the arrangement of pigment in such a way that it produced such gratification, and so it was appropriate to turn to painters for advice in visual matters. This is the origin of Knight's version of the picturesque (or *pictoresque*), which turns attention away from the objects which were painted to the artists who painted them. In addition to the pleasures which might be had from the arrangement of pigment as such, paintings also offered intellectual pleasures through the association of ideas, and Knight felt that 'in the higher class of landscapes, whether in nature or in art, the mere sensual gratification of the eye is comparatively so small, as scarce to be attended to'.[17] So for example the landscapes of Claude, which Knight loved, and collected when he could, were greatly enhanced by associating them with the poetry of Virgil. It was commonplace for someone with a good education in the eighteenth century to think of Virgil's evocations of a golden age of

14 M. A. Screech, *Montaigne and Melancholy* (London: Duckworth, 1983), p. 138.

15 Michel Eyquem de Montaigne, 'Of Drunkenness', in *Essays*, trans. John Florio, ed. L. C. Harmer, 3 vols. (London: Dent, 1910), vol. II, pp. 15 ff.

16 Farington, *Diary*, 5 September 1806.

17 *Principles of Taste*, p. 96.

peace and plenty while looking at a Claude landscape bathed in the glow of the setting sun, where:

> Soft spikes of grain will gradually gild the fields,
> And reddening grapes will hang in clusters on wild brier,
> And dewy honey sweat from tough Italian oaks.[18]

Knight said that it was such trains of thought as this which stimulated almost the whole of the response to a painting, not the arrangement of the pigment in itself. Moreover, the intellectual content of the aesthetic response could not be controlled by an act of will, but depended on individual experience:

> The habit of associating our ideas having commenced with our earliest perceptions, the process of it, whatever it was in the beginning, has become so spontaneous and rapid in adult persons, that it seems to be a mechanical operation of the mind, which we cannot directly influence or control: those ideas, which we have once associated, associating themselves again in our memories of their own accord; and presenting themselves together to our notice, whether we will or not. Hence agreeable and disagreeable trains of thought and imagery are often excited by circumstances not otherwise connected with them than by having before occurred to our minds at the same time, or in the same place, or in the same company; and these trains of thought will continue to haunt us in spite of all we can do to free ourselves from them; so that we feel ourselves in a situation not unlike that of a moth fluttering round a candle.[19]

This kind of thinking has perhaps most famously been explored by Proust, but in Knight's day 'associationism' was already a commonplace in aesthetic discussion.[20] It is, for example, the means by which the most trivial of objects can come to have 'sentimental value' and was firmly in place at the very inception of the idea of the picturesque. Sir John Vanbrugh sent a letter to the Duke of Marlborough in 1709 arguing that the old manor at Woodstock should be preserved. It was under threat of demolition for the sake of the landscape around Blenheim Palace, which was being built there by Vanbrugh for the duke. He said that the manor should be preserved not for the sake of its intrinsic beauty, or because it had any grace or elegance of form, but because it was old, and because it had been the scene of romantic royal deeds.[21] However, he did not suppose the form of the building to be devoid of charm, but importantly

18 Virgil, *Eclogue* IV, lines 280–3, in *Eclogues*, trans. Guy Lee (Liverpool: Francis Cairns, 1980), pp. 26–7.

19 *Principles of Taste*, p. 136.

20 H. F. Clark, 'Eighteenth-Century Elysiums: the Role of "Association" in the Landscape Movement', *The Journal of the Warburg and Courtauld Institutes* (London: 1943), pp. 165 ff.

21 11 June 1709, in *The Genius of the Place: the English Landscape Garden 1620–1820*, ed. John Dixon Hunt and Peter Willis (London: Paul Elek, 1975), pp. 119 ff; p. 120.

said that with a little adjustment it 'wou'd make One of the Most Agreable Objects that the best of Landskip Painters can invent'.[22] So the building was seen to have some affinity with the work of painters, and therefore to have aesthetic merit, but principally it deserved to be retained on account of its sentimental associations.

This way of thinking is to be found in the work of such notables as Joseph Addison (1672–1719) of the *Tatler* and the *Spectator*, and the poet Alexander Pope (1688–1744), both of them literary men with an interest in architecture and landscape design, and in that of William Kent (*c.*1685–1748) the architect and gardener.[23] It is also to be found in the lectures of Sir Joshua Reynolds (1723–92) an illustrious member of the Society of Dilettanti,[24] of whom Knight spoke admiringly (but not completely uncritically). He composed the Latin epitaph on Reynolds's tomb and adopted some of his views, including his view that associations of ideas were important in the viewer's response to a painting, so that the artist needed to attend not only to truth, but had to work with custom, prejudice and opinion in order to achieve his effects,[25] which is to say that the work of art had to take account of its cultural context.

The principle of the association of ideas in aesthetics was taken to its furthest theoretical extreme by the Reverend Archibald Alison (1757–1839), another Scot[26] and a friend of Dugald Stewart, Reid's most distinguished student.[27] Knight drew on Alison's *Essays on the Nature and Principles of Taste* (1790),[28] which were dedicated to Stewart 'in whose friendship the author has found the happiness of a lifetime'.[29] In them Alison argued that the association of ideas could account for the whole of any aesthetic response and that there was no need to draw on any other ideas. Francis Jeffery (1773–1850), who in 1802 founded, and subsequently edited, the *Edinburgh Review* (to which Knight contributed), endorsed Alison's views in a review of a second edition of the *Essays* which is so detailed and thorough as to amount to a condensed and improved version of Alison's text, and had more influence than the original.[30] Jeffery took issue with Knight's assertion that sensory pleasure was to be found in colour, but in taking Alison's part Jeffery exaggerated the difference between Knight's and Alison's points of view. He treated Knight's *Inquiry* with respect, calling it 'acute and philosophical', but on the face of it misrepresented Knight by saying that in his publication 'a very high degree of intrinsic beauty is supposed to reside in tints, and combinations of tints, and the mere optical impression of broken or mingling masses of light and shadow'; and he made the point that 'In so far as they are mere variations of tint, they may be imitated by

22 Ibid., p. 121.

23 Clark, 'Eighteenth-Century Elysiums', pp. 166–71.

24 Lionel Cust, *History of the Society of Dilettanti* (London: Macmillan, 1898), p. 265. Reynolds was a member of the society from 1766, and became the first President of the Royal Academy in 1768. He painted many of the society's portraits.

25 Sir Joshua Reynolds, 'Discourse VII, Delivered to the Students of The Royal Academy, on the Distribution of the Prizes', 10 December 1776, in *Discourses On Art*, ed. Robert R. Wark (New Haven: Yale University Press, 1975), pp. 122–3.

26 He was not sanctimonious: his sermons were admired, and some were printed, but they showed 'more study of the "Spectator" than of the masters of theological eloquence'. Alison would generally lie in bed 'reading or thinking' until two in the afternoon. *Dictionary of National Biography*, vol. I, pp. 286bff.

27 See chapter 3, p. 81.

28 Knight, *Principles of Taste*, pp. 120, 307.

29 Archibald Alison, *Essay on the Nature and Principles of Taste* (Edinburgh: 1790), dedication page.

30 Francis Jeffery, review of Alison, *Essay on Taste*, in *Edinburgh Review*, May 1811.

unmeaning daubs of paint on a pallet; – in so far as they are *signs*, it is to the mind that they address themselves, and not to the organ.'[31] So according to Jeffery the intrinsic beauty in colours was 'so slight as scarce to merit attention',[32] whereas Knight said that there was 'a very high degree' of it. Knight certainly took pleasure in describing the effects of broken lights and tints, and did so often and at some length, but when it came to ascribing a theoretical source to that pleasure he said that that deriving directly from the organ of sense was 'so small, as scarce to be attended to', which seems to put him in complete agreement with Alison. The only difference between their positions was that Alison said that the effect was slight and therefore neglected it, whereas Knight said that the effect was slight but nevertheless considered it. Jeffery responded to Knight's lingering descriptions of the play of colours, rather than to his theoretical position as stated. Knight was to clarify his position as being in agreement with Alison and Jeffery in a later publication, when he had Jeffery as his editor. 'As for the delight afforded by rich, mellow, and splendid harmony of colours and light and shade,' he said,

> we cannot but think that Sir Joshua Reynolds, though so successful in producing it, has unreasonably debased it in his Discourses, by treating it as a pleasure of mere sensuality. There are unquestionably some colours or modifications of light more grateful to the eye than others; but the mere organic pleasure that any of them afford, is so imperceptible amidst the higher gratifications, that it can in no case be properly called sensuality, any more than that arising from the melody of verse. Both are only grateful when employed as the vehicles of meaning; no person, we believe, having ever found pleasure in hearing verse recited in a language, which he did not understand; or in contemplating the materials spread out on the pallet. Yet, as far as they affect the organs of sense only, each must be the same in both instances.
>
> Even when painting or sculpture are unworthily employed to excite sensuality, they only do it through the medium of the imagination.[33]

However, despite a willingness to conform to the orthodoxy being laid down in Edinburgh, Knight fell into heresy because he was not consistent in his terminology. Reynolds had made a distinction between the sensual pleasure to be had from colours and the intellectual pleasure to be had from the painting's subject-matter, and the same distinction is to be found in both Kant and Rousseau, though in making it they, like

31 Ibid., p. 37.

32 Ibid., pp. 36–7.

33 Review of *The Life of Sir Joshua Reynolds, Knight, late President of the Royal Academy, &c.*, by James Northcote, the *Edinburgh Review*, vol. 23 (Edinburgh: 1814), pp. 263–92; p. 292.

Reynolds, made it clear that they thought of the enjoyment of colour as a distraction from the more important spiritual aspects of the work.[34] Knight endorsed both these varieties of pleasure, but in his theoretical discussions he supposed them both to be intellectual in character, being dependent on the action of the mind. However, when he discussed paintings he reverted to using the word 'sensual', as Reynolds had done, to describe the enjoyable effects of colour, failing to maintain the distinction which he had made. For example, in describing the flower paintings of Jan van Huysum he said that they formed 'the most perfect spectacle of mere sensual beauty that is any where to be found,' whereas in the great landscape paintings the imagination also was engaged and 'only a small part of those pleasures are merely sensual'.[35] Perhaps a delight in colour 'can in no case be properly called sensuality', but Knight himself did call it sensuality in his text. The enjoyment of the colour was not for Knight as abstract as might be supposed, but it was, as for Jeffery and Alison, related to its use in appropriate signification (for example a vermilion pigment would not seem beautiful if it were used to render the appearance of grass).[36] Jeffery tried to ridicule Knight by saying that 'A piece of putrid veal, or a cancerous ulcer, or the rags that are taken from it, may display the most brilliant tints, and the finest distribution of light and shadow. Does Mr. Knight, however, seriously think, that either of these experiments would succeed?'[37] Mr. Knight did indeed think that such experiments would have some chance of success, at least in the hands of the right artist. Jeffery's suggestions, even though they were intended to sound outrageous, extend hardly at all the list of disgusting objects which Knight said might yet make good paintings. 'Decayed pollard trees, rotten thatch, crumbling masses of perished brick and plaster, tattered worn-out dirty garments, a fish or a flesh market,' he said,

> may all exhibit the most harmonious and brilliant combinations of tints to the eye; and harmonious and brilliant combinations of tints are certainly beautiful in whatsoever they are seen; but nevertheless, these objects contain so many properties that are offensive to other senses, or to the imagination, that in nature we are not pleased with them, nor ever consider them as beautiful. Yet in the pictures of Rembrandt, Ostade, Teniers, and Fyt, the imitations of them are unquestionably beautiful and pleasing to all mankind.[38]

Knight thought that the work of painters could usefully be consulted for ideas about how to gratify the sense of sight, whether by sensual or

34 Immanuel Kant, *Critique of Judgement* (1790), trans. James Creed Meredith (Oxford University Press, 1952), 'Critique of Aesthetic Judgement', p. 67. Jean-Jacques Roussseau, *Essai sur l'origine des langues* (1761), trans. John H. Moran, *On the Origin of Language* (New York: Frederick Ungar, 1966), p. 53.

35 Knight, *Principles of Taste*, p. 63.

36 Jeffery, review of Alison, *Essay on Taste*, p. 38.

37 Ibid.

38 *Principles of Taste*, pp. 70–1; compare with Knight, *The Landscape: A Didactic Poem*, 2nd edn (London: 1795), p. 22n.

intellectual means, and looked for a visual manner characteristic to painting.[39] He found it in the principle of 'massing', by which he meant the blurring of detail into broad masses. So that, for example, it would be characteristic of this painterly procedure to represent a tree full of minute leaves, or a head covered in fine hairs, as a single relatively undifferentiated mass,[40] and

> the greatest painters of the Venetian and Lombard schools; and afterwards those of the Flemish and Dutch, carried this principle of massing to a degree beyond what appears in ordinary nature; and departed from the system of direct imitation in a contrary extreme to their predecessors. Instead of making their lines more distinct, and keeping their tints more separate, than the visible appearance of the objects imitated warranted, they blended and melted them together with a playful and airy kind of lightness, and a sort of loose and sketchy indistinctness not observable in the reality, unless under peculiar circumstances and modifications of the atmosphere; and then only in those objects and combinations of objects, which exhibit blended and broken tints, or irregular masses of light and shadow harmoniously melted into each other.[41]

Knight credited Giorgione with the invention of this style, and Titian with its perfection;[42] artists whom Henry Fuseli in his Royal Academy lectures particularly associated with the 'inferiour but more alluring charm of colour' (colour being inferior to but more alluring than draughtsmanship, chiaroscuro and composition).[43] Fuseli, incidentally, credited Titian with the invention of the genre of landscape painting. 'Landscape,' he said, 'whether it be considered as the transcript of a spot, or the rich combination of congenial objects, or as the scene of a phænomenon, dates its origin from him.'[44] Knight found the highest excellence in the works of Giorgione and Titian, and in those of Claude, whom he saw as their successor. He praised their deep shadows and soft twilights, and contrasted them with the hard-edged style of the medieval painters, in whose works Knight praised the richness of colouring.

The best arrangements of pigment, though, were to be found where tints were 'happily broken and blended, and irregular masses of light and shadow harmoniously melted into each other'.[45] If by some association of ideas in the mind these appealing combinations of colour were associated with the works of painters, then a natural scene before the eyes might reasonably be said to be picturesque, whether or not it fitted Price's

39 Knight, *Principles of Taste*, p. 151.

40 Ibid., pp. 149–50.

41 Ibid., p. 150.

42 Ibid.

43 Henry Fuseli, *Lectures on Painting*, 2nd edn (Edinburgh: 1829), p. 63.

44 Ibid., p. 65.

45 Knight, *Principles of Taste*, p. 151.

definition.[46] A scene might indeed become picturesque when overtaken by a light mist or in the glow of evening sunshine, when the range of colours in the view might be made more harmonious than usual and so call to mind the artist's controlled use of a palette of colours.

Criticism of Burke and Price

Knight's responses to paintings and natural scenery were always framed in terms of the allurements of colour, together with the pleasures of the association of ideas, and he did not dwell on the form-related ideas which preoccupied Price and Burke. If we turn to Knight's treatment of Burke's ideas then we find him in characteristically knockabout mode, accusing Burke of having confused an idea in the mind (a 'power') with a sensation from an organ of sense:

> An eminent author, who makes terror to be a principal source of the sublime, has . . . conceived a notion . . . of stinks being sublime; though he acknowledges that he never could bring his mind to act in unison with his nose, so as to satisfy himself that he had really smelt a sublime stink . . . In this, however, as well as in many other instances, this truly great author has most unphilosophically mistaken a power for a sensation: a mistake, for which no excuse can be made but the early period of life at which *The Inquiry into the Sublime and Beautiful* was written; and his having soon after, unfortunately for his peace of mind, abandoned himself to more active pursuits, 'and to party given up [*sic*] what was meant for mankind'. But, nevertheless, at this early period, his feelings were generally right, even where his judgement was most wrong; so that he *felt*, though he did not *know* that, in the description it is a *power* only, and in the reality the *sensation* only, that affects the mind, or is at all perceived by it. But of this more hereafter: at present I shall merely observe, in justice to his memory, that, in his latter days, he laughed very candidly and good-humouredly at many of the philosophical absurdities, which will be here exposed; and I must add, in justice to myself, that I should not have thus undertaken to expose them, had they not been since adopted by others, and made to contribute so largely to the propagation of bad taste.[47]

The allusion which Knight put into quotation marks was to an 'epitaph' which Oliver Goldsmith composed in 1774 as a *Retaliation*:

46 See chapter 3, pp. 79–85.

47 *Principles of Taste*, pp. 27–8.

> Here lies our good Edmund, whose genius was such,
> We scarcely can praise it, or blame it too much,
> Who, born for the Universe, narrow'd his mind,
> And to party gave up, what was meant for mankind.[48]

There is a glance to his political affiliations, which had been opposed to Knight's, and as the war with France developed Knight must have thought Burke's abandonment of philosophical contemplation in favour of political activity was unfortunate for more than Burke's peace of mind. Burke, who had actually died in 1797, long after Goldsmith's verse, but before the publication of Knight's *Inquiry*, was introduced into Knight's text with the utmost respect; but we are left in no doubt whatsoever that in Knight's view Burke's aesthetics were completely misconceived. Burke's laughing about his early ideas is treated benevolently enough, but the anecdote trivialised views which Price took seriously, and he would certainly have found it insulting. The 'bad taste' which was propagated on account of these views was not, however, Price's, in which Knight expressed his confidence, but was particularly that of the landscape designer 'Capability' Brown, who will figure in chapter 7. Knight's treatment of Burke did not continue in the same respectful vein. There had been a time when Burke had acted in Parliament with Charles James Fox, and, as Knight put it, 'became the disinterested patron of remote and injured nations, who had none to help them'. At that period 'his character was truly sublime'.[49] However, according to Burke's own system sublimity is closely related to terror, and it can be heightened by astonishment, so taking one logical step after another, Knight suggested that

> If, during this period, he had suddenly appeared among the managers in Westminster-hall without his wig and coat; or had walked up St. James's street without his breeches, it would have occasioned great and universal astonishment; and if he had, at the same time, carried a loaded blunderbuss in his hands, the astonishment would have been mixed with no small portion of terror: but I do not believe that the united effects of these two powerful passions would have produced any sentiment or sensation approaching to the sublime, even in the breasts of those who had the strongest sense of self-preservation, and the quickest sensibility of danger.
>
> From this system the author has deduced many strange principles of taste.[50]

48 Oliver Goldsmith, *Retaliation* (1774), in *Collected Works of Oliver Goldsmith*, ed. Arthur Friedman, 5 vols. (Oxford: Clarendon Press, 1966), vol. IV, p. 353, lines 29–32.

49 *Principles of Taste*, p. 383.

50 Ibid., pp. 383–4.

In short Knight found Burke's ideas 'so strange and unphilosophical, that were it not for the great name, under which it has been imposed on the world, I should feel shame in seriously controverting it'. He went so far as to claim that he had 'never met with any man of learning, by whom the philosophy of the *Inquiry into the Sublime and Beautiful* was not so much despised and ridiculed, as the brilliancy and animation of its style were applauded, and admired'. The single solitary exception to this generalisation was 'my friend above mentioned', which is to say Mr Uvedale Price.

Knight tells us that Burke's doctrines concerning beauty were classified under six heads by Price, 'the most eminent and distinguished of his disciples', and this, 'if it prove nothing else, shows at least to what degree the most discerning mind may be occasionally deprived even of the ordinary powers of perception by the fascination of a favourite system'.[51] So far as architecture was concerned

> 'No building', says Mr. Price, 'is more universally admired for its beauty than the temple of the Sibyl at Tivoli. Let us then consider what are the qualities of beauty according to Mr. Burke, and how far they apply to beautiful buildings in general, and to that in particular. Those qualities are, I. to be comparatively small: II. to be smooth: III. to have a variety in the direction of the parts: but, IV. to have those parts melted, as it were, into each other: V. to be of a delicate frame, without any remarkable appearance of strength: VI. to have the colour clear and bright, but not very strong and glaring. The temple I have just mentioned, has, I think, as much of those chief principles as architecture will allow of: it is circular, surrounded by columns detached from the body of the building; it is light and airy; of a delicate frame; in a great measure free from angles; and comparatively small. I am speaking of it, as it must have been in its perfect state, when the tint of the stone, and the finishing and preservation of the parts, corresponded with the beauty of its general form.'[52]

Knight did not take issue with the idea that this building was beautiful, which would have been futile, but pointed out, quite correctly, that it was not the building in its perfect state which had been so widely admired, but the building in its present state of ruin. He did not question Price's evaluation of the building's merit, only his 'systematic' analysis of its merits. Price was determined to find in the building the characteristics which Burke had said should be there, but Knight found nothing of the sort.

51 Ibid., p. 76.

52 Ibid., pp. 76–7. This is not in fact a direct quotation from Price, but a concise (and fair) paraphrase of part of Price's 'Essay on Architecture and Buildings', in *Essays on the Picturesque*, vol. II, pp. 355–6.

> Compared with the Pantheon or the Parthenon, it was certainly small; but, compared with any edifice of similar plan (the proper object of comparison), it was by no means so: for though smaller in diametre [*sic*] than that of the same goddess at Rome, it appears to have been altogether a larger, more massive, and more considerable building, than either that or any other of the kind known.
>
> So far from being smooth, it is all over rough with sculpture, and built of the most rugged, porous, unequal stone, ever employed in a highly wrought edifice.
>
> The parts, instead of having any variety or even difference in the direction, all converge to one centrical point; as they necessarily must in a building completely circular . . . Instead of being free from angles, every thing is composed of angles: the entablature consists of angles projecting beyond each other; the capitals are clusters of angles . . .
>
> So far from being of a delicate frame, or with little appearance of strength, it is remarkable for nothing more than the compact firmness of its construction . . . The colour is that of the rough Tiburtine stone, which could never have been other than a dingy brown.[53]

In fact Knight found that the principles of beauty listed by Burke were to be found not in the universally admired temple at Tivoli, but in the 'hindoo domes', which he seems to have found self-evidently ridiculous.[54]

We have seen, then, how Knight dealt with the sublime and the beautiful, taking rules from Burke and Price and making them look completely absurd. It is already understandable that Price would have felt hurt and humiliated by his treatment at Knight's hands, but when he turned to the subject of the picturesque, the third category, and the one which Price had formulated himself, Knight was at his most completely destructive. Here the reason for Price feeling hurt could well have been very much more personal. William Wordsworth met Uvedale Price and his family at a dreadful dinner in London:

> On Tuesday at Rogers's, present the B[eaumont]s Mr Price Lady Caroline, Miss Price and her Brother; . . . [who is a] very well looking & agreeable Young Man. Nothing could be more deplorable than the rest of the Party: Miss P – a little deformed Creature, with a most strange enunciation, sitting by Mr Jekyll a celebrated Wit, and

53 *Principles of Taste*, p. 77–9.

54 Ibid., p. 80.

> quite pert and to use a coarse word ever rampant upon him. She is, as Sir G[eorge Beaumont] observed in expression of countenance & manner just like the bad Sister who does all the Mischief in a Faery tale. Lady Caroline was coquetting away with General Fitzpatrick her old Paramour, who is a most melancholy object, with a complection as yellow as a frog, a tall emaciated Figure & hobbling with the gout. He creeps abroad yet, poor Man, and may fairly be said to have one foot in the grave. It was lamentable also to see poor Price overgorging himself at dinner as he did, and falling into a lethargic sleep immediately after, from which he had not power to preserve himself two minutes together. This was truly a piteous sight for Price is a man of genuine talents, and gifted by Nature with a firm Constitution which he is destroying by gluttony. He invited me to go to Foxley, and if you could ride so far I should be glad to go with you to shew you the place.[55]

Price clearly was not being guided by philosophy in his eating habits. It was not the first time Wordsworth had met the Prices, and not the first time that he had expressed most of these views, but in this letter to his wife, Mary, he was unguarded and the views are clear. In an earlier letter, to Sir George Beaumont, Wordsworth let it be known that he had visited Foxley in the autumn of 1810, and Price had shown him round.[56] He was pleased enough by the scenery, but did not much enjoy the visit as a whole, partly because he was uncomfortable about the presence of the same Fitzpatrick, who had not in fact stepped into the grave, but was in Wordsworth's view altogether *too* comfortable in the presence of Price's wife, 'snugly and peaceably content with each other', but had no rapport at all with Price himself. Then there was Price's daughter who, Wordsworth said, 'put me out of tune by her strange speech, looks, and manners'. Joseph Farington had noted in his diary in 1806 that 'There is insanity in the family of Mr. Price. His eldest daughter 22 or 3 years old, has been confined, but now visits with them. She is deformed & has many singularities.'[57]

One of Price's illustrations of the picturesque with which Knight made characteristically facetious play could have been drawn from his own particular personal circumstances: his example of 'the good old parson's daughter', attractive in a 'picturesque' way (according to Price's but not Knight's principles) but not at all beautiful,

> made upon the model of her father's house: her features are as irregular, and her eyes are inclined to look across one another, like

55 William Wordsworth to Mary, 1 June 1812, in *The Love Letters of William and Mary Wordsworth*, ed. Beth Darlington (Ithaca, New York: Cornell University Press, 1981), p. 212.

56 William Wordsworth to Sir George Beaumont, 28 August 1811, in *Memorials of Coleorton*, ed. William Knight, 2 vols. (Edinburgh: 1887), vol. II, pp. 133–4.

57 *Diary*, 13 October 1806.

> the roofs of the old parsonage; but a clear skin, clean white teeth, though not very even, and a look of cheerfulness, in spite of these irregularities, made me look at her with pleasure; and I really think, if I were of the cloth, I should like very well to take the living, the house, and its inhabitant.[58]

Knight's reply to this line of Price's argument was merciless and, given Miss Price's general appearance, at least insensitive and possibly downright cruel.

> My friend, Mr. Price, indeed admits squinting among the irregular and picturesque charms of the parson's daughter, whom (to illustrate the picturesque in opposition to the beautiful) he wishes to make appear lovely and attractive, though without symmetry and regularity further than to the features of the face; though to make the figure consistent and complete, the same happy mixture of the irregular and picturesque must have prevailed through her limbs and person; and consequently she must have hobbled as well as squinted; and had hips and shoulders as irregular as her teeth, cheeks, and eyebrows. All my friend's parental fondness for his system is certainly necessary to make him think such an assemblage of picturesque circumstances either lovely or attractive; or induce him to imagine, that he should be content with such a creature, as a companion for life.[59]

Price must surely have seen these remarks as absolutely outrageous personal abuse, hence his response, which was publicly made on a philosophical plane, albeit prefaced by a cry of 'foul', but which privately led him to break off contact with Knight. Knight compounded the suspicion, and therefore the offence, in the preface which he added to the second edition of his book (published in 1805) in which he repeated the association of Price's fondness for irregular picturesqueness with his 'parental affection', in the general context of hoping that his remarks would be taken philosophically and would not cause offence, saying that Dr Johnson and Sir Joshua Reynolds,

> while living in the most familiar intimacy of the strictest friendship with Mr. Burke, entirely rejected, in their writings, the principles which he had endeavoured to establish in the 'Inquiry into the Sublime and the Beautiful;' without, indeed, naming the Author, or citing the book; and this mode of proceeding, I adopted with reference to such of Mr. Price's opinions, as I could not acquiesce

58 Knight quoting Price, *Principles of Taste*, p. 202n.

59 Ibid., pp. 202–4.

> in or approve: in this mode too I should have persevered, had he not, in his dialogue, made a pointed attack upon the adverse opinions, which I had simply professed; and a pointed attack necessarily produces a pointed attack in return; since it is impossible wholly to separate measures of defence from those of offence.
>
> Having, however, never embraced any speculative opinion with that eagerness of parental affection, which engages the feelings of the heart in support of the theories of the head, I shall feel no perturbation of temper at finding any, that I have embraced, proved to be false or erroneous: but can even share the triumph of a candid adversary, if it appears to be, at the same time, the triumph of truth; which, being the fundamental principle of both taste and morality, ought to be the ultimate object of every writer; and which, if steadily kept in view, will equally exclude the irritability of passion, the presumption of prejudice, and the dogmatical pride of system.
>
> In all controversy, the mildest mode is, in every respect, the best: but, nevertheless, there are occasions, where it is impossible not to employ ridicule: for when a ludicrous light is the natural and proper light to any ill-founded argument or erroneous position, it comes upon it, as it were, of its own accord; and the fairest and simplest, becomes the most ridiculous statement of it. In such circumstances, all I can say is, that, as I have always taken good-humouredly what has appeared to be meant good-humouredly, I trust that reciprocal indulgence will be granted me.[60]

Price was not persuaded. Lord and Lady Oxford knew the artist Robert Smirke, and also his son the architect Robert Smirke (1780–1867), whom they employed in 1806–7 to rebuild their house at Eywood (in a Capability Brown landscape) and whose best-known work was to be the British Museum (1823–46).[61] Lady Oxford spoke to Smirke senior about the quarrel, and he then told Joseph Farington about it, who confided in his diary that Price was so upset

> that it required the intervention of Lady Oxford to make it up. She told Robert that Mr. Knight wrote a letter of explanation to Her to be shown to Mr. Price. She said she really believed Mr. Knight did not mean to offend Mr. Price, but in his writing, as in his conversation, when He means to assume lightness & vivacity of

60 *Principles of Taste*, 2nd edn only (1805), pp. iv–vi.

61 The house was demolished in 1955, but some of the ancilliary buildings remain, and the general disposition of the landscape is still recognisably Brownian.

> remark, He becomes satirical. She thinks Knight very learned, but Mr. Price more elegant & agreeable, & that he has better taste.[62]

In the light of this incident Lady Oxford's verdict seems sound. As a friend of both parties she was faced with some delicate problems, being apprehensive that Knight might meet up with Price and his family at Eywood in the autumn of 1806.[63] Knight, who spent a good deal of his time in London, was not liked in the country,[64] but Price, less affluent because his estate remained agriculturally based and without the industrial production of Knight's, spent more time cultivating Foxley and the people of the county. Knight and Price evidently avoided one another for a time, but would have heard about one another by way of mutual friends. For example, Knight warned Price off a public confrontation with Dugald Stewart by sending a letter to Lord Aberdeen, saying:

> Corresponding associations are so necessary to produce a sense of the delicacy of pictoresque [*sic*] beauty that not only very clever men but the most learned and refin'd judges of imitative art, as far as it has been employ'd upon Forms, have never acquired it. Such was the late Charles Townley, and if there needed any further proof of the fallacy of Price's system of its belonging to a distinct class of objects, this would be sufficient. If he attacks Dugald Stuart so as to provoke a reply the whole will be blown at once into oblivion; for Stuart will be under no restraints of personal friendship, and is really a metaphysician, which his antagonist is not in any degree.[65]

He could have counted on the message being relayed to Price, who wrote to Aberdeen frequently and at length. Relations between Knight and Price had begun to thaw by 1812, when Knight went hunting and mentioned that he had seen 'my brother farmer Price last week at Foxley, too unwell to join in enjoying the pursuit, though not dangerously or very seriously ill', and their friendship later grew to be again quite warm.[66]

The public exchange of philosophical argument had certainly become overheated and upset Price when the attack on his aesthetic principles became inseparable from personal abuse. Although Knight's book was widely read, the documents which were subsequently published in defence of the different positions made strangely arcane reading. The architect George Dance (1741–1825), who moved in this circle, followed the argument but did not feel enlightened for having done so. 'What stuff it is', he said.[67] Knight set himself against 'system',

62 *Diary*, 21 June 1806.

63 Ibid., 13 October 1806.

64 Ibid.

65 Knight to Lord Aberdeen, 12 October [1810?] British Library, Additional MSS, (Aberdeen Papers) 43230, fol.74.

66 Knight to Lord Aberdeen, 28 September 1812, and 28 July 1818; ibid., 43230, fols. 147 and 318.

67 Farington, *Diary*, 4 March 1810.

and his polemic was directed mainly against Price, whom he accused of having surrendered his wits to a system. Nevertheless he thought that Price's prescriptions admirably showed the practical means to gratify the eye with sensual pleasure and the mind with pleasant trains of thought, and that Price's practical advice should be followed. However, it was only the latter type of pleasure, the intellectual pleasure which arose from the association of ideas, which could properly be called 'picturesque', or even more properly 'pictoresque'.

Erasmus Darwin

Erasmus Darwin (1731–1802), grandfather of the more famous Charles, published a long poem, *The Botanic Garden*, in two volumes in 1789 (volume II) and 1792 (volume I), which seems to have had some influence on Knight's poem *The Landscape*, although the influence cannot readily be disentangled from that of their common source, Lucretius.[68] Darwin seems to have absorbed Epicurus' philosophy as completely as did Knight. They shared some behavioural traits, such as combining temperance with an idiosyncratic morality.[69] Darwin was as hostile as Knight to Christianity, and was also familiar with d'Hancarville's ideas, which he treated seriously but not uncritically. *The Botanic Garden* was prefaced with a quotation from Lucretius, and was loosely modelled on *De Rerum Natura*, enlisting 'Imagination under the banner of Science' in a characteristically Lucretian way.[70] Darwin's reputation as a poet currently has about the same standing as Knight's, his use of verse being, according to a recent Oxford Professor of Poetry, 'idiotic'.[71] Again the attempt to present the material in an engaging and attractive way now acts as an obstacle to its acceptance (or even its notice). In the Epicurean scheme of things there was no scope for divine intervention as a means to create life, and therefore it introduced an idea of evolution, which Darwin also held, though he was vague about the details of any mechanisms through which it could possibly work (his grandson was to make some suggestions about them). Although the idea of evolution can seem to date more importantly from the nineteenth century, when Charles Darwin's evidence and arguments made it very persuasive and difficult to resist, and when it became contentious, Erasmus Darwin was not alone in endorsing the idea two generations earlier. Intellectuals who had come into contact with Enlightenment ideas found the notion intuitively plausible and accepted it readily enough without strong argument. For example James Burnet, Lord Monboddo (1714–99), a Scottish judge, was

68 Erasmus Darwin, *The Botanic Garden*, 2 vols.: vol. I, *The Economy of Vegetation* (London: 1792), vol. II, *The Loves of the Plants* (London: 1789).

69 An anonymous obituary notice in the *Monthly Magazine*, vol. 13 (1802), p. 458 said that, 'in his youth Dr. Darwin was fond of sacrificing to both Bacchus and Venus; but he soon discovered that he could not continue his devotions to both those deities without destroying his health and constitution. He therefore resolved to relinquish Bacchus, but his affection for Venus was retained to the last period of his life.'

70 Darwin, *Botanic Garden*, vol. I, p. v.

71 'Of all the idiot uses to which poetry has been put – Christmas cracker rhymes, phoney epics, and the scientific verses of Erasmus Darwin.' Peter Levi, *The Noise Made by Poems*, 2nd edn (London: Anvil Press, 1984), p. 60.

particularly celebrated for his idea that man may be related to the orang-outang.[72] He also said that men had at one time had tails, and that the beaver was at a state of development similar to that of man before the development of language.[73] Knight referred to Monboddo's work,[74] and he certainly accepted the idea of evolution, and in both *The Progress of Civil Society* and *An Analytical Inquiry into the Principles of Taste* presented early man as black.[75] As his authority he cited 'the late great physiologist' Dr John Hunter (1728–93), an eminent surgeon and a noted collector of dead bodies, who, Knight said, 'used to maintain (and I think he proved it), that the African black was the true original man'.[76]

Knight's reason for introducing the 'true original man' into his discussion about the principles of taste was to combat the idea that a universal standard of taste could be established by referring the matter back to our primitive origins, for

> what more infallible criterion can there be for judging of the natural taste and inclination of mankind, than the most natural and original of the species? We can neither weigh nor measure the results of feeling or sentiment; and can only judge whether they are just and natural, or corrupt and artificial, by comparing them with the general laws of nature, which fall under our observation: for of the real laws of nature we know nothing; these deductions amounting to no more than rules of analogy of our own forming; by which, we judge of the future by the past, and form opinions of things, which we do not know, by things which we do.[77]

This is a statement of Knight's belief in the methods of natural philosophy as set down by Bacon and modified by Hume: that there are no unquestionable principles which are definitely known, only rules which humans have inferred from their limited experience, rules which may be subject to revision. The passage quoted above posited a hypothesis which was then undermined as Knight, addressing an audience which considered the likes of Lady Hamilton and Lady Oxford to be great beauties, thought that the original 'natural' man would

> view with pity and contempt the marked deformity of the Europeans; whose mouths are compressed, their noses pinched, their cheeks shrunk, their hair rendered lank and flimsy, their bodies lengthened and emaciated, and their skins unnaturally bleached by shade and seclusion, and the baneful influence of a cold climate. Were they to draw an image of female perfection, or a

72 James Burnet (or Burnett), Lord Monboddo, *Of the Origin and Progress of Language*, 6 vols. (1773–92), vol. I, p. 289: 'the Ouran Outangs . . . are proved to be of our species by marks of humanity that I think are incontestible . . . they walk erect. They live in society, build huts, joined in companies to attack elephants, and no doubt carry on other joint undertakings for their sustenance and preservation; but have not yet attained the use of speech.' See also Arthur Lovejoy, 'Monboddo and Rousseau', *Essays in the History of Ideas* (Baltimore: Johns Hopkins University Press, 1948), pp. 38 ff.; and the footnotes to Thomas Love Peacock, *Melincourt* (1816).

73 Elizabeth Carter, *Memoirs of the Life of Mrs. Elizabeth Carter*, ed. Montagu Pennington (Boston: Greenleaf, 1809), p. 472: 'The most fashionable object in all polite circles at present is Lord Monboddo, who you know has writ to prove, that all human creatures, in their natural state, have tails like a cat'; quoted E. L. Cloyd, *James Burnett, Lord Monboddo* (Oxford University Press, 1972), p. 44.

74 *Principles of Taste*, p. 110.

75 *The Progress of Civil Society: A Didactic Poem* (London: 1796), pp. 97, 108.

76 *Principles of Taste*, p. 15.

77 Ibid.

> goddess of love and beauty, she would have a broad flat nose, high cheeks, woolly hair, a jet black skin, and squat thick form, with breasts reaching to her navel. . . . perhaps at Tomuctoo the fairest nymph of St. James's, who . . . displays her light and slender form through transparent folds of muslin, might seem a disgusting mass of deformity; and who shall decide which party is right, or which is wrong?[78]

The taste of a 'natural' man such as this was not Knight's taste, and he presented as absurd the idea of making use of such a man's taste as a standard of judgement. This undermined any attempt which might have been made to argue from a Rousseauist position, that true taste was taste uncorrupted by contact with civilisation. Intuitively of course Knight thought that the truest taste was that of the Greeks of the fifth and fourth centuries BC, who were manifestly civilised, even though they were in touch with nature.[79] Hume had in practical terms come to much the same conclusion as Knight, but his views found expression in much less colourful terms, and unlike Knight he did suppose that there was a universal standard of taste. 'The general principles of taste are uniform in human nature', he said, but variety crept in where there was 'diversity in the internal frame or external situation', and that such diversity cannot be praised or blamed.[80] In practice the diversity could not be eliminated, which made the proposition an impossible one to test, but the belief that there were principles of some sort which were uniform in human nature led Erasmus Darwin to formulate a theory of aesthetics, which combined ideas from Hume with some from Hogarth, in an attempt to resolve the two rival theories. Hogarth, and of course Price, thought that the distinguishing quality of beauty was the smoothly curving serpentine line, a point which Darwin too accepted. However he sought to explain the phenomenon not by supposing the curve to be inherently beautiful, but by supposing that such a curve would have pleasant and deep-rooted associations. In *The Temple of Nature* (1803), another long poem with elaborate footnotes, Darwin annotated a reference to 'wavy lawns' at some length, declaring, 'When the babe, soon after it is born into this cold world, is applied to its mother's bosom, its sense of perceiving warmth is first agreeably affected; next its sense of smell is delighted with the odour of her milk; then its taste is gratified by the flavour of it.'[81] He developed this further, and elaborated it with circumstantial details, concluding :

> All these various kinds of pleasure at length become associated with the form of the mother's breast . . . And hence at our maturer

78 ibid., pp. 13–15.

79 See chapter 2, pp. 29–45.

80 David Hume, 'Of the Standard of Taste', in *Philosophical Works*, ed. Green and Grose, 4 vols. (1886), vol. III, pp. 280–1.

81 Erasmus Darwin, *The Temple of Nature* (London: 1803), p. 100n.

> years, when any object is presented to us, which by its waving or spiral lines bears any similitude to the form of the female bosom, whether it be found in a landscape with soft gradations of rising and descending surface, or in the form of antique vases, or in other works of the pencil or the chisel, we feel a general flow of delight, which seems to influence all our senses . . . And thus we find, according to the ingenious idea of Hogarth, that the wavy lines of beauty were originally taken from the temple of Venus.[82]

In Darwin's thinking Venus acted much as Priapus did in Knight's; they are, after all, both sexual principles, but Darwin was more attracted to Venus. He described her as being born out of the great Egg of Night (which was usually the way that Priapus or Cupid came into the world),[83] but then 'Immortal Love' was also to be found at the same time outside the egg, warming it and making atoms in chaos bind together. Knight and Darwin were at most points in agreement, however, for example in supposing that beauty was not inherent in wavy lines, but that if there were beauty in a wavy line then it was because of the association of ideas. Darwin also said that the eye could be pleased by direct stimulus,[84] as did Knight; and Darwin claimed that emotions 'as of sublimity, beauty, utility, novelty; and the objects suggesting other sentiments, which have lately been termed picturesque' were caused by associations of ideas, as did Knight;[85] but they were not in complete agreement. Knight could not accept that the wavy line was the only, or even the most significant, stimulus for an aesthetic response. As when dealing with other theories with which he disagreed, his response to Darwin's theory was to apply it in a way which showed it to be ridiculous:

> I am aware, indeed, that it would be no easy task to persuade a lover that the forms on which he dotes with such rapture, are not really beautiful, independent of the medium of affection, passion and appetite, through which he views them. But before he pronounces either the infidel or the sceptic guilty of blasphemy against nature, let him take a mould from the lovely features or lovely bosom of this masterpiece of creation, and cast a plum-pudding in it (an object by no means disagreeable to most men's appetites) and, I think, he will no longer be in raptures with the form, whatever he may be with the substance.[86]

So Knight held that beauty did not lie in any particular attribute of an object, neither its shape, nor its size, nor its resemblance to any part of the

82 Ibid.

83 Ibid., p. 1.

84 Ibid., p. 143n.

85 Ibid., p. 143.

86 *Principles of Taste*, pp. 185–6.

body, but mainly in its power to stimulate the mind to make associations (and to a much lesser degree by being pleasurable to the eye by virtue of its colour). The associations in the mind *could* be made on account of the form of the object, but could equally well be made on account of its colour, its odour or some detail which escapes conscious recognition. If the associations attached to the form are not congruent with those which attach to the substance (as was the case in the plum pudding in the form of a breast) then the reaction could well be confusion or distaste, the considerations of form failing to impress themselves as of paramount importance where there is a contradiction.

Flux

The associations on which Knight's theory of aesthetics depended are specific to limited social groups. These groups may be defined by climate, political organisation, geography or something else altogether, the critical difference being that each group has its own culture. If the principles of taste are to be rooted in the principles of association then it follows that there can never be certainty in matters of taste, because any given object will be assimilated into a different culture by different observers. Tastes may coincide when the observers share the same culture, but there can be no guarantee of an underlying universality to any set of principles of taste. So that whereas Hogarth's purpose in trying to analyse beauty was to find a constant principle of beauty which underpinned all the more superficial beauties which were paraded in the vagaries of fashion, Knight came to the conclusion that no such principle could ever be established. Words like 'genius' and 'taste' did not attach to any particular range of objects, but were simply terms of approbation 'which men apply to whatever they approve, without annexing any specific ideas to them'.[87] If there were to be no single principle underlying all others in matters of taste then it followed that taste cannot have fixed rules, applicable in all places and at all times. Moreover, in any given situation it would not be desirable to establish fixed rules of taste because

> Change and variety are . . . necessary to the enjoyment of all pleasures; whether sensual or intellectual: and so powerful is this principle, that all change, not so violent as to produce a degree of irritation in the organs absolutely painful, is pleasing; and preferable to any uniform and unvaried gratification . . . Thus, if we suppose the world and its inhabitants to be fixed

87 Ibid., p. 435.

> in one unchangeable state for ever, deprived of all variation of seasons, and of every kind of progressive or successive growth, decay, or reproduction, how perfect soever we may suppose that fixed state to be, we should soon become so tired of it, were it realised, that we should eagerly covet any change, and agree with the poet that even death itself is to be reckoned among the gifts or benefactions of nature.[88]

So there can be no fixed rules; the only certainty in matters of taste is the certainty of change. Were any universal principles of taste actually enforced, then they would soon be universally condemned, and we would find that 'a state of abstract perfection would . . . be a state of perfect misery'.[89] The conclusion was clearly in sympathy with Knight's general hostility to 'system' and regulation, and no doubt he reached it as much by way of his personal prejudices as by rigorous reasoning, but nevertheless he reached a conclusion which is more easily acceptable in the twentieth century than it was in the early nineteenth. Whilst others were searching for universal constants in matters of taste, Knight was, at a theoretical level, fully prepared to abandon them. This was a radical move, and an extreme one, which had not previously been made so clearly or to so wide an audience.

Addison, for example, had made the association of ideas an important part of his aesthetic theory, but because his frame of reference was that of the educated classes, to whom his essays in the *Tatler* and the *Spectator* were addressed, his version of the theory had made its appeal to learning and reflective contemplation in a way which was completely supportive of the existing patterns of learning, culture and taste. In Knight's hands the case was different, because he introduced an anthropological element into the equation and saw the association of ideas to be culturally specific and a discussion of taste possible only in relation to a given culture. It would have made no sense to say that Lady Hamilton was not beautiful simply because her beauty would not have been appreciated in 'Tombuctoo', as it certainly would have been appreciated in St James's. And if this were the case, and the beauty was in the mind of the observer, then why should not the African Venus be really beautiful when she is seen to be so in her own culture? The analysis of beauty had been made a cultural study. Moreover, even within a given culture the principles of taste were not fixed, and any attempt to fix them would bring only boredom and misery.

The idea of the world being in an ever-changing state is particularly

88 Ibid., pp. 432–3 and 474–5. 'The poet' is Juvenal, and the allusion is to his tenth *Satire*.

89 Knight, *Principles of Taste*, pp. 475–6.

90 Heraclitus of Ephesus, *Fragments*, ed. T. M. Robinson (University of Toronto Press, 1987), p. 55. The remark is only dubiously associated with the historical Heraclitus, and is to be traced back to a possible misrepresentation of him by Plato, in *Cratylus*.

91 Lucretius, *De Rerum Natura*, bk. V, line 280: 'assidue quoniam fluere omnia constat'; ed. Cyril Bailey (Oxford: Clarendon

associated with the presocratic philosopher Heraclitus, who is famously credited with saying that one could never step in the same river twice.[90] It was endorsed by Lucretius, for whom the world was in constant flux,[91] and is in some measure related to the general enthusiasm for progress, which is associated with the Enlightenment and was very much a part of Knight's own culture.[92] Although Newton seemed to have found some very basic universal laws, his whole understanding of the physical world was predicated on the idea that we must understand change as a constant, and he developed his theory of fluctions in order to help him do it: a theory which was developed independently at about the same time by Leibniz, as the more familiar infinitesimal calculus.[93] These developments in mathematics allowed change to be expressed arithmetically as a constant. In Newton's universe everything changed at a constant rate, unless a force acted, in which case the rate of change changed. Knight's conclusion that change is inevitable and necessary was grounded in his observations on the mechanisms of the senses, which respond not so much to the starting and stopping of a stimulus, but to variation, 'because the commencement of a new sensation is never from absolute inaction ... a certain degree of irritation being always kept up ... by the mere stimulus of the blood, or by the necessary operation of vital warmth and motion'.[94] Knight, like Newton, and following his example, saw his analysis to be based not on a static system which was set in motion by the action of forces, but on a state of affairs which was, from the outset, dynamic.

In the eighteenth century the idea of progress, 'the March of Mind',[95] became normal, and brought with it a concern for the vanished and vanishing past in antiquarian studies and in speculations about the most distant past. A concern to trace the development of civilisation, such as there is in *The Progress of Civil Society*, entailed a discussion of the origins of society and its attributes. However, there are tensions in Knight's understanding of things which make his own brand of progress highly problematic. He certainly did not suppose that everything was getting better in every way and that there was a straightforward improvement in the human condition and lot: far from it. There were three principal axes in Knight's thought, against which the state of a society and its arts might be judged. First, there was the continuous change which was necessary in order to prevent stagnation, a continuous refreshment and creativity, which did not in itself bring about any improvement as such, but a bad state of affairs would arise were it to be stopped (were that possible). This rate of change would vary from one culture to another; the

Press, 1947), p. 447, 'it is certain that all things are constantly flowing away'; trans. C. H. Sisson (Manchester: Carcanet, 1976), p. 145, 'there is perpetual flux'; trans. Ronald Latham (Harmondsworth: Penguin, 1951), p. 179, 'it is an established fact that everything is in a perpetual flux'.

92 J. B. Bury, *The Idea of Progress, An Inquiry into its Origin and Growth* (London: Macmillan, 1920).

93 Leibniz discovered the infinitesimal calculus in 1675 and published his findings in 1684, before Newton, who had made his own discovery of the same principles (which he called his theory of fluctions) in 1666. The two systems used different methods of notation. The one devised by Leibniz was simpler and is in general use today. See G. Macdonald Ross, *Leibniz* (Oxford University Press, 1984), pp. 30 ff.

94 *Principles of Taste*, p. 20.

95 Thomas Love Peacock, *The Works of Thomas Love Peacock*, ed. H. F. B. Brett-Smith and C. E. Jones, 10 vols. (London: Halliford, 1924–36), vol. IV, *Crotchet Castle* (1831), chapter 2, 'The March of Mind', p. 22: 'I am out of all patience with this march of mind. Here has my house been nearly burned down, by my cook taking it into her head to study hydrostatics, in a sixpenny tract, published by the Steam Intellect Society.'

'neutral' position would be one in which changes of taste would be freely made, but they could on the one hand be suppressed, and lead to a stultified society like ancient Egypt, or on the other change could be too rapid and one would become a victim of fashion. Secondly, there was the more clearly beneficial change of technical innovation and scientific progress, which did improve things, and made possible things which were not practicable before. It was possible to move in both directions along this axis, either progressing towards knowledge and reason, or regressing towards ignorance and superstition, so this progress was related not to the passage of time as such, but to the degree of enlightenment which a society enjoyed. The third axis is the most problematic, because, despite theoretically endorsing change in matters of taste, Knight believed that the cultural conditions and the sculptural works from Greece in the fifth and fourth centuries BC had greater merit than any others. This axis therefore indicates the distance from the ancient Greek conditions which combined civilised life with an understanding of and proximity to nature. So there was a complex interaction of different conceptions of change in Knight's thought: change as a condition of life, change as the progress of reason and change as retrieval of an ancient ideal.

Paintings and painters

The strongest of the contradictions is that between Knight's philosophical argument that aesthetic values are all culturally specific and subject to change, and his unshakeable personal conviction that the ancient Greeks had produced greater art than anyone before or since. He did accept, however, the possibility of progress in the arts. He may have been convinced that the genuine works of Homer and Phidias would never be surpassed, but he did think that painting had advanced since ancient times and was a patron of modern art, and living artists, as well being a collector of ancient bronzes and Old Master drawings. When Knight was living at Stonebrook Cottage he gave an illustration of one way in which his relish for his situation would not have been possible for an ancient Greek:

> The Greeks and Romans certainly never had a complete relish for these gratifications, owing to their never having been acquainted with the perfection of landscape painting, and consequently having no corresponding objects of association, and it is only through the association of ideas that imagination comes to the

> aid of the senses, and refines and exalts its pleasures. The mere sensualist is in fact only half a sensualist, his gratifications being not only very limitted [*sic*] and transitory, but very imperfect and incomplete.[96]

There had been some landscape painting in the ancient world. According to Knight it was first practised by 'one Ludius of Lydius, in the time of Augustus, who seems to have been little better than a scene painter',[97] and landscapes of a sort were to be found at Pompeii, though 'they were rather grotesques than landscapes; and certainly very undeserving of being ranked with the ancient efforts of the art in Greece and its colonies'.[98] Still less did it deserve to be ranked with the landscape painting of Giorgione, Titian and Claude; so in Knight's view it was possible to progress and improve upon the ancient world even in some areas of artistic endeavour, and the intellectual pleasures which could result from developing the mind extended the range of pleasurable activity beyond the merely sensual into something wider and longer-lasting. Moreover the indulgence in intellectual pleasure was in no way damaging to the health of the body, especially when it enabled Knight to relish the scenery which he saw when he was taking his daily exercise. Again we see Knight explaining his actions and his taste in terms of the pursuit of pleasure, even here where his scholarly endeavours could have been shown in a much more conventionally worthy light.

Whilst Knight was prepared to make some stipulations about painting which were deduced from his understanding of the sense of sight, concerned with the physiology of the eye, he was not prepared to suggest that any particular manner of painting was necessarily to be favoured above others. Showing again his dislike of general rules, he was theoretically opposed to the kind of developments which might have led to stylistic regularity, such as the institutional teaching of artists. He said that the academies which the sovereigns of the various states of Europe had set up for the study of the arts seemed to be in a good position to foster the talents of their students, but had in fact failed to produced a single significant artist. The institutions announced, regularly enough, that they had produced 'Heaven-born geniuses', but once sent out into the world they all 'returned through the same beaten track of mediocrity', having acquired at the academy 'enough of the art to make them miraculous boys, and contemptible men'.[99] 'France produced several great painters' before the French *Académie des Beaux Arts* was set up, though 'it has not produced one since'; but

96 Knight to Lord Aberdeen, 3 September 1810, BL (Aberdeen Papers), 43230, fol. 72.

97 Knight, *The Landscape*, p. 64n.

98 Ibid., p.64n.

99 *Principles of Taste*, pp. 240–2.

> Happily our own academy has hitherto escaped the contagion of system; and every artist taken up a style of his own, suited to his taste or talents; so that an English exhibition displays more variety than all those on the continent together. By thus continuing to apply the principles of British liberty to British art, we may reasonably hope to reach a degree of excellence in painting, which has never yet been attained: for painting, in modern Europe, has never approached that state of abstract perfection, which we admire in the sculpture of ancient Greece; and there can be no reason in the nature of things why it should not attain it.[100]

The reasons are characteristically anti-systematic and political. Progress in the art of painting is explicitly held out as a possibility, in contrast with the state of affairs in sculpture, where a 'state of abstract perfection' was reached in ancient Greece.

Knight did not explain what he thought would be the consequences of this for the sculptor. He said that a state of abstract perfection, if it were continued indefinitely, would be a state of perfect misery; which is to say that a state of abstract perfection would not be perfect. This contradiction indicates the strains in Knight's thought, where he needs on the one hand to use a rhetoric which saw progress as leading towards perfection, even though, on the other, he thought perfection would be unbearable and that we need change, not perfection. Theoretically Knight thought that even a change for the worse might be preferable to unchanging goodness (we might welcome even death, as a relief) but when considering the state of the arts in his own day his response was to reinscribe the same contradictions as he had in other fields of thought. The modern sculptor should aspire to produce what had been produced in ancient Greece, whereas a painter should aim to go beyond anything yet attained.

Knight's antipathy to the academies, whilst it may well have been justified, undoubtedly sprang from a conviction that his own highly unsystematic education had given him an ability to think for himself, in contrast to his more respectably schooled peers. The antipathy applied not only to schools of painting but to schools in general, 'the complete corruption and decline of Latin eloquence' dating from the early second century, when schools were set up to teach it.[101] That the Royal Academy had, at least at that time, escaped the 'contagion of system' was evident in Reynolds's *Lectures,* which were intended to give guidance to students. Reynolds supposed that there were no fixed rules to govern painters who were established masters, but advice to be given to a student was quite

100 Ibid., p. 241n.

101 Ibid., p. 245.

different from that to be given to an accomplished artist. The latter might produce wonderful work if left to follow his intuitions and inspirations, but the student had first to acquire some fundamental mechanical skills. Knight followed Reynolds and made a division between liberal and mechanic arts.[102] A liberal art would engage the intelligence, whereas a mechanic art was merely skilled manual labour; the 'great characteristic difference' between them

> which gives to the former all its superiority, is feeling or sentiment; a quality, that is always easily perceived, but incapable of being described. It is this which gives, in different ways, those inexpressible charms and graces to the works of Corregio [*sic*], of Rubens, of Rembrandt, and of Claude: which, amidst inaccuracies, that every student of every academy knows how to reprobate and avoid, still continue to fascinate every beholder; and will continue to do so, as long as a trace of them shall remain. Had these great artists been bred in the trammels of an academy, they also would have avoided their inaccuracies: but the same causes, that restrained their deviations one way, would have restrained them another; and, by preventing them from transgressing rules, prevented them from soaring above them. Their knowledge in this case might have been more correct, and their practice more regular: but their observation would have been less various and extensive; their use and application of it less free and vigorous; and their execution more mannered, and less adapted to the respective subjects, upon which it was occasionally employed.
>
> If, however, academical science and precision can be united with feeling and sentiment, there is no doubt that the result would be a degree of perfection hitherto unknown to the art; and which perhaps the limited powers of human nature are not capable of reaching. Annibal Caracci has combined them in a greater degree than any other painter: but yet how inferior is he, in the first, not only to the great artists of antiquity, but to Raphael; and, in the second, to the great Flemish painters, Rubens, Vandyke and Rembrandt! In the expression of sentiment and passion, he is, indeed, superior to all the moderns, except Raphael; but the sentiment or feeling, of which I am now treating is of a different kind; and belongs to the execution, rather than the subject or design of the picture. It is that felicity in catching the little transitory effects of nature and expressing them in the imitation,

102 See Joshua Reynolds, *Discourses on Art,* ed. Robert R. Wark (New Haven: Yale University Press, 1975), pp. 64–5.

> so that they may appear to be dropped, as it were, fortuitously from the pencil, rather than produced by labour, study, or design: it is that, in short, which distinguishes a work of taste and genius from one of mere science and industry; and which often raises the value of an inaccurate original above that of the most correct copy.[103]

The mechanical part of painting might be taught at an academy, but it should always be kept subservient to the high ideas which are to be expressed, which the artist would be unable properly to feel and develop without the ability to think independently of system and to make instinctive judgements. 'One of the evils of academies' was that they stifled individual instinct, and 'in common with all corporations in literature and art' tended to be animated by

> the spirit of corporate pride and vanity engendered and nourished in them. The importance which the body derives even from its members, communicates itself to each individual member; and an *academician*, like a doctor, has acquired the authority of professional rank, how small soever may be his other acquirements. An assembly of such dignitaries becomes, in their own estimation at least, a legislative synod of taste and science; which fixes arbitrarily the *criteria* of excellence, and thus sanctions and renders systematic every error, which the caprice of fashion or wantonness of theory may have accidentally brought into practice. As talent for debate in such assemblies gives more influence and authority than professional talent, it becomes the first object of ambition; and to *talk* well upon painting, rather than *paint* well, the means of honourable distinction. Thus the business of conducting the institution counteracts its purposes, and the arts of management take place of those professional arts, which it was alone meant to facilitate and promote. Divisions and factions arise; and every member, in proportion as he is neglected and despised as an artist, endeavours to make himself conspicuous and important as a partizan; in which the very want of professional employment to divert his attention generally enables him to succeed.[104]

In order to be able to practise the higher branches of art, such as history painting, the artist would need a liberal education, in order to be able to entertain appropriate associations of ideas; but improving only an artist's critical skills would not enable him to produce good art.

103 *Principles of Taste*, pp. 243–4.

104 [Richard Payne Knight], Review of *The Works of James Barry, Esq. Historical Painter; with some Account of his Life and Writing*, the *Edinburgh Review*, vol. 16 (Edinburgh: 1810), pp. 293–326; p. 311.

Whatever class of art was to be engaged upon manual dexterity in the control of paint, particularly with reference to draughtsmanship, would be needed, and this should be the artist's unfailing and diligent concern. When artists lost sight of this, as Knight felt they did in academies, then they ceased to develop beyond the stage of being talented and promising 'prodigies'. Surprisingly, given Knight's own extensive travels, he did not think that the influence of Italy on artists was necessarily to be recommended. It depended upon what they did with themselves when they were there. If, as they tended to, they went and admired the Sistine Chapel and the Raphaels in the Vatican and came away thinking that they should be doing similar things, then the influence was entirely bad. What Knight said they should be doing was learning accurate draughtsmanship, which could be done by drawing from the work of ancient sculptors in Italy or elsewhere, but this should be done for the sake of improving the artist's skill, not in order to re-educate his taste. The taste should be innate, and should be developed, rather than learnt by rule and through imitation, because 'There is something, perhaps, of more prolific energy and active vigour in the acquisitions which a man makes himself, than in those which he receives from others. They have a tone and character of originality derived from Nature; and neither crampt, enfeebled, nor distorted by passing through any other vehicle than that of the mind which conceived them.'[105] This is characteristically Romantic thinking, looking to the individual's uniqueness as a stamp of authenticity and nature.

One particular defect which artists who studied in Italy tended to acquire was a belief that large paintings were best. Knight did not think so; indeed, he said, 'We are so far from agreeing' in the notion of

> the vast space of the Vatican walls or Farnese ceiling being necessary to display the talents of a Raphael or Annibal Caracci, that we are convinced that both these great artists would have displayed more talent, and deserved more reputation, had they only been employed upon easel pictures of moderate size.[106]

He argued the point physiologically:

> When the whole of a picture does not come within the field of vision, from the point of distance best adapted to show the beauties of particular expression and detail in the parts, it is too large; since its effect on the mind must necessarily be weakened by being divided, and the apt relation of the parts to each other, and to the whole, in which the merit of all composition consists, be

105 Knight, Review of *Life of Reynolds*, p. 279.

106 Knight, Review of *Works of Barry*, p. 308.

> less striking when gradually discovered, than when seen at once. That the great patriarchs of the art should have been so much employed upon such works, we much regret; not only because they might have been better employed, but because the skill and science displayed in them have given authority to false principles; and, by perverting laudable ambition from its proper objects, obstructed instead of promoting the expansion of succeeding talents.[107]

These remarks are from Knight's review of writings by the painter James Barry (1741–1806) who had studied at Rome and, according to Knight's account, been ruined by the experience. It had warped his taste so that he felt he should be painting on a heroic scale and that nothing less would do for him. Knight criticised heavily Barry's draughtsmanship, and bitterly regretted the fact that Barry's Italian experience had left him blind to the merits of superior painters. 'In Turin,' said Barry, 'I saw the royal collection of pictures; but, except a picture or two of Guido, which I did not like, all the rest are Flemish and Dutch, Rubens's, Vandyke's, Teniers's, Rembrandt's, Scalken's, &c. – they are without the pales of any church; and, though I will not condemn them, I must hold no intercourse with them.' Knight could scarcely contain himself. '*He will not condemn, but yet must hold no intercourse with them!*' he exclaimed, 'With what? With the finest specimens of the greatest masters of the art, considered abstractedly as the art of painting – that is, the art of employing colours to imitate visible objects with the greatest possible degree of skill, judgement, taste and effect.'[108] The Italian masters might have dealt with nobler themes in their paintings, but the northern painters were unsurpassed in their ability fluently to reproduce visible appearances on the canvas. In Knight's view even Reynolds's work done in Italy had not escaped the baleful influence of Michelangelo and Raphael, but in his case it recovered once he had returned home.

Benjamin Robert Haydon of course fell foul of Knight's judgement about the size appropriate to paintings, being drawn to grandiose themes and huge canvases in the same way as Barry; and his estimate of Knight is made clear in chapter 2 (see pp. 46–56). Like Barry he died miserably, there being no patrons grandiloquent enough to sustain the production of the images he was determined to provide. Sir Thomas Lawrence, more modest in his aims and more happily adapted to the culture of the picture-commissioning class, benefited from Knight's early patronage before becoming the most brilliant and fashionable portrait painter of the

107 Ibid., pp. 308–9.

108 Ibid., p. 299.

day. He had an early introduction to Knight, and made his acquaintance soon after his arrival in London, on account of Lawrence's father having been helpful to Knight in the elections at Ludlow.[109] His painting of Homer reciting his verses was commissioned by Knight in 1788, when Lawrence was only 19 years old, and it was evidently worked on with care, as it was not finished until 1790. He was later twice to paint Knight's portrait, and though they did not always agree, Lawrence did not find Knight unreasonable, at least when he met him privately.[110]

Knight took artists with him to Sicily, and then on his return employed a meticulous topographical artist, Thomas Hearne (1744–1817), to make copies for publication of the Sicilian scenes, and to record the appearance of the landscape at Downton in a series of twelve views. He also bought drawings of ruffians and banditti from John Hamilton Mortimer (1740–79), and treated him generously when he was in difficulties.[111] However, the artist whom Knight patronised most extensively and who seemed most closely to fit his idea about what an artist should be was Richard Westall (1765–1836).

The earliest documented sighting of Westall in Knight's company was in May 1796, when he was one of Knight's dinner guests,[112] but they probably met some years earlier through Thomas Lawrence, who shared a house in Soho Square, on the corner of Greek Street,[113] with Westall between 1790 and 1794. Knight praised his work highly, describing 'Mr. West's General Wolfe, [figure 6] Mr. Westall's Storm in a Harvest, and Mr. Wright's Soldier's Tent' as 'some of the most interesting and affecting pictures, that the art [of painting] has ever produced'.[114] Westall's depiction of harvesters sheltering under trees at the edge of a cornfield from a storm which could be on the point of wiping out their year's industry and ruining them, dates from 1795. It was originally a watercolour, but Knight commissioned a version in oils (figure 15).[115] It included a depiction of an elderly man with a highly irregular physiognomy, a strongly hooked nose and chin, who, like the parson's daughter, could not be called beautiful, but was interesting and agreeable enough in a picture. It seems to have been Knight's earliest purchase from Westall, and the correspondence between picturesque ideas and Westall's realisation of them in the painting shows that he was already open to Knight's influence. In the relationship between them there was a clear imbalance of power as the patronage was Knight's to dispense, therefore Westall was dependent upon Knight's holding a good opinion of him, though not cravenly so, as he had no shortage of commissions from others. Westall was always described as polite, whereas Knight was given to pontificating and he

109 Farington, *Diary*, 16 January 1794.

110 Ibid., 24 August 1805; 2 February 1808; 6 March 1810.

111 John Thomas Smith, *Nollekens and His Times* (London: 1828), p. 21.

112 Farington, *Diary*, 4 May 1796.

113 Campbell Dodgson, entry for Westall in *Dictionary of National Biography*, vol. XX, p. 1,258. In 1794 Westall moved to 54 Upper Charlotte Street, Fitzroy Square, but remained on good terms with Lawrence.

114 *Principles of Taste*, pp. 311–12. The 'Soldier's Tent' is now known as *The Dead Soldier* (1979) by Joseph Wright (1734–97).

115 In *Arrogant Connoisseur*, ed. Clarke and Penny, p. 186.

Figure 15. Richard Westall, *Harvesters in a Storm*, 1795.

published his views in writing. The consequence is that we know Knight's views on a good many subjects and Westall's on few. That there is much common ground between them where painting was concerned is not surprising, given the circumstances, as had there not been Knight would have patronised another artist. It is possible that the views we know as Knight's could have been reached by way of conversations with Westall, but on the strength of his poetry Westall was not an intellectual and seems to have been willing to turn his hand to what was asked of him, especially later in life, when he was in financial difficulties and became a prolific illustrator of books, as well as drawing tutor to the future Queen Victoria, whose portrait (as a girl) he painted.

Knight entertained Westall at Downton in August 1806,[116] and perhaps on other occasions, and they both spent at least the winter in London, but it is not clear how close they became. Knight's treatment of the artist has been described as 'almost paternal',[117] and it can confidently be said that Knight was solicitous for Westall's well-being.

116 He had returned to London and told Farington about his visit by 5 September; Farington, *Diary*, 5 September 1806.

117 Michael Clarke, 'Collecting', *Arrogant Connoisseur*, p. 107.

Knight's patronage could well be interpreted as a consequence of an infatuation with Westall at some level, but this is not to say that it led them into a romantic involvement, as each would have been inhibited by custom. Moreover, in a letter to Lord Aberdeen in 1809 (which has all the appearance of frankness), Knight seemed to say that he had not known romantic love, but spoke bluntly about finding sexual partners among the peasantry, without sentiment becoming involved in the transactions.[118] His sentimental friendships therefore may not have involved sexual acts, and the relationship with Westall may better be described as 'homosocial'.[119] Westall was younger than Knight, 41 to Knight's 55 years, and although Knight was just about the same age as his father had been when he had married, he was on the point of giving up Downton Castle and moving into Stonebrook Cottage. One can imagine Knight feeling lonely and meditative: Price was avoiding him, Townley had died, the castle had been damaged by fire and Fox was ill (he would die in September). In 1808 Westall, encouraged by Knight, published a small book of verses, *A Day in Spring*.[120] One wonders at Knight's judgement as the verses are slight, but one of them, which might have been sent to Knight as an expression of thanks for the hospitality which he had enjoyed, seems to be set at Downton, in a mythologised form.

'Once on a day, alas the day!
Love, whose every month is May,'
Discern'd me on a bank reclin'd,
With listless limbs and vacant mind.
Beside me lay my idle lyre,
Unfit for song, with loosen'd wire
. . .
Dress'd like a rustic youth he came,
Nor shew'd his form, nor told his name
. . .
'Shepherd,' he said, 'thy lyre I'll string;
'Rise, idle shepherd, rise and sing'.
Thus as he spoke, he seiz'd my lyre,
And snatch'd away the trembling wire;
And unperceiv'd, with smiling face,
He stretch'd his bow-string in its place.[121]

And so on. The poem mentions a rippling brook, an awful grove, a humble cottage, and the mighty castle in a high place, and indeed sheep, which are all to be found at Downton, and in summer it can still be as

118 Knight to Lord Aberdeen, 28 November 1809, BL (Aberdeen Papers), 43230, fol. 58. See above, p. 133.

119 G. S. Rousseau 'The Sorrows of Priapus', in *Sexual Underworlds of the Enlightenment*, ed. G. S. Rousseau and Roy Porter (Manchester University Press, 1987), pp. 101–53.

120 Farington, *Diary*, 21 April 1808, mentions the encouragement.

121 Richard Westall, *A Day in Spring and Other Poems* (London: John Murray, 1808), pp. 131–3.

sleepily enchanting as Westall described, whether or not we are visited by a rustic youth whose influence turns friendship into love, a love which seems to be regretted ('alas the day!'). It conveys something of Westall's languid arcadian mood at Downton, but stops well short of being evidence for any actual events or deeds.

Knight certainly treated Westall indulgently, and his enthusiasm for Westall's work is not immediately explicable to modern tastes (it has, indeed, been called 'a remarkable lapse of judgement')[122] but could partially be accounted for by association with an enthusiasm for his person. However, this influence should not be overestimated, as Westall was much more highly regarded in his own day than he is in ours, and Knight showed how confident he was that Westall's work would be seen as self-evidently brilliant by hanging it in the most distinguished company. When Knight moved to Soho Square he built an iron-vaulted room which acted as a museum and gallery, the iron being chosen for its fire-resistant properties, which would have been especially important to him after the fire at Downton. The most celebrated of his pictures there was, he thought, by Rembrandt, and showed a cradle scene (figure 16). On 10 February 1808, for 150 guineas, he bought another cradle scene from Westall, his 'Exposition of Moses' (figure 17), which he hung between two pictures by Old Masters 'to show that the moderns can stand with them'.[123] Some small paintings by Westall showing simple rustic figures in cottages seem to have been designed to hang alongside Knight's small seventeenth-century Dutch and Flemish pictures,[124] and there were many more purchases or commissions, most notably *The Grecian Wedding* (figure 18) commissioned in 1811 for a thousand guineas,[125] a spectacular sum, which clearly shows Knight indulging Westall, as he could certainly have had the work done by him for very much less. However, by this means Westall was enabled to spend much longer than usual working on the painting, which had been exhibited by 1814.[126] Westall had been a Royal Academician since 1794, but he seemed in Knight's view to have survived the educational system, and this commission was, as *Homer Reciting his Verses* (see figure 5) had been for Lawrence, an example of the kind of patronage which Knight said was necessary for a painter's development. 'The best encouragement . . . that can be given to an artist, more especially a young one,' he said,

> is employment adapted to his capacity and acquirements, sufficient to enable him to live comfortably, by severe toil and study, exerted in accurate and finished, rather than numerous and

122 Messmann, *Richard Payne Knight: The Twilight of Virtuosity* (The Hague: Mouton, 1974), p. 125

123 Farington, *Diary*, 11 February 1808.

124 *Arrogant Connoisseur*, ed. Clarke and Penny, p. 186.

125 Farington, *Diary*, 8 July 1811.

126 Described by Knight in 1814, as being 'in [a] late exhibition'. Knight, review of *Life of Reynolds*, p. 287.

Figure 16. School of Rembrandt, *Cradle Scene*.

extensive works – but not without it: for, in an art of such laborious and difficult attainment, the stimulants of want are no less necessary than the allurements of ambition.[127]

Knight cited the finished painting as an example of how 'rich and splendid colouring' could enhance the 'utmost purity and dignity of heroic character and composition':[128] the two could develop together, without the sensuality of the colour undermining the nobility of the composition; a rebuttal of Reynolds's views on the matter:

> Such as suppose that the great stile might happily be blended with the ornamental, the simple, grave and majestick dignity of Raffaelle could unite with the glow and bustle of a Paulo [Veronese], or Tintoret, are totally mistaken. The principles by which each are attained are so contrary to each other, that they seem, in my opinion, incompatible, and as impossible to exist

127 Knight, review of *Works of Barry*, pp. 324–5.

128 Knight, review of *Life of Reynolds*, p. 287.

Figure 17. Richard Westall, *The Exposition of Moses*, 1808.

together, as that in the mind the most sublime ideas and the lowest sensuality should at the same time be united.[129]

Westall's best work was done for Knight, and is in some ways impressive, but it is not adapted to modern taste; nor was it universally admired in its day. His aberrations can be revealing, showing not only his weaknesses but also Knight's indulgence of them. For example the saccharine *Orpheus* shows the direction in which Knight's taste moved when it lapsed (figure 19). This painting was one of a group of three, the others depicting *Flora Unveiled by Zephyrs* and *Vertumnus and Pomona,* the mythological characters of the title being surrounded by a plethora of cherubs, flowers, fruit or animals; in each case a riot of colour.[130] Knight's fondness for colour in paintings, as well as doubt about his fondness for Westall, was remarked upon by his contemporaries. In 1807 when Westall's *Flora* was exhibited, Sir George Beaumont said that he 'hoped Knight had enough of what He liked in Westall, in his picture of Flora;

129 Reynolds, *Lectures*, pp. 64–5.

130 See *Arrogant Connoisseur*, pp. 186–7. The paintings, however, were not framed as a group of three. *Flora* and *Pomona* were given matching frames, but *Orpheus* was given a larger and more ornate frame, matching *Damocles'*, and are considered as a pair below.

Figure 18. Richard Westall, *The Grecian Wedding*, 1811.

meaning the gaudiness of it';[131] and another of Farington's friends thought 'Westall very unsuccessful in his Flora painted for Mr. Knight. He has taken much pains with the flowers but had not been successful.'[132] Samuel Rogers considered Knight's enthusiasm for Westall's *Flora* to be 'an additional proof of his bad taste'.[133] The most extreme judgement against Westall was made by 'Antony Pasquin', who said that Westall's picture of *Hesiod instructing the Greeks* (exhibited at the Royal Academy in 1796) was 'such an effort, as no person, possessing taste and knowledge, can regard with satisfaction; yet it involves that trickery and finery which is so captivating to vulgar minds'.[134] But these adverse opinions were being voiced as a corrective to the great enthusiasm for Westall's work which was prevalent, and we should not suppose that Knight had altogether taken leave of his judgement in voicing such extravagant praise. It was reported that at the Royal Academy in 1793 'the artist whose work aroused most enthusiasm among the critics was Richard Westall',[135] and Walpole was particularly impressed. He thought the Hesiod 'by far one of the finest compositions ever painted in England', while the portrait of *Sappho Chanting the Hymn of Love* was 'beautiful

131 Farington, *Diary*, 8 May 1807.

132 Ibid., 19 June 1807.

133 Ibid., 6 and 8 May 1807.

134 Antony Pasquin [pseud. for John Williams], *A Critical Guide to the Royal Academy for 1796* (London: 1796), p. 24.

135 Quoted in W. T. Whitley, *Artists and Their Friends in England 1700–1799*, 2 vols. (London: Medici Society, 1928), vol. II, p. 178.

Figure 19. Richard Westall, *Orpheus,* 1811.

beyond description'.[136] When Westall (apparently at Knight's suggestion) staged a huge exhibition of his work in 1814, the list of the works' owners included a healthy proportion of nobility and royalty. George IV presented a Westall to All Souls, Langham Place, as an altarpiece, thinking that he had 'never seen anything to equal' Westall's drawings.[137] Disraeli, Lord Byron and (despite the remark quoted above) Samuel Rogers owned Westalls,[138] as did J. M. W. Turner (*The Descent from the Cross*) and Sir John Soane (*Milton Composing Paradise Lost*). Despite the waspish remarks of some of his friends, Knight's taste for Westall's paintings would not have seemed eccentric at the time, however inexplicable modern commentators have found it. William Hazlitt's remarks are helpful here, because they are fair-minded and attest to the vogue for Westall, without sharing the enthusiasm. 'Of this artist's works we always wish to speak well from our respect to the public taste,' he said, 'and are only sorry that we cannot, consistently with any regard to our own.'[139]

Hazlitt saw Westall's works, or at least those of them exhibited at the British Institution, as following Sir Joshua Reynolds's teachings in avoiding the accidental appearances of particular circumstances in favour of a more elevated generalised image. If we were to follow this line of thought then we would have to accept that

> the argument of a poem [must be] better than the poem itself, – or the catalogue of a picture than the original work. Where shall we stop in the easy down-hill pass of effeminate, unmeaning insipidity? There is one circumstance, to be sure, to recommend the system here objected to, which is, that he who proposes this ideal perfection to himself, can hardly fail to succeed in it. An artist who paints on the infallible principle of not imitating nature, in representing the meeting of Telemachus and Calypso, will not find it difficult to confound all difference of sex or passion, and in pourtraying the form of Mentor, will leave out every distinctive mark of age or wisdom. In representing a Grecian marriage he will refine on his favourite principles till it will be possible to transpose the features of the bridegroom and the bride without the least violation of propriety; all the women will be like the men; and all like one another, all equally young, blooming, smiling, elegant, and insipid. On Sir Joshua's theory of the *beau ideal*, Mr. Westall's pictures are perhaps the best that ever were painted, and on any other theory, the worst; for they exhibit an absolute negation of all expression, character, and discrimination of form and colour.[140]

136 *The Yale Edition of Horace Walpole's Correspondence*, ed. W. S. Lewis, 48 vols. (New Haven: Yale University Press, 1937–83), vol. XV, p. 404, Sir Horace Walpole to Miss Berry, 25 June 1796.

137 Richard J. Westall, 'The Westall Brothers', *Turner Studies*, vol. 4, no. 1 (London: Tate Gallery, 1984), pp. 24 and 37, n. 81.

138 Ibid., p. 29, quoting Westall's Pall Mall exhibition catalogue of 1814.

139 William Hazlitt, 'British Institution (1814)', in *Complete Works*, ed. P. P. Howe, 21 vols. (London: Dent, 1930–4), vol. XVIII, p. 15; the remarks concern *Christ in the Temple* and *Margaret of Anjou* by R. Westall, RA.

140 'On the Ideal (1815)', in ibid., pp. 77–8.

In Westall's work, Hazlitt tells us, we find 'the refined essence and volatilized spirit of art,' and 'we constantly meet with the same classical purity and undeviating simplicity of idea – one sweet smile, one heightened bloom diffused over all'.[141] 'Are we,' he asked, 'to confound the difference of sex in a sort of hermaphrodite softness, as Mr. Westall, Angelica Kauffman, and others have done in their effeminate performances?'[142] The reason for the hostility to Westall was not however on account of the quality of his work but, as his contemporary the artist James Northcote remarked, because he had 'run away with nearly all the popularity of [his] time'.[143] 'I confess,' replied Hazlitt, 'I never liked W[estall]. It was one of the errors of my youth that I did not think him equal to Raphael and Rubens united, as Payne Knight contended.'[144]

When Knight said that the painters of his age could outdo the performances of the ancient Greeks, Westall was the painter he had in mind. The commissioned paintings were intended to hang alongside Old Masters to show that new art, of the sort being encouraged by the British Institution, could hold its own in their company. Knight thought that they were entirely successful, and the qualities which Westall's paintings have were the qualities which he valued: richly coloured, well drafted and affecting, and the right size to be seen comfortably in a domestic gallery, set alongside the best work of the past, which they neither overwhelmed with bombast, nor were shown up in that company as inferior work.

Orpheus

In 1811, when Knight commissioned *The Grecian Wedding*, he bought two other paintings with Greek subjects from Westall for 150 guineas each. These were *Orpheus* and *The Sword of Damocles*, both paintings with political subjects; they were given matching frames. *Damocles* has been discussed in chapter 2, and was particularly admired by Thomas Hope (1769–1831) an enthusiastic connoisseur of the Grecian taste, who wrote *Household Furniture and Interior Decoration* (1807) and *Costume of the Ancients* (1809). He commissioned a larger version of *Damocles* for himself, to join his other Westalls, also of Greek subjects.[145]

Orpheus who, along with Pomona and Flora, was shown against the background of ancient forest, is portrayed as a melancholy youth with a soulful expression, playing a lyre and charming an implausible array of animals with his music: an eagle, a lion, a tiger, a leopard, a stork, a stag, some squirrels, snakes and brightly coloured birds are gathered around him, harmoniously. The scene anticipated one of Westall's most widely

141 'Mr. West's Picture of Christ Rejected (1815)', in ibid., p. 29.

142 Hazlitt, 'On the Elgin Marbles (1822)' in ibid., p. 152.

143 Northcote (in conversation with Hazlitt), published 1830. In Hazlitt, ibid., vol. XI, p. 284.

144 Ibid.

145 David Watkin, *Thomas Hope 1769–1831 and the Neoclassical Idea* (London: John Murray, 1968), pp. 43–4.

circulated images, *The Peaceable Kingdom of the Branch* (1813) which illustrated Isaiah, 11:6, and became well known in America in Edward Hicks's many versions of it.[146] While Flora's flowers and Pomona's fruit link them straightforwardly with their rural settings, Orpheus was important in Knight's mythology, and invites further interpretation. Explaining the origin of the mystical rites of ancient Greece, Knight said that 'General tradition has attributed the introduction of the mystic religion into Greece, to Orpheus, a Thracian; who, if he ever lived at all, lived probably about the same time with Melampus, or a little earlier.'[147] Orpheus was, therefore, at least symbolically the founder of Greek religion, and thereby of Greek civilisation, a point which can be clarified by turning, as Knight might have done, to Giambattista Vico, who said that 'Orpheus, the founder of Greece, with his lyre or cord or force ... met his death at the hands of the Bacchantes (the infuriated plebs), who broke his lyre to pieces (the lyre being the law).'[148] Orpheus taming the animals is seen symbolically as a representation of him civilising the barbarian population by binding them in a social contract with the cord of the law, which is stretched and turned into a musical instrument whose harmonies have a similar civilising effect.[149] Here we find music becoming political, the harmonious relations between sounds finding a counterpart in the unexpectedly sociable relation between the wild beasts: both music and politics are arts of relationship.[150] It is a recurrence of Knight's refrain of making connections between the benefits of wild nature and the benefits of civil society, and bears some comparison with the origin of language, according to Rousseau, who supposed that people expressed their emotions through song before they developed conventional speech;[151] Orpheus plays his lute and conjures an ideal society into being. Orpheus was hung, along with Flora and Pomona, in the gallery at Soho Square: tokens of the countryside which show the forest as the haunt of pagan gods, embodying natural principles. Flora shows the sensual beauty of nature in her body and in the richly coloured flowers; Pomona, surrounded by fruit, is emblematic of fertility, and is shown in an amorous dalliance with Vertumnus; while Orpheus brings harmony and civilisation to the scene. Despite a few sarcastic remarks, these paintings were tremendously admired, and it would not have been Knight but his acquaintance Sir George Beaumont who would have seemed eccentric in his taste for commissioning paintings of natural scenery from John Constable: paintings which may have had a good deal of the natural about them, but none of the high-minded associations of ideas which were to be expected in the highest class of art.

146 Eleanore Price Mather, 'A Quaker Icon: The Inner Kingdom of Edward Hicks', *The Art Quarterly* (London: Spring/Summer 1973), pp. 84–99.

147 Richard Payne Knight, *The Symbolical Language of Ancient Art and Mythology. An Inquiry*, ed. Alexander Wilder (New York: 1876), p. 11, sections 21–2.

148 Giambattista Vico, *Scienza nuova,* 3rd edn (Naples: 1744), paragraph 659; trans. Thomas Goddard Bergin and Max Harold Fisch, *The New Science of Giambattista Vico* (Ithaca and London: Cornell University Press, 1968), p. 248.

149 Bergin and Fisch, *Vico,* pp. 227–8.

150 Gilles Deleuze, *Périclès et Verdi: la philosophie de François Châtelet* (Paris: Editions de Minuit, 1988).

151 Jean-Jacques Rousseau, *Essai sur l'origine des langues*, ed. Charles Porset (Paris: Nizet, 1970), p. 139: 'les prémiérs discours furent les prémiérs chansons' [accents *sic*]; 'the first discourses were the first songs'.

Taste and morals

To say that tastes would always change was not the same as saying that there could be no good and bad taste; Knight made that very clear. The standard against which taste was to be judged was always that of nature, and bad taste was always marked out by its lack of connection with natural impulses and desires. When the outward form of something, whether it be the form of a building, or a form of behaviour, was copied, and adopted as an outward form, then it was to be condemned as affectation. Firm rules could only ever regulate outward forms, and were therefore operating in the realm of affectation and artificiality, never in the realm of natural feeling and genuine inspiration. Instead of setting up a system of rules against which to judge the merit of surfaces, what Knight proposed was the cultivation of an ideal sensibility, which would mean that the genuine man would simply not be able to act in ways which could ever be adjudged to be in poor taste; the state of his mind would be such that, as in ancient Greece, every idea and every gesture would be graceful and harmonious. This was a condition which was reached by artists after long practice in their art, so that their marks on the canvas might appear light and spontaneous, but they would, if produced by a master's hand, be perfectly judged. The manual skill was developed to such an extent that the hand could accomplish exactly what the mind directed it to do; the mind being in contact both with the realm of inspired ideas and able to direct the hand of the accomplished craftsman.

Knight took artistic production of this sort as an illustration of unaffectedly 'natural' behaviour, and applied it elsewhere. For example, in speaking of the 'untutored but uncorrupted feelings' of Homer's contemporaries, he said that 'men, in the early stages of society, when manners are the general substitute for laws, are scrupulously observant of whatever custom or public opinion has established as a criterion of politeness or good breeding; the principles of which . . . are the same in all ages and all countries, howsoever the modes of showing them may vary'.[152] The principles on which good manners operated, in Knight's thinking, were not excruciatingly correct, but were 'easy and negligent' without ever descending into the 'coarse and slovenly';[153] and the ancient Greeks in particular were singled out because

> civilisation had just arrived to that state, in which the manners of men are polished, but yet natural; and consequently their attitudes and gestures expressive and emphatical, without ever being coarse

152 *Principles of Taste*, p. 316.

153 Ibid., p. 292.

> or violent. All the more noble and amiable sentiments of the mind were indicated by the correspondent expressions of the body; while those of a degrading and unsocial cast were suppressed and concealed.[154]

It followed that the people who were possessed of the most perfect taste might never give the matter any thought at all, and be surprised to find that others might suppose them to be obeying rules of any kind. It was the authenticity of the action which made a work genuine, whether it was a work of high art or humble craftsmanship; affectation could only take a hold when the link between the impulse and its expression was broken.

The person who genuinely feels and acts, therefore, is like an artist who should have a consummate command of the means of expression which the local society makes available, and should use it to express such authentic feelings and insights as are noble and contribute to social well-being, whilst keeping any impulses of a degrading and unsocial cast suppressed and concealed.

The moral character of Knight's subjects was therefore brought under scrutiny in terms of the practical politics of living in a society. Degrading acts would be those which would bring one into disrepute, and, if performed, they were to be kept secret; whereas unsocial acts would be bad for others, and they were to be avoided altogether. It was portrayed as a purely practical matter, with no metaphysical dimension, and seems to be regulated by a fear of shame rather than by any sort of guilt or fear of supernatural retribution, following pagan rather than Christian practice. For Knight it did not seem to be important whether or not artists, novelists or poets depicted heroes who were worthy of emulation. The characters in art would not significantly influence the ends of the actions of people in life, though they might possibly influence the forms of those actions. The important thing was to make the characters plausible and genuine, and therefore affecting. In fact Knight, in the example he gave, consistently argued against models of conventional morality in fiction, arguing on aesthetic rather than moral grounds, and in favour of good Epicurean characters.

Generally speaking, Knight's view of religion in the *Principles of Taste* seems, for him, unusually moderate. There is even a description of a Roman Catholic Mass which at first would seem to be quite rapturously appreciative. Its context, however, encourages the association of ideas in the way that one would expect as characteristic of Knight: it comes between pagan worship and theatrical exhibitions, darkness, vacuity and

154 Ibid., p. 214.

silence.[155] The general tenor of Knight's remarks remained here as elsewhere anti-Christian and pro-Epicurean.

Knight and Burke would have found themselves on opposite sides of the House when Fox's bill to abolish the Church of England came before Parliament. It is clear from the *Enquiry* that Burke had a tendency towards piety, even though his aesthetic system was informed by Lucretian atoms. For example, he drew an illustration from Lucretius to show the effect of the perception of power, in this case the power of nature:

> These things brought me a certain etherial pleasure
> And yet an awe that nature so by your insight
> Should be laid bare and every cover withdrawn.[156]

Burke found this passage from the would-be destroyer of all religion unsatisfactory, and remarked that 'the scripture alone can supply ideas answerable to the majesty of the subject'; and he gave a quotation from the Bible to make his point.[157] Knight was not given to biblical quotation, but in his *Principles of Taste* he quoted a very similar passage from Virgil, saying by way of introduction that 'there is no image in poetry wrought up with more true sublimity and grandeur than the following of Virgil'.[158]

> From the night of thunderclouds Jupiter hurls bolts.
> His right hand gleams. The earth shakes far and wide
> As the blow falls. Wild animals run for cover,
> Men feel their hearts grow small with terror.[159]

This was for Knight an unusually generous assessment of Virgil, and at first it is difficult to see why he should accord this particular passage such exceptional praise, since its image of the heavenly father is easily adapted to Christian ends. Reading a little further, however, we find that Knight was not making an uncharacteristic judgement at all; Virgil had evidently stolen his thunder, because: 'the principle [*sic*] features of this sublime image are taken from one, at least as sublime, and far more spirited, of Lucretius':

> whose mind is not contracted with fear
> Because of the gods? whose body is not afraid
> When the parched earth trembles under the lightning
> And the great rumblings of thunder cross the sky?
> Are not whole nations terrified? Kings may be proud
> But they stoop quickly enough when they fear the gods,

155 Ibid., p. 369.

156 Lucretius, *De Rerum Natura,* bk. III, lines 28–30; ed. Cyril Bailey, p. 302, trans. C. H. Sisson, p. 77.

157 *Sublime and Beautiful*, p. 69.

158 *Principles of Taste*, p. 371.

159 Virgil, *Georgics*, bk. I, lines 329–32; trans. Robert Wells (Manchester: Carcanet, 1982), pp. 38–9.

> Afraid that for some one crime or even a word
> The day of reckoning may suddenly have come.[160]

Knight's opinion of Virgil was distinctly muted, unusually so, as it was normal in Knight's day to think Virgil the finest of the Latin poets. Knight found him an unconvincing representative of pagan culture because he had proved to be so acceptable to the Christians. This was on account of a celebrated passage in the fourth *Eclogue* which the early church wrongly understood to be predicting the birth of Christ, and which led to him being accepted virtually as an honorary Christian himself (and as a consequence guided Dante through the *Inferno*).[161] Knight reserved his most extravagant praise for Homer, whom he believed shared his religious beliefs; but Virgil by contrast was timid, bound by established rules and no more than 'the most modest of [Homer's] imitators'.[162] In Knight's estimate a mark of Virgil's limitation was that he did not dare to break rules. Knight supposed that had the *Odyssey* not been composed before Aristotle formulated his rules for poetic composition (in the *Poetics*), that the rules which Virgil followed would not have made allowance for descriptions of scenery. It was fortunate, then, that Aristotle's rules were drawn up after the *Odyssey* had been written, because Virgil's timidity when faced with established rules would have meant that we would have lost the best parts of Virgil. The fortunate circumstance that the *Odyssey* preceded Aristotle

> allowed the taste and genius of Virgil to display itself in those various changes of scenery, which he was so eminently qualified to describe and embellish; but which, nevertheless, the natural cautiousness and modesty of his disposition would not have allowed him to introduce contrary to the established rules of criticism; though those rules were nothing more than general deductions from the particular, and, in many instances, accidental practice of such poets as himself.[163]

Knight considered Virgil to be a model for corrupt taste, saying that he acted 'in defiance of truth and nature' so as to please 'courtly critics' who would have found him 'judicious and elegant'.[164] In portraying Laocoon he 'debased the character, and robbed it of all its sublimity and grandeur of expression'.[165] Whereas Knight thought Homer the greatest Greek poet, in Latin, despite the fact that in the world at large Virgil's reputation certainly stood higher, Knight gave the palm to Lucretius, whose 'style and manner I consider as perfect'.[166]

160 Lucretius, *De Rerum Natura,* bk. V, lines 1,217–25; Bailey, p. 496; Sisson, pp. 169–70.

161 Virgil, *Eclogue* IV, lines 4–10.

162 *Principles of Taste*, p. 286. See also pp. 276, 289, 318, 340, 434.

163 Ibid., p. 275.

164 Ibid., p. 289.

165 Ibid., p. 340.

166 *Civil Society*, p. v; *Principles of Taste*, p. 371.

To take another example: John Milton, was, and remains, one of the most admired, revered and conspicuously pious of Christian poets. Knight acknowledged his greatness, but found him confused, obscure and inverted.[167] Where Milton advanced a case for non-rhyming poetry, following classical models, Knight (who generally adopted classical models when he could) found rhyming couplets more idiomatic in English verse.[168] No one would rank Knight with Milton, but that did not prevent him from criticising Milton (who fared badly when Knight compared him with Homer) whom he defended in one point only: his characterisation of Satan. 'Milton has been censured for making the devil too amiable and interesting a character,' he said, 'but Milton could not have done otherwise, without destroying all the interest of his poem . . . Throughout the poem, the infernal excite more interest than the celestial personages, because their passions and affections are more violent and energetic.'[169] Knight was acting as the devil's advocate, saying that even if Satan in fact were not attractive it would be necessary for Milton, on technical literary grounds, so to present him: the attractiveness of Satan would be required because of the effects of rhetoric, not because evil itself were attractive.

In fact we can go further than this and show that Knight was very clearly on the same side as Milton's Satan if we take Milton's Comus as one of Satan's avatars. In Milton's *Maske Presented at Ludlow Castle* (1634) the pursuit of pleasure was portrayed as evil and a cult of chastity was promoted. The language used for this drew on the ancient rivalry between the Epicureans and the Stoics. Milton's sympathies were entirely Stoic, and he sought to reconcile the Stoic virtues of chastity and abstinence with Christianity. (That it led him into heresy need not detain us here.)[170] The argument of the masque answers that of Ben Jonson's *Pleasure Reconcild to Vertue* (1618) which portrayed Comus, the god of revelry, as its hero. Jonson's Comus was introduced to the stage riding in triumph to the song

> Roome, roome, make roome for ye bouncing belly,
> first father of Sauce, & deuiser of gelly.[171]

Milton portrayed Comus in this way, as a character of wanton appetite, and the indulgence of his followers turned them into animals. Milton not only made Comus present his own (Comus') views in the language of Epicurus *as misunderstood by the Stoics*, he also made Comus denigrate those who favoured chastity by calling them Stoics:

167 *Principles of Taste*, pp. 125, 405.

168 Ibid., p. 50.

169 Ibid., pp. 363–4.

170 George N. Conklin, *Biblical Criticism and Heresy in Milton* (New York: King's Crown Press, 1949).

171 Ben Jonson, *Pleasure Reconcild to Vertue* (1618), lines 13–14.

retaliatory preface and extensive footnotes, which greatly increased the gardening content of the book.

At first *The Landscape* seems to be a typically bucolic piece of gentlemanly versification, modelled on Virgil's *Georgics*, which celebrated the life of the countryside of Augustan Rome;[3] but that it was in fact something much more explosive is shown by Horace Walpole's reaction, in denouncing

> this pretended and ill-warranted dictator to all taste, who Jacobinically would level the purity of gardens, would as Malignantly as Tom Paine or Priestley guillotine Mr Brown . . . I did ardently wish you had overturned and expelled out of the gardens this new Priapus, who is only fit to be erected in the Palais de l'Egalité.[4]

Walpole was writing to the Reverend William Mason (1725–97), author of *The English Garden* (published in four books, 1771–81), an extraordinarily long poem in blank verse which suffered from all the faults which Knight ascribed to Virgil, being the very model of polished and polite verse-making. What is clear is that Walpole was reacting as much to the political outlook expressed in the poem as he was to any proposals which Knight made about garden design. This was perfectly understandable, as the poem had a good deal of political content, although Walpole reacted to it without understanding it with great precision. The point to be made here is that if we look to *The Landscape* solely for the sake of its advice about landscape design, then we miss an important part of its content. Indeed, the poem was structured in such a way that if we see it as being principally about landscape design then it will seem to digress to such a degree as to lose sight of its object. Knight divided *The Landscape* into three 'books', not one of which ends by drawing conclusions about landscape design. If, on the other hand, we read it as a poem about politics and religion, which uses landscape as a source of metaphor, then it makes much more coherent sense.

In the lyrical descriptions of landscape Knight's model was Virgil's *Georgics*, particularly in the translation by John Dryden; but the polish of conventionally tasteful versification is abandoned in lengthy passages of *The Landscape* in favour of a heightened emotional range which is used at the end of each of the three books to make a resonant conclusion, which in books I and II is a point about the evil of superstition, while in book III it is about the state of France and the mass bloodshed there. These are important passages which have no parallel in Virgil, but seem

3 Jay Appleton, 'Richard Payne Knight & "The Georgics"', *The Picturesque*, no. 5 (Hereford: The Picturesque Society, 1993), pp. 1–8.

4 *The Yale Edition of Horace Walpole's Correspondence*, ed. W. S. Lewis, 48 vols. (New Haven: Yale University Press, 1937–83), vol. XXIX, p. 338, Walpole to William Mason, 22 March 1796.

to be drawn from the example of Lucretius. For example, when Knight gave his reason for adopting a poetic form to convey his ideas, he explained that the listener would be charmed by the verse into hearing unpalatable truths. He made use of a specifically Lucretian image:

> For as the doctor's wig, and pomp of face,
> Announce his knowledge of the patient's case,
> And harmless drugs, roll'd in a gilded pill,
> From fancy get the power to cure or kill;
> So our poor palliatives may chance to acquire
> Some fame or favour from their gay attire.
> (I, 11–16)[5]

Lucretius gave as his reason for presenting a treatise on physics and philosophy in verse the fact that poetry was more palatable than dry dissertation. He compared his philosophy with bitter medicine, and his poetry with honey smeared round the rim of the bowl from which the medicine was being quaffed. The patient, encouraged by the sweetness at the rim, would be able to drink the bitter contents which would effect a cure.[6] Knight's position is more extreme because he suggests that the medicine itself has no power at all, the whole of its effectiveness is brought about through its presentation. This image is less successful than the original because it tends to undermine the distinction which Knight himself made between the 'plain truth' which is made charming by being put into a 'flowery dress'. The strategy of the poem however is made explicit: the reader should be beguiled into reading but come away having learnt serious lessons.

When we see that in each book Knight moved *away* from the conventional lyrical treatment of pleasant rural themes *to* the difficult and contentious matter concerned with politics and religion, then we can see him adopting a deliberately Lucretian means of conveying his serious messages.

Superstition and religion

The conclusions of books I and II of *The Landscape* both attacked Christian superstition. Book I's ending described a monk:

> The monk, secluded by his early vow,
> The blessings of retreat can never know
> (I, 391–2)

5 Richard Payne Knight, *The Landscape, A Didactic Poem* (London: 1794) references to 2nd edn (London: 1795).

6 Lucretius, *De Rerum Natura*, bk. IV, lines 11–25, ed. Cyril Bailey (Oxford: Clarendon Press, 1947), pp. 362–3.

Dark rankling passions on his temper prey,
And drive each finer sentiment away;
Breed foul desires; and in his heart foment
The secret germs of lurking discontent.
(I, 395–8)

The continuation to this passage alluded to book II of *De Rerum Natura*, which Dryden translated (using exactly the same metre and rhyme-scheme as he did in his translation of the *Georgics*) in which Lucretius argued that it was not necessary to over-indulge in order to find happiness; little more than good health was needed:

For Nature wisely stints our appetite,
And craves no more than undisturb'd delight;
Which minds unmix'd with cares, and fears, obtain;
A Soul serene, a body void of pain.
So little this corporeal frame requires;
So bounded are our natural desires,
That wanting all, and setting pain aside,
With bare privation, sence is satisfi'd

. . .

These bugbears of the mind, this inward Hell,
No rayes of outward sunshine can dispel;
But nature and right reason, must display
Their beames abroad, and bring the darksome soul to day.[7]

Knight, finding himself arguing against Christian self-denial rather than pagan self-indulgence, put a contrary case tending towards the same moderate position

In vain to distant Hope, Religion calls,
When dark vacuity his mind appalls: –
Without, a dismal sameness reigns around;
Within, a dreary void is only found.
  From mere privation nothing can proceed,
Nor can the mind digest unless it feed;
For understanding, like the body, grows
From food, from exercise, and due repose.
(I, 403–10)

The conclusion to book II of *The Landscape* drew on similar material. Knight inveighed against religion in a highly Lucretian manner,

7 Lucretius, bk. II, trans. Dryden, lines 20–7, 64–7, in *The Works of John Dryden*, ed. H. T. Swedenberg, E. Miner and V. A. Dearing (Berkeley: University of California Press, 1969), vol. III, pp. 44–66.

comparing Christians with Vandals, and finds the Vandals to have been relatively harmless. [Roman culture sleeps . . .]

> But short its slumbers: – see fierce bigots rise!
> Faith in their mouths, and fury in their eyes;
> With mystic spells and charms encompass'd round,
> And creeds obscure, to puzzle and confound;
> While boding prophets in hoarse note foretell
> The ripen'd vengeance of wide-gaping hell;
> And pledging round the chalice of their ire,
> Scatter the terrors of eternal fire.
>   Touch'd by their breath, meek Science melts away;
> Art drooping sinks, and moulders to decay;
> Books blaze in piles, and statues shiver'd fall,
> And one dark cloud of ruin covers all.
>   Much injured Vandals, and long slander'd Huns!
> How are you wrong'd by your too thankless sons;
> Of others' actions you sustain the blame,
> And suffer for your darling goddess Fame:
> For her, or plunder, your bold myriads fought,
> Nor deign'd on art to cast one transient thought;
> But with cold smiles of cold contempt pass'd by
> Whate'er was fashion'd but to please the eye;
> The works of Glycon and Apelles view'd
> Merely as blocks of stone, or planks of wood.
>   But gloomy Bigotry, with prying eye,
> Saw lurking fiends in every figure lie,
> And damned heresy's prolific root
> Grow strong in learning, and from science shoot;
> Whence fired with vengeance and fierce zeal, it rose
> To quench all lights that dared its own oppose.
> (II, 406–33)

And so on. From this point Knight moved on to praise developments in painting from Titian to Claude, the 'one perfection, e'en to Greece unknown' (line 439), and then concluded with a passage which again drew on Lucretius, this time relishing the calm of retreat from the world. Dryden translated Lucretius as saying

> If Golden Sconces hang not on the Walls,
> To light the costly Suppers and the Balls;

If the proud Palace shines not with the state
Of burnish'd Bowls, and of reflected Plate,
If well tun'd Harps, nor the more pleasing sound
Of voices, from the vaulted roofs rebound,
Yet on the grass beneath a poplar shade
By the cool stream, our careless limbs are lay'd,
With cheaper pleasures innocently blest,
When the warm Spring with gawdy flow'rs is drest.
Nor will the rageing Feavours fire abate,
With Golden Canopies and Beds of State:

. . .

these useless toyes of every kind
As little can relieve the lab'ring mind.[8]

Knight echoed this, some fifteen years before he actually moved into Stonebrook Cottage.

Vain is the pomp of wealth its splendid halls,
And vaulted roofs sustain'd by marble walls. –
In beds of state pale sorrow often sighs,
Nor gets relief from gilded canopies:
But arts can still new recreation find,
To soothe the troubles of the afflicted mind.
(II, 458–63)

The anti-Christian sentiments expressed in *The Landscape* can be startling, but its pagan imagery is hardly noticeable not because it is absent, but because it was such a commonplace of eighteenth-century poetry. In Knight's work it is not mere convention, but is the means by which we can see his deepest feelings about landscape design. Knight's thinking can be seen to be close to that of the Romanticism of Wordsworth and Coleridge, but he did not share their taste for motionless lakes and mountainous scenery.[9] He worshipped nature, but did so through a range of symbols which now seem too lightweight to be convincing: nymphs and dryads sound too whimsical to do serious duties, but they haunted the dark places in *The Landscape*; and Knight's practical project in gardening seems to have been to restore their presence in the natural landscape. 'The Nymphs', he said, were the 'emanations of the female productive power of the universe'; and 'Upon the monuments of ancient art, they are usually represented with Fauns and Satyrs, frequently in attitudes very lascivious and indecent; but in the Homeric

8 Ibid., lines 28–39, 44–5.

9 'Oft have I heard the silly traveller boast / The grandeur of Ontario's endless coast; / Where, far as he could dart his wandering eye, / He nought but boundless water could descry. / With equal reason Keswick's favour'd pool / Is made the theme of every wondering fool'; *The Landscape*, bk. II, lines 128–33.

Figure 20. Claude Gellée, called le Lorrain, *Landscape with Narcissus and Echo*, 1644.

times, they seem to have been considered as guardian spirits or local deities of the springs, the valleys, and the mountains.'[10] Nymphs are to be found, for example, in Claude's evocative *Landscape with Narcissus and Echo* (figure 20), a painting which Knight greatly admired.[11] One nymph is apparently asleep by a pool, failing to attract Narcissus' attention, the others, one of them Echo herself, lurking in the bushes, hardly visible, merging harmoniously into the scene.[12] Knight favoured gardens which were rampant and unchecked, preferring even old formal gardens to those designed by Brown because, although the old gardens had worked against nature, Knight argued (as we shall see) that so did Brown's, and his unnatural designs were far more extensive:

> kings of yew, and goddesses of lead,
> Could never far their baneful influence spread;
> Coop'd in the garden's safe and narrow bounds,

10 *The Symbolical Language of Ancient Art and Mythology. An Inquiry*, ed. Alexander Wilder (New York: 1876), p. 141, section 189.

11 Farington, *Diary*, 17 April 1803.

12 Jean Badoin, *Recueil d'Emblemes divers avec des discours moraux, philosophiques et politiques*

They never dared invade the open grounds;
Where still the roving ox, or browsing deer,
From such prim despots kept the country clear;
While uncorrupted still, on every side,
The ancient forest rose in savage pride;
And in its native dignity display'd
Each hanging wood and ever verdant glade;
Where every shaggy shrub and spreading tree
Proclaim'd the seat of native liberty
(II, 29–40)

But ah! how different is the formal lump
Which the improver plants, and calls a clump!
Break, break, ye nymphs, the fence that guards it round!
With browsing cattle, all its forms confound!
(II, 51–4)

This is nature worship in the guise of politics. The old order, of kings and goddesses, was despotic but not very powerful, and the ancient forest retained its sacred mystery. By contrast Brown's gardens threatened the forest, and therefore natural forces (personified as nymphs) were justified in rising up to overthrow the despotic oppression, just as the people of America and France had overthrown despotic rule. Knight seditiously roused trees and nymphs to break down fences and to 'spread promiscuous o'er the plains' (III, 2). The voluptuous fertile landscape was to be settled by ancient gods, and Knight's imagery was both religious and erotic.

Ye woodland nymphs, arise,
And ope your secret haunts to mortal eyes!
Let my unhallow'd steps your seats invade,
And penetrate your undiscover'd shade.
(III, 9–12)

Knight's landscape was imbued with religious feeling, albeit of a pagan turn. A good Christian who gave full weight to Knight's religious symbolism would have thought it demonic.

(Paris: 1638), n. 50, pp. 216–17, saw Narcissus 'less as an example of self-love and more as the type of man who retires to the country to lead a solitary life, so failing to work for the public benefit or to become involved in political affairs'. Humphrey Wine, *Claude: the Poetic Landscape* (London: National Gallery, 1994), p. 43.

Politics

We can see, perhaps, in the above-quoted lines an allusion to Alexander Pope's *Windsor-Forest* (1713):

Thy Forests, *Windsor*! and thy green Retreats,
At once the Monarch's and the Muse's Seats,
Invite my Lays. Be present Sylvan Maids!
Unlock your Springs, and open all your Shades.[13]

Pope's movement between forest scenery and politics is in some ways similar to Knight's, linking the prosperity which is visible in the landscape to the fact that 'a Stuart reigns', but the general tone is different because Pope rhapsodised the current state of affairs, whereas Knight was understandably more troubled and critical. The political imagery in Knight's discussion of the landscape was pervasive and persistent, and the basic argument about landscape advanced in the poem was that the countryside should be well governed. Formality was condemned as a form of despotism; this seems to have become a habit of mind, as casual remarks about the management of his estate show him thinking in these terms. For example, describing the cultivation and sale of trees for timber, he remarked that he had been 'prescribing for sale some of the Oppressors, as well as transplanting considerable Numbers of the oppressed into situations where they may have Room to thrive'.[14] In discussing different types of tree in book III of *The Landscape,* Knight offers us the fir's 'unsocial shade' (line 59), the oak as 'King of the woods' (line 63) with the most extended treatment given to the cedar

lord supreme o'er all this formal race, [of trees]
The cedar claims pre-eminence of place;
Like some great eastern king, it stands alone,
Nor lets the ignoble crowd approach its throne,
Spreads out its haughty boughs that scorn to bend,
And bids its shade o'er spacious fields extend;
While, in the compass of its wide domain,
Heaven sheds its soft prolific showers in vain:
Secure and shelter'd, every subject lies;
But, robb'd of moisture, sickens, droops, and dies.
O image apt of man's despotic power!
Which guards and shelters only to devour,
Lifts high in air the splendours of its head,
And bids its radiance o'er the nations spread;
While round its feet in silent anguish lie
Hunger, despair and meagre misery.
(III, 111–26)

13 Alexander Pope, *Windsor-Forest*, in *The Poems of Alexander Pope,* ed. John Butt (London: Methuen, 1963), p. 195, lines 1–4.

14 Knight to Lord Aberdeen, 2 November 1817, British Library, Additional MSS (Aberdeen Papers), 43230 fol. 314.

The elm, meanwhile, was in an uncongenial climate here, 'abandon'd and forlorn', 'divorced' from the vine (line 138). Lists of trees with particular attributes are to be found in both classical and modern literature, in Virgil and Ovid, Chaucer and Spenser,[15] but Knight's trees tended to the political. In *The Landscape* they are described both as botanical specimens and as symbols, and seem to be most closely related to the plants which open Thomas Gray's *Alliance of Education and Government.*[16] Knight was explicitly to draw on the later parts of this 'exquisite'[17] fragment in *The Progress of Civil Society,* but its opening seems to have informed the tree symbolism in *The Landscape*:

> As sickly plants betray a niggard earth,
> Whose barren bosom starves her generous birth,
> Nor genial warmth, nor genial juice retains,
> Their roots to feed, and fill their verdant veins:
> And as in climes, where winter holds his reign,
> The soil, though fertile, will not teem in vain,
> Forbids her gems to swell, her shades to rise,
> Nor trusts her blossoms to the churlish skies:
> So draw mankind in vain the vital airs,
> Unform'd, unfriended, by those kindly cares,
> That health and vigour to the soul impart.[18]

Gray was writing about education and government and was drawing on plants for imagery, whereas Knight was supposedly writing about plants and drawing on politics for imagery. Gray's plants could in fact be transplanted into Knight's poem and be completely at home: neither imagery, nor rhyme, nor metre would be disrupted in the move. Gray's influence in *The Landscape* was less extensive than that of Virgil and Lucretius, but it can be found with certainty in a passage which deals with a colony of rooks, which owed much to Gray's celebrated *Elegy Written in a Country Church Yard.* The passage about rooks begins:

> Then homeward as I sauntering move along,
> The nightingale begins his evening song;
> Chanting a requiem to departed light,
> That smooths the raven down of sable night.
> (I, 345–8)

This compares closely with the opening of Gray's *Elegy*, which compressed into the same small compass ideas of a mourned dying day, slow

15 See, for example, the notes to Chaucer's 'The Parliament of Fowls', lines 176–89, *The Works of Geoffrey Chaucer*, ed. F. N. Robinson (New York: Houghton Mifflin, 2nd edn 1957), pp. 793–4; and Edmund Spenser, *The Faerie Queene*, bk. I, canto I, stanzas 8 and 9, ed. A. C. Hamilton (New York: Longman, 1977), p. 32.

16 All quotations from Gray from *The Poems of Gray, Collins and Goldsmith*, ed. Roger Lonsdale (New York: Longman, 1969).

17 *The Progress of Civil Society: A Didactic Poem* (London: 1796), p. 65n.

18 Gray, *The Alliance of Education and Government*, lines 1–11.

walking, darkness and the countryside, as well as sharing the same scheme of rhyme and rhythm:

> The curfew tolls the knell of parting day,
> The lowing herd wind slowly o'er the lea,
> The plowman homeward plods his weary way,
> And leaves the world to darkness and to me.[19]

Gray went on to reflect that the simple folk who lay buried in the churchyard had much the same feelings and abilities as did the grander people who moved in the world of politics and great affairs. The difference between the two groups of people – one prominent, the other obscure – was that the great developed and realised their abilities, whereas the obscure did not. So we find Gray imagining that in the churchyard there lay 'some mute inglorious Milton' or a 'Cromwell guiltless of his country's blood' (lines 51–2). The forces of good and evil were at work among these simple folk in exactly the same way as they were at work in the highest levels of society, but, lacking power, their influence was not felt by others. Knight's strategy was the same, but he found his microcosm in a colony of rooks rather than in the rustic life of villagers:

> e'en these little politicians know
> The ills, that from a social compact flow
> (I, 363–4)

> Here, while I view their feuds of petty strife,
> I learn, unfelt, the ills of public life;
> And see well acted, in their little state,
> All that ambition aims at in the great.
> (I, 373–6)[20]

Knight finished Book III of *The Landscape,* his major conclusion, with a vision of peace and prosperity, not a restatement of a theme clearly related to the landscape, but a peace which remained when 'tides of blood' withdrew.

> What heart so savage, but must now deplore
> The tides of blood that flow on Gallia's shore!
> What eye, but drops the unavailing tear
> On the mild monarch's melancholy bier!
> Who weeps not o'er the damp and dreary cell,
> Where fallen majesty is doom'd to dwell;
> Where waning beauty, in the dungeon's gloom,

19 Thomas Gray, *Elegy*, lines 1–4.

20 However if we return to lines 345–8 quoted above (p. 199), we can also find Miltonic overtones. Line 348 alludes to *Comus*: [the wings / of silence] / 'At every fall smoothing the raven down / Of darkness'. 'A Masque Presented at Ludlow Castle', lines 248–51, in *The Shorter Poems of John Milton*, ed. John Carey (New York: Longman, 1968), p. 189.

The nightingale in Knight seems also to have been borrowed from Milton, this time from *Il Penseroso*, where a similarly reflective melancholy is evoked, in connection with oaks, woods and shaved lawn:

> Philomel will deign a song,
> In her sweetest, saddest plight,
> Smoothing the rugged brow of night,
> While Cynthia checks her dragon yoke
> Gently o'er the accustomed oak;
> Sweet bird that shunn'st the noise of folly,
> Most musical, most melancholy!
> Thee chauntress oft the woods among,
> I woo to hear thy even-song;
> And missing thee, I walk unseen . . .

'Il Penseroso', lines 56–65, in *Milton*, ed. Carey, p. 142. 'Cynthia' is the moon.

Feels, yet alive, the horrors of the tomb!
Of all her former state no traces left,
But e'en of nature's common needs bereft;
Through days of solitude, and nights of woe,
Which, hopeless still, in long succession flow,
She counts the moments, till the rabble's hate
Shall drag their victim to her welcome fate!
(III, 401–14)

This passage, already substantial, was annotated with several pages of observations on the French Revolution (a footnote to III, 405) which was still current news. Lucretius concluded *De Rerum Natura* with a description of calamity and death in the plague of Athens, an example which Knight seems to have used as a formula, since all three of his major poems concluded with political turmoil and blood. Knight's radical side is shown in the closing lines, where, having described some of the horror and terror, he concluded by supposing that it might, in the long term, be a good thing:

Yet, from these horrors, future times may see
Just order spring, and genuine liberty:
Split into many states the power that hurl'd,
So oft, destruction o'er the affrighted world;
May hence ambition's wasteful folly cease,
And cultivate the happy arts of peace.
(III, 415–20)

If the major influences on the poetry were Virgil and Lucretius, and to a lesser extent Gray, another influence, which perhaps led Knight to adopt a poetic form for the presentation of his discourse, was Erasmus Darwin's very Lucretian poem *The Botanic Garden*, published in two parts in 1789 and 1791. *The Botanic Garden* is about botanic gardens in about the same measure that *The Landscape* is about landscapes. Knight would have found Darwin's poem most congenial in its range of sympathies, and indeed Knight and Darwin were satirised in parallel in *The Anti-Jacobin*.[21] Darwin gave as his reason for adopting a verse form exactly the same Lucretian reason as Knight: 'to inlist Imagination under the banner of Science'.[22] Darwin's poem had enjoyed very recent success, and it probably gave Knight the immediate prompt to cast his ideas into verse. There are strong similarities between Knight's and Darwin's verse, and in the end the influence might not all have been

21 Again, though, it was *The Progress of Civil Society* rather than *The Landscape* which was the object of the satire. See Frank J. Messmann, *Richard Payne Knight: The Twilight of Virtuosity* (The Hague: Monton, 1974), pp. 88–93.

22 *The Botanic Garden*, vol. I [vol. I was published after vol. II], *The Economy of Vegetation* (London: 1792), p. v. See p. 157.

acting in one direction. Darwin knew of Thomas Andrew Knight's work as a botanist,[23] and it seems likely that he knew also *The Progress of Civil Society*, to judge by the parallels in the following passages. Knight began by wondering

> Whether primordial motion sprang to life
> From the wild war of elemental strife;
> In central chains, the mass inert confined
> And sublimated matter into mind?[24]

While Darwin, in 1803, wrote:

> Say, MUSE! how rose from elemental strife
> Organic forms, and kindled into life;
> How Love and Sympathy with potent charm
> Warm the cold heart, the lifted hand disarm;
> Allure with pleasures, and alarm with pains,
> And bind Society in golden chains.[25]

Whilst some of the similarity can be accounted for by the fact that both Darwin and Knight owed their ideas in these passages to Lucretius, nevertheless there is perhaps a sufficient degree of correspondence for us to suspect that here is a rare example of Knight's poetic skills being valued and emulated. This does not amount to an argument that Darwin strongly influenced the content of *The Landscape*, but shows a strong affinity between the two in their ideas about the use of verse, and that Darwin's example was one which Knight could have adopted as a fellow-traveller.

The Landscape was not wholly concerned with promoting the idea of the picturesque, but moves in each of its three books away from its declared material towards more serious and contentious matters. The fact that the same move is made three times over shows that it is not simply a matter of Knight being unable to control his material and needing to resort to continual digression, though that is certainly how it seems if we suppose that *The Landscape* is exclusively concerned with garden design. When read for the sake of Knight's views on the picturesque the structure of the poem is highly unsatisfactory and has led to him being judged as a worse poet than he was. The verse in *The Landscape* which dealt with the landscape itself was derived from Virgil's treatment of rustic life in the *Georgics*, but it was incorporated into a larger design which worked partly by using features of the landscape as imagery with which to make political and religious points, rather

23 *The Temple of Nature* (London: 1803), p. 57.

24 *Civil Society*, bk. I, lines 1–4.

25 *The Temple of Nature*, canto I, lines 3–8.

after the manner of Thomas Gray, and partly by openly discussing political and religious concerns in the conclusion to all three books. The material moves from the honeyed, to the veiled and then to the openly medicinal. This larger design follows both the advice of Lucretius to sweeten harsh teachings, and his example of the formulation of what is said therein.

Knight thought that Virgil was a great poet, but within polite limits. He was suitable as a model for the parts of *The Landscape*, concerned with the promulgation of good taste in the design of gardens, but when it came to the heightened language necessary to the uncomfortable themes of religious bigotry and political bloodshed, Knight turned to Lucretius.

The picturesque

Nevertheless Knight's poem was, *inter alia,* about the picturesque, and it has been best remembered in that context, largely on account of the two illustrations by Thomas Hearne which succinctly summarised the new aesthetic around which argument revolved (figures 21 and 22). The first shows a house set in grounds which were supposed to have been laid out in the manner of 'Capability' Brown: a vaguely Palladian house with mown lawns around it, with paths, a stream and the undulating ground all following the smoothly regulated 'line of beauty' which Hogarth had adopted as his talisman. This was contrasted with an exuberantly shaggy scene exhibiting picturesque beauty, in which the same elements are shown in a vigorously overgrown state, and highly irregular forms, bursting with life, have overtaken the tidiness and control of the former scene. As we have seen, Knight thought it mistaken to think that objects could be picturesque in themselves, though they could be seen as picturesque. He stressed the Italian derivation from '*pittoresco*': 'According to the idiom of the Italian language, by which the meaning of all adjectives ending in *esco* is precisely ascertained, *pittoresco* must mean, *after the manner of painters*'.[26] Knight found this initial meaning exact, and more useful than its later corruption into English, the particular manner of painters being the adoption of the principle of 'massing' (see pp. 147–9), explained in the last chapter. *Pittoresco,* or the French *pittoresque*, refers to painters rather than paintings, and therefore implies a connection with painters' methods rather than with finished pictures.

> The English word refers to the performance, and the objects most suited to it: the Italian and French words have a reference to the

26 *An Analytical Inquiry Into the Principles of Taste*, 4th edn (London: 1808), p. 148.

Figure 21. Thomas Hearne, *A landscape in the manner of 'Capability' Brown*. Plate from *The Landscape*, 1794.

> turn of mind common to painters; who, from the constant habit of examining all the peculiar effects and combinations, as well as the general appearance of nature, are struck with numberless circumstances, even where they are incapable of being represented, to which an unpractised eye pays little or no attention.[27]

Indeed, Knight never used 'picturesque' as a noun, only ever as an adjective: never 'the picturesque', but always 'picturesque landscape', 'picturesque improvement', 'picturesque circumstances' and so on. According to this definition it is not the irregularity of form or variety of hues and shades as such which makes for picturesque beauty, but the manner of representation, which cannot be intrinsic in the object itself. This manner of representation is sometimes brought to mind in natural scenes, for example when a haze or mist evenly mutes the colours in a scene, and the scene might then be said to have picturesque beauty

27 Uvedale Price, *Essays on the Picturesque*, 3 vols. (London: 1810), vol. I, pp. 44–5.

Figure 22. Thomas Hearne, *A picturesque landscape.* Plate from *The Landscape,* 1794.

because it has brought to mind the manner of painters. But Knight thought it absurd to suggest that the objects in the scene might *be* picturesque, independent of their circumstances. He was proposing not that landscape designers should aim to copy paintings, but that they should learn to think like painters, to see scenery appreciatively with a painterly eye and, where practical improvements were possible, to remove blemishes and eyesores, glaring disharmonies of colour, awkward abruptness and so on. The point of studying paintings was to learn to see the world through artists' eyes. The idea of studying paintings is to bring about a change in the observer so as to make possible an aesthetic response to scenes which would otherwise seem to lie beyond aesthetic appreciation and therefore to stand in need of improvement. Where Price sought to teach how scenery could be made intrinsically picturesque, Knight tried to teach how to look in the manner of painters.

In addition to painting, Knight's taste in landscape had two major influences. One was the scenery of the Herefordshire countryside in which he had grown up, a very productive and fertile part of the country. The second was the English tradition of landscape design, about which Horace Walpole had written in his important essay, *History of the Modern Taste in Gardening* (1771), a tradition which had a precursor in the descriptions which Milton had given of the Garden of Eden in *Paradise Lost*,[28] but which really began, he said, with William Kent (1685–1748), who designed gardens by means of associating them with paintings. Kent was

> painter enough to taste the charms of landscape, bold and opinionative enough to dare and to dictate, and born with a genius to strike out a great system from the twilight of imperfect essays. He leaped the fence and saw that all nature was a garden . . . Thus the pencil of his imagination bestowed all the arts of landscape on all the scenes he handled. The great principles on which he worked were perspective, and light and shade. Groups of trees broke too uniform or too extensive a lawn; evergreens and woods were opposed to the glare of the champain . . . Thus selecting favourite objects, and veiling deformities by screens of plantation, sometimes allowing the rudest waste to add its foil to the richest theatre, he realised the compositions of the greatest masters in painting.[29]

This was enough to ensure Kent a place in Knight's esteem: he too thought it essential to consult the work of painters in designing gardens, but even earlier, 200 years before the publication of Knight's poem, Francis Bacon had recommended that at least part of a garden ought to be perfectly natural. 'I should wish it to be framed,' he said,

> as much as may be, to a natural wildness. Trees I would have none in it; but some thickets, made only of sweet-briar and honeysuckle, and some wild vine amongst; and the ground set with violets, strawberries, and primroses . . . I like also little heaps, in the nature of mole-hills (such as there are in wild heaths), to be set, some with wild thyme; some with pinks; some with germander, that gives a good flower to the eye; some with periwinkle; some with violets; some with strawberries; some with cowslips; some with daisies; some with red roses; some with lillium convallium; some with sweet-williams red; some with bear's foot; and the like low flowers, being withal sweet and sightly. Part of which heaps to be

28 Milton, *Paradise Lost*, canto IV, lines 131–263.

29 Horace Walpole, 'History of the Modern Taste in Gardening' (1771/80) in *The Genius of the Place*, ed. John Dixon Hunt and Peter Willis (London: Paul Elek, 1975), pp. 313–14.

> with standards of little bushes pricked upon their top, and part without. The standards to be roses; juniper; holly; berberries (but here and there, because of the smell of their blossom); red currans [*sic*]; gooseberries; rosemary; bays; sweet-briar; and such like. But these standards to be kept with cutting, that they grow not out of course.[30]

This is what Bacon meant when he spoke of a 'completely natural' garden. It would not have looked completely natural to Knight. Nevertheless Bacon did belong to the tradition of English gardening in making this appeal to nature: Walpole's friend, the Reverend William Mason (1724–97), for example, who supported Brown's ideas, traced the genealogy of Brown's designs back through to Bacon's suggestions. He called 'Bacon the prophet and Milton the herald of true taste in gardening'.[31] Mason evidently could not bring himself to praise so unguardedly the work of Sir William Temple (1628–99). He suggested that if the reader compared Lord Bacon's description of a princely garden

> with that which Sir William Temple has given us in his essay, intituled *The Garden of Epicurus*, written in a subsequent age, he will find the superiority of the former very apparent; for though both of them are much obscured by the false taste of the times in which they were written, yet the vigour of Lord Bacon's genius breaks frequently through the cloud, and gives us a very clear display of what the real merit of Gardening would be when its true principles were ascertained.[32]

It is worth noting that Mason clearly believed that the rules of gardening (which he thought had been perfected by Brown) were laws of nature as firmly fixed as Newton's laws of motion: not stylistic innovations which had been invented, but underlying principles which had been discovered. Both Bacon's and Temple's accounts of the garden were concerned with relatively formal designs, but each gave a hint of 'that adorned natural wildness which we now deem the essence of the art'.[33] In *The Gardens of Epicurus* Temple said (and Mason quoted him in part) that

> Among us, the beauty of building and planting is placed chiefly in some certain proportions, symmetries, or uniformities; our walks and our trees ranged so, as to answer one to another, and at exact distances. The Chinese scorn this way of planting, and say that a boy that can tell an hundred, may plant walks of trees in straight

30 Bacon, 'Of Gardens', in *Essays,* ed. J. Spedding, R. L. Ellis and D. B. Heath (London: Dent, 1915), pp.141–2.

31 William Mason, *The English Garden*, bk. I, n. 8, line 493, in *The Works of William Mason M.A.*, 4 vols. (London: Cadell and Davies, 1811), vol. I, p. 394.

32 Ibid., p. 390.

33 Ibid., p. 394.

> lines, and over against one another, and to what length and extent he pleases. But their greatest reach of the imagination, is imployed in contriving figures, where the beauty shall be great, and strike the eye, but without any order or disposition of the parts, that shall be commonly or easily observed . . . And whoever observes the work upon the best Indian gowns, or the painting upon their best screens or purcellans, will find their beauty is all of this kind, without order. But I should hardly advise any of these attempts in the figure of gardens among us; they are adventures of too hard achievement for any common hands; and though there may be more honour if they succeed well, yet there is more dishonour if they fail, and 'tis twenty to one they will.[34]

Mason was unimpressed by this, though in fact it is the clearest indication of a starting-point for the type of gardening which he endorsed. It found a more responsive reception with Sir Nikolaus Pevsner, who thought it 'one of the most amazing [passages] in the English language', crediting it with starting 'a train of thought and visual conceptions which were to dominate first England and then the rest of the world for two centuries. It is the first suggestion ever of a beauty fundamentally different from the formal, a beauty of irregularity and fancy.'[35]

Temple had been a friend of Walter Charleton and a disciple of Epicurus.[36] So pious a man as the Reverend William Mason would have had little sympathy for Temple's character, but he could accept at face value the conventional piety which Bacon displayed in public, and this seems to have led him to play down the importance of Temple's suggestions. For Mason the true principles of garden design were those which had been practised by Capability Brown, the epitaph on whose tombstone Mason composed, praising him not only as a genius but also as a virtuous 'Christian, Husband, Father, Friend!'[37] Knight, of course, might have shaped this tradition differently, and the representative of the true taste in Brown's generation would have been someone who worked in a much more associative way, for example William Shenstone (1714–63) who not only made himself a famously accomplished garden (The Leasowes, in Worcestershire) but was also a friend of Knight's cousin, Edward Knight of Wolverley. Shenstone died when Richard Payne Knight was only13 years old, and given his uneducated state at that time it is unlikely that they met; but it does seem likely that Shenstone's influence was felt, as it could have been both through his writings and through

34 William Temple, *Upon the Gardens of Epicurus: or, Of Gardening, in the Year 1685* (1692) in *Genius of the Place*, ed. Hunt and Willis, p. 99.

35 Nikolaus Pevsner, 'The Genesis of the Picturesque', *Studies in Art, Architecture and Design*, 2 vols. (London: Thames and Hudson, 1968), vol. I, p. 82.

36 Clara Marburg, *Sir William Temple: a Seventeenth-Century 'Libertin'* (New Haven: Yale University Press, 1932).

37 William Mason, *Epitaph: On Lancelot Brown, Esq.*, in *Works*, vol. I, p. 143.

Edward's mediation. Shenstone was well respected as a poet in his day, though his poems, like Knight's, have not worn well; and he gave aphoristic advice on garden design. He lived poetically and beyond his modest means at his *ferme ornée*, which would have been more productive of material comfort had it been less decorative. Shenstone's means were much more modest than Knight's, but he was certainly often in agreement with his advice. For example, Shenstone in one of his maxims said that 'Art should never be allowed to set a foot in the province of nature, otherwise than clandestinely and by night. Whenever she is allowed to appear here, and men begin to compromise the difference – Night, gothicism, confusion and absolute chaos are come again.'[38] This mixing of art and nature was what Knight had singled out as Brown's great crime: he claimed to show nature in an idealised state, but in fact he left behind him evidence of his own intervention. In Knight's conception of the garden there was a place for art, but it should either be clearly recognised as artifice, as might be the case near the house, for example, or else the artifice should be completely concealed: there was no room for compromise or confusion. Art and nature, however, might happily be found side by side, for example in the 'ivy'd balustrade',[39] where the associations were at their most pleasant when nature seemed to be regaining control.

Both Shenstone and Knight placed a particularly high value on the ability of objects in the garden to prompt pleasant trains of thought, doubtless because they were both men of letters and poets and had particularly well-stocked minds. 'An able gardener,' said Shenstone, 'should be able to avail himself of objects, perhaps not very striking; if they serve to connect ideas, that convey reflexions of the pleasing kind.'[40] The weakness of a garden which relies on objects which are not in themselves very striking is that it will have little effect on an observer whose mind is not similarly stocked with appropriate ideas. Such a garden, therefore, can have only limited appeal, though in an age when all educated men shared a common culture, the appeal could be fairly widespread among the visitors Shenstone would be likely to have had. Nevertheless, in Shenstone's case the principle of the association of ideas seems to have been particularly highly developed: he planted fragments of verse in the garden at strategic points, to help the ideas flow. Although Knight made strong associations between literature and the garden he did not go so far as to introduce it into his garden in so literal a fashion. Whatever the pleasing and poetical associations The Leasowes may have had for their designer, they did not strike Thomas Jefferson when he made a visit in 1786, and made notes, saying

38 William Shenstone, *Unconnected Thoughts on Landscape Gardening* (1764) in *Genius of the Place*, ed. Hunt and Willis, pp. 289 ff.

39 Ibid., p. 293.

40 Ibid., p. 290.

> the waters small. this is not even an ornamented farm. it is only a grazing farm with a path round it. here & there a seat of board, rarely anything better. architecture has contributed nothing. the obelisk is of brick. Shenstone had but 300.£ a year, & ruined himself by what he did to this farm. it is said that he died of the heart-aches which his debts occasioned him. the part next the road is of red earth; that on the further part grey. the 1st and 2d cascades are beautiful . . . the walk through the woods is umbrageous and pleasing . . . many of the inscriptions are lost.[41]

Jefferson's designs for his own garden at Monticello suggests that he would have found Brown's landscapes more to his tastes. While Shenstone and Knight were in accord about many things, their agreement was not complete. For example, Knight thought that hedges were sometimes an asset in a landscape,[42] whereas Shenstone thought that they were universally bad.[43] Shenstone felt that they disclosed the presence of art in the province of nature, but Knight was happy to grant the products of rural industry the status of 'honorary nature' and did not criticise the scenic effect of useful landscapes, or useful elements within a landscape.[44] The 'accidental' character of the countryside should always be the starting-point for the scene, which should be developed with the minimum of physical change. By 'accidental' character he meant

> that which every cultivated country derives from the style of husbandry, building, and planting of its inhabitants. Where that originally given is very grand and fine, the less of any other is preserved the better; and the neglected style of forest scenery is preferable to all others: but before the improver ventures to take accidental or artificial character away, he should take care to have some other to put in its place; the usual substitute of an overgrown piece of pasture dotted with clumps, and surrounded by a broad hedge-row of trees having absolutely none. Scarcely any parts of our island are capable of affording the compositions of Salvator Rosa, Claude and the Poussins; and only the most picturesque parts those of Rysdael, Berhem, and Pynaker; but those of Hobbima, Waterloe, and Adrian Vandervelde (which have also their beauties) are to be obtained everywhere. Pastures with cattle, horses or sheep grazing in them, and enriched with good trees, will always afford picturesque compositions; and inclosures of arable are never completely ugly, unless when lying in fallow, which, I believe, is very generally disused in the present state of husbandry.[45]

41 *Memorandums Made on a Tour to Some of the Gardens in England* (1786), in *Genius of the Place*, p. 336.

42 *The Landscape*, pp. 41n., 45n.

43 *Genius of the Place*, p. 295.

44 *The Landscape*, p. 44n.

45 Ibid., pp. 44–5nn.

Knight here was proposing that the scenery should not all be adapted to an ideal state such as Claude depicted, and to which his own garden quite readily adapted, but the lower-status genre scenes could also be used as models by those blessed with less exceptional scenery.[46] For example Hobbema's *Wooded Scene with Cottage* (now in the National Gallery, London) could be used as a model to make a picturesque association of ideas with a modest dwelling, and can be compared with Stonebrook Cottage. For Knight, agricultural scenes were charged with the resonances of Georgic poetry which celebrated the life of the countryside at work, so the association of ideas was pleasant enough,[47] and he held against the pleasure grounds made by Brown the fact that they lacked utility. (On scenic grounds, he would have objected to the modern 'set aside', but Price might have favoured its shagginess.) Part of the sub-text to the type of improvement suggested by Knight and Price was the fact that it was possible for an estate cultivated in a picturesque manner to be at the same time an object of taste and a profitable concern. Timber could be grown for profit and enjoyed for its scenic effect.[48] Knight and Shenstone were united in the most important principle in the composition of scenery; as Shenstone said, 'Landskip should contain variety enough to form a picture upon canvas; and this is no bad text, as I think the landskip painter is the gardiner's best designer.'[49] Knight made the point that there are many possible models for the landscape: he did not instruct everybody to expect to be able to live in ancient forest which might have come from a Claude or a Salvator Rosa, though he himself did manage it at Downton. Knight's advice in this respect was practical: the character of the place was to be preserved and enhanced, not mechanically 'improved' in the direction of a single ideal of beauty which might in some circumstances be difficult or impossible to attain. The adaptations should of course be such that the 'hand of art' was not apparent; the landscape should ideally seem neglected, and the picturesque scene a happy accident. It was not necessary that the examples afforded by paintings should be very closely followed, only that the principles of painterly composition should be applied to the objects from which the scene was composed; and those objects should be found naturally in the place to be improved. For example, Knight mentions the principle whereby a picture is divided into 'foreground', 'middle-distance' and 'background'; and also the principle that the tints of pigment should be 'mixed and blended' into a general harmony. When applied to a house and grounds the result, in Knight's verse, ran:

46 On the status of different types of landscape see John Barrell, 'The Public Prospect and the Private View: the Politics of Taste in Eighteenth-Century Britain', *The Birth of Pandora and the Division of Knowledge* (London: Macmillan, 1992), pp. 41–62.

47 Herefordshire was particularly associated with eighteenth-century Georgic poetry; John Barrell, *The Dark Side of the Landscape* (Cambridge University Press, 1980), p. 173, n. 99.

48 Stephen Daniels and Charles Watkins, 'Picturesque Landscaping and Estate Management: Uvedale Price and Nathaniel Kent at Foxley', in *The Politics of the Picturesque*, ed. Stephen Copley and Peter Garside (Cambridge University Press, 1994), pp. 13–41.

49 *Genius of the Place*, p. 291.

Well mix'd and blended in the scene, you shew
The stately mansion rising to the view.
But mix'd and blended, ever let it be
A mere component part of what you see.
For if in solitary pride it stand,
'Tis but a lump, encumbering the land,
A load of inert matter, cold and dead,
The excrescence of the lawns that round it spread.
   Component parts in all the eye requires:
One formal mass for ever palls and tires.
To make the Landscape grateful to the sight,
Three points of distance always should unite.[50]

In *The Landscape* Knight set out his reasoning for giving paintings prominence in his theory of landscape design, in terms which he would develop further in his *Inquiry into the Principles of Taste:*

For nought but light and colour can the eye,
But through the medium of the mind descry;[51]

Paintings eliminated all but visual effects and made their appeal solely to the eye, but in a real garden there were other charms, because

   in nature oft the wandering eye
Roams to the distant fields, and skirts the sky,
Where curiosity its look invites,
And space, not beauty, spreads out its delights;
Yet in the picture all illusions cease,
And only nature's genuine beauties please;[52]

It is not at all clear why Knight should have thought that visual pleasure was the only pleasure legitimate in a garden, nor why he should think that all illusions cease in a picture. The other pleasures here seem to be dismissed out of hand as 'delusions'. For Price the term 'beauty' was rooted in the visual sense, but Knight argued against the restriction of its application only to objects of vision.[53] It would have been understandable that Price might have insisted that visual beauties were the only ones to be genuine, but not Knight; and here it is the 'delights' of space, rather than its 'beauties' which are being dismissed as spurious distractions. This seems perfectly extraordinary and is a needless inconsistency in Knight's thought. According to Knight one of the reasons for Brown's failure as a garden designer was that he was 'ignorant of painting and

50 *The Landscape*, bk. I, lines 217–28.

51 Ibid., lines 263–4.

52 Ibid., lines 247–52.

53 Knight, *Principles of Taste*, p. 9.

incapable of judging picturesque effects';[54] and it would seem here that Knight was prepared to elevate paintings, or nature seen through paintings, even above nature itself as the appropriate standard against which to make a judgement of landscape garden. Knight resolved this contradiction, after a fashion, by endeavouring to reassure us that 'in general, art and nature love the same'[55], but he saw the need to defend his questionable position, introducing a seven-page footnote into the second edition of the poem. In it he used the expression 'picturesque beauty' to designate purely visual beauty, 'because painting, by imitating the visible qualities only, discriminates it from the objects of other senses with which it may be combined', and which could overpower it in the case, for example, of a disgusting object, which nevertheless was full of interesting colour-combinations.[56] This is a second definition of 'picturesque': beauty after the manner of painters here being beauty which made its appeal, as paintings did, only to the sense of vision.

Picturesque beauty was purely visual beauty, and any other pleasures which a garden might offer, such as space, or the pleasant perfumes of plants, were not picturesque and had nothing to do with landscapes. As such they were irrelevant so far as the design of landscape gardens was concerned, and Knight said that if 'an improver of grounds chooses to reject this criterion, and to consider picturesque beauty as not belonging to his profession', then he had no quarrel with him, 'the objects of our pursuit being entirely different'. All he asked was that 'if he takes any *professional title*, it may be one really descriptive of his profession, such as that of *walk maker, shrub planter, turf cleaner,* or *rural perfumer*; for if landscapes are not what he means to produce, that of *landscape gardener* is one not only of *no mean*, but of *no true pretension*'.[57] This passage was directed against Repton, who took issue with Knight's prescriptions, and did indeed call himself a landscape gardener. It is in the term 'landscape' that Knight's argument finds its force, because to look at a garden *as* a landscape one must, of course, be familiar with paintings, and it was in so far as Brown's 'improvements' were to be considered as landscapes that his ignorance of painting handicapped him.

The case against Brown

Brown, in his ignorance of pictures, was charged with adopting a formula for the production of landscape, and applying it wherever he went in the name of making the scene look natural, but ideal. One way of obscuring the fact that man had intervened in the landscape was to avoid the use of

54 Knight, *The Landscape*, p. 43n.

55 Ibid., line 270.

56 Ibid., p. 22n.

57 Ibid., p. 23.

geometric figures, such as were usual in the grand gardens of the French châteaux and Italian villas. Knight more or less approved of that, but disapproved of the fact that Brown altogether avoided straight lines for paths, even when a straight line would have been most convenient, and the line in which a path would most 'naturally' have developed; and he further disapproved of the fact that Brown tended to adopt a serpentine curve, very like Hogarth's 'line of beauty' for any lines which might appear in the landscape. The constant use of this figure marked out the countryside in which it occurred as artificial, in as clear a way as any geometric figure would have done. The particular forms of Brown's system were different from those of the old-fashioned and the continental gardeners, but they were no less artificial, and bound by rule. This argument was presented in various insulting terms.

> Curse on the pedant jargon that defines
> Beauty's unbounded forms to given lines!
> (I, 79–80)

> Nature in all rejects the pedant's chain;
> Which binding beauty in its waving line,
> Destroys the charm it vainly would define;
> For nature, still irregular and free,
> Acts not by lines, but general sympathy.
> (I, 140–4)

This 'systematic' gardening was an affront to the goddess Nature, and drove away the sacred spirits with which Knight could feel the natural landscape to be populated.

> See yon fantastic band,
> With charts, pedometers, and rules in hand,
> Advance triumphant, and alike lay waste
> The forms of nature, and the works of taste!
> To improve, adorn, and polish, they profess;
> But shave the goddess, whom they come to dress;
> Level each broken bank and shaggy bound,
> And fashion all to one unvaried round;
> One even round, that ever gently flows,
> Nor forms abrupt, nor broken colours knows;
> But wrapt all o'er in everlasting green,
> Makes one dull, vapid, smooth, unvaried scene.
> (I, 275–86)

Hence, hence! thou haggard fiend, however call'd,
Thin meagre genius of the bare and bald;
Thy spade and mattock here at length lay down
And follow to the tomb thy favourite Brown;
Thy favourite Brown, whose innovating hand
First dealt thy curses o'er this fertile land;
First taught the walk in formal spires to move,
And from their haunts the secret Dryads drove;
(I, 297–304)

The areas of open ground, covered with mown grass, were the basis of Brown's garden designs, bringing the green expanses of the open countryside right up to the walls of the house itself, apparently uninterrupted by walls, fences or hedges (though a ha-ha might invisibly be separating grazing animals from the mansion). The open space would, according to Knight, be surrounded by a belt of trees, the idea of which was to suggest that the open space was a clearing in a vast forest, an idea of which Knight would have approved, had it worked. His objection stemmed from the fact that the practical effect was, he said, quite different: the belt of trees did not in fact call an ancient forest to mind, because it was too narrow to do that. What it did very effectively was to mark out the boundary of the estate, thereby impressing visitors; and so Knight facetiously said that

> Mr Brown, though ignorant of painting, and incapable of judging of picturesque effects, was a man of sense and observation, and had studied mankind attentively: he therefore knew that when a large sum of money had been expended in inclosing, levelling, and dressing (or rather undressing) a very extensive desmesne, the proprietor would not dislike to have the great extent of his supposed improvements so distinctly marked, that all who came within sight of his place might form just notions of his taste and magnificence: for this purpose the belt is admirably contrived; and, if so intended, does honour to the sagacity and ingenuity of the inventor.[58]

Knight suggested that the same instinct could be gratified with less wasteful extravagance by hanging up a map of the estate at the porter's gatehouse. After the 'belt' and the open space, the third principal element in Brown's landscape was the 'clump' of trees arranged in a supposedly informal group, which would be disposed about the

58 Ibid., p. 43n.

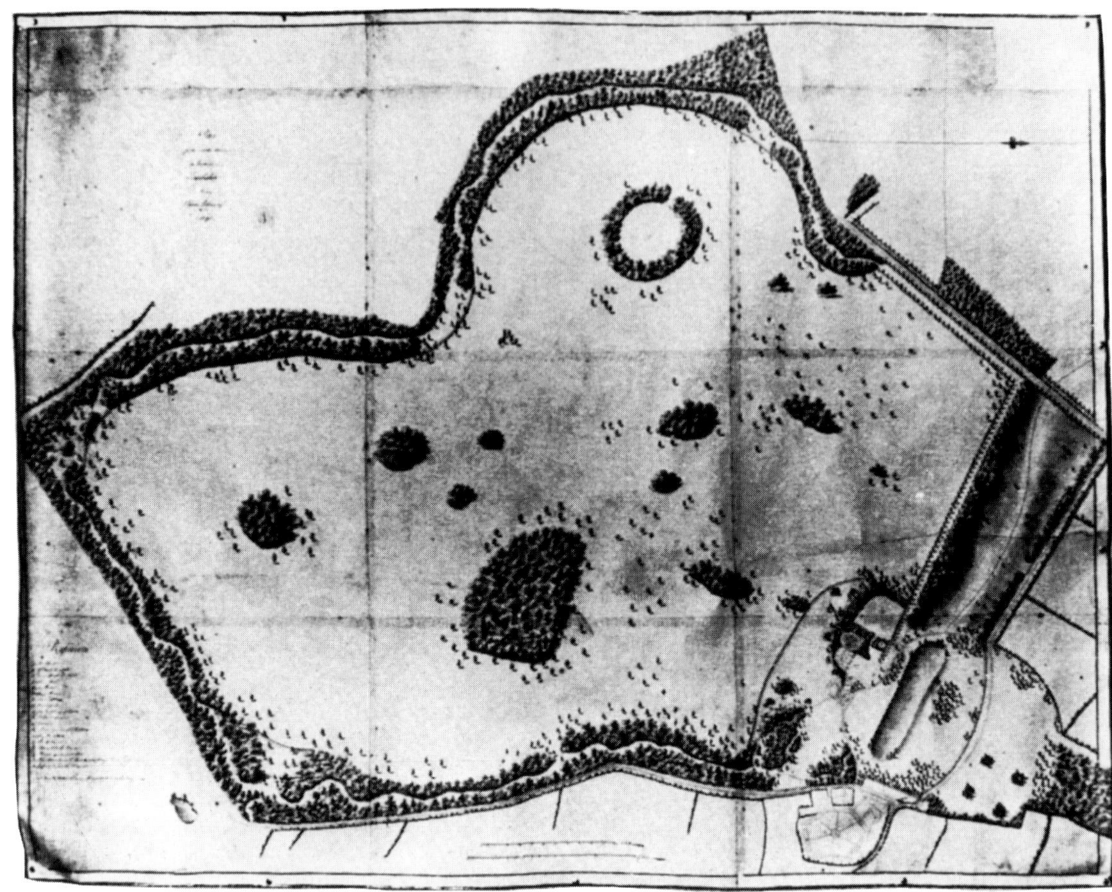

Figure 23. Plan of Lancelot Brown's layout for Brocklesby, 1771. Lord Yarborough.

continuous lawn so as to give some variety, and to break up the wide expanses, though not enough to satisfy Knight. These 'clumps' were not large enough to have deeply shaded areas within them, and did not have the effect of forest scenery, in which the spirits of nature might live.

This description of course undervalues Brown's achievements, but it must be admitted that he did lay out at least some of his gardens in precisely this way. His design for Brocklesby, for example, is perfectly diagrammatic (figure 23) and some others, such as those for Ashburnham and Wimpole, are hardly less so. The design for the grounds of Lowther Castle, recently described as 'typical of the plans that Lancelot Brown was producing at the height of his career'[59] shows a slight variation on the basic pattern. Knight knew well the Brown landscape of the Cornewalls' estate, Moccas Court, but the grounds at Eywood and Berrington are more interesting in this case, because their layouts are very similar both to one another and to the formula which Knight accused Brown of adopt-

59 David Jacques, *Georgian Gardens, The Reign of Nature* (London: Batsford, 1983), p. 78.

ing. They belonged to Lord Oxford and his brother Thomas Harley: Berrington was in Herefordshire, and Eywood across the border in Wales, but both made much the same of their landscapes, with serpentine driveways, clumps and belts of trees and streams which were dammed to make lakes.

Knight's argument against the Brownian landscape was that it was mechanical, and took account neither of the genius of the particular place, nor of the means by which taste operated, which is to say by means of the operation of the association of ideas. Hogarth's theory was applied as if it would give rise to beautiful effects, but that was not the case, the theory was wrong and landscape design could not be treated as a mechanical art: it could only work by means of the association of ideas, which meant that a gardener could not be a mere nurseryman, like Brown, but would need a liberal education, in order to be able to call to mind appropriate trains of thought. Knight did not trust garden designers who did not aim to call pictures to mind. The gardens mechanically set out by Brown had become formulaic and did not have the appearance of nature, but of the Brownian system, which was as rigid and unyielding as the tyranny of the Bourbons. Furthermore, by way of a different line of argument, the gardens had the effect of ostentatiously showing off the patron's estate, and, far from being a display of artistry and taste, had become a sop to vanity and display. So Brown bound up beauty, he cramped nature's freedom and drove the dryads from the forests, and though he claimed to 'polish' and idealise the landscape, in fact what he did was to 'shave' the goddess Nature.

The defence of Brown, from various quarters

Brown had died in 1783, so the criticisms of his landscapes in Knight's poem of 1794 were not directed against him personally, but against the ideas for which he stood. Those who took offence on account of the attack, in which *The Landscape* was supported by Price's essay, were such as William Mason who had known Brown personally, and others who depended on exploiting Brown's ideas for their livelihood. Knight called this second group the 'tasteless herd of followers'[60] and the most prominent among them was Humphry Repton, who was seen as Brown's apostolic successor. It fell to him to defend Brown in public, against Knight's and Price's accusations of ineptitude, which he did by publishing *A Letter to Uvedale Price* (1794). While Knight's attacks on Brown were more vicious than those made by Price, it is understandable that

60 *The Landscape*, p. 100.

Repton should have addressed his reply to Price because the *Essay on the Picturesque* was concerned with landscape design far more consistently than was Knight's poem, with its marked tendency to digress. Repton did not write the letter himself, but commissioned it from William Combe (1741–1843), an industrious literary hack who scribbled in secret and published for the most part anonymously so as to present himself to the world as an indolent gentleman.[61] His best-known work was to be a satire on Gilpin's picturesque tours called *The Tour of Doctor Syntax in Search of the Picturesque* (1812), and he also organised Repton's thoughts for publication as *Sketches and Hints on Landscape Gardening* (1795).[62] Combe would have been particularly willing to accept a commission to attack Price, because he had nursed a grudge against him since having been unjustly accused of pilfering whilst staying at Foxley.[63]

Reading the letter to Price it quickly becomes clear that much of the criticism levelled by Price and Knight was fully justified; Repton did not attempt to argue that it was not, but only that they had chosen the wrong target. It would, he said, have been aimed more appropriately at others who – while professing to follow Brown – did not understand Brown's genuine principles. In trying to realise arcadian landscapes after the master's example these incompetents failed miserably, and Repton argued that it was unfair to blame Brown and himself for the failures of others, explaining

> it is necessary to enter something farther into the detail of his practice of what has been ludicrously called *clumping* and *belting*. No man of taste can hesitate betwixt the natural group of trees composed of various growths, and that formal patch of firs which too often disfigure a lawn, under the name of a clump; but the most certain method of producing a group of five or six trees, is to plant fifty or sixty within the same fence, and this Mr. Brown frequently advised, with a mixture of firs to protect and shelter the young trees during their infancy; but, unfortunately, the neglect or bad taste of his employers would occasionally suffer the firs to remain long after they had completed their office as nurses, while others have actually planted *firs only* in such clumps, totally misconceiving Mr. Brown's original intention. Nor is it uncommon to see these black patches surrounded by a painted rail, a quick hedge, or even a stone wall, instead of that temporary fence which is always an object of necessity, and not of choice . . . The clump, therefore, is never to be considered as an object of present beauty,

61 Harlan W. Hamilton, *Doctor Syntax: A Silhouette of William Combe Esq.* (London: Chatto and Windus, 1969).

62 Ibid., p. 183.

63 Ibid., pp. 32–3.

> but as a more certain expedient for producing future beauties, than young trees which very seldom grow when exposed singly to wind and sun.[64]

So Repton was fully prepared to admit that there were gardens as badly mis-handled as Knight and Price claimed, but he was not prepared to acknowledge that Brown's works were among their number. Repton in his defence of Brown adopted Knight's way of thinking, finding in Brown's landscapes the virtues of the British constitution

> seeing great affinity betwixt deducing gardening from the painter's studies of wild nature, and deducing government from the uncontrolled opinions of man in a savage state. The neatness, simplicity, and elegance of English gardening, have acquired the approbation of the present century, as the happy medium betwixt the wildness of nature and the stiffness of art; in the same manner as the English constitution is the happy medium betwixt the liberty of savages, and the restraint of despotic government; and so long as we enjoy the benefits of these middle degrees betwixt extremes of each, let experiments of untried, theoretical improvement be made in some other country.[65]

Knight, as we have seen, approved of the British constitution, but that did not mean that he was unable to feel sympathy for the revolutionaries in France and America: he felt that they were trying to make their own countries as well-run as Britain. Where Knight had compared Brown's landscapes, by implication, with the tyranny to be found in France before the Revolution, Repton compared them with the freedom in England, and therefore made Knight appear to be far more radical than he was by leading one to suppose that he was advocating revolutionary change in England. This was a misrepresentation on Repton's part which fitted the mood of the time, and whether it was done wilfully or through misunderstanding is not clear. Knight answered Repton in the footnotes to the second edition of *The Landscape,* apparently denying that he had made any connection whatsoever between gardening and politics, and suggesting that Repton was wrong to make such links. 'To say that his own system of rural embellishment resembles the British constitution,' said Knight, 'and that Mr. Price's and mine resemble the Democratic tyranny in France, is a species of argument which any person may employ, on any occasion, without being at any expense either of sense or science.'[66] This is an outrageous dissimulation. Knight accused Repton of making

64 Humphry Repton, *Letter to Mr. Price* (1794), in Price, *Essays*, vol. III, pp. 10–13.

65 Ibid., p. 10.

66 *The Landscape*, p. 101.

connections which were not in the poem, which is fair, but Knight did make connections which were different only in their sympathies. He was in no position to condemn the whole 'species of argument' having used it extensively himself, albeit to different ends. Knight concluded with some very carefully chosen words which seem to deny everything while in fact denying nothing at all, entreating that his readers would 'not at this time, when men's minds are so full of plots and conspiracies, endeavour to find analogies between picturesque composition and political confusion; or suppose that the preservation of trees and terraces has any connection with the destruction of states and kingdoms'.[67] Knight himself of course made analogies between picturesque composition and politics, but he made the comparison not between the picturesque and political confusion, but between the picturesque and political freedom. The preserved trees and terraces may not have been connected with the destruction of states and kingdoms, but the unruly tramplings of woodland nymphs certainly were (see p. 197); and though Knight's critics should not 'at this time' find such analogies, Knight gives us leave to find them at some other time. The passage is not a denial, but an evasion.

So far as aesthetic matters were concerned, there was little in *The Landscape* or in Price's essay to arouse controversy. Repton claimed in his letter that his own position in practical matters was much the same as Knight's and Price's, except with regard to the authority of painting. This would seem to be a perfectly fair statement of the position. Repton in fact did not practice according to the same precise rules as had Brown, for example, in 1790 he had advised the retention of terraces and spoken dismissively of the 'too frequently repeated line of beauty'.[68] His problems, where Knight and Price were concerned, seem to have stemmed at least in part from the fact that although he did not practice according to the example of Brown, he nevertheless – for the sake of attracting important clients – assumed the mantle of Brown's successor, and therefore found himself defending his mentor even though he had departed from his practice. However, the heat of the controversy which followed the publication of *The Landscape* did not arise from arguments about aesthetic practice or theory. One of the most bitter attacks on Knight came from the Reverend William Mason, who was not only the author of Brown's epitaph, but was also Thomas Gray's literary executor.

Knight found Gray's ideas congenial: he expressed admiration for Gray's poetry and absorbed ideas from him into *The Landscape* and *The Progress of Civil Society*; and Knight clearly assumed that Gray's ideas were not unlike his own. Indeed an affinity between the poetry of Gray

67 Ibid., p. 104.

68 Nikolaus Pevsner, 'Humphry Repton' in *Studies in Art, Architecture and Design*, vol. I, p. 145.

and Lucretius has been noted before now,[69] but not by Mason, and there are phrases from Lucretius (as well as a great many other classical poets) woven into the fabric of Gray's poems.[70] Mason, in responding to *The Progress of Civil Society*, objected indignantly that Knight was enlisting Gray in support of his Epicurean cause, and although Knight actually wrote praising Gray, Mason's comments read in isolation would lead one to suppose that Gray had come under attack. Knight's method of attack, as Mason construed it, was by means of poison: contaminating Gray's purity by including it in paraphrase in Knight's own poem. By the time he had read the poem Mason already detested Knight,on account of *The Landscape* and *The Worship of Priapus*. Knight must have seemed to him to have been an emissary of the Secretary of Hell (see p. 25): he had defiled the poetry of one of Mason's friends, poured scorn on the garden designs of another, and had even dared to mock Mason's God. Mason retaliated in verse, casting Gray and Brown in a heroic mould, but comparing Knight with a pig, the classical disparagement for an Epicurean.[71]

Old as I am, I yet have powers to sneer
  At him, who dares debase the gold of Gray
  With his vile dross, and by such base allay,
Hope to buy off the critic's frown severe;
Him too, whose page e'erwhile had dar'd appear
  With shameless front the symbols to display
  Of pagan rites obscene, and thence convey
Shame to each eye, profaneness to each ear.
  Methinks, through fancy's tube, my friend I spy
Thron'd on a cloud in yon etherial plain,
  'Smiling in scorn;' methinks, I hear him cry,
'Prosaic Poetaster, cease to drain
  'The filthy dregs of Epicurus' sty;
'They shall not mix with my nectareous strain!'[72]

The poem was written in circumstances which Mason described to Walpole. 'A friend of your Lordship's and mine and of Mr Gray's sent me by the last post,' he wrote,

> an extract of what he says is a very long poem by the author of *the landscape*, the principles of which have been so completely confuted by various hands, that I should have imagined he would ere this have felt the less than mediocrity of his talents, and have forborne to trouble the public with any more of his trash . . . And

69 George D. Hadzsits, *Lucretius and his Influence* (New York: 1963), p. 331.

70 A. L. Lytton Sells, *Thomas Gray: His Life and Works* (London: George Allen and Unwin, 1980), pp. 152, 158, 165, 261.

71 Thomas Love Peacock, *The Works of Thomas Love Peacock,* ed. H. F. B. Brett-Smith and C. E. Jones, 10 vols. (London: Halliford, 1924–36), vol. V, *Gryll Grange*, p. 13n: 'The old philosophers accepted good-humouredly the disparaging terms attached to them by their enemies or rivals. The Epicureans acquiesced in the pig, the Cynics in the dog, and Cleanthes was content to be called the Ass of Zeno, as being alone capable of bearing the burthen of the Stoic philosophy.'

72 William Mason, *Sonnet XIII, occasioned by a Didactic Poem, on the Progress of Civil Society*, in *Works*, vol. I, p. 134; 'Smiling in scorn' see Gray's *Elegy*, line 105; 'Prosaic Poetaster' see *Walpole's Correspondence*, vol. XXIX, p. 338, Walpole to Mason, 22 March 1796.

> when I was told also that the thing was wished to be considered as a continuation of our friend's fine fragment on education and civil government, I became still more indignant. For I could not bear to think that Gray, who thought like Montesquieu upon those subjects, should be brought into company with that madman Lucretius. [73]

Mason was reacting not to the content of *The Progress of Civil Society*, of which he had read only half a dozen lines from the first page,[74] but *ad hominem* to Knight, whom he knew to be wicked because he had written sceptically about Christianity, had endorsed Lucretius and dismissed Brown. Therefore it was of no consequence to him that Knight too thought like Montesquieu, and was in full agreement with Gray where matters of education and government were concerned. Mason was not prepared to recognise any affinity whatsoever between Gray and Lucretius because he had known Gray as a decent friend and thought of Lucretius as a disciple of the Secretary of Hell. He was responding to reputations rather than the particular poem. Mason's letter was written in 1796 in outraged response to the appearance of *The Progress of Civil Society*, but his correspondent, Walpole, had been aware of Knight from the inception of his literary career.

The Worship of Priapus included an illustration of an ancient object from Walpole's collection, a woman with a bull sitting on her lap, and on his first acquaintance with the work he did not seem at all shocked or hostile. Far from thinking the book instantly to be a shameless affront he politely, if faintly, praised it and, on returning to Joseph Banks the copy which he had been lent to see how his antique had been treated, plainly hinted that he might be given a copy, and the gift was made.[75] However, in 1794 after the appearance of *The Landscape* we find that Walpole disapproved not only of the new book but also of the earlier one. By this time *The Worship of Priapus* was no longer a curious work which Walpole would like to own, but was laughable;[76] and by 1796 with the appearance of *The Progress of Civil Society* things had deteriorated still further. Walpole was reported as saying

> I cannot go to Mr. Knight's to see his antique bronzes, which I excessively admire, because I have abused his literary works. I think him as an author arrogant and assuming. His manner is picked up from others, having little originality. The absurdity of his making Lucretius his model is a proof of bad taste. His dictatorial manner is very offensive, and his placing Goldsmith

73 Ibid., p. 134n. Mason justified himself by quoting Gray: 'the doctrine of Epicurus was ever ruinous to society. It had its rise when Greece was declining, and, perhaps, hasteded its dissolution, as also that of Rome. It is now propagated in France and England, and seems likely to produce the same effects in both'.

74 Knight's sympathies should have been clear to someone who had read the poem. The reviewer in the *Critical Review* (March 1796), p. 334, understood well enough: 'the state of France, and the misery arising from the revolution to that country, are forcibly represented. The author deprecates the day when Great Britain, from the improvidence and profusion of its rulers, may be exposed to similar calamities.'

75 *Walpole's Correspondence*, ed. W. S. Lewis, 48 vols., vol. XXIV, p. 193, Walpole to Sir Joseph Banks, 31 March 1787. 'I return you the book, with many thanks. It is a most curious one; and as I readily lent my Ceres to be drawn for it, I confess I should have been much pleased if it had been thought fit to give me one. I should still be glad at least, if I could obtain one or two impressions of my Ceres; as I gather as many prints as I can of the pictures and curiosities in my collection. I have not the pleasure of knowing Mr Knights; but I think he would not refuse me such a trifling request.'

76 Farington, *Diary*, 29 April

> in the rank which he has done is proof of want of judgement. Goldsmith in his *Deserted Village* had some good lines, but his argument 'that commerce destroys villages', is ridiculous. There are occasionally smooth lines, among a great number of very bad ones, in Knight's publications, but pretending to a great deal, he has little power.[77]

Mason invited Walpole to join forces with him against Knight. They had both written about landscape design in the past, but had quarrelled; and it was through finding a common enemy in Knight that they were reconciled to one another in old age. Walpole wrote to Mason giving as his excuse the fact that 'He is a great favourite of a very near relation of mine ... whom I should mortally disoblige', and 'Weak and broken as I am and tottering to the grave at some months past seventy-eight, I have not spirits or courage enough to tap a paper-war.'[78]

Walpole's praise of William Kent was certainly one of the influences on Knight's thinking, and *The Landscape* was not in any sense an attack on the principles of garden design which Walpole had endorsed, only on Brown's unsatisfactory attempts to realise them. One element of Brown's landscapes which came in for particular criticism from both Knight and Price was the gravel walk. They found it unnatural, whereas Brown apparently did not: he arranged them in sinuous waving lines. In the case of a gravel path in a supposedly natural landscape the associations connected with the shape of the path were far outweighed by the fact that it was manifestly unnatural, and the associations were therefore unpleasant. Knight and Price both found the shape of these serpentine paths to be pedantically regulated, and suggested that the 'natural' line for a path would often be straight, advancing directly towards its destination unless its course was deflected by obstacles. The shape of a path was thus referred back to its function, not to an ideal of beauty. The objection to gravelled paths brought in response a sonnet from Mason, in which he found them to have practical advantages over the picturesque tracks of beaten earth; but the poem concluded by charging the path with symbolism in such a way as to make Knight's attack on it again appear in the guise of an attack on the British constitution.

> Smooth, simple path! whose undulating line,
> With sidelong tufts of flow'ry fragrance crown'd,
> 'Plain in its neatness', spans my garden ground;
> What, though two acres thy brief course confine,
> Yet sun and shade, and hill and dale are thine,

1794. Farington reports that Walpole 'laughs at the systematising plan of Knight, Towneley etc. who attempt to prove the lascivious designs of antiquity to be merely emblematic of the creative power'.

77 Ibid., 24 July 1796.

78 *Walpole's Correspondence*, vol. XXIX, p. 338, Walpole to William Mason, 22 March 1796.

And use with beauty here more surely found,
Than where, to spread the picturesque around,
Cart ruts and quarry holes their charms combine!
Here, as thou lead'st my step through lawn or grove,
Liberal though limited, restrain'd though free,
Fearless of dew, or dirt, or dust, I rove,
And own those comforts, all deriv'd from thee!
Take then, smooth Path this tribute of my love,
Thou emblem pure of legal liberty![79]

This was playing Knight at his own game. It is of course unfair, and the effect of the poem is ludicrous, but what it makes abundantly clear is that Mason realised that Knight's poem worked by making links between the landscape and political symbolism. Again if we compare Mason's and Knight's rhetoric about the aesthetics of landscape design we find, unsurprisingly, that they both appealed for nature to be used as the standard of judgement, but Mason clearly preferred nature's gentler arcadian moods, whereas Knight preferred nature to be rugged and turbulent, favouring above all the neglected forest. Had the debate been confined to this level then the exchanges would have been more polite than in fact they were, and very much less energetic, but once the discussion had been charged with political and religious symbolism the whole perspective and scope were changed and the stakes raised. Where Mason and Walpole favoured Brown's arcadian vision of nature, from which the old gods, notably Priapus, had been excluded, Knight would have seen such a landscape as having been emasculated and secularised. He preferred to think that a garden should symbolise the unknown workings of nature and the natural freedom of man. Mason and Walpole understood this to mean that Knight favoured atheism and anarchy; so their attacks were directed much more forcefully against Knight's supposed anarchist sympathies than against his ideas about the landscape as such. In fact Knight's landscape was far from atheistical, and sought not to banish God from the garden but to reinstate a sense of the numinous: his whole sense of the landscape was imbued with religious feeling, albeit of a pagan turn.

Although Walpole and Mason misunderstood and misrepresented Knight's political and religious intentions, they did at least understand his rhetoric on the level at which it was intended to communicate, despite Knight's protests to the contrary. When the poem was attacked without an awareness of the symbolic programme the criticism wilted into point-

79 William Mason, *Sonnet XII, To a Gravel Walk*, in *Works*, vol. I, p. 133.

lessness. For example, William Marshall (1745–1818), an agricultural writer, published a review of the poem which understood its trees simply as trees and as no more than that, and its paths as no more than paths. The result looks very foolish. Marshall's case against Knight rested on the assertion that Knight supposed all scenery to be naturally wooded until the landscape designer made his appearance. Knight would indeed have been showing a lack of practical common sense if he had set out from this assumption, but in fact he did not. He thought that forest scenery was best, but readily admitted that it was not everywhere available. This may seem a slight point on which to take issue with Knight, but in fact it was the only point on which Marshall made any attempt to argue. The rest of his 'review' was composed entirely of blustering abuse which was launched on the flimsiest and most ridiculous of pretexts. His technique in rhetoric relied very heavily on the fact that his audience would find Knight's suggestions self-evidently preposterous, and he strengthened the force, but not the sense, of his condemnations by larding them with elided curses. For example, when he turned to criticise the engraved plate in *The Landscape* which purported to show a garden set out after the manner of Brown, he said that the picture travestied Brown's designs. This was not because the bareness of the landscape had been exaggerated (this being the point of Knight's criticism) but because a vital element was missing:

> It has no practicable coach-road to it. The immediate approach takes the house in full front, as if to pass through it, rather than to approach it. It must, therefore, either be *wilful misrepresentation*, or be taken from some place, in the more recluse parts of the island, where Ladies still Darby-and-Joan it, or pay visits in pattens. It would make our English coachmen stare, and, perchance, bl–st the fool of a fellow who made it; for how, and be d–'d to him, were they to set down at the hall door.[80]

A much more intelligent, and no less spirited, performance came from Dr John Matthews (1758–1837). He lived at Belmont in Herefordshire and was well informed about discussion in the Price–Knight circle, and was probably personally known to Price and Knight. He liked Price's essay, but thought 'very moderately' of Knight's poem, which he thought didactic 'only in the title';[81] which is to say that it conveyed little information about landscapes. Matthews published anonymously his satirical poem, *A Sketch from the Landscape*, quoting in the preface parallel passages from Knight's *The Landscape* and William

80 William Marshall, *Review of 'The Landscape'* (London: 1794), pp. 6–7.

81 Farington, *Diary*, 31 August 1794.

Mason's *The English Garden*, which showed some close similarities. He remarked that

> The charge of borrowing from Mr. Mason is positively denied by Mr. K. He declares that he never read the English Garden. The assertion of a man of honour must be credited. One passage only from each of these poets is given below, not to support the accusation, but to justify the suspicion. It was scarcely possible to have conceived a Professor sitting down in his dictatorial chair to teach the world how to set to create landscape, who could be so perfectly satisfied with his own notions as not to wish to know what had been said before on the same subject in one of the most beautiful poems in the English language.[82]

It is difficult to believe that Matthews' evaluation of Mason's poem was completely sincere (it has been described as 'long and tedious'),[83] but in its day it was popular enough, and it was clearly in the interests of Matthews' argument to over- rather than under-value it. In the preface Matthews wrote in his own voice, but in the poem he affected to take Knight's point of view, in order to burlesque it. Then *The English Garden* became 'a Poem which *has had* its admirers' but which was not worth rescuing from oblivion except for those 'few thoughts from it which are already *embalmed* in THE LANDSCAPE, as the attentive reader will easily discover'.[84]

Matthews made fun of Knight's politics, connecting him, as had Walpole, with such radicals as Thomas Paine (whose name, rendered with a 'Y', made him appear to be one of Knight's relations), and Mary Wollstonecraft.[85]

> PAYNE blusters for the Rights of Man;
> Of Woman, on the same bold plan,
> The fair Miss WOLLSTONCROFT does prattle:
> I trust your patience to be heard
> Whilst softly *I* put in a word
> In favour of the Rights of Cattle.
>
> ...
>
> the free-born Muse bewails
> Those curs'd despotic things call'd pales
> Which bar these commoners from browsing:
> Ye rustic Nymphs! hedge-breaking lasses!
> Oh! tear 'em up – drive horses, asses,
> Pigs, goats, sheep, oxen, calves, and cows in.[86]

82 [Dr John Matthews], *A Sketch from 'The Landscape'* (1794), p. ii.

83 Nikolaus Pevsner, *Oxfordshire* (Harmondsworth: Penguin, 1974), p. 729 n.

84 Matthews, *Sketch,* p. 9.

85 Mary Woolstonecraft, *A Vindication of the Rights of Woman* (1792).

86 Matthews, *Sketch*, pp. 16–17.

And Matthews took up Knight's accusation that Brown set about shaving the goddess Nature (whom he professed to have come to dress) by making another connection between luxuriant growths and politics:

> Of all the innovations and improvements planned by the unfortunate PETER the third, the scheme of shaving the Clergy is supposed to be that which more immediately led to the revolution which placed the present illustrious Empress upon the throne of all the Russias. A few days after this event, all the world knows he died *rather suddenly*.[87]

The means to political stability, therefore, were clear enough:

> Shave, then, no more, good friends, but friz
> The lovely locks round Nature's phiz,
> The weedy honours of her head.[88]

Knight's abuse of the gravel walk also was satirised, Knight having found the formal garden of Moorfields in the city of London, the site of Bedlam Hospital, more picturesque than Brown's shaved and polished gardens:

> Prim gravel walks, through which we winding go
> In endless serpentines, that nothing show;
> Till tired, I ask, *Why this eternal round?*
> And the pert gardener says, *'Tis pleasure ground.*
> *This pleasure ground!* astonish'd, I exclaim,
> *To me Moorfields as well deserve the name:*
> Nay, better; for in busy scenes at least
> Some odd varieties the eye may feast,
> Something more entertaining still be seen,
> Than red-hot gravel, fringed with tawdry green.
> (III, 225–34)

Matthews transmuted this into:

> To Bedlam rather let me travel,
> Than here in endless windings view
> Discordant tints of glaring hue
> And walk tormented by the gravel![89]

And Brown was remembered, by Matthews, with an appropriate epitaph:

87 Ibid., p. 6 n.

88 Ibid., p. 7; cf. Ovid, *Artis Amatoriae*, bk. III, lines 249–50, quoted by Thomas Love Peacock, *Works*, vol. V, *Gryll Grange*, pp. 34–5, 35n: 'Ugly is a field without grass, / a plant without leaves, or a head without hair,' trans. J. H. Mozley, *The Art of Love and Other Poems*, Loeb edition (London: Heinemann, 1929), pp. 134–5.

89 *Sketch*, p. 17.

Figure 24. Brown's tomb, vignette from [John Matthews] *A Sketch from The Landscape.*

Death has mown thee – his heavy paw
Has swept thee down his deep ha-ha,
　Thou great defacer of the nation!
Well did he use his scythe and broom!
And now, with glee, upon thy tomb
　I'll pour a suitable libation.[90]

At this point the reader is referred to a vignette showing the contents of a chamber pot being thrown at Brown's tomb (figure 24).

A suitably Epicurean reason was suggested for Knight's preference for functionally direct drives over those which wandered round the bounds of the estate, which he had condemned as ostentatious.

When dinner calls, pray tell me who
Would ride about to see a view?[91]

While the satire concluded with an image of Knight's symbolic apotheosis

Thy statue of Colossal size
In ductile yew, shall nobly rise –
　(Think not thy modesty shall 'scape us)
The *God of Gardens* thou shalt stand,
To fright improvers from the land,
　A huge and terrible *Priapus*.[92]

90 Ibid., pp. 13–14.

91 Ibid., p. 10.

92 Ibid., pp. 21–2.

Figure 25. Topiary, vignette from [John Matthews] *A Sketch from The Landscape*.

A second vignette shows this extravagant topiary from behind, its frontal view understandably causing some winsome young ladies to blush (figure 25). Knight paid Matthews the compliment of including a snatch of his verse in the preface to the second edition of *The Landscape*, but the price for its inclusion was that it be insultingly dismissed as 'blundering dullness vainly attempting wit, and producing nonsense'.[93] Marshall's work was treated even more scathingly and was ignored altogether, unworthy even of contempt.

Ostentation

In the first edition of the poem, Knight had anticipated that he would be charged with misrepresenting Brown's followers; therefore to show that they were indeed concerned with ostentatious display, and that Knight was not being unfair, he quoted a passage from

> the most skilful and eminent among them. Mr. Repton, in his plan for improving Tatton Park, in Cheshire, with which he means to

93 *The Landscape*, p. xiii.

> favour the public in the general collection of his works, and in which he has professedly detailed the principles of his art, suggests many expedients for shewing the extent of property, and among others, that of placing the family arms upon the neighbouring mile-stones.[94]

Repton took angry exception to this, but his defence was feeble. He claimed that Knight had wilfully misread 'mile-stones' for what he had actually written, which was 'mere stones'. In itself this was correct, but in context it was an insubstantial misreading, as Knight sarcastically pointed out. Repton had referred to 'mere stones with distances', and Knight queried what on earth these 'mere stones with distances' could have been, if not 'mile-stones': 'So far from intentionally *misquoting, in order to ridicule him*, as he has thought proper to insinuate, the author took the instance, and employed the interpretation, which he thought the least ridiculous.'[95] This exchange was commemorated by Thomas Love Peacock in *Headlong Hall,* written some twenty years later. There, a landscape designer by the name of Mr Milestone put forward Brown's ideas as represented by Knight, using Knight's pejorative language (shaving and polishing, clumping and belting) to describe his wonderful intentions which, inevitably when so described, appear ridiculous, or, in context in the novel, enjoyably comic.[96]

It would of course be unfair to suppose that Repton and Brown had no more to offer than Knight and Price suggested: they are now acknowledged as the greatest garden designers of their times. But it would equally be unfair to Knight and Price to suppose that there was no substance or justification in their attacks. The issue is complicated by the fact that whilst Repton was defending Brown he was nevertheless adapting his own practice to bring it more closely into line with what Price and Knight were recommending. Knight's evaluation of Repton in *The Landscape* seems to be perfectly sincere and justifiable, and he gave an account of how he first came into contact with Repton, and his subsequent disillusion.

They met when Repton was engaged to work on a 'small, but romantic place' near Downton, Ferney Hall, in 1789.[97] Knight had felt some apprehension when he heard that 'an improver' was to be employed to work on the grounds, but his 'fears were suddenly changed into the most pleasing expectations, which were still heightened and confirmed when I heard him launch out in praise of picturesque scenery, and declare that he had sought the principles of his art, not in the works of Kent or Brown,

94 Ibid., p. 12 n.

95 Ibid., p. v.

96 Knight was acknowledged by Peacock. See Marilyn Butler, *Peacock Displayed* (London: Routledge, 1979), pp. 26 ff.

97 Hazel Fryer, 'Humphry Repton in Herefordshire' in *The Picturesque Landscape: Visions of Georgian Herefordshire*, ed. Stephen Daniels and Charles Watkins (Nottingham University, 1994), p. 80.

but in those of the great landscape painters'.[98] It had long been Knight's wish, he said, that 'a man of liberal education, conversant (in some degree at least) with almost every branch of polite literature, and skilled in the art of design' should rescue the landscape 'from the hands of mere gardeners, nurserymen, and mechanics' (such as Brown);[99] and he thought that he had found just such a person in Repton. 'But alas!' said Knight, 'my triumph was of short duration: – the plans of improvement which he produced for the place above mentioned instantly undeceived me; and he will do me the justice to allow, that I did not, through affected delicacy or hypocritical politeness, conceal my disappointment from him.'[100] This is a polite way of saying that he was very rude to him. Knight was not given to diplomacy, and Repton was to find Knight's public abuse of him 'indecently personal',[101] so it was scarcely surprising that 'Since that time,' Knight said, 'I have not had the pleasure of much of Mr. Repton's conversation.' On the other hand, he went on,

> I have had the misfortune to see many of his performances designed and executed exactly after Mr. Brown's receipt, without any attention to the natural, or artificial character of the country, or the style of the place. In his Letter, too, to Mr. Price, he has avowedly become the patron and defender of this system, and professedly abandoned the school of the painter for that of the gardener; he having, as he says, *found, after mature consideration, and more practical experience, that there is not so great an affinity betwixt painting and gardening as his enthusiasm for the picturesque had originally led him to fancy*. I, it seems, had the good fortune first to enjoy his conversation, when this original enthusiasm for the picturesque was in its full vigour; and the ill fortune to become first acquainted with his works just as it was gone off, and he was animated with all the zeal of a new proselyte for the adverse system.[102]

So Brown, and Repton if he was following him, was deep in error in Knight's eyes. First, his aesthetics were misguided: he had no knowledge of pictures and could therefore lay out continuous undulating lawns with no thought given to foregrounds and backgrounds; the result was not merely dull, but even painful. Secondly Brown (and even more particularly Repton) was said to be pandering to the vanity of his employers by arranging their gardens not according to the rules of art but so as to give the maximum opportunity for ostentatious display. Thirdly, according to Knight, Brown's contribution to landscape design was a 'system', which

98 *The Landscape*, p. 98.

99 Ibid., p. 99.

100 Ibid., p. 100.

101 Repton, Red Book for Sufton, 1 July 1795, in David Whitehead, 'Repton and the Picturesque Debate: The Text of the Sufton Red Book', *The Picturesque*, no. 1, p. 6.

102 *The Landscape*, pp. 99–100. Price told much the same story, rather more ingratiatingly:

> I remember your being consulted about the improvements at Ferney Hall, a small place in the neighbourhood of Mr. Knight, the most striking feature of which is a rocky dell near the house. I was extremely pleased to hear that you had asked Mr. Knight's advice with regard to the management of that part, acknowledging that you had not been so conversant as himself in that style of scenery.
>
> This instance of your diffidence, and of your wish to draw knowledge from others, not merely to impress them with an idea of your own, was what first made me desirous of being known to you. The character I heard of your drawings added to that desire; and as I was persuaded that the same diffidence, and readiness to listen to advice, would lead you to correct any defects they might have, I felt great hopes that the art of landscape-gardening would be fixed on better

was applied uniformly wherever he went, and did not respond to the accidental character of the place. This linked Brown to medieval ways of thought and portrayed him as a fanatical believer in an indefensible faith. By contrast, a genuinely inspired non-systematic gardener (ideally an 'analytical' gardener) would first have examined evidence, and tried in an enlightened way to perfect the given situation.

Repton had been employed with some regularity in Knight's part of the country, and it can easily be imagined that his freshly planted schemes would contrast unfavourably with the mature established landscapes to be found cultivated at, say, Croft Castle (which belonged to Knight's family) or Brampton Bryan (which was another of the Earl of Oxford's properties), both of which have magnificent ancient trees, and could be found uncultivated in the case of Downton's craggy gorge (when Knight found it). Scenery such as this could not be conjured from nothing by any designer, but at least the mature and irreplaceable delights of a place should not be wiped out. For example, Repton was quick to point out that crags, such as the Teme Gorge, could not be created out of flat country, but nevertheless he can be found smoothing out such a feature when presented with it,[103] whereas Knight would have preferred its retention and enhancement.

Wild theory

All in all the 'Picturesque Controversy' did not have a clear victor, since nobody conceded ground, still less admitted defeat. Repton eventually published his opinion that Knight and Price were correct in denigrating the work of most gardeners, but that he, Repton, should not have been their target:

> When I compare the picturesque scenery of Downton Vale with the meagre efforts of art which are attributed to the school of Brown, I cannot wonder at the enthusiastic abhorrence which the author of 'The Landscape' expresses for modern gardening: especially as few parts of the kingdom present more specimens of bad taste than the road from Ludlow to Worcester; in passing over which . . . surrounded by plantations of firs, and larches, and Lombardy poplars, I saw new red houses, with all the fanciful apertures of Venetian and pseudo-Gothic windows, which disgust the traveller, who looks in vain for the picturesque shapes and harmonious tints of former times.[104]

principles than it had hitherto been; for I little imagined that you would strive to lessen the consequence of that art, to which you are indebted for your superiority in your own.

Those drawings of your's [*sic*] which were shewn me, (when considered as those of an improver, and not of a professed artist) manifested talents which made me wish to know the author. You will forgive me, however, if I mention in my own justification, and by no means with an intention of hurting you, that they still (according to my conceptions) pointed out reasons for recommending to you what I did, and do strongly recommend – a study of the higher artists; for it is a study which never should be remitted, either by the painter, or the improver.'

Price to Repton, in Price, *Essays*, vol. III, pp. 89–91.

103 Repton said that he favoured moderation in these matters: 'I trust that the taste of this country will neither slide into the trammels of that smooth shaven *genius* of the bare and bald which [Knight] so justly ridicules, nor enlist under the banners of that shaggy and harsh-featured *spirit*, which knows no delight but in the scenes of Salvator Rosa'; *Sketches and Hints on Landscape Gardening* (1794), ed. J. C. Loudon (London:

This was published in 1816, long after the event; Repton insisted that his own principles were, in practice, very close to those of Knight and Price, and that really there was no need to argue; the 'elegant and gentlemanlike manner in which Mr. Price has examined my opinions, and explained his own, left no room for further controversy'.[105]

But to consider the argument about landscape design in isolation would be to exclude from consideration the factors which gave the argument its heat; Repton, unlike Knight and Price, was arguing not just for his principles but for his livelihood; he had been very active in the years before the controversy, and suddenly his income halved.[106] The reason for this was certainly not the attacks made upon him, which could only have brought him greater celebrity and have made potential clients feel less secure about their own tastes, and therefore the more ready to reach for professional advice, however firmly Price and Knight advised against it. The war with France had brought inflation and tax increases as well as the fear of political instability, so both the mood and the means of the landed gentry did not favour Repton at that time, or any other gardener or architect.

The most vitriolic criticisms were made by William Mason, who poured scorn on Knight's Epicureanism and his supposedly radical political sympathies, using the landscape as his means for doing so. This was perfectly justified, as Knight had made the landscape into a vehicle for precisely such contentious ideas, but on the other hand Mason did misrepresent Knight's views, probably because he did not understand them, as he seems not to have read any more of Knight's work than was necessary to his purpose. However, it is clear enough from Mason's remarks that what Knight had to say about the landscape as such exercised him relatively little. *The Landscape* addressed the problems of practical garden design only as a matter of secondary interest, and delegated responsibility for this matter to Price, to whom the reader was referred. Knight's concern was to portray the garden as a landscape of ideas, symbols and metaphors, so that when the reader was presented with real scenery it would start appropriate and enjoyable trains of thought. *The Landscape* was a catalogue of associations, not of practical advice. If we are to find a wholly sympathetic response to Knight's poem then we must find someone whose political and religious views were in sympathy with his own, and we need not look far, because Knight helpfully published an encomium from his friend Sir Edward Winnington in the second edition. Winnington, according to the *Gentleman's Magazine*, was above all else 'an amiable, entertaining and instructive

Compendium edition, 1840), p. 191. References are to this edn except where stated otherwise.

104 Repton, *Fragments on the theory and practice of Landscape Gardening, including some remarks on Grecian and Gothic Architecture* (London:1816), p. 440; originally from the Red Book for Stanage Park.

105 Repton, *Sketches and Hints*, p. 352.

106 Repton quoted Whitehead, 'Sufton Red Book', *The Picturesque*, no. 1, p. 6.

companion',[107] the Member of Parliament for Droitwich and a member of the Society of Dilettanti.[108] Winnington made the same use of language as Knight had done, using light-related and freedom-related words to describe virtues, and the verse's twenty-four lines concerned landscape to roughly the same extent as Knight's poem, being mentioned in three of the lines, two of which appear here.

O liberty and nature, kindred powers,
Shed on this favour'd isle your genial beams!
Arch our high groves, and weave our tangled bowers,
Pile our rude rocks, and wind our lucid streams![109]

The landscape was used exclusively as a source for images of liberty and nature. Six lines of the verse praised Knight's abilities, and no fewer than seven were given over to a description of a horse; no ordinary steed, but one capable of bearing a particularly heavy burden of metaphor:

His flowing mane, by barbarous art unshorn,
Floats on a neck by no rude yoke oppress'd;
While nature's beauties all his limbs adorn,
And conscious freedom swells his ample chest.[110]

Knight's use of symbolism was understood by his friends as well as his more enlightened enemies: Winnington's verse summarised the content of Knight's poem, using different symbols to represent that content. Those with sympathies a little less liberal than Knight's own, however, understood his expressions of concern for freedom to mean that he favoured anarchy and revolt in England; and they understood that his 'nature' was not rooted in the Garden of Eden, but in the Gardens of Epicurus. The central practice of Knight's picturesque was the forging of links between objects and ideas, which in itself was far from novel; but it was radicalised because on the one hand the objects in question were often quite commonplace and on the other the ideas were contentious. What his poem did was to gather together a great collection of metaphors drawn from the landscape, and use them to illustrate points, many of which are not remotely useful to the garden designer. For example, the flowing water of a river (like the Teme) is seen as an image of liberty, in contrast to the dammed stream with which a landscape designer such as Brown had formed a lake.

As the dull, stagnant pool, that's mantled o'er
With the green weeds of its own muddy shore

107 *Gentleman's Magazine*, January 1805, p. 91.

108 Ibid.

109 Edward Winnington, quoted by Knight, *The Landscape*, p. xiv.

110 Winnington, quoted in ibid.

No bright reflections on its surface shows,
Nor murmuring surge, nor foaming ripple knows;
But ever peaceful, motionless and dead,
In one smooth sheet its torpid waters spread:
So by oppression's iron hand confined,
In calm and peaceful torpor sleep mankind;
Unfelt the rays of genius, that inflame
The free-born soul, and bid it pant for fame.
But break the mound, and let the waters flow;
Headlong and fierce their turbid currents go;
Sweep down the fences, and tear up the soil;
And roar along, 'midst havock, waste, and spoil;
Till spent their fury:– then their moisture feeds
The deepening verdure of the fertile meads;
Bids vernal flowers the fragrant turf adorn,
And rising juices swell the wavy corn:
So when rebellion breaks the despot's chain,
First wasteful ruin marks the rabble's reign;
Till tired their fury, and their vengeance spent,
One common interest bids their hearts relent;
Then temperate order from confusion springs,
And, fann'd by freedom, genius spreads its wings.
(III, 377–400)

So far as practical advice about gardening is concerned, then, flowing water is preferable to confined water; but the argument is not made by considering visual effects, rather it is seen as a moral imperative to liberate nature, and the rest falls into place once freedom has been established, even though there is some regrettable but necessary destruction along the way. It is not clear whether such a passage as Knight's describing the cedar would lead one to plant cedars, but clearly the tree in Knight's hands became political.[111] Again it is not clear that his passage about a colony of rooks would lead one to encourage rooks to nest in one's trees, but it did mean that coming across one by chance it could be enjoyed as an improving spectacle.[112] Repton was undoubtedly thinking more of Knight than of Price when he made reference to 'the wild theory of improvement which has lately sprung up in Herefordshire'.[113] It is no doubt clear by now that despite being united in their opposition to Repton, Knight and Price had quite different personalities, tastes and projects. Repton remarked that

111 See p. 198.

112 See p. 200.

113 Repton, quoted Whitehead, 'Sufton Red Book', p. 6.

> there is a shade of difference betwixt the opinions of Mr. *Price* and Mr. *Knight*, which seems to have arisen from the different characters of their respective places: *Foxley* is less romantic than *Downton*, and therefore Mr. Price is less extravagant in his ideas, and more willing to allow some little sacrifice of picturesque beauty to neatness, near the house.[114]

This is accurate, if underplayed. Knight's interests were much more overtly political and philosophical, and his personal manner was highly combative, to the point of being insulting, whereas Price was very much more emollient, his great project being to distinguish an aesthetic category, the picturesque. His considerations of what is appropriate in a garden are constantly discussed with reference to it, which gives the work a meticulous and obsessional quality, quite different from Knight's racy enthusiasm. In the body of his poem Knight made no use at all of the word 'picturesque': in the first edition it figured just once (in a footnote to page 52) compounded in the term 'picturesque beauty', which was objectionable to Price. Associations of ideas played a lesser role in Price's discussion, but he accepted that they shaped responses in a very significant way. In a natural scene every eye would be pleased 'with a happy combination of forms, colours, lights and shadows', but 'other considerations proceeding from the mind only, are often imperceptibly blended' and

> From the force of this association, places of celebrity are viewed with much more delight, than those which are little known, though of equal, or greater beauty: and, I believe, it would be difficult for a man of poetical enthusiasm, to judge impartially between a beautiful scene in some obscure district, and one in the classic regions of Greece,
>
> 'Where not a mountain rears its head unsung.'[115]

Beautiful and sublime landscapes would, according to Price, have an immediate effect on even an untrained observer, but a picturesque landscape could seem undistinguished to someone who was not versed in the study of pictures, as 'a scene may, and often does exist, in which the qualities of the picturesque, almost exclusively of those of grandeur and of beauty, prevail; and . . . persons unacquainted with pictures, either take no interest in such scenes, or even think them ugly, while painters, and lovers of painting, study and admire them'.[116] It is not at all clear why he did not move from here to conclude, as Knight did, that only lovers of painting

114 Humphry Repton, *Sketches and Hints on Landscape Gardening Collected from Designs and Observations now in the Possession of the Different Noblemen and Gentlemen, for Whose Use they were Originally Made. The Whole Tending to Establish Fixed Principles in the Art of Laying Out Ground* (London: 1795), p. 77.

115 Price, *Essays*, vol. II, pp. 247–9

116 Ibid., vol. I, p. 219.

could enjoy such scenes because only they could make the appropriate associations in the mind. Price seems to have thought that the study of paintings heightened visual awareness so that one became aware of things which would otherwise pass unnoticed, things which were not beautiful, nor imposing. The logical outcome of making such a study, and implementing the principles thereby learned, would be the production of landscapes about which nothing would seem remarkable except to connoisseurs. Such landscapes would be, in Price's view, the most purely picturesque, having nothing of beauty or grandeur about them; but it is not at all clear why such landscapes should be thought the best.

Despite Price's political outlook, his instincts were conservative. Where he had made radical change to the surroundings of his own house he bitterly regretted having done so. His writing took on a very personal confessional tone when he described how, having fallen victim to the mania promoted by Brown, he did away with an ornamental terrace.

> I may perhaps have spoken more feelingly . . . from having done myself, what I so condemn in others, – destroyed an old-fashioned garden. It was not indeed in the high style of those I have described, but it had many circumstances of a similar kind and effect: as I have long since perceived the advantage which I could have made of them, and how much I could have added to that effect; how well I could in parts have mixed the modern style, and have altered and concealed many of the stiff and glaring formalities, I have long regretted its destruction. I destroyed it, not from disliking it; on the contrary, it was a sacrifice I made against my own sensations, to the prevailing opinion. I doomed it and all its embellishments, with which I had formed such an early connection, to sudden and total destruction; probably much upon the same idea, as many a man of careless, unreflecting, unfeeling good-nature, thought it his duty to vote for demolishing towns, provinces, and their inhabitants, in America: like me (but how different the scale and the interest!) they chose to admit it as a principle, that whatever obstructed the prevailing *system*, must be all thrown down, all laid prostrate: no medium, no conciliatory methods were to be tried, but whatever might follow, destruction must precede.[117]

He made this 'frank confession' of his 'errors' in the hope that others might be persuaded to trust their own judgement, and not persuaded to sweeping irrevocable acts by the advice of 'systematic' improvers of land-

117 Ibid., vol. II, pp. 118–20.

scape, who professed to know what the taste of the day required and imposed it whatever the particular circumstances might be, because the 'system' demanded it. Where Knight's rhetoric was rousing, calling for the liberation of repressed nature, Price's was affecting and sentimental. Price's authority for making his pronouncements was that of the repentant sinner, the reformed character who had once succumbed to the allurements of wrongdoing, but now knew better and hoped to help his readers avoid his own pitfalls.[118] This stance is not overtly religious, but suggests a sympathy for Christianity in general, in marked contrast with Knight. Price's essay had fewer political and religious overtones than Knight's poem, and those it had were carefully framed so as to be clearly conservative: the changes being proposed are incremental and aim to improve the situation without sudden catastrophic change. The revolutionary changes, sweeping away all that was there before, belonged to the fashionable 'system' which did not accord with Price's own tastes. His aim was to overturn the practices (of the previous generation, led by Brown) which Price stigmatised as 'new', and to institute a new way of looking at the landscape, which he portrayed as 'old'. His taste favoured nature, to be sure, but also the aged; and not particularly ancient things which were well preserved, but rather things which exhibited symptoms of age. For example, Price evocatively and nostalgically described the formal terrace which he had demolished, then went on

> I now can only lament what it is next to impossible to restore; and can only reflect, how much more difficult it is to add any of the old decorations to modern improvements, than to soften the old style by blending it with a proper proportion of the new. My object (as far as I had any determinate object besides that of being in the fashion) was, I imagine, to restore the ground to what might be supposed to have been its original state; I probably have in some degree succeeded, and, after much difficulty, expence, and dirt, I have made it look like many other parts of mine and of all beautiful grounds; with but little to mark the difference between what is close to the house, and what is at a distance from it; between the habitation of man, and that of sheep.[119]

Price had supposed before he destroyed his terrace that his only reasons for enjoying it had been sentimental, but in retrospect he was convinced that part of his pleasure had been physiological, and derived from the irregularity which William Gilpin had described as characteristic of the picturesque.[120]

118 Ibid., pp. 126–7.

119 Ibid., pp. 125–6.

120 William Gilpin, *Three Essays on Picturesque Beauty; on Picturesque Travel; and on Sketching Landscape: to which is added a poem, on Landscape Painting* (London, 1792); Price, *Essays*, vol. II, p. 123.

121 Price seems to have had in mind the contrast between his own grounds at Foxley and Knight's at Downton when he wrote:

> Of this description are the two most renowned of all didactic poems, those of Lucretius and Virgil; and they are the best illustrations of the manner in which the useful and the ornamental, in places of great natural beauties, should be combined together.
>
> Those who wish for as great a degree of elegance and high polish as is compatible with grandeur and energy, will imitate Virgil; but, like him, they will avoid all flat effeminate smoothness. Like him, they will leave those masterly touches which give a spirit to the rest, though they will give to the whole of their scenery a more general appearance of polish, than those who take Lucretius for their model. In him certainly the contrast

between what answers to the picturesque, the sublime, and the beautifil, that is, between the rough, and seemingly neglected parts – the forcible and majestic images he at other times presents – and the extreme softness and voluptuousness of his beautiful passages – is much more striking than in Virgil; and therefore by many his style has been preferred to that of his more equal, but less original rival.

Price, *Essays* vol. III, pp. 54–7. Virgil of course was much more generally preferred to Lucretius, and when Price said here that Lucretius was preferred 'by many' we may suppose that he meant by Knight and Fox (and see p. 110).

Price's arguments, then, were framed in such a way as to persuade his readers to sympathise with them, whereas Knight's seem by contrast to have excited alarm and anxiety. Price's arcadian vision of the landscape fitted securely into the general picture of the development of the Virgilian landscape, from William Kent onwards, and his ideas could easily have been accepted as a judicious refinement of a continuing tradition had they not been associated with Knight's inflammatory poem and his Lucretian landscape.[121] If we take *The Landscape* to be a poem about designing gardens, then it is remarkable for the length and prominence of its digressions. It is more centrally concerned with the dynamic forces of nature, standing against their repression. Knight embodied this theme not only in the landscape, which he described as being repressed by Capability Brown, but also in other manifestations. For example in politics, where he described the oppressed French overturning a cruel tyranny, and in religion, where human nature (which the ancient Greeks understood) was seen to have been warped by Christianity and abstinence. This theme rages through the poem as confidently as the Teme through Knight's gorge: it is not an arcane undercurrent, but its vital force. In the name of the liberation of nature the poem proposed a radical programme of restoration: of the landscape to the old gods, of freedom to the individual and of justice to society.

8 A house and a garden

The gothic idea

The house which Knight commissioned to be built for his own use and to his own design, and which came to be known as Downton Castle, was an extraordinary edifice to find being erected in the Herefordshire countryside in the 1770s (see figure 3). Absolutely the most extraordinary thing about it is that it would have been relatively normal fifty or a hundred years later, when the nineteenth-century gothic revival was under way. In retrospect the house does not look like an eccentric departure from normal behaviour, as it surely must have done at the time, but it looks prophetic. As ever with Knight, though, the building had its own very particular frame of reference, within which it was not wilfully eccentric, and he could not have known what course future events would take. That he might have intended to build his dwelling in a medieval manner is incredible, given his philhellenism, and it seems as astonishing an aberration as his failure to recognise outstanding merit in the Parthenon marbles. It was not absolutely inconceivable that an eighteenth-century gentleman might build himself a gothic country seat, as an interest in the gothic was gaining ground at the time, especially in the Society of Antiquaries of which Knight was a member. Horace Walpole had turned his villa at Twickenham into the resplendently gothic Strawberry Hill, which could have guided Knight's thinking, but despite some occasional sympathetic remarks, the gothic in Knight's writings was something to be regretted. He complained that the Society of Antiquaries had been overrun by Goths,[1] and, far from setting himself up as a medieval baron, in a building evocative of the Castle of Otranto, he seems to have intended his house to have been more properly classical than the

1 Knight to Lord Aberdeen, undated [1812] British Library, Additional MSS (Aberdeen Papers) 43230, fol. 88: 'The society is so numerous, promiscuous and thoroughly Gothicised, that I fear it will [be] impossible to turn its attention to objects of real Taste and Elegance, or employ its funds to their cultivation and promotion.'

Palladian building which he could reasonably have been expected to build.

Gothic architecture, a product of the medieval era, the age of religious superstition, suffered an appalling and insuperable handicap, in Knight's eyes, in its disadvantaged origin. He supposed that the gothic style had evolved in a vicious and barbarous age in which everything of value from classical civilisation had been either forgotten or destroyed by Christianity's depredations. For Knight, gothic buildings stood unredeemed, victims of their unfortunate birth, but, having accepted this obvious handicap, he did his best to appreciate it. He felt that in some respects it was better than Greek architecture, but showed no sign at all of a prophetic anticipation of the attitudes which would come to the fore in the nineteenth century, when gothic would be seen as embodying spirituality and goodness,[2] but, on the contrary, he adopted a condescending tone when discussing it. Knight's estimate of the worth of gothic architecture was normal for an Enlightenment thinker, but increasingly unusual in the nineteenth century.

Ancient classical architecture, which was pagan, preceded the Christian gothic architecture, but Knight thought of it as more developed. The first gothic architecture had arisen, he said, in a time of ignorance, and he therefore saw the earliest gothic work as a mere step away from the primitive, saying that 'the pointed arch, which we call Gothic, is the primitive arch'.[3] The only reason that pointed arches were used in medieval times, he thought, was that people at that time, in their ignorance, were unable to construct the round Roman arches, which required a knowledge of centring, building a temporary timber framework in order to hold the incomplete arch in place. He explained what he thought gothic architecture was like:

> At this time, when the taste for Gothic architecture has been so generally revived, nothing is more common, than to hear professors, as well as lovers, of the art, expatiating upon the merits of pure Gothic; and gravely endeavouring to separate it from those spurious and adscitious ornaments, by which it has lately been debased: but, nevertheless, if we ask what they mean by *pure Gothic*, we can receive no satisfactory answer: – there are no rules – no proportions – and consequently, no definitions: but we are referred to certain models of generally acknowledged excellence; which models are of two kinds, entirely differing from one another; the one called the castle, and the other the cathedral or

2 Michael McCarthy, *The Origins of the Gothic Revival* (New Haven: Yale University Press, 1987).

3 *An Analytical Inquiry Into the Principles of Taste*, 4th edn (London: 1808), p. 166.

> monastic; the one having been employed in the fortresses, and the other in the churches and convents of those nations, which divided the Roman empire, and erected the states and kingdoms of modern Europe upon its ruins.[4]

The call to purify gothic came most clearly from the Abbé Laugier, who favoured a clean athletic gothic which displayed its structural principles in making elegant vaults, and when he wrote about the gothic he saw the applied ornament as merely additional blocks of stone which weighed down the essential structure.[5] By contrast Knight felt that ornament was of the essence of the style, and he made a distinction between the visible appearance of lightness and the mechanical fact of lightness:

> That visible effect, which we call lightness, proceeds, like all other beauties of this kind, from the association of ideas: for the specific gravity of bodies is not measured by the eye; and we all know that neither statues of brass or marble, nor buildings of brick and stone, are, in reality, light . . . Attempts at lightness, unless supported by extreme richness, either of material or ornament, either of colour or form, almost always produce meagreness, poverty, and weakness of effect . . . In the Gothic churches . . . a profusion of elaborate ornament, how licentiously soever designed or disposed, seldom failed to produce this effect: but the modern fashion of making buildings neither rich nor massive, and producing lightness of appearance by the deficiency rather than the disposition of the parts, is of all tricks of taste the most absurd, and the most certain of counteracting its own ends.[6]

Knight clearly imagined the gothic style to be cluttered and ornate, but his remarks about the complete lack of regulation should not be taken as condemnation. This licentiousness may have made the style difficult to define, a difficulty which was compounded by the fact that for Knight the term 'gothic' was supposed to cover all the products of the Middle Ages, 'from the third to the thirteenth century inclusive',[7] including therefore styles which would now be separately distinguished and classified as late Roman, Anglo-Saxon and Romanesque, as well as gothic, but such virtues as the gothic did possess stemmed, in Knight's understanding, precisely from this anarchy. The gothic masons may have been in the grip of superstition and a prey of every species of religious enthusiasm and zeal, but whatever their spiritual and intellectual state, they

4 Ibid., p. 162.

5 Marc-Antoine Laugier, *Essai sur l'architecture* (Paris: 1753); trans. *Essay on Architecture*, by Wolfgang and Anni Herrmann (Los Angeles: Hennessey and Ingalls, 1977), pp. 100 ff: 'Our Gothic churches are still the most acceptable. A mass of grotesque ornaments spoils them, and yet, we are awed by a certain air of greatness and majesty.' See also Laugier, *Observations sur l'architecture* (The Hague: 1765), and Andrew Ballantyne, 'First Principles and Ancient Errors: Soane at Dulwich', *Architectural History* (London: Society of Architectural Historians of Great Britain, 1994), pp. 96–111.

6 *Principles of Taste*, p. 180.

7 [Richard Payne Knight], Review of *The Works of James Barry, Esq. Historical Painter; with some Account of his Life and Writing*, the *Edinburgh Review*, vol. 16 (Edinburgh: 1810), pp. 293–325; p. 297.

were in their architecture at least free from that radical vice, the spirit of system. In spite of everything that weighed against them, because the 'contrivers of this refined and fantastic Gothic' trusted their judgement and acted without reference to rules, they produced architecture of merit. They seemed

> to have aimed at producing grandeur and solemnity, together with lightness of effect; and incompatible as these qualities may seem, by attending to the effect only, and considering the means of producing it as wholly subordinate, and in their own power, they succeeded to a degree, which the Grecian architects, who worked by rule, never approached.[8]

This shows that Knight's hostility to rules was even greater than his considerable prejudice against the Middle Ages. When the Greeks worked according to rules, even they could be surpassed; but his enthusiasm for gothic architecture was more limited than might be supposed from this appreciation. He thought that the gothic arch was adopted because of ignorance, not by design, and that the rest of the architecture was adapted from classical models. He supposed, unconventionally but quite reasonably, that medieval battlements had been copied from earlier Greek and Roman ones, an idea which is borne out by some of the small statues which he owned. He also, quite correctly, saw the cathedrals as having ultimately been adapted from classical antecedents, being

> manifestly a corruption of the sacred architecture of the Greeks and Romans, by a mixture of the Moorish or Saracenesque, which is formed out of combination of the Ægyptian, Persian, and Hindoo. It may be traced through all its variations from the church of Santa Sophia at Constantinople, and the cathedral of Montreale near Palermo, the one of the sixth, and the other of the twelfth century, down to the King's chapel at Cambridge, the last and most perfect of this kind of buildings; and to trace it accurately would be a most curious and interesting work.[9]

Had he entertained a rosier view of the Middle Ages then he would have seen gothic architecture *developing* from the architecture of the Romans, as a further flowering from the same productive roots, rather than being a corruption. It can be seen from the passage given here that Knight lumped together all the non-classical styles of architecture as a general barbaric assortment, not making punctilious distinctions among

8 *Principles of Taste*, p. 176.

9 Ibid., p. 166.

them. He did not have the benefit of the researches of the architect Thomas Rickman (1776–1841), who codified and clarified the different styles of English gothic architecture in his immensely influential book *An Attempt to Discriminate the Styles of English Architecture* (1817), a familiarity with which would have enabled Knight to have seen much more reason in medieval architecture than in fact he did. Knight could not have been familiar with Reynolds's remark, given in a lecture in 1784 after the house had been built, that

> Architecture certainly possesses many principles in common with Poetry and Painting. Among those which may be reckoned as the first, is, that of affecting the imagination by means of association of ideas. Thus, for instance, as we have naturally a veneration for antiquity, whatever building brings to our remembrance ancient customs and manners, such as the Castles of the Barons of ancient Chivalry, is sure to give this delight. Hence it is that *towers and battlements* are so often selected by the Painter and the Poet, to make a part of their ideal Landskip; and it is from hence in a great degree, that the buildings of Vanbrugh, who was a Poet as well as an Architect, there is a greater display of the imagination, than we shall find perhaps in any other.[10]

Nevertheless this is the cultural milieu in which Knight was moving; he too praised Vanbrugh,[11] and illustrated the value of imaginative associations of the same kind in *The Landscape:*

> Bless'd is the man in whose sequester'd glade,
> Some ancient abbey's walls diffuse their shade;
> With mouldering windows pierc'd, and turrets crown'd,
> And pinnacles with clinging ivy bound.
> Bless'd too is he, who 'midst his tufted trees,
> Some ruin'd castle's lofty towers sees;
> Imbosom'd high upon the mountain's brow,
> Or nodding o'er the stream that glides below.[12]

The verse itself has associations with Virgil's

> Happy the Man, who, studying Nature's Laws,
> Thro' known Effects can trace the secret Cause.
> His mind possessing, in a quiet state,
> Fearless of Fortune, and resign'd to Fate.
> And happy too is he, who decks the Bow'rs
> Of Sylvans, and adores the Rural Pow'rs.[13]

10 Sir Joshua Reynolds, 'Discourse XII, Delivered to the Students of The Royal Academy, on the Distribution of the Prizes', 10 December 1784, in *Discourses On Art*, ed. Robert R. Wark (New Haven: Yale University Press, 1975), pp. 241–2.

11 Knight, *Principles of Taste*, p. 227.

12 Knight, *The Landscape: A Didactic Poem*, 2nd edn (London: 1795), bk. II, lines 280–7, p. 53.

13 Virgil, *Georgics*, bk. II, lines 490–5, translated by John Dryden (1697), bk. II, lines 698–703. See also Jay Appleton, 'Richard Payne Knight and the *Georgics*', *The Picturesque*, no. 5 (Hereford: The Picturesque Society, 1993), pp. 1–8; and Andrew Ballantyne, 'Bloodshed and Rankling Passion: Lucretius in *The Landscape*', *The Picturesque*, no. 7 (Hereford: The Picturesque Society, 1994), pp. 1–6.

14 Knight's early correspondence is at Herefordshire County Records Office in Hereford.

15 John Harris, 'Pritchard Redivivus,' *Architectural History*, vol. 11 (London: Society of Architectural Historians of Great Britain, 1968), pp. 17 ff.

16 The extent of Pritchard's involvement was settled by Nicholas Penny, 'Architecture and Landscape at Downton', in *The Arrogant Connnoisseur*, ed. Clarke and Penny (Manchester University Press, 1982), pp. 32 ff; see also Howard Colvin, *A Biographical Dictionary of*

And, incidentally, Virgil here was alluding to Epicurus, but, more to the point, the castle's romance was linked back to the work of painters and poets.

Downton

Knight's house was built at Downton-on-the-Rock, west of Ludlow, between 1772 and 1778, but, just before construction began, Knight himself left the scene of activity for France and Italy. Mostly in his absence, the work was supervised by his maternal uncle, Samuel Nash, and a few scraps of correspondence between them survive.[14] The Sicilian journal, from this stage of his life, shows that he was already well read and that his most characteristic enthusiasms were already established.

Originally Knight had commissioned a design for the house from a professional architect in Shrewsbury, Thomas Farnolls Pritchard (1723–77),[15] but his involvement with the house can only have been slight.[16] Pritchard had already been employed by Knight's relations at Croft Castle, a genuinely medieval fortress which Pritchard had been called on to renovate, and which he did with great success with elaborately gothick plasterwork, in a rococo manner which might have met with Walpole's approval (figure 26). The house at Downton, however, had none of this character, and it seems very unlikely that Pritchard was chosen on account of his expertise in the medieval manner. What Pritchard does seem to have done at Downton is to have designed and built a handsome stone bridge across the River Teme,[17] known as the Castle Bridge, which carried the original driveway across the river to the house, and spans the current with three gracious elliptical arches, solid and substantial (figure 27). A second well-designed stone bridge, which seems to have been built later, is somewhat less than a mile downstream. Originally it stood beside the Bringewood Forge, which is now completely ruined but was once an important source of the Knight family's wealth. The Forge Bridge has a castellated parapet and spans the river in a single dramatically high arch, with a smaller span across the mill-race (figure 28).

The building work at Downton should have been under way by 25 September 1772, but there had been a delay: Knight sent a letter from Calais to his uncle at Downton in which he apologised for the fact that he had not written sooner. He explained by way of excuse that he had hoped to include a plan for the house with the letter, but he had found that there was much about the design which should be reconsidered. The letter shows us that Knight was concerned with detailed technical aspects of

British Architects 1660–1840, 3rd edn (New Haven and London: Yale University Press, 1995), p. 783, where 'designs' for Downton Castle are mentioned in the entry for Pritchard; and Alistair Rowan, 'Downton Castle, Herefordshire', in *The Country Seat: Studies in the History of the British Country House Presented to Sir John Summerson*, ed. Colvin and Harris (London: Allen Lane, 1970), p. 170, imagined stylistic affinity between Pritchard's work and the house at Downton.

17 Pritchard was paid for 'bridge work' at Downton, but its extent is not certain. Pevsner (*Buildings of England, Herefordshire* (Harmondsworth: Penguin, 1963), p. 118) attributed the Forge Bridge to Pritchard; and Penny (*The Arrogant Connnoisseur*, p. 32) added the Castle Bridge. The two bridges do seem to be handled in much the same way, and the geometry of the Forge Bridge certainly inclines one to attribute it to Pritchard, as its geometry either anticipated or perhaps derived from that of Pritchard's most celebrated work, the iron bridge at Coalbrookdale. In the absence of records of the involvement of any other architects at the time it seems perfectly reasonable to accept these attributions. However, there is an estate map which shows the house and the Castle Bridge on it, but not the Forge Bridge, which should indicate that the Forge Bridge was not there and was not by Pritchard. Julia Ionides, personal communication.

Figure 26. Staircase at Croft Castle with decorative plasterwork by T .F. Pritchard.

the design, in a way he would not have needed to have been had a professional architect been in his employment: 'I find that the present method of building is to make all the inside beams of Deal which is better and cheaper, so you need not fell any oak. Let Pritchard's bill be paid, but do not tell him that I have no design of imploying him again.'[18] So Knight's house was to be constructed using the most modern techniques and according to his own plan. Pritchard was 49 years old at the time and an experienced architect; Knight was 21 and out of the country. Clearly he

18 Knight to Samuel Nash, 25 September 1772 (MS, Downton Castle Papers, Hereford).

Figure 27. Thomas Hearne, *View of the Castle Bridge, Downton Castle.*

was extraordinarily confident in his abilities and was interested in making the building suit his own ideas. Quite how extraordinary and unconventional those ideas were to be was still not apparent even in November 1772 when Samuel Nash wrote to complain to his nephew about the delay. He could not make a start on the foundations because he had no idea where the walls were to be; and he noted that: 'Mr Pritch[d] has this day sent his bill viz a tending 3 times at Downton to fix on a spot for the new byllding, consulting a bout muterriells and making plans.'[19] This makes it clear that Pritchard had drawn up a plan (which has since been lost) for the house and also that Knight had chosen to disregard it in favour of one of his own – as yet undevised. Pritchard's practical experience might have led Knight to take his advice in technical matters, but even here we find Knight taking his own decisions. Pritchard's influence can, as Nicholas Penny has observed, hardly have gone further than the provision of a technical specification for the foundations.[20] Clearly the design of the house itself was Knight's work: he dismissed his architect before the plan had been settled and before the foundations were laid. The link between Downton Castle and Croft Castle would be an attrac-

19 Samuel Nash to Knight, 2 November 1772 (MS, Downton Castle Papers, Hereford).

20 Penny, *The Arrogant Connnoisseur,* ed. Clarke and Penny, p. 34.

Figure 28. Forge Bridge, Bringewood.

tive one to make, because Croft was the house of Knight's cousin and friend Thomas Johnes (1748–1816), who shared many of his ideas about landscape design, and arranged a superlatively romantic and picturesque estate at Hafod.[21] Johnes outdid Knight in almost every way, except for moderation and prudence. His ambitions overreached his resources, and his hopes sustained him for a surprising length of time against spectacular bad luck, so that his life story is one of grand Romantic doom. For Knight to have been influenced by his aesthetic ideas would have been highly plausible, and Knight's initial choice of architect goes some way towards supporting the notion, but unfortunately nothing remains of Pritchard's suggestions for Downton, and in the building which Knight did erect there is nothing of the rococo gothick of Croft, or the romantic gothic of Hafod. However, we may tentatively suppose that the house was not from the outset imagined as a castellated structure, from the fact that of the two bridges at Downton the only one to be equipped with castellations is that which is at a remove from the house, and the one which, moreover, was probably built later. Most importantly Croft Castle, for all its medieval character, has symmetrically organised façades and there-

21 Elisabeth Inglis-Jones, *Peacocks in Paradise* (London: Faber, 1950); Caroline Kerkham, 'Hafod: Paradise Lost', *Journal of Garden History*, no. 11 (London: The Garden History Society, 1991), pp. 207–16; *A Land of Pure Delight: Selections from the Letters of Thomas Johnes of Hafod, 1748–1816*, ed. Richard J. Moore-Colyer (Llandysul, Dyfed: Gomer, 1992); Andrew Sclater, 'Sublime Irregularities and the Design of Hafod', *The Picturesque*,

fore could not possibly have influenced the free planning which was Downton's most revolutionary innovation.

It is claimed that Knight's house was the first country house of any importance to have been erected in Europe since the Renaissance that was designed from the outset to have an irregular plan.[22] Such notably asymmetrical houses as Vanbrugh's castle at Blackheath or Walpole's Strawberry Hill, which would at first seem to anticipate Downton in this respect were originally symmetrical buildings and were only later adapted into their well-known irregular states.[23] It was, however, Walpole's intention from the outset to make Strawberry Hill irregular. 'I am going to build a little Gothic castle', he wrote, saying something which, significantly, Knight never did,[24] but Walpole made it clear that he had something asymmetrical in mind when he said that he was 'as fond of Sharawaggi, or Chinese lack of symmetry, in buildings as in grounds or gardens'.[25] Therefore he clearly anticipated Knight in allowing the discipline of the English landscape garden to take over the composition of a dwelling, in marked contrast to the earlier practice of allowing the discipline of the symmetrical house to be extended out into the landscape, such as can be seen at its most extensively developed at Versailles. Knight's notion of landscape design was to enhance as sympathetically as possible the accidental character of the place which he had very carefully selected, and the task of placing a building in this setting involved accepting the natural surroundings as given. It would have been expected that he would have erected a house with a symmetrical frontage with a central portico, which was generally deemed proper by the fastidious man of taste, but Knight made it clear that it would not have pleased him:

> Since the introduction of another style of ornamental gardening, called at first oriental, and afterwards landscape gardening (probably from its efficacy in destroying all picturesque composition) Grecian temples have been employed as decorations by almost all persons, who could afford to indulge their taste in objects so costly: but, though executed, in many instances, on a scale and in a manner suitable to the design, disappointment has, I believe, been invariably the result. Nevertheless they are unquestionably beautiful, being exactly copied from the models, which have stood the criticism of successive ages, and been constantly beheld with delight and admiration. In the rich lawns and shrubberies of England, however, they lose all that power to please which they so eminently possess on the barren hills of

no. 8 (Hereford: The Picturesque Society, 1994), pp. 17–23.

22 Nikolaus Pevsner, 'Richard Payne Knight', *The Art Bulletin*, vol. 30 (1949), reprinted in *Studies in Art, Architecture and Design*, 2 vols. (London: Thames and Hudson, 1968), vol. I, pp. 109 ff; Penny, *The Arrogant Connoisseur*, pp. 42–3; Christopher Hussey, 'A Regency Prophet of Modernism', *Country Life Annual* (London: Country Life, 1956), p. 48.

23 Pevsner, 'Richard Payne Knight', pp. 111–12.

24 *The Yale Edition of Horace Walpole's Correspondence*, ed. W. S. Lewis, 48 vols. (New Haven: Yale University Press, 1937–83), vol. XX, p. 111, Horace Walpole to Horace Mann, 10 January 1750. See McCarthy, *Gothic Revival*, p. 63.

25 *Walpole's Correspondence*, vol. XX, p. 127, Walpole to Mann, 25 February 1750.

Figure 29. Thomas Hearne, *Distant view of Downton Castle.*

> Agrigentum and Segesta, or the naked plains of Paestum and Athens. But barren and naked as these hills and plains are, they are still, if I may say so, their native hills and plains – the scenery, in which they sprang; and in which the mind, therefore, contemplates them connected and associated with numberless interesting circumstances, both local and historical – both physical and moral, upon which it delights to dwell. In our parks and gardens, on the contrary, they stand wholly unconnected with all that surrounds them – mere unmeaning excrescences.[26]

The most important of Knight's pictorial sources for advice about landscape and architecture was certainly Claude, whose example was clearly evoked in Thomas Hearne's distant view of the house (figure 29). Knight's collection was to include many Claude drawings and one of his paintings, but they were not in his ownership when the house was being built. Claude did paint classical temples in the landscape, and in doing so had influenced the connoisseurs of whom Knight spoke; but this example was not the one to follow in England, where:

26 *Principles of Taste*, pp. 169–70.

> The best style of architecture for irregular and picturesque houses, which can now be adapted, is that mixed style, which characterises the buildings of Claude and the Poussins . . . it is distinguished by no particular manner of execution, or class of ornaments; but admits of all promiscuously . . . In a matter, however, which affords so wide a field for the licentious deviations of whim and caprice, it may be discreet always to pay some attention to authority; especially when we have such great authorities as those of the great landscape painters above mentioned; the study of whose works may at once enrich and restrain invention.[27]

This remark had evidently been absorbed by the author of a guide to Ludlow published in 1821, who remarked that

> The singular irregularity of the house, which has proved the greatest source of fretful remark, had its origin in the very design of the builder, whose intention was not so much to copy the style of any particular age or country, as to produce a comfortable, pleasant and elegant dwelling, under an outward form which might serve as a principal, and not unsuitable feature for the wild, romantic, and picturesque scenery of his desmesne.[28]

Close to the Welsh border, where Knight chose to build his house, no large-scale building type is more securely sanctioned by precedent than is the castle. Croft Castle is a particularly comfortable example, having been thoroughly refurbished, but there are others in every state of preservation and decay, such as the highly picturesque Stokesay or the romantic ruin at Wigmore which had once been the home of the Harley family (the Earl of Oxford's family). Every village in Downton's vicinity seems to have a castle of some sort to its name, even if (as is the case at Downton village) all that remains is an inconspicuous turfed mound. The most spectacular of all these relics is the great castle at Ludlow; but while this may seem to set an attractive example to follow, it could be seen alternatively as so outstandingly excellent as to deter imitations which would inevitably seem inferior. Certainly this latter view was taken by Geoffrey Lipscomb, who visited Downton Castle in 1802 and saw fit to publish his remarks, describing how he 'turned into a dirty lane on the right, passed a deep and narrow valley, full of wood, crossed a turnpike road, and soon arrived at the seat of Richard Payne Knight Esq':

> Before we visited Downton I could not help remarking that the man who presumed to imitate an ancient castle within an hour's

27 Ibid., p. 225.

28 *Felton's New Guide to the Town of Ludlow* (Ludlow: 1821), p. 158.

> ride of Ludlow, ought at least to possess no small share of that species of fortitude which would enable him to withstand the criticism of those who might be inclined to view it with a scrutinising eye; because the perfect specimen of feudal splendour which Ludlow furnished as a model, would be fresh in the memory of almost every traveller likely to visit Downton; and, in a certain degree, would enable even very unskilful persons to form a tolerable judgement of the comparative merits of the imitation.[29]

Another possible influence which could have led Knight to think of building himself a castle was his cousin Edward Knight of Wolverley, a friend of Shenstone and an admirer of the work of Sanderson Miller (1716–80), a gentleman architect. Edward Knight took measurements of the tower which Miller had built near his seat to commemorate the battle of Edge Hill, at Radway.[30] Again this was an exercise in gothicism, and although the building was asymmetrical it, like other towers built by Miller, was a mere folly, a garden ornament, not a dwelling of consequence, and Knight's house had a seriousness of purpose which is lacking in Miller's charming, but deliberately quaint, structures and, though it might be seen as a 'parent of Downton',[31] the offspring certainly was no obedient heir. Miller's building not only had a very different functional role, but its irregular shape was not derived from the consideration of practical utility, and it also made use of deliberately gothicising detail – painted glass, window tracery, a drawbridge – which Knight avoided.

In short there are, local to Downton, a good many precedents for the adoption of a medieval style; but this should not lead us instantly to suppose that any or all of them, separately or in combination, had any decisive effect on Knight's thinking. Despite the fact that Knight felt his house should be connected with the character of the place in which it was located, he did not design it when he was at Downton but while he was travelling in France and Italy, and though his friends and cousins may have discussed the design with him at an early stage of its development he was, while making his final design, far removed from their suggestions and the influence of buildings close to Downton. If it had been Knight's intention to build an imitation of Ludlow Castle then he would not have posted the design home from Italy. Moreover, as Knight's instructions were sent to his uncle by post they were certainly worked out on paper, so he was in a position to see his design in highly abstract terms, and for his vision – to a perfectly remarkable degree – to remain unclouded by the contingencies of practical reality.

29 Geoffrey Lipscomb, *A Journey into South Wales* (London: 1802), pp. 265–7.

30 Diana Uhlmann, *Croft Castle* (London: National Trust, 1982), p. 10. Edward Knight quoted by McCarthy, *Gothic Revival*, p. 52.

31 David Watkin, *The English Vision* (London: John Murray, 1982), p. 51.

As Knight thought of the Middle Ages as a completely dreadful time of darkness, destitute of philosophy and riddled with superstition and 'priestcraft', it is unlikely that he would have wanted his house to be seen as gothic; and if it is judged as an essay in medievalism then inevitably it is found sorely wanting, but nevertheless some visitors judged it to be a half-hearted attempt at an essay in the medieval manner. Geoffrey Lipscomb, for example, thought that the house hardly tried at all to present itself as a castle, but nevertheless supposed that this was what it was trying feebly to do, and he condemned it, saying:

> It is embattled, and built of stone, in which particulars only it can, with propriety, be said to resemble an ancient castle; for the windows are all square modern sashes, and the door-way is equally fashionable, and equally inconsistent. One of the angles of the building is terminated by an octagon tower, the other by a diminutive circular turret, containing a closet with a square sash window.
>
> Nothing within sight of the building bears the slightest appearance of the antique . . . if Mr. Knight had expended half the sum which it has cost him to provoke satirical reflections on his extraordinary taste in building, in repairing the roads near his seat, he might have possessed one of the most elegant and complete residences, – one of the prettiest villas which this country can boast, without the mortification of finding every visitor a critic, – without incurring the frowns of the fastidious, – or provoking a comparison of this *avowed* imitation of the ancients, with works which must every day bring it not only into disrepute, but even into contempt . . . the modern-antique mansion of Downton is unworthy of the dignified title of a castle. [32]

If we turn elsewhere in Lipscomb's account of his travels we find that he was consistently more sympathetic to the Middle Ages than was Knight. In the passage quoted above, Lipscomb preferred to use the word 'antique' (rather than 'gothic') to mean *medieval*, as 'gothic' had etymologically pejorative connotations. The parts of the house which Lipscomb did not hesitate to label as 'modern' would today be recognised as classical. Knight would have approved of that, but it is clear that Lipscomb and Knight had very different views of the world, the most important being that Lipscomb presented himself in this account as a pious Christian. Although both he and Knight shared a passion for nature, their passion stemmed from quite different preoccupations, and

32 *A Journey into South Wales,* pp. 268–71.

Figure 30. View of Downton Castle, from Neale's views of seats.

stood in marked contrast to one another. Lipscomb's is best illustrated in his reactions to natural scenery rather than to buildings, as, for example, when he visited the Rhydoll waterfall, and was thrown into a transport of religious ecstasy. 'I was rivetted to the place,' he said,

> and experienced that thrilling horror, that reverential awe, that holy dread, which an assemblage of the grandest scenery alone can inspire; nor did I leave this sacred temple of solitude until I had humbly adored the Creator and Preserver of all around me. – the great, the mighty Lord! and Father of the Universe!!![33]

One need hardly add that when Lipscomb looked over the house at Downton nothing remotely akin to holy dread affected his judgement. The house was not only a man-made work, it suffered also from being the work of a notorious infidel, and it is only to be expected that Lipscomb would have scorned it, which he did by saying that 'It would . . . be very easy, by levelling the battlements, and removing the towers, to convert into a modern looking house, that which is so very improperly termed Downton castle'.[34] There is a view which clearly shows the sash windows (figure 30) and Lipscomb was not alone in seeing Knight's house as an

33 Ibid., p. 145.

34 Ibid., p. 270.

Figure 31. Downton Castle, north front.

inept exercise in the gothic style. In 1797 the *Gentleman's Magazine* had carried an article which remarked that:

> Instead of that clutter of towers and pinnacles which makes a Gothic building so picturesque, the whole is long and flat; and, on a closer examination, there has been such carelessness about the minuter parts of the style, that even the battlements want *copings*. The inside of the house is modern, but affords little to be admired.[35]

In looking at Knight's house in the twentieth century we are handicapped by a problem caused by commentators such as these, who saw the building as a failed attempt to build in the gothic style as did a later owner, Andrew Johnes Rouse Boughton Knight, who in the 1860s had it treated so as to supply its deficiency. He added a clutter of towers, along with some carved gothic tracery in the windows, oriels and copings for the battlements. The north side of the house today, which has become the entrance front, is composed almost entirely from elements which were added at this time (figure 31). If we look at the house from the north then the only element of the composition which remains from Knight's building is the circular tower at the extreme right, and even that has undergone change: its battlements were replaced and there is a window with gothic tracery exactly where Lipscomb complained of a modern sash. The additional towers and turrets certainly helped to variegate the skyline, but it is unfortunate that Christopher Hussey should have chosen this particular view as the most effective, and suggest that the house anticipated the craze for medievalism prompted by the vogue for

35 *Gentleman's Magazine*, June 1797, p. 473 (unsigned).

Figure 32. Downton Castle, stableyard.

Sir Walter Scott's novels.[36] The gothic tracery at Downton was not 'ahead of its time', but was added later; indeed the only part of the building externally to retain its pre-Victorian character is the stable yard, and even here there were some alterations, such as the storey which was added above the kitchen (figure 32).

It is not surprising that Knight's house was seen as gothic because it made use of such elements as towers and battlements which were most readily associated with medieval castles; and it is not surprising that having accepted the building as gothic, it should have seemed to have been in need of 'improvement', or correction. As the popularity of the gothic style gained ground many existing buildings were transformed into gothic piles, and the conversion of Downton could be carried out more sympathetically than in some other cases. There is a drawing by James Sheriff of Downton in its original state, which shows that the house was much plainer than the castle which can be seen today (figure 33). The building shown in Sheriff's drawing is also much smaller than the present house: there were fewer and shorter towers, with the central square one looking particularly squat. On the right of the central tower Sheriff showed the wing which housed the servants' offices, which was

36 Christopher Hussey, 'A Regency Prophet of Modernism', p. 46.

Figure 33. James Sherriff, *View of Downton Castle.*

then a storey lower than it is today; also, whereas the bay which figures at the extreme right of Sheriff's drawing simply broke forward without a change in the parapet's height, the equivalent bay today can be seen to be developed more fully into a tower. The windows in this section of the building in Sheriff's drawing clearly have arched openings, but it is not absolutely clear from the drawing whether or not the arches are pointed. Presumably the windows depicted here matched those which have survived in the stable-yard; but even if we regard these windows as definitely pointed then we are not led immediately to the conclusion that Knight intended thereby to signify a gothic building. The pointed arch was the primitive arch, and in Knight's house it was used only in the servants' wing, and so can be taken to indicate that it had a lower status. The house without its battlements, as Lipscomb remarked, would not have seemed gothic at all, and Knight did not think that castellations belonged to the Middle Ages any more than did the pointed arch. He believed that there was nothing worthy of the name 'architecture' extant in Europe prior to the occupation by the Roman Empire; therefore, he argued, when the gothic masons began to build they had for guidance only the ruins which remained from classical civilisation; so he confidently asserted

> That the military architecture of the Greeks and Romans consisted . . . of walls and towers capped with battlements is certain; but in what manner those battlements were formed and finished is not so easily ascertained; there being no perfect specimen of them extant. It is probable, however, that they differed in different ages, accordingly as the modes of attack and defence were varied. The overhanging battlements, now called Gothic, were certainly known to the Romans.[37]

Knight went on to claim that the proportions of these fortifications followed no rules but those of convenience and effectiveness; and that similarly Roman villas were laid out irregularly, spreading in every direction as convenience suggested – something that Knight's own house most conspicuously did. So where Knight is concerned it is a mistake to suppose that battlements signal 'gothic'. For him they were part of classical civilisation and were merely copied by the barbaric Christians who laid waste to genuine culture and learning. In *An Analytical Inquiry into the Principles of Taste*, Knight said

> It is now more than thirty years since the author of this inquiry ventured to build a house, ornamented with what are called Gothic towers and battlements without, and with Grecian ceilings, columns and entablatures within; and though his example has not been much followed, he has every reason to congratulate himself upon the success of the experiment.[38]

It is worth noting here the distance Knight put between himself and the towers and battlements which 'are called Gothic', by some but perhaps not by Knight himself, as his intention at Downton seems to have been to build a modern house, which is to say a classical house. At Downton the interiors are all very clearly and conventionally classical, and they were seen by Knight's visitors as unexceptionably, even uninterestingly, modern; there was no problem here: antique classical forms and decorations could be used in conjunction with modern elements (such as sash windows) without any sense of awkwardness because both were understood as 'modern'. But the outside of the house was very different, and could not be seen as modern in the same way, even though (if we take Knight's own definition of his terms) there is no reason to suppose that it was not intended to be classical throughout, both inside and out. Knight wrote:

> A house may be adorned with towers and battlements, or pinnacles and flying buttresses; but it should still maintain the

37 *Principles of Taste*, pp. 163–4.

38 Ibid., p. 223.

> character of the age and country in which it is erected; and not pretend to be a fortress or monastery of a remote period or distant country: for such false pretensions never escape detection; and, when detected, necessarily excite those sentiments, which exposed imposture never fails to excite.[39]

In view of this firmly stated opinion it is most unlikely that Knight would have attempted to build a house which was intended to be anything other than English and modern, and it would be a mistake to suppose that Knight was trying in his house to imitate the forms of the buildings of a remote age or country such as Greece in the classical age, or medieval England. Yet despite this apparent desire to build in the manner of the country and the age in which he lived we do not find at Downton the conventionally pretty 'modern villa' which Lipscomb recommended. The basic house was straightforwardly modern in its decorative style (but remarkably and daringly planned on principles which could conceivably be called 'Chinese' clearly with the intention of linking the building to the surrounding landscape) and to this basic design Knight added his 'adornments': towers and battlements. Apart from these elements there is externally hardly any decoration at all: only a thin line running round the base of the parapet, nothing more. The outside of the building was unusually bare, the blank surfaces of the walls being relieved only by the doors and windows which were introduced where they were made necessary by the internal functioning of the building. A more experienced, or a more conventionally grounded, eighteenth-century architect faced with façades as empty as those at Downton might well have proposed the use of architectural devices to give the building a less forbidding aspect. Modelled window-surrounds, blind windows or realistically faked windows were introduced as a matter of course into eighteenth-century designs; but Knight made no use of them in his façades, and this was certainly a matter of design, not of ignorance. He did not feel that it was against his principles to use such things, as he did not avoid them internally: in his circular dining room, modelled on the Pantheon in Rome, there was a false window glazed with mirror to balance the genuine window across the room; and in his drawing room a doorway on one side of his Doric fireplace, which led through into his study, was symmetrically matched with a second which led into a cupboard. Nevertheless from the outside the house appeared wildly and unaccountably irregular, though it was actually quite rigorously disciplined from within, as we shall see. Its layout was certainly classical so far as Knight was concerned: irregular planning was not only permitted in a

39 Ibid., p. 224.

house which sought to imitate the true principles of the ancient Greeks, it was actually entailed in the attempt. Knight believed that only the temples and the town houses of antiquity were symmetrical, whereas country houses sprawled at their convenience. Had Knight designed himself a symmetrical country house then he would have been betraying classical principles as he understood them.[40] When Knight's contemporaries saw the building as Gothic then they condemned it, but they need not have seen it in that way; for example, Henry Skrine, who visited Downton in 1795, felt puzzled by it, but his reaction was not dismissive. 'This modern castle,' he said, does not

> in any respect, either of figure or position, resemble those ancient fortresses which abound in that quarter of the kingdom. Still, irregular and unaccountable as it appears, the eye is rather pleased than offended with it, and the assortment of apartments within, some of which are very splendid, does not lessen its effect.[41]

Whereas Lipscomb's description suggested a building which tried (and miserably failed) to seem ancient, Skrine's suggests something new (so avant-garde as to perplex) but successful. Lipscomb felt that the house resembled an ancient fortress in only one respect, that is, its inadequately modelled battlements, whereas Skrine described the house as 'modern' and tells us that it did not in any respect resemble an ancient fortress. Skrine's reading was much more sympathetic than Lipscomb's, and he was, in his travels, in search of quite different objects of contemplation, taking delight for example in the sight of the activity of the many forges and furnaces at Coalbrookdale (where the Knight family had interests); and it is worth noting that Knight did not find the Bringewood Forge an intrusion in his landscape, though its presence must have been apparent, and it was later demolished; but Knight had it refurbished in 1784 and let it out for the next thirty-one years.[42] Skrine's outlook was readier to accept the experimental and the progressive than was Lipscomb's, which had a greater sympathy than Knight's for 'ancient' gothicisms.

Planning

Knight's plan for the house, when it eventually arrived, was remarkable: internally its arrangements abided by the conventions of the day, but the conventional rooms were grouped to startlingly original effect, giving

40 Ibid., pp. 167–8. 'The system of regularity, of which the moderns have been so tenacious in the plans of their country houses, was taken from the sacred, and not from the domestic architecture of the ancients . . . These regular structures [the temples] being the only monuments of ancient taste and magnificence in architecture, that remained at the resurrection of the arts [i.e. the Renaissance], in a state sufficiently entire to be perfectly understood, the revivers of the Grecian style copied it servilely from them, and applied it indiscriminately to their country as well as their town houses.'

41 Henry Skrine, *Two Successive Tours Throughout the Whole of Wales with several of the adjacent English Counties; so as to form a comprehensive view of the Picturesque Beauty, the peculiar manners, and the fine remains of antiquity, in that interesting part of the Island* (London: 1795), reprinted in *A General Collection of the Best and Most Interesting Voyages and Travels in all parts of the World*, ed. John Pinkerton (London: 1808), p. 641.

42 Tom Wall, 'The Verdant Landscape: the practice and theory of Richard Payne Knight at Downton Vale' in *The Picturesque Landscape: Visions of Georgian Herefordshire,* ed. Stephen Daniels and Charles Watkins (Nottingham University Press, 1994), p. 55.

Figure 34. Downton Castle, dining room

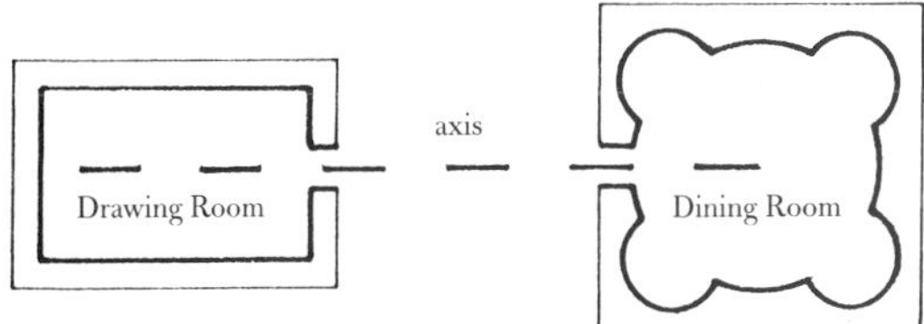

Figure 35. Plan showing alignment of dining room and drawing room at Downton Castle.

Figure 36. Downton Castle, drawing room.

rise to the irregular and unaccountable appearance of the exterior. The analysis of the plan which follows is not an attempt to imagine the design process through which Knight went in order to arrive at his design; there must have been a variety of trials and experiments before Knight arrived at so original a conclusion, but no record of them survives and without drawings to record the development of the ideas, no such reconstruction is possible: what can be done, though, is to analyse it and show that it works in a reasonable way. In examining the house plan it quickly becomes apparent that utilitarian concerns took priority over any notion of geometric regularity.

The central and the grandest room was the dining room, domed like the Pantheon, with a coffered ceiling and Corinthian columns, giving formal meals a setting almost of sanctity, which seems appropriate in an Epicurean (figure 34). The room was centralised, with four axes of approximate symmetry, illuminated principally from a lantern (corresponding with the oculus in the original Pantheon), which was blocked up when an extra storey was added in the Victorian extension.

From the dining room, along one of its axes, a line can be extended to form the processional route from the drawing room (figures 35 and 36), a configuration which happily accommodates the usual social arrangements, whereby guests would assemble in the drawing room and, when the signal was given, men and women would link arms in pairs and process through to the meal. The dining room and drawing room in eighteenth-century houses are often axially aligned, and at Downton there was no need to forsake this desirable axis for the sake of the building's external appearance.

Next to the drawing room was a range of rooms which included the library and some smaller rooms (which were probably bedrooms for guests, but they have since been converted into a ballroom).[43] These rooms were arranged so that they were aligned along only one wall at a time, which meant that no room's size was compromised by the size of its neighbours. The library was shorter than the drawing room, but one wall ran straight across one end of both of them. The bedrooms were shorter than the library, but they shared a continuation of the library's external wall. The bedrooms were all the same length as one another – which is understandable since they all had the same function – but if the function had demanded variations then the aesthetic could easily have accommodated them (figure 37).

A corridor connected the dining room with the kitchen, perhaps running as a covered walk for part of its distance in order to stop the spread of cooking smells.[44] The servants' offices were arranged to lead off the corridor, the coherence of which disciplined the rooms' arrangement: as the inner wall of each room made a part of a long straight circulation route, the outer walls were adjusted freely so as to make rooms of convenient sizes for the activities they were to house (figure 38).

43 Penny, *Arrogant Connoisseur*, p. 34.

44 It is necessary to walk in the open air between the kitchen and the dining room at Berrington, where the offices were grouped in a symmetrical court behind the main block of the house. The location and sizes of the service rooms at Downton is conjectural, as they were largely obscured by Victorian alterations, though the kitchen survives.

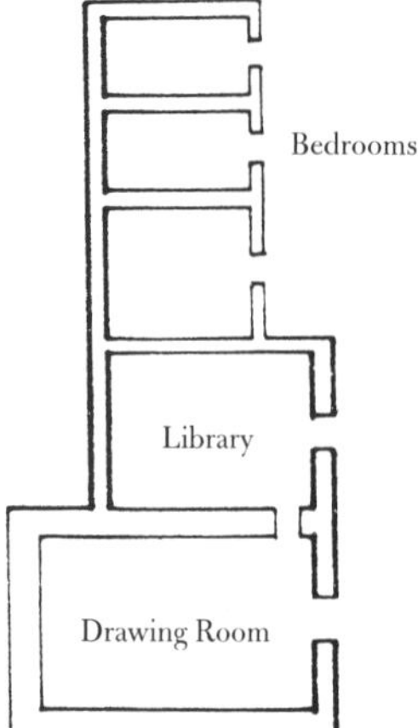

Figure 37. Plan showing alignments of walls from drawing room to library, and library to bedrooms at Downton Castle.

The dining room at meal times was the space which would have demanded the most attention from the servants, and it was therefore appropriate for it to be closely linked with the servants' offices. Sheriff's drawing shows that the roofs over the offices were noticeably lower than those above the principal rooms, so not only the disposition of their rooms, but also their heights, were related to their function, without uniformity of external appearance.

As described so far the house is divided into two parts, and near the Mediterranean it could conceivably have remained that way, but in Britain's climate it made sense to enclose the space given over to circulation. A corridor was introduced in order to reach the guest rooms, and the central space between the dining room and the drawing room extended back far enough to meet it. The other end of the hallway was defined by placing a wall across it, as close as possible to the axially related doorways into the two principal rooms – allowing enough space for the elaborate door-surrounds. The entrance to the house was originally made through this wall, placed again axially between the two reception rooms, and a porch developed about the entrance (figure 39). The central circulation area was subdivided so as to give differing degrees of privacy, separating the entrance hall from the staircase hall, which left the library and the guest rooms in a slightly more secluded state. The library, which would have been visited by learned guests, was made accessible directly from the drawing room (and a fake doorway introduced in order to balance the symmetry).

One of the advantages which this plan had over more conventional

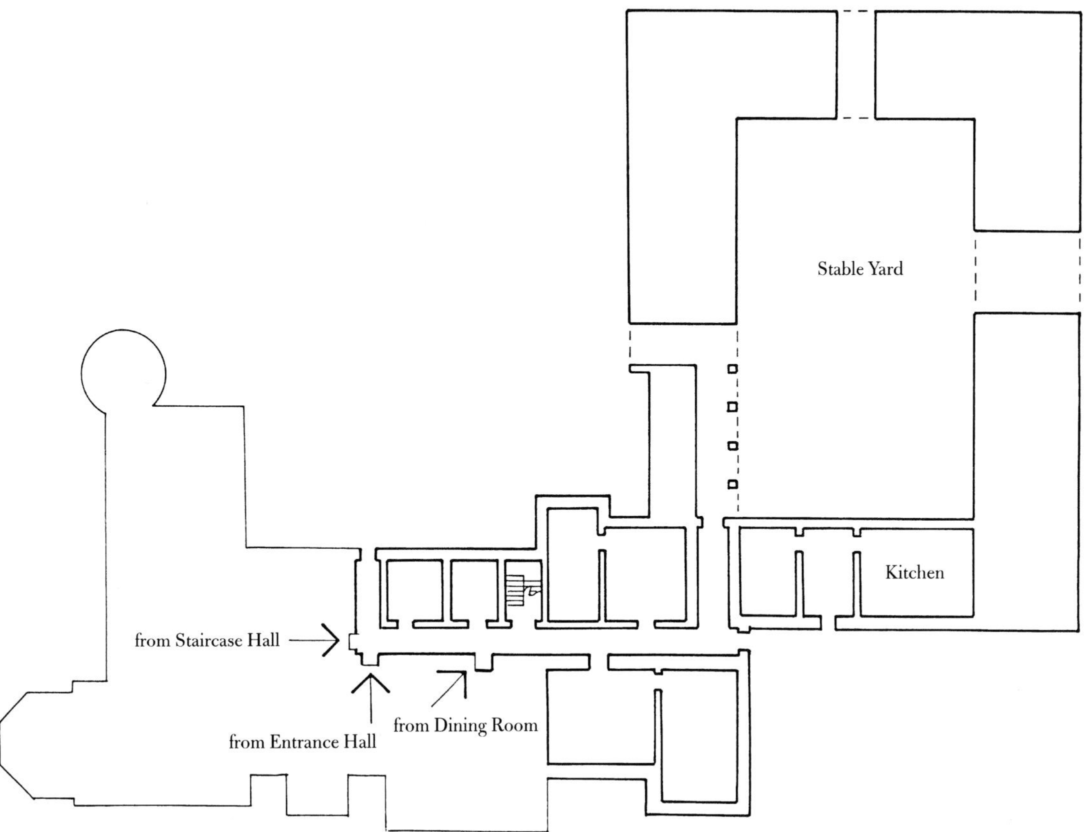

Figure 38. Arrangement of domestic offices at Downton Castle.

alternatives was that it could be extended: the two corridors could be made as long as necessary in order to reach as many rooms as might be ranged along them. The irregular aesthetic would not be disturbed by the inclusion of additional elements. The ingenuity of Knight's plan lay in the fact that it allowed for each and every room to be adjustable in size and shape; and, because there was no concern for overall symmetry, or for any simple overall shape, there was no need for the proportions of one room to be sacrificed (or even adjusted) for the sake of another's.

A good example of a conventional house plan of the time is at Berrington Hall, the house which was built for Thomas Harley at virtually the same time that Knight's house was being built (1778–81) (figures 40 and 41).[45] The architect was Henry Holland (1745–1806), who married Capability Brown's daughter, and enlarged Carlton House for the Prince of Wales (1783–95) and, also for the latter, designed the modest

45 See p. 267.

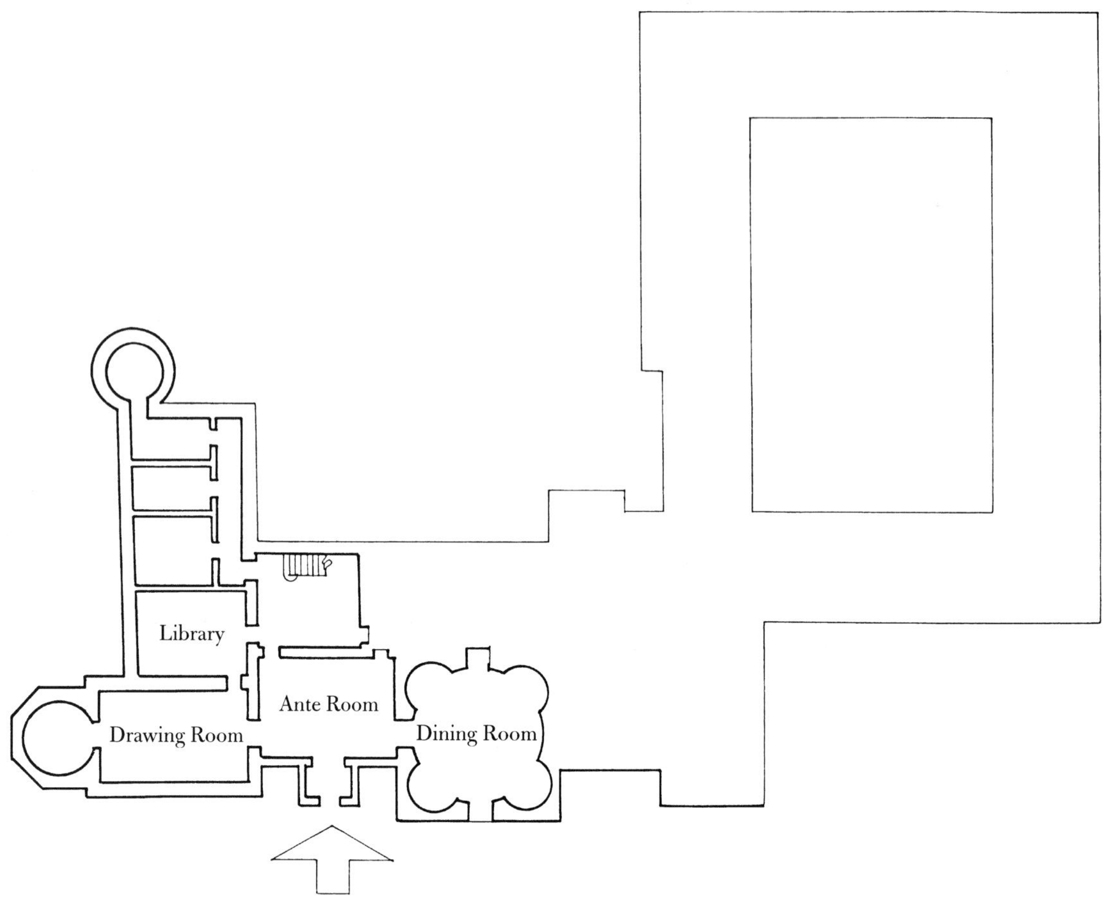

Figure 39. Plan of Downton Castle's original arrangement.

pavilion which later flourished into the Indian extravaganza at Brighton. At Berrington his ingenuity was engaged in organising the house so as to combine convenient arrangements inside with symmetrical compositions outside, and there was a constant tension in the planning between, which involved for example making the drawing room and the billiard room the same size, whether they needed to be or not, and introducing an apse into the boudoir, in order to have its window central in the wall; and the outside of the building was made regular by the introduction of at least eight large fully modelled fake windows. Knight used such devices inside his house, where propriety demanded regularity in the layout of the rooms, but externally he had abandoned convention and embraced freedom. If we compare the plan of Downton with that of Strawberry Hill (figure 42), then the latter looks very whimsical in comparison. The importance of Knight's plan lies in the fact that he achieved the scenic

Figure 40. Henry Holland, Berrington Hall, Herefordshire, 1778–81.

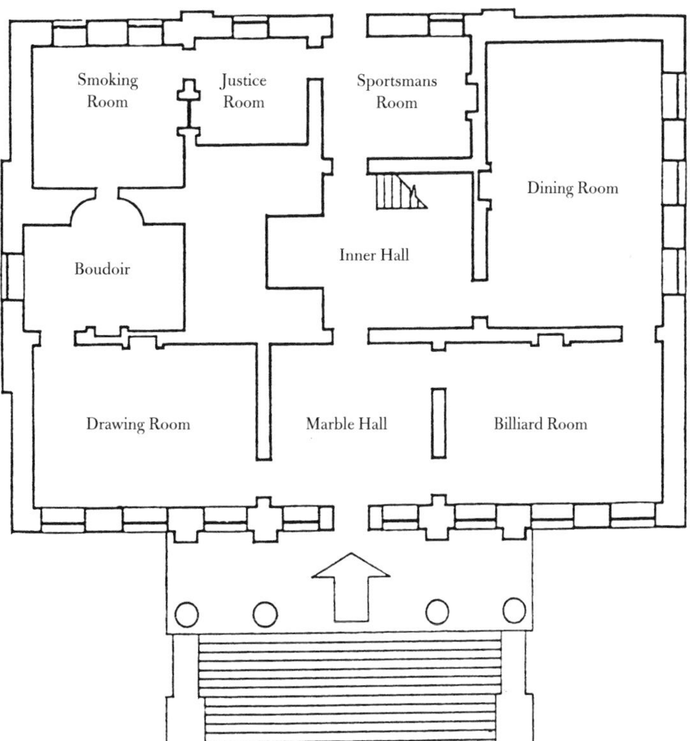

Figure 41. Plan of Berrington Hall.

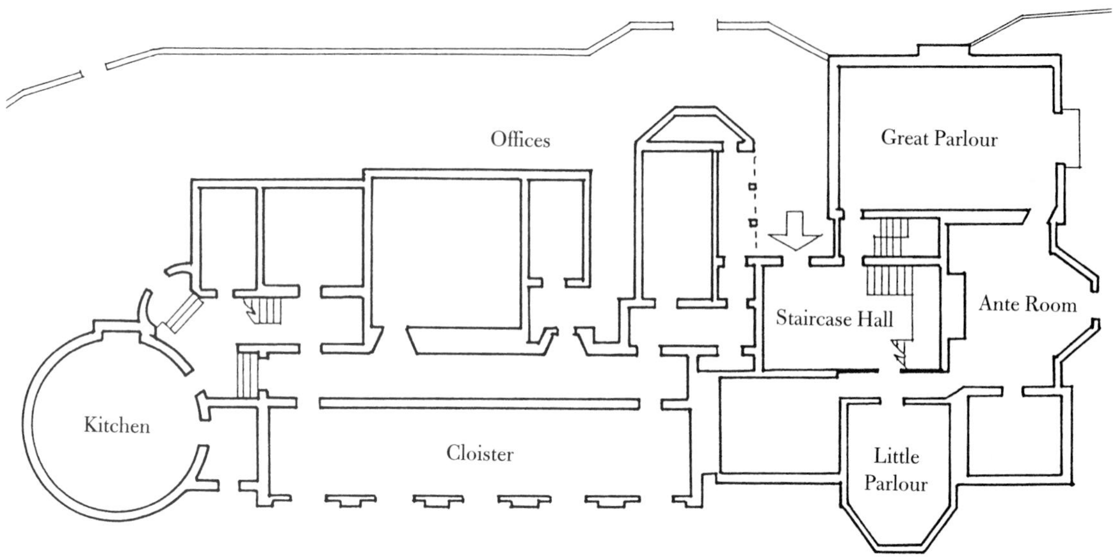

Figure 42. Plan of Strawberry Hill, Twickenham. Horace Walpole, 1750–81.

effect of irregularity without sacrificing anything at all by way of convenience.

Imagery

When Knight adapted his house from its original form he did so in such a way as to follow the more determinedly his advice about picturesque principles. He made the original hallway into a more habitable music room by moving the main entrance to the north of the house (figure 43). This may have helped the serviceability of the approach from Ludlow, of which Lipscomb had complained, but the first sight of the house would certainly have been made less dramatic, and the entry was now along a dark passageway. The original porch was replaced by a bay window, which was different from the other already in the house, being Elizabethan in style, like the house which was shown in Hearne's plate of the picturesque dwelling in *The Landscape* (see figure 22). A sketchy watercolour survives showing this window, the dining room tower and a stretch of wall to the right of it which, curiously, has no battlements, even though they were recorded as being there before and after the date of the picture; so perhaps they were removed in order further to variegate his building's appearance. The artist is not known for certain, but of Knight's visitors at Downton Richard Westall seems to be the most likely,

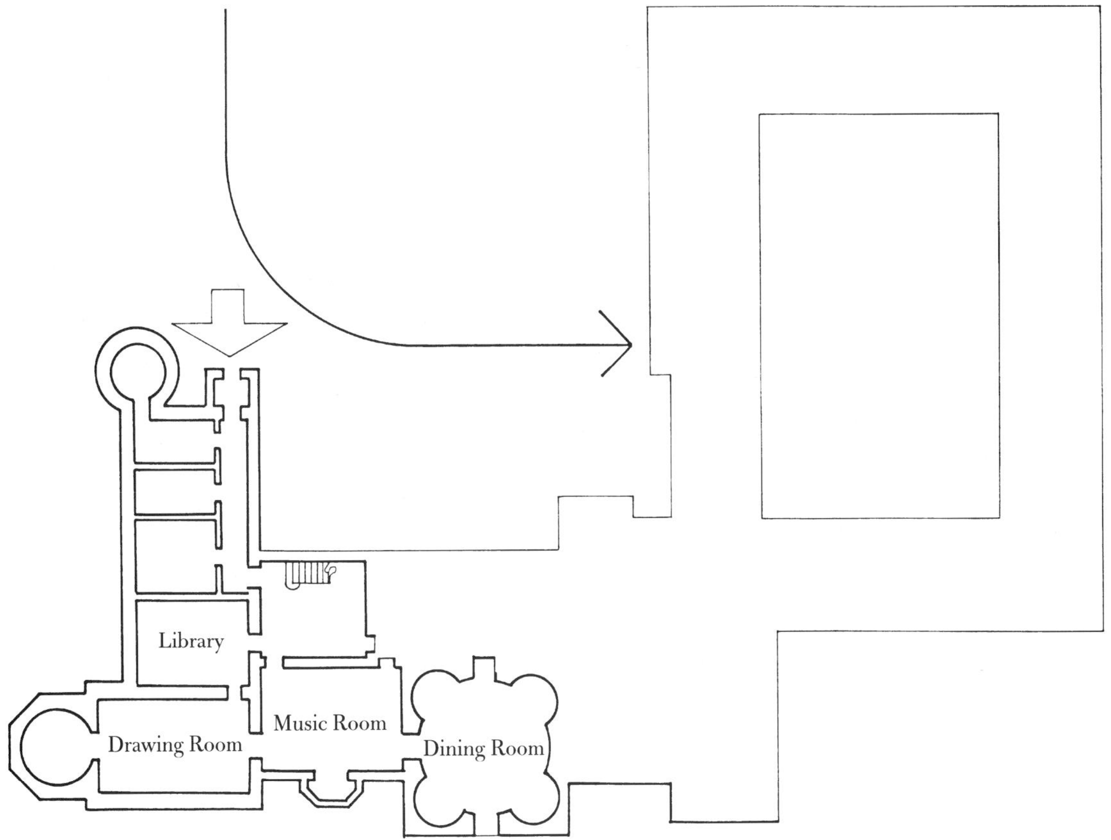

Figure 43. Revised plan of Downton Castle, entrance to the north.

on stylistic grounds (given that this was a sketch and not a highly finished work) and because it could plausibly show the house in 1806, when he is known to have visited. At different times the battlements around the house were all remodelled, with the exception of those in the tower of the stable-yard, which had no impact on distant views.

Knight was also to add to the composition an isolated tower, for his own use after his brother's family had moved into the main house and Knight himself had taken himself off to Stonebrook Cottage. A precedent for the addition can be found in Claude, and the tower neatly expresses Knight's role at a distance from the family home (figures 44 and 45).

Looking to Lucretius for imagery which might have informed Knight's design, there is disappointingly little to be found about buildings; certainly *De Rerum Natura* gives no clear instructions about house design, however, he did give a description of Nature as personified by the Greek poets. Nature/Venus/the Earth, he tells us

Figure 44. Downton Castle, isolated tower.

is called the Great Mother and the mother of beasts;
She is the actual progenitor of our bodies.
The wise old poets of Greece have represented her
Sitting back in a chariot and driving two lions
High in mid-air, by way of making the point
That the earth must not be thought of as resting on earth.
They chose wild beasts as an indication that offspring,
However wild, are bound to submit to their parents.
They put a crown like a wall around her head
Because there are towns and fortresses in high places.
It is with these insignia that the Great Mother
Is carried about now amidst a general shudder.[46]

The 'crown like a wall' in the original Latin was a '*corona muralique*', the 'mural crown' which was presented to the first soldier to breach the wall of a town under siege.[47] It survives as a heraldic device, and was being worn by some of the silver statuettes, depicting the personifications of towns, in Knight's collection of antiquities (figure 46). So perhaps Knight's intention was less to model a 'castle' as such than to model a walled town; the house is in a high place, and when seen from the

46 Lucretius, *De Rerum Natura*, bk. II, lines 598–609; trans. C. H. Sisson, *Lucretius: the Poem on Nature* (Manchester: Carcanet, 1976), p. 60.

47 *Oxford Latin Dictionary* (London: 1968), p. 1146c (muralis 3).

Figure 45. Claude Gellée, called le Lorrain, an isolated tower.

gorge can certainly be imagined 'crowning' the hill. Nature was absolutely central to Knight's philosophy, and so was Lucretius, and, given his later productions, he would certainly have been drawn to noticing the symbolic potential of his dwelling. He was inclined to favour elaborate symbolism, and described one of the silver figures in his collection (figure 47) as

> A female Pantheistic figure in silver with the borders of the drapery plated with gold, and the whole finished in a manner surpassing almost anything extant, was among the things found at Macon on the Saone, in the year 1764, and published by Count Caylus. It represents Cybele, the universal Mother, with the mural crown on her head, and the wings of pervasion growing from her shoulders, mixing the productive elements of heat and moisture, by making a libation upon the flames of an altar from a golden patera, with the usual knob in the centre of it, representing, probably, the lingam. On each side of her head is one of the Dioscuri, signifying the alternate influence of the diurnal and nocturnal sun; and, upon a crescent supported by the tips of her wings, are the seven planets, each signified by a bust of its

Figure 46. Silver figure (personification of a town, wearing a mural crown) from the Macon horde.

Figure 47. Silver figure (Cybele) from the Macon horde.

> presiding deity resting upon a globe, and placed in the order of the days of the week named after them. In her left hand she holds two cornucopiae, to signify the result of her operation on the two hemispheres of the Earth; and upon them are the two busts of Apollo and Diana, the presiding deities of those hemispheres, with a golden disk, intersected by two transverse lines, such as the barbarians of the North employed to represent the solar year, divided into four parts, at the back of each.[48]

The symbolism is interpreted very closely indeed, perhaps over-interpreted, but highly characteristic, and demonstrative both of Knight's erudition and his inclination to see symbolism where others might not: to see fertility symbolised in the cornucopiae was within the normal range of expectations, but to see a phallus (lingam) in the golden patera certainly was not. To find the connection between the mural crown and the Earth Mother is relatively very straightforward; for example Thomas Love Peacock (1785–1866), whose outlook was sympathetic to Knight's, did it in a description of a fanciful game of chess, played as a dance, in which the pieces were people in fancy dress. The rooks, which conventionally look like castles, were 'enveloped in a sort of mural robe, with the headpiece formed on the model of that which occurs in the ancient figures of Cybele'.[49] Peacock was not the most popular of authors, but he had read Lucretius; and Knight, using the same symbolism, might have expected it to be recognised by his classically-educated friends. This could explain the supposed deficiencies of the building's detailing, since a mural crown would not have copings. Moreover, the surviving builders' bills for the house refer not to 'battlements', 'crenellations' or 'castellations' but to the row of battlements as a 'cornice', which is etymologically so close to the word 'crown' that in Latin a single word carries both meanings.[50] In *The Progress of Civil Society* the town appeared as an emblem of civilisation

> The throng'd city spread its ample round,
> And raised its walls, with lofty turrets crown'd;[51]

This again shows that Knight thought of the town as being crowned (and turreted, like his house); and the closest correspondence between the house and the buildings in Claude's paintings is not with the palaces and temples which he depicted, but with the distant hill-top towns, such as the one in the background of *Cephalus and Procris reunited by Diana* (figure 48). Knight knew it as part of the Angerstein collection, which was

48 *The Symbolical Language of Ancient Art and Mythology. An Inquiry*, ed. Alexander Wilder (New York: 1876), p. 145, section 193 and note.

49 J. J. Mayoux, *Un épicurien anglais: Thomas Love Peacock* (Paris: PUF, 1933); Marilyn Butler, *Peacock Displayed* (London: 1979); Thomas Love Peacock, *Works*, ed. H. F. B. Brett-Smith and C. E. Jones, 10 vols. (London: Halliford, 1924–34), vol. II, *Melincourt*, p. 302.

50 Downton Castle Papers, quoted by Penny, *Arrogant Connoisseur*, p. 36.

51 Knight, *The Progress of Civil Society: A Didactic Poem* (London: 1796), bk. IV, lines 179–80.

Figure 48. Claude Gellée, called le Lorrain, *Cephalus and Procris reunited by Diana*, 1645.

bought for the National Gallery in 1824, soon after Knight's death. Such a model not only looks more like Downton Castle than does Ludlow Castle, but making the association of ideas is also very much more sympathetic to Knight's outlook; moreover, although such towns were not local to Downton, they were local to Knight when he was designing the building on his travels.

If we think of the house as following the pattern of the town, then, in functional if not in physical terms, there was a central square given over to circulation from which the rooms for public entertainment were to be reached. In addition there were two streets: one of them select and residential, the other lined with offices. We have seen that the house was composed from elements, the rooms, which were in themselves regular, and it is characteristic of Knight's thought that he was not concerned with the regularity of the whole at the expense of the parts. (The general model for this was Bacon's understanding of science, in which natural philosophy was seen to be based an a body of self-evident facts from which generalisations could be drawn).[52] Just as natural philosophy's 'laws' were regulated by reference to facts, not to God-given principles, and just as a society should be regulated by reference to the governed individuals, and not only by tyrannical decree; so Knight's house embodied the ancient Greeks' freedom from systematic constraint, and spread itself out as it required, taking on as it did so the poetical appearance of a fortified town, which served Knight as an emblem of civilisation. And it is as such a symbol that it appeared when seen from the dynamic and primitive ancient forest in the gorge, down below, which Repton described with some generosity, given the treatment he had received at Knight's hands. 'A narrow, wild, and natural path,' he said,

> sometimes creeps under the beetling rock, close by the margin of a mountain stream. It sometimes ascends to an awful precipice, from whence the foaming waters are heard roaring in the dark abyss below, or seen wildly dashing against its opposite banks; while, in other places, the course of the river Teme being impeded by natural ledges of rock, the vale presents a calm, glassy mirror, that reflects the surrounding foliage. The path, in various places, crosses the water by bridges of the most romantic and contrasted forms; and, branching in various directions, including some miles in length, is occasionally varied and enriched by caves and cells, hovels, and covered seats, or other buildings, in perfect harmony with the wild but pleasing horrors of the scene. Yet, if the same picturesque objects were introduced in the gardens of a villa near the capital, or in the more tame yet interesting pleasure grounds which I am frequently called upon to decorate; they would be as absurd, incongruous, and out of character, as a Chinese temple from Vauxhall transplanted into the vale of Downton.
>
> 'Whate'er its essence, or whate'er its name,
> Whate'er its modes, 'tis still in all the same;
> 'Tis *just congruity* of parts combin'd
> Must please the sense, and satisfy the mind.'[53]

The quotation here is from Knight himself,[54] and Repton makes it clear that the mood within Downton Vale (as he called it) was very varied, and could be quite different from the Claudian serenity in the view of the house. The gorge was darkened by the great overhanging trees, and the Teme could appear either tranquil or turbulent. The painters who come to mind here include Salvator Rosa and Ruisdael, as well as Claude.

52 See pp. 74–5.

53 Humphry Repton, *An Enquiry into the Changes of Taste in Landscape Gardening to which are added some observations on its theory and practice including a defence of the art* (London: 1806), pp. 138–9.

54 Knight, *The Landscape*, bk I, lines 37–40.

Knight discussed the merits of the horse chestnut (which he said bore shade better than any other large tree) and the Spanish chestnut (which he said was widespread in Italy, and 'the tree which Salvator Rosa chiefly studied')

> Next to the elm, let either chestnut claim
> The place of honour, and the crown of fame:
> The one, with pointed foliage light and gay,
> Opening its quivering masses to the day;
> Whilst the other gloomy, with imbowering leaves,
> Aloft its dark and clustering summit heaves,
> Or under the tall oak, extends its shade,
> Excludes the sun, and deep imbrowns the glade:
> The one long since to classic climates known,
> Has learn'd the painter's mimic skill to own;
> And lightly brilliant from Salvator's hand,
> Diffus'd its charms o'er many a distant land.[55]

Knight's skill in laying out the walks through the gorge was in seeming to have left everything almost perfectly natural, whilst contriving a richly varied sequence of sensory experiences. The associations which the imagination would bring into play in response to these sensory stimuli would be those set out in his poem, and explored in chapter 7 above, as this landscape perfectly embodied Knight's ideas: it was the means by which he generated them.[56] So that, for example, the free-flowing river might put us in mind of other sorts of liberty, and so on. The path, as Repton's account makes clear, and enough of the route remains to be able to follow it today, was sometimes very close to the edge of the river, and sometimes ran along the top of a steep slope, or a cliff. In such circumstances a climb up a relatively short distance, soon accomplished, can appear to have carried one to a great height, and the contrast between the experiences, the suddenness with which one succeeds the other, certainly contributes to their effectiveness. The bridges, alas, have gone, but one of Hearne's watercolours shows an Alpine bridge, made from fallen trees, with their branches and bark still in place, an essay in extreme rusticity, appropriate in this place in the garden, surrounded by the spirits of the forest, the principles of nature at work on all sides (figure 49). The bridge crossed the river to a path which led up a short distance to a bath house, which survives in ruins and in a watercolour by William Owen (figure 50). This was an exercise in the most primitive gothic: a small gothic window is just visible at the left of the building in the water-

55 Ibid., bk. III, lines 155–66.

56 Tom Wall, 'The Verdant Landscape', discusses the correspondence between Knight's principles and his garden.

Figure 49. Thomas Hearne, *View of Alpine Bridge, Teme Gorge, Downton.*

colour, and the entrance was made up of two great stones, which made a primitive, which is to say a gothic, arch. There was also a series of caves, the best of which was entered by way of a tunnel cut through the rock. The chamber of the cave opens up on one side, very dark indeed, but illuminated from close to its highest point by a fissure in the rock, perhaps recalling the lighting from the oculus in the Pantheon, or the dining room, but here, in the forest by the river, it recalls a Greek temple, of the type in which Pan was worshipped: caves were set up with shrines to him in ancient Greece, as Knight knew,[57] and moreover he identified Pan with Priapus.[58]

The most strikingly original of all Knight's designs to have survived, though, is an extraordinary little tunnel built in rough stone, unprepossessing in itself. It was arranged on the path which runs along the very edge of the river; following it along, heading upstream, the view of the river is progressively cut off by a wall which increases in height, and then the path is roofed over. Hinges survive to show where there was once a door which would have opened to reveal a view, again from very close to the river; but the river now has a completely different character: the

57 Knight, *Symbolical Language*, p. 48.

58 Ibid., p. 141.

Figure 50. William Owen, *View of Mr. Knight's Cold Bath, Teme Gorge, Downton.*

tunnel was placed at a point where the river's bed changes from being rocky to being smooth, so that on the way upstream the river changes from being calm to being animated. It is a brilliant coup, and Hearne was commissioned to paint the view. From this point the path at first appears to have nowhere to go, but in fact it doubles back, up some steep steps, to emerge at high level and go on to the Alpine bridge. The sequence was marvellously well contrived, so that the visitor was, and is, given a series of surprises which are all the more effective for seeming effortless. Yet this little structure, curious and awkward in itself, is perfectly judged to bring about an intensification of the visitor's experience of the landscape: without it we might walk through without noticing the river's strongly differentiated qualities and moods, or without relishing the proximity to the water or the drop below us. The structure hardly qualifies as architecture, as it is scarcely an object of attention, but serves as a device to direct its user's attention elsewhere: to the water, the trees and their harmonious combination.

At Downton we have in the house an emblem of civilisation, not imposed on the countryside, but responding to and growing out of its surroundings: an emblem of civilisation which is in touch with nature, as in Homeric Greece. From it we can move out into the kind of landscape which painters populated with mythical figures, and which Knight, in his poetry, populated with nymphs and dryads, and evidently in conversation with Sir George Cumberland with Comus and his band of revellers.[59] The range of associations which can be developed around the house and garden is as rich as can be found anywhere, but they derived rather idiosyncratically from Knight's own, sometimes abstruse, learning and have been assimilated in ways other than he would have seen them himself. When he retired to Stonebrook Cottage it was so that he could be still closer to the landscape, becoming inseparable from it, becoming a part of it.

59 See p. 187.

9 Conclusion

Peace of mind

At a personal level Knight's most important achievement was *ataraxia*, a state of psychological serenity, free from guilt and anxiety, as well as from physical discomfort. From a distance, seeing him in a comfortable position of high privilege, it is easy to take for granted that his life would be more or less serene, but we should not do so without noticing that there were those of a similar sensibility among his contemporaries who tended romantically to self-destruction in one way or another. Knight's means were considerable, but he did live within them, unlike many of his friends. He criticised Lady Oxford's extravagance; Richard Westall, despite a briefly brilliant career, became financially embarrassed well before the taste for his work had passed; Uvedale Price's gluttony got the better of him; Thomas Johnes's ambitious schemes at Hafod were beset by various disasters and led to both financial ruin and personal calamity. Figures who made a much more powerful impact on the cultural scene of the time included, for example, Lord Byron, whose career was a glorious and inspiring trail of self-destruction, leaving various ruined lives and ending in his early death; and William Beckford managed to squander the most colossal fortune in setting up Fonthill as a place of stupendously exotic exile, leaving us with a spellbinding but insubstantial vision of what can be achieved when almost unlimited resources are put at the disposal of capricious whimsy.

Knight by contrast maintained a philosophical outlook, and adhered to a disciplined regimen of very limited self-indulgence. He managed to keep the various parts of his life in balance, and though he might have achieved a more lasting reputation had he concentrated all his efforts in one direction, he might have had a less contented life. Had he thrown all his energies and all his resources Byronically into a great cause he might have produced something dazzling and memorable, but it would have been at the sacrifice of his peace of mind, which was not a price he was prepared to pay for the sake of securing so elusive a possession as an imperishable public reputation. Knight was not driven by vainglory, but was not without vanity: he was ready enough to act in the public arena, and to attract attention with disconcerting remarks, but he was not prepared to sacrifice his personal well-being on the altar of fame. Knight moved into his cottage, into his retirement, when he was approaching his sixtieth year, which is to say when he was 58. He enjoyed good health for at least another decade, and could have continued in public life had he felt so inclined. His sense of his identity, and of his duties to himself, however did not require it of him. He performed his public duties, but they did not take hold of him and come to define him, so that he was not ambitious to wield any power in national politics beyond the vote which went with his seat. He never spoke in Parliament, despite holding a seat there for twenty-five years, but he endorsed the worthiest of causes, but, unlike Charles James Fox or Edmund Burke he did not sense the urgency and import of issues in such a way that they turned into personal crusades, and he was never fired with the kind of enthusiasm which might have led him to try, by force of will, to drive legislation through Parliament. He was allied with Fox, and therefore always in opposition to the leadership of the day, and must be seen as principled, but as a practical politician he was uninspired and completely without distinction. He subordinated his public duties to more private enthusiasms, which he had the means and leisure to pursue, and which brought him recognition, some of it appreciative, some of it hot-tempered. If his career was not one of spectacular service to his country, to a great cause or to the amassing of spectacular wealth, then it was because his primary ambition was to possess leisure – not for the sake of simple idleness, but for philosophical contemplation. He had a very contented life into old age, and would have counted that as his major success, seeing everything else as means to that end, which allowed him, as he grew less active, to continue to relish the associative pleasures of his imagination.

If Knight had focused all his talents on one subject then it would probably have been classical scholarship, and had he done that then he would not have been remembered more than, say, his illustrious contemporary Richard Porson. Eighteenth-century classical scholars in England are overshadowed by the more illuminating work which was done in Germany at the time, and even Porson's reputation does not inspire tremendous enthusiasm, brilliant and respectable though he was. Scholars who are remembered tend to be remembered for something other than their scholarship, which is superseded if it is fruitful, and neglected to gather dust if it is not. Winckelmann, for example, is remembered as a great scholar, and his general schema of Greek art remains as an orthodoxy in the field (its authorship generally passing unnoticed, as if it were a natural fact) but his scholarship is now known to be faulty, and when he is actually read it is on account of his ability to communicate his own state of mind: the enthusiasm he felt for the ancient statuary he studied. Similarly, Knight's achievements as a scholar of Greek were real enough, and his enthusiasm for ancient statuary was scarcely less than Winckelmann's (though he lacked the literary means to communicate it infectiously); but his lasting reputation in connection with ancient Greece is not that of a learned scholar, but of an idiotic philistine, who was so ignorant as to be blind to the merits of the greatest statues the world has ever seen: the Parthenon marbles. This reputation is undeserved, produced when he made a scholarly slip in circumstances which had become highly charged and fraught with malice on account of the stakes. Knight's public persona, as an opinionated connoisseur whose remarks merited wide attention, was skewered by a Damoclean sword when the thread of public confidence finally snapped.

A state of grace

Knight managed to fuse his two greatest enthusiasms, so that his concern for ancient Greece on the one hand and the Herefordshire countryside on the other became different aspects of the same passion, reflected in the paintings he collected, which included ideal landscapes and rustic scenes, some of them commissioned works. The rustic scenes include pictures of cottages on his own estate as well as rustic structures such as his alpine bridge and cold bath. They represent the countryside as simple and quaint, the seat of contentment and domestic virtue, and can be associated with, say, the sentiments to be found in Goldsmith's 'Deserted Village'.[1] The Herefordshire landscape is more fertile and benevolent than that of the Lake District, in which William Wordsworth's rustics had to show a sterner and more heroic stoicism. Knight's experience of the countryside was of a gentler place, not without its anxieties (which we see in Westall's painting of the harvest storm; see figure 15) but as altogether more bountiful than the harsh slatey conditions in which Wordsworth's *Lyrical Ballads*' characters

1 There is an approving reference in Knight, *The Progress of Civil Society: A Didactic Poem* (London: 1796), p. xiv.

scratched their livings. The peasants in Knight's rustic paintings tended to be absorbed contentedly in commonplace life, untroubled by great ideas or the affairs of the world, with the means of subsistence adequately provided. They were, without knowing it, in a state of grace: they had peace of mind, like the philosopher Knight tried to be. This complete freedom from affectation and false values was also to be found, Knight thought, among the Homeric Greeks (see figure 5), and he supposed that everything they thought and did was thought and done unselfconsciously, and consequently with an ideal grace, each action of the body being directed spontaneously by the impulse of the mind.

This state of affairs was possible for them because they enjoyed liberty and were in touch with nature, and Knight tried to follow their example. This was no small feat, and involved him in associating ideas drawn from various fields, to establish (at least in his own mind) a web of connections which enabled his thought to move easily between aesthetics, politics, religion and morals. To some extent Winckelmann had already made such connections, but Knight pursued them further. However, his prospects as a hero of the Grecian taste were blasted utterly, both by his failure to recognise the Parthenon marbles' quality, and by a general failure on the part of others to notice that his house was built on Greek principles as well as being stocked with Greek treasures. He did not communicate his associations of ideas particularly effectively. His aesthetic theory met with some applause when he explained it, but his politics caused anxiety, his ideas about religion seemed downright scandalous and he seemed to have no morals at all. This led Hazlitt, for example, to say that he laid 'somewhat more stress on the value of the Fine Arts than Mr. Payne Knight, who considers them (we know not for what reason) as an elegant antithesis to morality. We think they are nearly related to it.'[2] This casts Knight as an immoralist aesthete, in a role which would be played more deliberately by Oscar Wilde. In fact Knight made very strong links between art and morality, but his moral system was Epicurean and his moral character was as misunderstood as the ancient Epicureans had been.[3] Also he did not suppose that the connection between art and moral character operated symmetrically, because on the one hand it was necessary, if good art were to be produced, to have a moral system which did not suppress the free operation of instinctive and 'natural' behaviour (so that the operations of the mind could be translated uninhibitedly and gracefully into actions of the body), but on the other hand Knight did not think that works of art decisively shaped the moral character of the people who looked at them. A certain morality was

2 William Hazlitt, *Complete Works*, ed. P P. Howe, 21 vols. (London: Dent, 1930–4), vol. XVIII, p. 101.

3 Walter Hipple calls Knight 'a moralist of stature' on account of his views linking art and morality, but without appreciating (or at least without explaining) the basis of his moral philosophy. Hipple, *The Beautiful, The Sublime & The Picturesque In Eighteenth-Century British Aesthetic Theory* (Carbondale: The Southern Illinois University Press, 1957), p. 277.

necessary to good art, but good art was not to be relied upon to produce good morals. The links which he made were therefore utterly different from the pieties which would link art and morality in the wake of Pugin and Ruskin in the nineteenth century, and which Wilde resisted. The links which Knight made followed Winckelmann's example in associating ancient Greek freedom with artistic genius and quotidian grace, to recapture which involved flight from the artificialities of modern life. This line of thought found expression in Knight's pictures of ideal landscape, in which the figures of gods were sometimes to be found. His Claudes, and some of the views of the Teme Gorge at Downton, including Hearne's distant view of Downton Castle, portrayed the scenes' arcadian qualities. This side of the landscape is well represented in paintings such as Claude's *Landscape with Narcissus and Echo* (see figure 20) in which mythological figures populate the scene, so that although the effects of light and vegetation are accurately portrayed, the landscape is securely located in Arcadia, in an ideal golden age of the world. The religious paintings which Knight commissioned from Westall, depicting pagan gods in what looks like the ancient forest at Downton, show how Knight imaginatively populated his woods with personifications of the forces of nature (see figure 19). Knight's woods themselves were carefully husbanded into an appearance of total neglect, and the hand of art was not visible in them, but in Knight's imagination as he walked along the paths of beaten earth which he set up to take him on his daily wanderings, these forces were at work all around him. His feeling for the landscape involved a sense of the numinous, and his walks were in effect a form of religious devotion.

Gardening in the mind

Knight made a distinction between the manual dexterity involved in painting and the affective aspects of the work which prompted sentimental responses, including the recognition of beauty. The accurate portrayal of physical likenesses was only a small part of his interest in the higher class of paintings, and he thought of it as something which could more or less be taken for granted by the critic in considering the best work (though it should not be forgotten by the artist). It belonged to the category of mechanical skills, and was to be found in a diligent artisan; the great artist had to accomplish much more than accuracy of physical likeness and attain a higher form of expression. What really mattered to Knight were the emotions and ideas which the pictures prompted in his well-stocked mind. Mechanical skill might be learnt by a craftsman, but it took a liberal education to be able to feel the high-minded sentiment which could be prompted if the subject-matter were properly considered and properly treated. A painting was not only an arrangement of pigment, but operated through the play of associations of ideas, and the artist's mind would need to be well stocked with a store of appropriate culture if he were to be able to call its influence into play in order for the picture to achieve its effects. He would also need to develop the mechanical skills to portray his ideas, but it was far from being the whole of what was needed.

Knight transferred this way of thinking about paintings to his consideration of the landscape. His poem *The Landscape* attacked Capability Brown, who had trained as a gardener, and whom Knight accused of reducing the liberal art of landscape design to a mechanical formula. Instead of making drastic changes to the landscape, in order to bring it into conformity with Hogarth's abstract ideal of beauty, Knight's policy was to alter as little as possible, enhancing the established character of the place in question by changing only the jarring elements in a view, leaving nature (or the day-to-day activity of the countryside) to do the rest. An overall effect of visual harmony should be achieved, but then for the landscape to yield its most abundant pleasures it was necessary to have a developed sensibility which could respond in a sympathetic manner. *The Landscape* is a catalogue of appropriate responses to landscape which takes in not only pictorial but also religious and political associations of ideas.

Knight's landscape is to be found only very partially in the arrangement of objects: a substantial proportion of it is formed by the ideas in the minds of its observers. Capability Brown did not have a liberal education, had no wide acquaintance with works of art and was therefore, Knight said, incapable of seeing picturesque effects, which Knight thought were the surest guide to the production of the best possible landscapes. The point was not so much that the gardens should be made to look like the scenes in landscape paintings, as that the observer should think like a painter, should mentally construct the landscape images and should respond to them as if they were works of art placed in a tradition of painting. The garden in practice would be arranged so as to make this feasible and satisfying, removing such elements of a scene as became obstacles to thinking of the scene as a work of art, and adding minimal prompts in order to enhance the production of pleasant trains of thought. At its most extreme this would involve the observer in a great deal of mental activity, and the gardener in none at all. In effect, it is tantamount to saying that the observer who is properly to appreciate landscapes must in effect be a painter in all the high-minded aspects of art, but can be exempted from having the mechanical skill of transferring the landscape to canvas, and fixing it in pigment. It should be expected therefore that painters would make good landscape designers, but a mere gardener without an appreciation of painting simply could not have the appropriate cultural apparatus to bring to bear on the problem; and Knight had no expectation of excellence in Capability Brown's work. In general he thought that these matters were best left in the hands of cultivated and well-educated gentlemen with the leisure to contemplate their desmesnes, rather than being delegated to a jobbing gardener. This was, naturally enough, construed by Humphry Repton as a threat to his professional livelihood, and so he fought back with some ferocity. Knight insisted, though, that because Repton had had a polite education he did have higher expectations of him than he had had of Brown. When he first met Repton they were agreed on the importance of paintings in the consideration of landscape designs, and he was disappointed that Repton had gone on to repudiate this position. For Knight the landscape could be a more completely intellectual form of painting, as surely as it could be more concrete.

Knight's way of construing the landscape was based on his reading of Hume. Since beauty is in the mind of the observer, rather than in the objects which are seen, the practice of appreciating landscape becomes an art to be practised by the observer. A landscape gardener is not always needed, as it is possible to find and enjoy (to compose in the mind) landscapes in which a gardener has played no part. This had already been William Gilpin's practice on his 'picturesque tours', though he had complicated the matter by taking a sketch book along, and he gave no satisfactorily philosophical account of his activity. Knight's important contribution here was to stress the mental operations involved, and to play down the role of the practical gardener, so that the appreciation of even natural beauty became a fusion of image and idea. The practice is not without precedent, and had been at work in the more obviously cultivated eighteenth-century gardens, such a Stourhead or Stowe, but Capability Brown's 'mechanical' practice, which Knight saw as dependent upon a discredited physiological theory of beauty, had come to dominate, and Knight put his theory forward in order to counteract that tendency. Wordsworth expressed the importance of the activity of the mind when he visited Knight's part of the country on a tour in 1798, explaining how his response to the objects in the scene was caught up with the ideas in his mind

> Therefore am I still
> A lover of the meadows and the woods,
> And mountains; and of all that we behold
> From this green earth; of all the mighty world
> Of eye and ear, both what they half-create,
> And what perceive; well pleased to recognize
> In nature and the language of the sense,
> The anchor of my purest thoughts, the nurse,
> The guide, the guardian of my heart, and soul
> Of all my moral being.[4]

The *Lyrical Ballads* made virtually all eighteenth-century poetry sound old fashioned, and Knight's verse suffers cruelly from the comparison, but the sentiments belong securely to Knight's sense of the landscape. The feeling that the landscape is bound up with important religious and moral truths plays a part in both of their sensibilities, and this association of ideas was to become a regular practice of Romanticism.[5] It is quite different from Price's conception of what *he* was doing. Despite what Knight said in his preface to the second edition of *The Landscape*,[6] there do seem to have been practical, as well as theoretical, differences of taste between him and Price, whose landscape at Foxley was quite different in mood from Knight's at Downton. The aesthetic which Knight promoted differed both from the grandiose sublimity of the Lake District (which found favour with an increasing number of people) and from the Arcadian serenity which reigned at Foxley. The lively waters of the River Teme, the relatively small scale of the gorge through which they ran, and the surrounding ancient forest produced a landscape which Knight understood in terms of natural freedom and the direct actions of the forces of nature. In contrast with the Lake District's sublime indifference, one can sense here a human scale of involvement: the spirits of the place here are dryads among the trees, with Eros, Pan and Orpheus. The fusion of the landscape at Downton with this body of ideas was Knight's authentically great aesthetic achievement, and having made it, initially in his mind and then in verse and in his purchases of paintings, he was able to draw on it for sustenance later in his retirement. Where he was less successful was in being able to communicate his ideas beyond the circle of his friends. His vision is dispersed, and cannot have been pieced together by many from

4 William Wordsworth, 'Lines Written a Few Miles Above Tintern Abbey, on Revisiting the Banks of the Wye During a Tour, July 13, 1798' in *Lyrical Ballads* (London: 1798).

5 Kathleen Wheeler, *Romanticism, Pragmatism and Deconstruction* (Oxford: Blackwell, 1993).

6 *The Landscape: A Didactic Poem*, 2nd edn (London: 1795), pp. vi and vii.

his texts. The publication of *The Landscape* caused some excitement, but it caused more controversy, mainly on account of its political content, and because it insulted so established a figure as Capability Brown. The poem has kept Knight's reputation alive, but his ideas have been understood in a greatly simplified form. Thomas Hearne's illustrations effectively summarised the aesthetic differences between Capability Brown's gardens and the picturesque practice which Knight and Price approved (see figures 21 and 22), but Price's more practical advice on how to achieve picturesque effects has been understood the more readily: it was the more reassuringly presented, but was unillustrated, so Knight's illustrations have been made to explain Price's outlook, making the two of them into a Tweedledum and Tweedledee, with no substantial differences between them, only a tendency to quarrel.[7] Price was perhaps thinking of the difference between his own and Knight's landscapes when he wrote the following passage, in the published 'letter' to Humphry Repton. He defended Knight's use of the didactic poem as a vehicle for the communication of his ideas, comparing it (in a characteristically extended simile) with a *ferme ornée*. 'The two most renowned of all didactic poems', he said, were 'those of Lucretius and Virgil':

> Those who wish for as great a degree of elegance and high polish as is compatible with grandeur and energy, will imitate Virgil; but, like him, they will avoid all flat effeminate smoothness. Like him they will leave those masterly touches which give a spirit to the rest, though they will give to the whole of their scenery a more general appearance of polish, than do those who take Lucretius for their model. In him certainly the contrast between what answers to the picturesque, the sublime, and the beautiful, that is, between the rough, and seemingly neglected parts – the forcible and majestic images he at other times presents – and the extreme softness of voluptuousness of his beautiful passages – is much more striking than in Virgil; and therefore by many his style has been preferred to that of his equal, but less original rival.[8]

Lucretius was important to Knight, who was one of the 'many' (in actual fact a few) who preferred Lucretius to Virgil, and the contrast Price made here applies readily to the character of the scenery at Downton and Foxley. Knight's taste was, as Repton said, the more romantic.[9]

7 Jean-Jacques Mayoux, *Richard Payne Knight et le pittoresque* (Paris: PUF, 1932), p. 7.

8 Uvedale Price, 'A Letter to H. Repton, Esq. on the Application of the Practice as well as the Principles of Landscape-Gardening: Intended as a Supplement to the *Essay on the Picturesque*', in *Essays on the Picturesque*, 3 vols. (London: 1810), vol. III, pp. 56–7.

9 Humphry Repton, *Sketches and Hints on Landscape Gardening Collected from Designs and Observations now in the Possession of the Different Noblemen and Gentlemen, for Whose use they were Originally Made. The Whole Tending to Establish Fixed Principles in the Art of Laying Out Ground* (London: 1795), p. 77.

Irregular houses

The house which Knight introduced into this landscape in his twenties was to be his most enduring claim to fame. It made a bold departure from the established formula of the day: the symmetrically disposed Palladian mansion, organised into a regular block with a portico around a centrally placed entrance. Knight's rejection of it was a significant aberration from the norm, and signalled an unusual independence of mind and a rejection of conventional judgements, both social and aesthetic. It is appropriately placed between Horace Walpole's Strawberry Hill and William Beckford's Fonthill, as domestic monuments which rejected in varying degrees the established conventions of the day. Strawberry Hill and Fonthill were deliberately theatrical in their effects, and large parts of them were nothing but splendid showcases for the treasures which their owners collected, but Knight's house by contrast was a serious attempt to think afresh about domestic arrangements. The planning of the house is sensible, highly practical and tightly organised, and although there is a grand show in the Pantheon dining room, the house did not develop into a virtuosic display of architectural wonders. Its originality caused it to be noticed, but our attention is held, and the building's importance confirmed, because the originality was not wilful but was securely grounded, both practically and culturally. The house was not a whimsy but a new and winning formula.

As a work of architecture in its own right the house had its shortcomings: the exterior was unenlivened by the detailed attention which a more practised architect would have given it, either to make it less severe or to make it crisply unornamented. Its practical benefits did not have an immediate influence, but after it had been given a variety of more convincing architectural treatments by John Nash (1752–1835) the influence it exerted at second-hand was vast. Nash was to become the most successful and prolific architect of the age, though certainly not the finest. He is best remembered for developing Regent Street, and other works for the Prince of Wales, who was to become the Prince Regent and then George IV; Nash was responsible for the orientalising of Brighton Pavilion, for Buckingham Palace, and for Carlton House Terrace, as well as the spectacular palatial terraces which look out on to Regent's Park. The early part of Nash's career in property speculation had ended in financial ruin, and he retreated to Wales, where he recouped his resources before again making an assault on fashionable society. He was introduced into Knight's circle by Thomas Johnes, with whom he was involved at Hafod from 1793,[10] in remodelling the house there (which had symmetrical façades); and came into closer contact when he was engaged by Price in 1797 to build a house on the seafront at Aberystwyth. 'At first,' said Price, 'I thought of running up two or three nutshells of rooms, and got a plan from a common Welch carpenter.'[11] Nash's entrepreneurial flair and charm came into play, however, and he talked Price out of the idea of a cottage in favour of a larger house, which would have been 'a square bit of architecture' had Price not introduced him to picturesque principles. 'I told him,' Price said,

> that I must have, not only some of the windows but some of the *rooms* turned to particular points, & that he must arrange it in his best manner; I explained the reasons why I built it so close to the rock, showed him the effect of the broken foreground & its varied line, & how by that means the foreground was connected with the rocks in the second ground, all of which would be lost by placing the house further back. He was excessively struck with these reasons, which he said he had never thought of before in the most distant degree, & he has I think contrived the house most admirably for the situation, & the form of it is certainly extremely varied from my having obliged him to turn the rooms to different aspects.[12]

The house, which was to become known as the Castle House, ended up with a triangular plan (and a turret at each corner) so as to give, in different directions, views of the shoreline, a ruined castle and some cliffs. Downton's influence is not evident in the triangular plan, but Price presumably introduced Nash to Downton and to Knight as part of his education in the picturesque; and Nash had evidently visited before 1799, his first documented presence there.[13] Nash learned his lesson well, and applied it in the design of many buildings after that, more convincingly than Knight himself had been able to do, which is not surprising since Nash was an experienced professional architect, and Knight designed the house as a young amateur.

If the house which Nash designed for himself, East Cowes Castle on the Isle of Wight, begun 1798 (figure 51) is compared with Downton, it is immediately apparent that Nash's house had a much more extrovert character, and had very much more elaborate detailed treatment in its façades; but Downton had set the example for the planning and the irregular composition. Similarly, houses which Nash designed at Caerhays, Cornwall (*c.* 1808) and Luscombe, Devon, 1799 (figure 52) were unequiv-

10 John Summerson, *The Life and Work of John Nash, Architect* (London: George Allen and Unwin, 1980), p. 20.

11 'Nutshell' was used in this sense by a contemporary, to whom Price may well have been alluding, in a book about cottage architecture with a Grecian title: Jose Mac Packe [J. Peacock], *OIKIΔIA, or Nutshells: Being Ichnographic Distributions for Small Villas* (London: 1785). The title is a diminutive form of 'Οικος', house.

12 Uvedale Price to Sir George Beaumont, quoted by Summerson, *Nash*, p. 21.

13 Nash to P. C. Methuen, September 1799, quoted in Dorothy Stroud, *Humphry Repton* (London: Country Life, 1962), p. 96. 'What is certain is that some years before this the house had made a deep impression on him', Summerson, *Nash*, p. 24.

Figure 51. John Nash, East Cowes Castle, Isle of Wight, begun 1798 (demolished 1950).

ocally gothic in their style. There is no question of their having Grecian battlements. Nash was content to work within the established conventions of architectural style, and had no particularly scholarly programme to perturb his received wisdom. His ideas about architecture were philosophically and historically much less deeply rooted than Knight's, but he was efficiently capable of producing striking surface effects, which were perfectly well attuned to the taste and understanding of his day. One

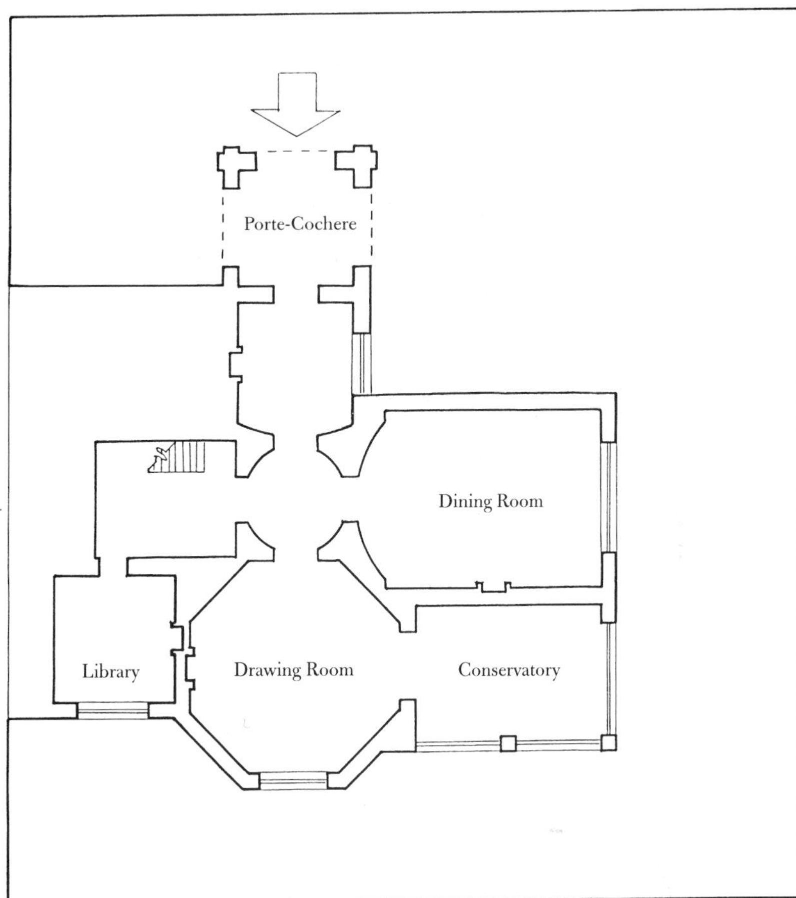

Figure 52. Plan of Luscombe Castle, Devon. John Nash, 1800–4.

of his most interesting essays in this regard is the villa he designed at Cronkhill in Shropshire, 1799–1802 (figure 53) for the steward of the Attingham estate, which is not far distant from Downton, and which made use of the same play of axiality to discipline the alignments of the rooms within, and irregularity to animate the massing of the exterior. Here the composition was picturesque in the same way, but the building was dressed in Italianate style, which made clearer the connection with landscape paintings by Claude and Poussin. Nash's castle-style houses were to feed a vogue for the gothic, which gained momentum under the influence of Sir Walter Scott, and became one of the main currents in nineteenth-century taste.

Among the next generation of architects, Robert Smirke (1780–1867) was clearly influenced by Knight and his circle, as he was regularly at Eywood, now in Powys, with Lord and Lady Oxford, and he rebuilt their

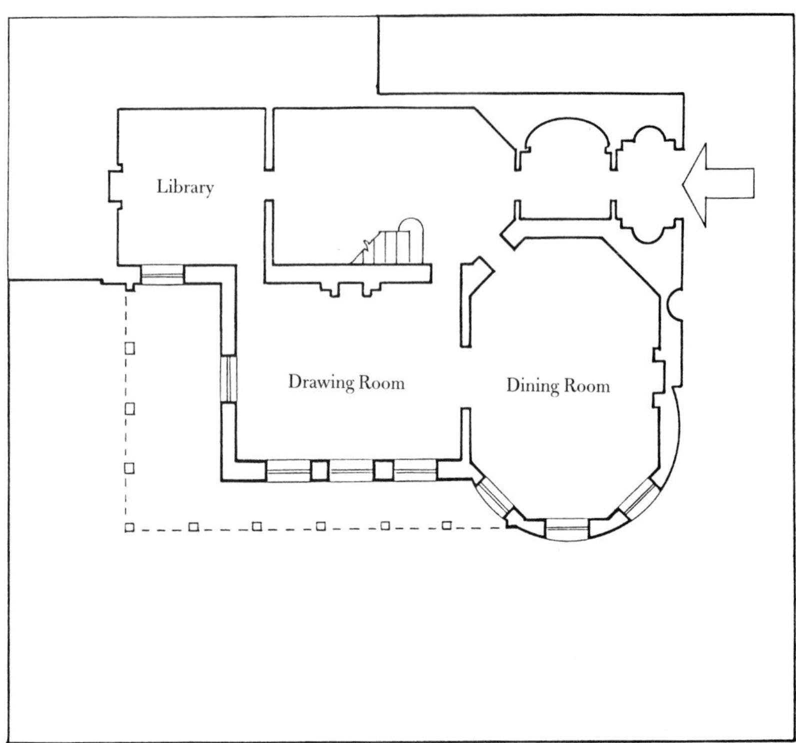

Figure 53. Plan of Cronkhill, Shropshire. John Nash, *c.* 1802.

house there. It is now demolished, but the decayed stables remain, along with fragments of the mansion's brick walls, with ornate stone dressings, still set in the Capability Brown landscape, itself rather shabby but still recognisable. Smirke's buildings in urban settings, such as the Shire Hall at Hereford (1815–17) and the British Museum (1823–46), adopted the most formal and meticulously detailed monumental Greek manner, but in the country he was sometimes freer, though he did not adopt Knight's irregular planning at Eywood or at Eastnor Castle, Herefordshire, 1812–20 (figure 54), which has a special link with Downton. When Downton was remodelled in the 1860s, a second circular tower was added on the north side of the building in order to improve the configuration about the entrance (see figure 31). The two towers were linked by a flying pointed arch, which strongly resembles the arrangement to be found at Eastnor, and it seems here that the influence was working in the opposite direction to that which might have been expected. Downton was being made into the building which it was thought it had all along been trying, but failing, to be: Downton's wide, if indirect, influence coming round full circle to reconfigure its own origins, and in the process making the house look more prophetic than ever.

Figure 54. Robert Smirke, Eastnor Castle, Herefordshire, 1812–20.

Another younger architect, William Wilkins (1778–1839), worked with Knight in 1814–15 on a publication for the Society of Dilettanti.[14] Up to this time Wilkins had been designing sternly symmetrical buildings, such as The Grange in Hampshire, a house designed in the form of a Greek temple; it was modelled minutely on the Hephaesteion at Athens (figure 55). Knight no doubt explained to Wilkins that his approach was misguided, as from 1814 he was working on a design for Dalmeny House in West Lothian, which was axial in its early drafts, but when finished was 'a new kind of house in Scotland',[15] and, importantly as evidence for Knight's influence, a new kind of house in Wilkins's output (figure 56). In one elevation symmetry was maintained, but battlements were used, and the planning bears a strong resemblance to Downton's. Unlike Downton in its original state, Dalmeny made overtly gothic gestures, with its stained-glass windows and long vaulted corridor, but the windows are large and were made with mullions and transoms like those of the Tudor windows shown in the house in Hearne's exemplary picturesque scene in *The Landscape* (see figure 22), and the skyline was variegated with gables, chimneys and pinnacles in the same manner.

14 R. W. Liscombe, *William Wilkins 1778–1839* (Cambridge University Press, 1980), p. 90.

15 James Macaulay, *The Gothic Revival 1745–1845* (Glasgow: Blackie, 1975), p. 319.

Figure 55. William Wilkins, The Grange, Hampshire, 1809 onwards.

Another of Wilkins's designs from this period, for Tregothnan in Cornwall, 1815 (figures 57 and 58) adopted the same method, and was planned in a way which still more closely resembles Downton (especially after Knight had moved the entrance to the north: see figure 43). Here the house combined Tudor signification in the façades with classically decorated interiors. Wilkins remained a champion of the Greek style, and used it in a conventional way (but with a particularly strong commitment to archaeological observation) in urban settings, such as at Downing College Cambridge (1807–20), London University (1825–7) and the National Gallery, London (1833–8). Knight's conviction that in country houses the Greeks had not erected symmetrical temple-like buildings could have relaxed his commitment to the use of archaeologically Greek forms in rural settings.

Knight's influence was felt less directly at Belsay Hall in Northumberland (1807–17), not in the house but in the garden. The house is remarkable, again the work of an amateur, but its interpretation of Grecian style could hardly be further from Knight's (figure 59). It was

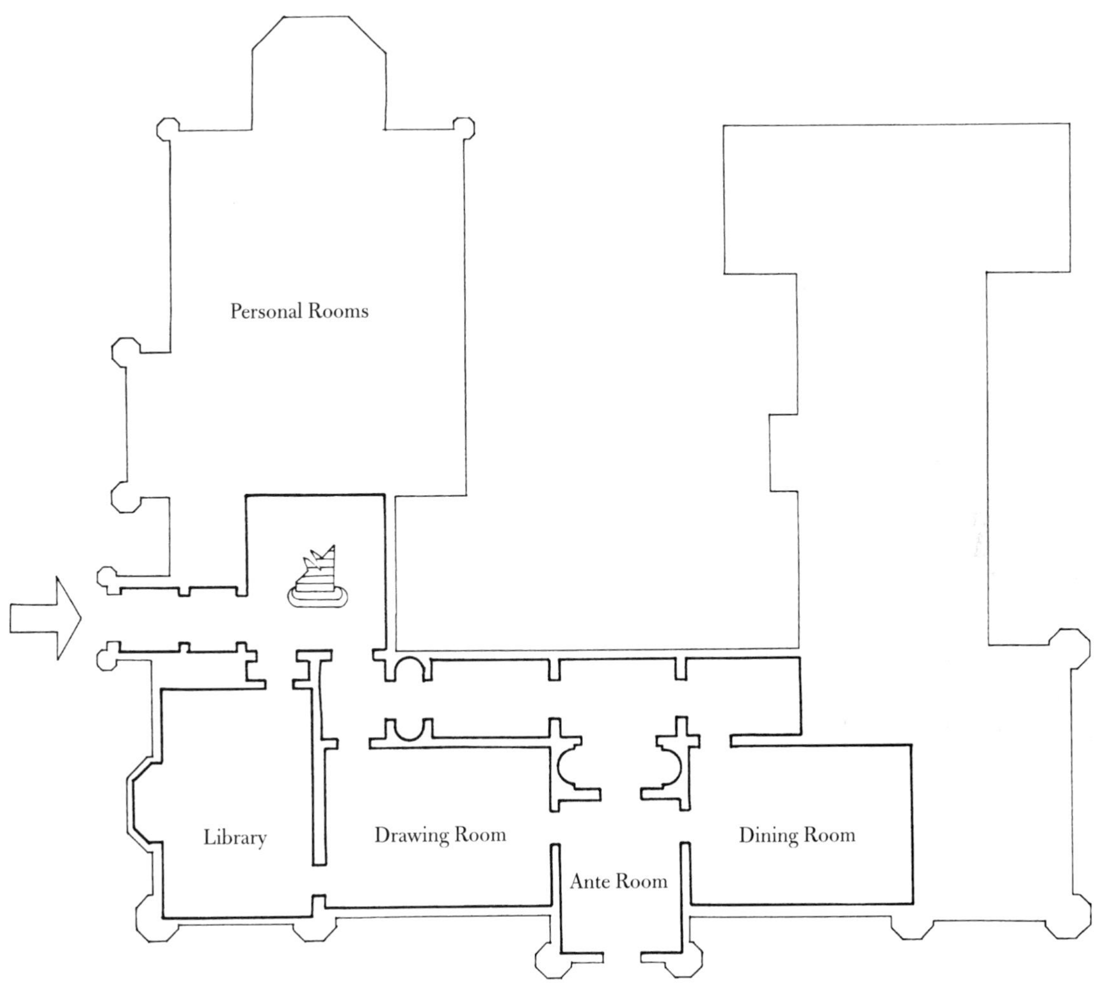

Figure 56. Plan of Dalmeny, West Lothian. William Wilkins, 1814–17.

a square bit of architecture if ever there was one, built by Sir Charles Monck, who spend his lengthy honeymoon in Greece, and sought architectural advice from Sir William Gell, whom he may well have met there.[16] The stone to build it, however, was quarried from the land nearby, and the resulting excavations landscaped into a craggily Romantic walk, leading to a ruined castle. The quarry garden lacks the animation which running water would give it, but otherwise is very much closer to Knight's than to Price's taste in the picturesque (figure 60).

The specific influence of Knight's aesthetic is difficult to isolate because it became so general, mixed of course with Price's, and promulgated by Nash and others. There were soon pattern books which showed

16 Nicholas Penny, 'Architecture and Landscape at Downton', in *The Arrogant Connoisseur*, ed. Michael Clarke and Nicholas Penny (Manchester University Press, 1982), p. 43; Christopher Hussey, *English Country Houses, Late Georgian 1800–1840* (London: Country Life, 1958), pp. 83 ff.

Figure 57. William Wilkins, Tregothnan, Cornwall, 1816–18.

17 E.g. William Atkinson, *Views of Picturesque Cottages with Plans* (London: 1805); Edmund Bartell Jr., *Hints for Picturesque Improvements in Ornamented Cottages, and their Scenery* (London: 1804); Robert Lugar, *Architectural Sketches for Cottages, Rural Dwellings, and Villas* (London: 1805); James Malton, *Collection of Designs for Rural Retreats* (London: 1802); W. F. Pocock, *Architectural Designs for Rustic Cottages, Picturesque Dwellings, Villas, with Appropriate Scenery* (London: 1807).

the uninitiated how to mimic picturesque effects without the liberal education which Knight insisted upon as essential.[17]

Cultural dislocation

The problem faced in appreciating the house at Downton is a problem faced in the appreciation of all Knight's work. It was designed in the context of one highly rarefied culture, but has been understood more generally in another, which has put a construction on things which is utterly at variance with Knight's own. In theory he could not complain. If everything depends on the association of ideas, then when we introduce an object into a culture wider than our own personal ideas we must expect a degree of reinterpretation. Whereas in Knight's own understanding his house was built on ancient Greek principles, it was seen by most of his contemporaries as a rather feeble attempt to evoke the grandeur of the medieval castles. Its position in the history books has not helped to correct this impression; when it is placed alongside

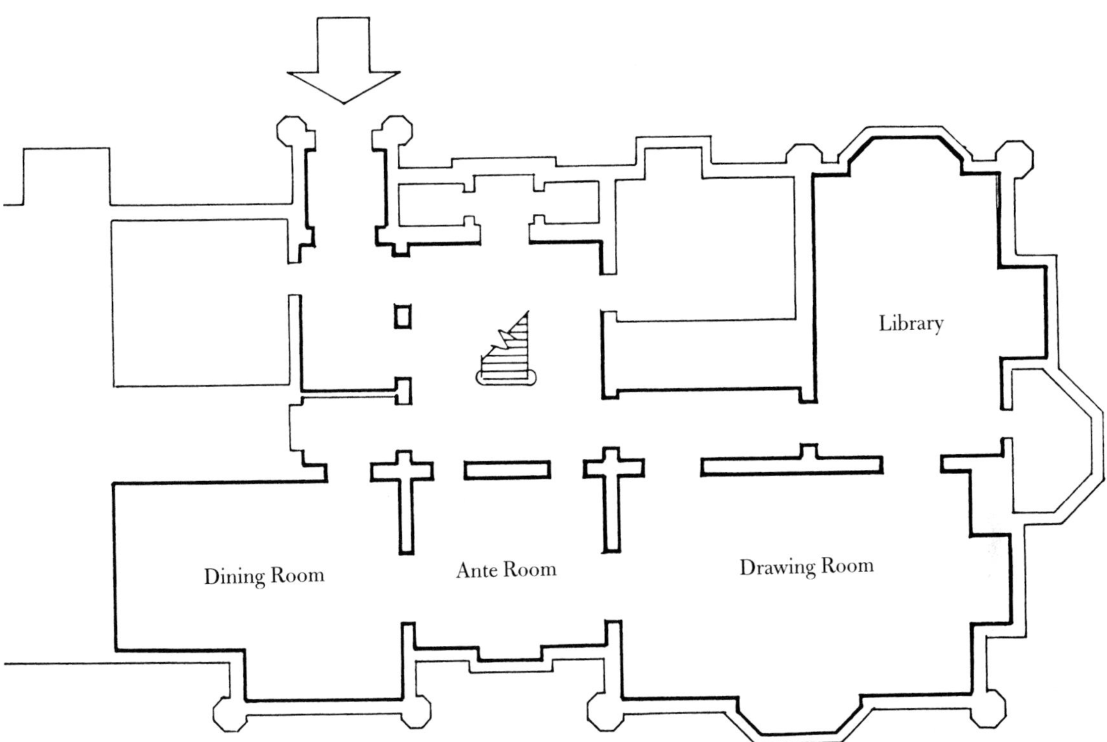

Figure 58. Plan of Tregothnan, Cornwall.

Strawberry Hill and Fonthill it seems as if it is part of a more general move in the direction of the gothic, and it is interpreted as, and therefore becomes, a precursor of the gothic revival, and it was eventually modified to make this interpretation more certain. Nash certainly made use of Downton's formula in the production of designs in the gothic style, and it has indeed contributed to the gothic revival exactly because it has been understood as a building in the gothic style. Once the gothic tracery had been added to the windows, then it was without ambiguity a gothic revival building. This is not necessarily a problem, but to see the building in this way is to see it quite differently from how Knight saw it.

This demonstrates that the meaning of the building is not intrinsic in the forms, that the architect's beliefs and intentions are not embodied in the stone, but remain as ideas associated in his mind. The meaning is inferred by the observer, and within a given culture there are recognised clues and signals as to which associations of ideas should be made. Knight did not deploy his signals with any great degree of success because his audience did not share his range of learning. If he

Figure 59. Charles Monck, Belsay Hall, Northumberland, 1807–17.

thought of battlements as somehow intrinsically classical, because he knew that they derived from classical sources, his visitors did not: for them battlements showed that the building was trying to evoke the Middle Ages, because for them battlements really did evoke the Middle Ages.

Knight's relationship with his audience was always problematic whenever he reached out beyond the elite circle with whom he might dine. The most sensational example was with the reception of *The Worship of Priapus*, which was appreciated and accepted within the Society of Dilettanti for whom it was intended, but met with scandalised derision when its existence became known to a wider public. Although Knight's last works remained decently obscure, *An Analytical Inquiry into the Principles of Taste* brought him a more appreciative as well as a wider audience. In it he said that he was not presenting original ideas, but was explaining his theoretical position on taste so that his remarks on the matter might be properly understood. The remarks were addressed to Price, in order to show how completely wrongheaded his aesthetic theory was. The demolition was done thoroughly and at times entertainingly, to the audience's apparent satisfaction; yet when Price's essays were reissued in 1842, their editor Thomas Dick Lauder added a critical apparatus which grounded Price's theories in associationism, which by then was an orthodoxy.[18] Had Price understood associationism, then the quarrel with Knight would never have

18 Thomas Dick Lauder, *Sir Uvedale Price on the Picturesque* (Edinburgh: 1842).

Figure 60. Charles Monck, Quarry Garden at Belsay, Northumberland.

arisen; and Lauder's version of Price is in effect a fusion of the practical advice from Price's essays with the Scottish aesthetics which Knight had propagated.

Authoritative taste

Knight's principal aesthetic doctrine was based on Hume's essay 'On the Standard of Taste' in which Hume argued that if one sensed beauty then one was feeling an emotion, a sentiment, about which there could be no argument. If beauty was not sensed then it was not there. Hume's ideas were known in academic circles, particularly in Edinburgh, and had formed the basis for Archibald Alison's more voluminous writings on aesthetics, but they had had relatively little influence in London when Knight published his thoughts. Hume's theory of taste made it a psychological matter: if each observer sees a different beauty, then one might expect each observer to form an individual sensibility and taste. However this was not Hume's position; nor was it Knight's, because if everyone's judgements were personal and had equal validity then Knight could have seen no role at all for arbiters of taste.

In order for taste to be seen as something more important than an aggregate of personal likes and dislikes it is necessary to make an appeal to some idea of authority, and the matter of taste thereby becomes in a sense political. Hume's philosophical theory of taste was accompanied by some sociological observations about the politics of taste, which he used to argue that despite tastes being individual and subjective, nevertheless some people's tastes had more prestige and importance than others. The reason for this lay in the division of labour. In a developed society people have their own varied specialisms, and do not all have the time or the sensitivity to develop a refined taste, and so in effect we delegate some members of society to do the investigation for us, and we accept their pronouncements on taste as more or less authoritative. That the members of society with the leisure and the ability to do this predominantly belonged to the wealthy and educated classes was theoretically incidental. Among the elite group of specialists in matters of taste there might be some room for dispute and contrary opinions, but it was not to be doubted that their taste was to be accounted the best. Knight fell securely into the category of person practised and skilled in making aesthetic judgements, and belonged to the class whose pronouncements were taken seriously as a matter of course; but in his ideal society taste would not have been a matter for experts and the need for them arose only on account of the specialism needed in a complex and vast modern state. In Homeric Greece every individual would have had, without considering the matter, perfect grace and taste, because the city-states were small, and every citizen a statesman. Adam Ferguson explained that the small republics of Greece,

> by their subdivision, and the balance of their power, found almost in every village the object of nations. Every little district was a nursery of excellent men, and what is now the wretched corner of a great empire, was the field on which mankind have reaped their principal honours. But in modern Europe, republics of a similar extent, are like shrubs, under the shade of a taller wood, choked by the neighbourhood of more powerful states.[19]

In the modern state the ordinary 'less enquiring' citizens, as Edmund Burke put it, receive their opinions 'from an authority which those whom Providence dooms to live on trust need not be ashamed to rely on'.[20] In a mass society everyone is doomed to live on trust so far as most issues are concerned, and in Knight's determination to investigate as many branches of knowledge as thoroughly as he could, we can see a symptom of his unwillingness to accept unchallenged the authority of others. It is another facet of his desire for the wholeness which he saw in ancient Greece: it led him first of all to strive to master the whole culture of his day, and then drastically to simplify his life.

19 Adam Ferguson, *An Essay on the History of Civil Society* (1767), ed. Duncan Forbes (Edinburgh University Press, 1966), p. 60.

20 *Reflections on the Revolution in France* (1790) in *The Works and Correspondence of the Right Honourable Edmund Burke*, 8 vols. (London: Rivington, 1852), vol. IV, p. 230.

Freedom from rules

The main point of departure between Knight and Hume was that Hume thought all educated judgements tended to a standard which was universal in human nature, and therefore there was a single universal standard of beauty, not because beauty could be defined in objective isolation from human sensibility, but because it could be grounded in a universal human nature. If the sensory make-up of mankind was everywhere the same, then it followed that proper considerations of the beautiful would have a rapport with it, and would tend to a universal standard.[21] Knight disagreed with this, arguing that a black African's idea of ideal beauty would be so completely different from the fashionable beauties in St James's that they could not possibly be adjudged by the same standard, and that moreover the 'African Venus' had a stronger claim to be thought the original ideal of beauty and therefore had the stronger claim to represent a universal standard.[22] He proposed that there was no universal standard of beauty, that these standards were culturally determined and subject to change.

In retrospect this seems to be an important step in the direction of the cultural pluralism which is an orthodoxy at the end of the twentieth century. We can see Knight's as an egalitarian sensibility, to contrast with Hume's. Where Hume was trying to reintroduce the established taste of his day as a universal norm in order to give new justification for what remained an aristocratic attitude to taste, we could see Knight as ushering in and promulgating a more individualistic bourgeois sensibility. This is not how it would have been understood at the time. Knight's interpretation would have appealed to some, but it would not have persuaded anyone who had been convinced by Hume's argument to abandon that position. 'There is a species of philosophy,' said Hume, 'which cuts off all hopes of success . . . and represents the impossibility of ever attaining any standard of taste.'[23] This would be the judgement of common sense, whereas it would take an uncommon understanding to see the permanent universal values which formed the basis of judgement in the art which was applauded by all nations at all times. The arguments which Knight presented would have seemed powerful to those who were inclined to agree with them, but unpersuasive to those who did not. There was no doubt that the common-place taste of the crowd was in a state of constant flux, but a very high-minded critic might rise above the fashion of the day. William Hazlitt, writing after the publication of Knight's book, still believed that he had to overcome the distracting

21 Hume, 'Of the Standard of Taste' in *Essays, Moral, Political, and Literary*, ed. Eugene F. Miller (Indianapolis: Liberty Fund, 1987), pp. 226–49; and see Richard Shusterman, 'Of the Scandal of Taste: Social Privilege as Nature in the Aesthetic Theories of Hume and Kant', in *Eighteenth-Century Aesthetics and the Reconstruction of Art*, ed. Paul Mattick, Jr. (Cambridge University Press, 1993), pp. 96–119.

22 *An Analytical Inquiry Into the Principles of Taste*, 4th edn (London: 1808), pp. 13–15; 97, 108; see also pp. 158–9.

23 Hume, *Essays*, ed. Miller, p. 229.

fluctuations of public taste in order to perceive the more durable works of art which would stand the test of time. He condemned the fashionable critics, whom he thought tended to follow public opinion rather than trying to guide and improve it. He called them 'common-place critics' and despised their common-sense judgements. Knight could not, even in Hazlitt's view, be called a commonplace critic, as he certainly thought for himself and made pronouncements which were not in line with public expectation, even flatly contradicting the most eminent authorities. Hazlitt's commonplace critics, though, had evidently picked up some ideas from Knight, who was just the type of person whose views they would respect (on account of his property and his tone of voice). Hazlitt compiled a long list of commonplace critics' views, presented as being wrong and dull and snobbish, boring Hazlitt when he was told once more that one could 'see no reason why artists of the present day should not paint as well as Raphael or Titian', or that 'there is something very elegant and classical in Mr. Westall's drawings'.[24] Knight did not carry opinion with him against the idea of universal taste. Hazlitt's commonplace critics said that it was 'difficult to prove the existence of any such thing as original genius, or to fix a general standard of taste', so the commonplace view in 1816 was perhaps vaguely supportive of Knight's contention, at the level of common sense, but very much less firm-minded about it. Knight's argument was that it was logically impossible for there to be a general standard of taste, not merely that it was difficult to find and that one had not yet been agreed.

In a broad view of the history of taste Knight's theoretical position is at an extreme of eclecticism. There was no single standard of beauty and therefore variant forms of beauty were possible, and there was no means to produce a permanent standard against which all work could be judged. What mattered was that the parts should make a harmonious whole, but it was important not to be trapped by 'system' into making foolish decisions. Even the Greeks were handicapped when they started to develop rules to regulate their architecture, while the gothic mason, who worked in the absence of rules and looking only to effect, could surpass them.[25] Knight abolished the idea of formal rules of any kind, which were as much of an obstacle to genuine art as ritualised forms of politeness were to genuine good manners. Genuine art, like genuine manners, should not be governed by adherence to rules about outward form, but should be graceful on account of being unaffected, they should be 'easy and negligent' without ever becoming 'coarse and slovenly'.[26] So Knight was tolerant of the wildest eclecticism provided that it was

24 Hazlitt, *Works*, ed. Howe, vol. IV, p. 139.

25 *Principles of Taste*, p. 176.

26 Ibid., p. 292.

unaffected and harmonious. He had no objection to the mixing of architectural styles in a single building, because there was precedent for it in the buildings which figure in the paintings of Claude and Poussin. Nor was it a problem for him if a building was, say, gothic outside and classical inside, which was how people took his own house to be decorated.[27] Knight's principles of taste were, in the end, almost no principles at all, but a directive to be high-minded and unaffectedly in touch with the genuine sentiments and passions of the mind. This is a Romantic theory, and could hardly have been more extreme. It belongs securely with the architectural eclecticism of John Nash and others of the age: the forms of buildings being adopted for the sake of the associations which they brought to mind. The only restriction is that the forms should be harmonious in their setting, and should belong to the place in which they were constructed, because otherwise a reaction of disgust would set in when the imposture was discovered. So perhaps Knight's principles would stop short of endorsing the wild extravagance of, say, the Brighton Pavilion (Indian outside, Chinese inside) which would be altogether too exotic for its setting. Nash learnt from Knight, but although he might adopt the practical advantages offered by reconciling convenient planning with a picturesque silhouette, it is unlikely that he was influenced by an understanding of Knight's more philosophical principles of taste. He would accept all the freedom they offered, and then some more besides.

Freedom was the central issue in Knight's aesthetics, freedom of expression in the absence of formal rules would give rise to the best possible works of all kinds. It was for this reason that he advocated particularly the work of the ancient Greeks, who had lived in a free society in touch with nature, before the development of formal rules in art. His study of the principles of taste was therefore concerned in the first place to restore this freedom, and its principal means of doing so was by showing how every accepted rule of art, even the most fundamental, was wrong. It was an attempt to clear the undergrowth, so that the fresh shoots of genuine unregulated creativity could flourish. It was a daring position to take, and shows a deeper understanding of and commitment to ancient Greek culture than that of most connoisseurs or artists who are more readily identified as neoclassicists. For Knight, the way to become Greek was not to imitate the antique, which the ancient Greeks themselves could not have done, but was to be as civilised as possible without losing touch with natural freedom: to harness the arts of civilisation in the service of the instincts.

27 Ibid., p. 225.

Doing well out of the Elgin marbles

The most extremely eclectic architect was Peter Frederick Robinson (1776–1858) who was responsible not only for the Swiss Cottage in St John's Wood, London, but also for the Egyptian Hall (Bullock's Chambers) which once stood in Piccadilly.

Robinson's style was picturesque, and could involve highly wrought changes in style from one building to another in a street, even if he designed the whole street to be built at one time. His aesthetics were of the associationist persuasion, in its least rigorous formulation ('it is generally admitted that the Parsonage should be erected in the old English character', etc.)[28] and his Grecian manner was as superficial as could be: 'it is well known that temples are the only existing building in Greece, and these but few in number, little can be done by the artists of the present day, than to apply porticos where favourable opportunities occur to introduce them'.[29] Robinson's culture was that of the successful practising architect, and his remarks expose the gulf between Knight's serious but arcane scholarship and Robinson's readily understood classicizing gestures. Robinson was the most commonplace of critics of classical architecture, but could blithely say that

> The fortunate acquisition of the Elgin marbles brought about an epoch of singular importance in the history of architecture in this country; and the opportunity thus afforded to our artists, by the liberality of the legislature, of studying the form and proportions of these wondrous productions of ancient art, together with the advantage, which may have been enjoyed, of visiting the superb temple from whence they were taken, to adopt it generally in this kingdom.[30]

The sculptures from the Parthenon were taken up by complacent philistines like Robinson as emblematic of the noblest taste, and Knight's reputation was completely ruined in the eyes of these people who were doomed to live on trust rather than think for themselves. There is a crueller irony yet, as it was in Bullock's Chambers, the Egyptian Hall, that Haydon had his final disastrous exhibition. He had shown genuine insight by recognising the sculptures' merits ahead of the crowd, but in arguing their case he poured scorn not only on Knight personally, but on the whole class of connoisseurs, who were the only people who might have commissioned large historical canvasses from him. He remained convinced that his paintings were works of genius, and that only the fact

28 *Designs for Village Architecture, Being a Series of Designs Illustrating the Observations Contained in the Essay on the Picturesque by Sir Uvedale Price* (London: 1830), notes to design no. XXXI.

29 Robinson, *Designs for Ornamental Villas* (London: 1825), p. 1.

30 Ibid., pp. 1–2.

that he had insulted the connoisseurs stood between him and recognition. The canvasses now look terrible, having most of the disadvantages of Westall's works with none of their charm or polish. Haydon lived embittered, in an increasingly wretched state of despair and poverty, coming to the conclusion that he could by-pass the need for the connoisseurs' approval if he made an appeal to a more popular audience, and to this end staged his exhibition in Piccadilly in 1846. The public flocked to the building in droves, because in another part of it T. P. Barnum was promoting a midget, General Tom Thumb. During the first week Barnum made £600, while Haydon made less than £8,[31] and Haydon, who was already seriously indebted and in a state of despair, bloodily did himself in with razor and pistol in his studio, having written a desperately tragic conclusion to his diary.[32] It was Robinson, not Haydon or Knight, who was fully attuned to the tenor of his times, and who actually made money by associating his work with the prestige of the Elgin marbles, something which Elgin himself had failed to do. When Robinson published a book of self-consciously 'picturesque' designs he did not acknowledge any influence at all from Knight, but gave it the carefully explanatory title: *Designs for Village Architecture, being a series of Designs illustrating the Observations contained in the Essay on the Picturesque by Sir Uvedale Price* (1830). By this time Knight's reputation was not helpful to the promotion of picturesque ideas.

'Utility' a problem

Knight's account of taste was more philosophically developed than any by his contemporaries in London, and was bracingly free from the standard judgements of polite society. Knight was not intimidated by reputation, and gave his own apparently unmediated views on artists of established merit, which could be astringent and dismissive. In presenting arguments to undermine the over-mechanical accounts of aesthetics given by Hogarth, Burke and Price, Knight adopted a knockabout style of argument, which is entertaining and effective, but which understandably left Price feeling hurt. In denigrating Michelangelo and Milton, Knight was on much less secure ground, as their works were already part of the canon, and a failure to appreciate them would tend to show a lack of discernment on the part of the critic. Curiously Knight's appreciation of Richard Westall's work would not have worried his readers at the time. There were members of the artistic elite of the day who had misgivings about Westall's work, but it was generally accepted

31 Eric George, *The Life and Death of Benjamin Robert Haydon, Historical Painter, 1786–1846,* 2nd edn, ed. Dorothy George (Oxford: Clarendon Press, 1967), p. 282.

32 Ibid., pp. 293 ff.

as being of the highest calibre, and Knight's enthusiasm for it would have lent credibility to his claims on their attention. It was his failure to recognise the secondary characteristics of Greek sculpture which led to his undoing, not his high valuation of Westall.

Knight's account of taste, and his sceptical and liberal conclusions, met with general approval. It remains, at a theoretical level, a remarkably astute account, and has a high degree of plausibility for a late twentieth-century audience raised on the uncertainties of postmodernism. Fredric Jameson has called postmodernism 'the cultural logic of late capitalism',[33] but it can be seen that the characteristic fragmentation and division, which generates first of all different areas of expertise and then different standards of judgement, was already in operation in the mid-eighteenth century: as soon as efficiency and the rate of production become important measures in a society, then the division of tasks and the development of specialised expertise proceeds apace. It is the role of an expert to have ventured beyond the horizon of common knowledge in order to report back to his fellows on the terrain which lies beyond their vision, and Knight did this convincingly enough to establish his credibility for a time, but the most important part of his report was that there were no firm principles to be found, only pearly mists and turbulent currents; only uncertainty and change. This was not particularly useful to the commonplace critics who wanted to be told what to think, who wanted to be able to tell from secondary characteristics what was tasteful and what was not so that they could praise and condemn with confidence and a good conscience. They supposed that there might yet be firm principles, but that Knight had not been the person to see them. Moreover, Knight's advice to artists was that they should act freely and not be under the influence of artificial constraints, which is good advice, but again it is not useful to the artists. If 'anything goes', then one is left in a state of indecision, and it is of far more use to the artist or the architect to be told to follow a certain limited range of formal principles, as it cuts down the need to think (which is the primary object of making divisions of labour). Therefore in the time which has elapsed between Knight's day and our own many theories have been advanced, which have been intellectually less substantial than Knight's, but which have briefly had more influence on account of their having, at least for a while, more practical benefits to offer the artist or architect who sought to act efficiently – in order to produce what passed serviceably enough as the high-minded art or architecture of the day.

33 Fredrick Jameson, *Postmodernism, or, the Cultural Logic of Late Capitalism* (Duke University Press, 1991).

The need for a public

Knight's account of taste assimilated Hume's, but of the responses to Hume he preferred those of Thomas Reid and other Edinburgh philosophers rather than Kant, whose views dominate twentieth-century accounts of Enlightenment aesthetics. They played no part in Knight's thinking, which was much more willing to accept uncertainty and change and the possibility of a multiplicity of ideals of beauty, at least at a theoretical level. This is not to say that he was in any danger of renouncing any claim to be able to make aesthetic judgements on behalf of others; far from it. He did not at any time transfer from his political thinking any idea that all aesthetic responses had equal value, because they were personal and sentimental. On the contrary, he retained the right to make his own pronouncements on matters of taste and expected others to accept them as authoritative. There was no confusion between the recognition that a work of art could be good or bad, independently of its popularity: artistic quality was not open to democratic dispute. Even if Knight's were the sole dissenting voice in the whole critical establishment, it would not have meant that he was wrong if he were relaying his own sincere independent judgement.[34] On the other hand the views of a Herefordshire farmer who had had little exposure to works of art and had spent little time reading philosophy would not have carried equal weight. Status accrued on account of the division of labour, and because different people specialise in different tasks.

This division of labour, here intellectual labour, gave Knight the authority to speak; but the authority of the public pundit has always had a very provisional legitimacy. It is not conferred by law, or by any official appointment; nor is it conferred irrevocably. The critic can make his pronouncements, but there is no public that is obliged to listen, and if the critic's authority is accepted, then it is because the audience allows itself to be told by him what it should think. The arrangement is sustained only for as long as the critic's claims to expertise in uncommon knowledge can be sustained, and any clear evidence of error is catastrophic.

34 Knight's views are implicit in what he said, but Hazlitt stated this position much more directly. His social views were more radical than Knight's, but even so he believed that the more popular a work of art was the more likely it was to be bad. When people knew which works of art were great, it was not from their own experience of the art, but because they had been informed by people with authority.

Discontinuity and the *flâneur*

In the time which has passed between Knight's day and our own, the number of divisions and specialisations has increased enormously, so that it is more difficult than ever to have a view of the whole. There are more pundits than ever before, with more narrowly defined constituencies. Recent attempts to take a wide overview, such as Jean-François Lyotard's widely noticed 'report on knowledge',[35] have tended to stress the awareness of discontinuity and lack of coherence as a distinctly recent trait, though it has certainly been in evidence for some time, and was seen to be embodied in the figure of the *flâneur*, whom Walter Benjamin saw as the manifestation of a distinctively new sensibility in Baudelaire.[36] The *flâneur* made his first appearance 1806, giving his opinion of pictures in the Salon at the Louvre.[37] He was to develop during the 1830s into a languid figure wandering the city in search of novelty, but in his earliest manifestations he seems to be a dilettante, making connections between the picturesque, philosophy and morality without producing actual works of art.[38] The division and separation of knowledge seemed already to be characteristic of a society which had taken a step away from a primitive state in Adam Ferguson's account of early industrial society,[39] but since 1767 the process has been carried very much further, and when we look back to the eighteenth century we must logically suppose that society was relatively unified. However, at the time the situation seemed as complex and as fragmented as it does to the best minds today. Knight's thought continually escapes the categories which a historian would most readily bring to bear on it now, but that was the case even in his own day. His own intellectual world was not identical with that of the commonplace critics of his day, who saw his house as gothic, his religion as pornography and who did not see his morals at all. There were, even within the critical establishment of his day, different cultures which set store by different things; so that when he argued in favour of Henry Fielding against Samuel Richardson (on the grounds that the former could write better) he was seen to be arguing against an author whose moral tales might influence his vast popular audience for the better.

Knight lived through a time of rapid and accelerating change which saw the industrialisation of the country, the abolition of the slave trade, revolutions abroad and the rise and fall of Napoleon. It was perhaps little wonder that he should have been inclined to see change as a constant, and to enshrine the idea in his thinking rather than look for ways to resist it. Everything in the modern world came to seem provisional, and Knight looked for stability and a stake in the future by communing with his forest and planting trees. Knight was a decathlete of culture: not pre-eminent in any single discipline, but doing surprisingly well across a broad range. Knight's thought belongs securely within the Enlightenment tradition, but he espoused these ideas a generation after they swept Europe with

35 François Lyotard, *Le condition postmoderne: rapport sur le savoir* (Paris: Les Editions de Minuit, 1979), trans. Geoff Bennington and Brian Massumi, *The Postmodern Condition: A Report on Knowledge* (Minneapolis: Minnesota University Press, 1984).

36 Walter Benjamin, *Charles Baudelaire: a Lyric Poet in the Era of High Capitalism*, trans. H. Zohn (London: Verso, 1983); Susan Buck-Morss, *The Dialectics of Seeing: Walter Benjamin and the Arcades Project* (Cambridge, Massachusetts: MIT Press, 1986); Eugene W. Holland, *Baudelaire and Schizoanalysis: The Sociopoetics of Modernism* (Cambridge University Press, 1993); *The Flâneur*, ed. Keith Tester (London: Routledge, 1994).

37 Priscilla Parkhurst Ferguson, 'The flâneur on and off the streets of Paris', in *The Flâneur*, ed. Tester, p. 26, referring to the anonymous pamphlet *Le Flâneur au salon ou M.Bon-Homme: examen joyeux des tableaux, mêlé de vaudevilles* (Paris: 1806).

38 [J. B. Auguste Aldéguier] *Le Flaneur* [*sic*], *galerie pittoresque, philosophique et morale* (Paris: 1826).

39 See pp. 4–5.

revolutionary force, so that instead of conversing with Hume he could only read his essays, and although Fox and Price did meet Voltaire, they did so when he was a venerable relic rather than an active force. Knight, whose outlook was shaped by reading Lucretius at an impressionable age, welcomed and absorbed Enlightenment ideas into his culture, but he made use of them in framing a way of looking at the world which was more concerned with the individual sensibility than with grounding thought in universal reason – an outlook which gave him more in common with the Romantics than his immersion in Enlightenment thought might at first lead one to suppose. His most significant achievement lay in piecing together a coherent view of the world; but he was not good at communicating this view, and it has been lost in fragments and footnotes distributed around his various works. If he had managed effectively to communicate it then he would long have been thought a great artist in some medium or other, and it is only in his landscape design that such a description could be sustained. His poetry has been thought bad, which it was not to any exceptional degree: it was ordinary, but when it is considered on its literary merits then it sinks without trace, along with most eighteenth-century verse. His house has earned him a secure place in architectural history, on account of its originality; the quality of thinking which went into it was excellent, and in the right light it can look evocatively Claudian, but it lacks the panache which Nash was to bring to bear on Knight's formula in his reworkings of the design. The garden at Downton, though, was an outstanding piece of landscape architecture which was much admired in Knight's day, and which attracted discerning visitors. It is now decayed, but this does not obscure its natural beauties, and steps are being taken to restore it to some degree. It was without doubt Knight's great work and, along with Homer, his abiding passion. However, even here there remains the problem that one appreciates the scene as the product of nature rather than the work of an ingenious eye and hand. Not until the landscape has been linked back to Knight's ideas can it be seen at least to some degree as it once was, part formed by his thoughts as well as our own.

Original legislation

Orpheus, like culture itself, was torn apart, limb from limb. The matter in which Knight was most skilled was the forging of links between ideas from different disciplines, in overcoming the scholarly division of labour, in resisting the professionalisation of knowledge, which, as specialisation increases, tends to mean that ever more of us are doomed to live by others' judgements in more parts of our lives, though we may be free to choose which expert's advice to follow. The values of the dilettante have been denigrated by professional culture over the last two hundred years in the name of excellence and efficiency, so that there is a general tendency to have a narrower expertise than at any time in the past, though it is disguised by the smattering of superficial information which easily finds its way into our minds. Knight made ready use of metaphor, because his thoughts frequently moved from one subject area to another, and he saw the whole of religion as a language of symbolic images which both conveyed and veiled meaning. If for his understanding of religion the most basic image was of fertility, the most fundamental for understanding Knight's morals was the image of the stomach, which had an appetite, but an appetite which could easily be satisfied, an image which he learnt from Epicurus. For understanding his intellect the key image was that of the pyramid of knowledge. These concepts are found in a realm of philosophical ideas and he used them in various practical applications; but he also used less generalised images from one area of interest to think about another: landscape, for example, was informed by politics, or politics by images of bodies of water. Associations between ideas, as Hume importantly determined, are external to the ideas themselves;[40] by linking ideas into a network we generate the world which we inhabit, or at least the part of it which is formed by thought. As the flow of unconfigured information continues to increase, we must find apt metaphors if we are to be able to deal with it. The beauty of Knight's range of metaphors is that they generated an illusion of coherence out of disparate material, and gave him an ability to deal with a wide range of subject-matter.

Of the Romantic poets, Knight has the most affinity with Shelley, who studied Knight's work on ancient mythology.[41] Shelley described a process whereby our ideas begin provisionally as metaphor: 'In the infancy of society every author is necessarily a poet, because language itself is poetry';[42] and poets

> are not only the authors of language and of music, of the dance, and architecture, and statuary and painting: they are the institutors of laws and the founders of civil society and the inventors of the arts of life and the teachers, who draw into a certain propinquity with the beautiful and the true that partial apprehension of the agencies of the invisible world which is called religion.[43]

40 Gilles Deleuze, *Empirisme et subjectivité: essai sur la nature humaine selon Hume* (Paris: Presses Universitaires de France, 1953), trans. Constantine Boundas, *Empiricism and Subjectivity: an Essay on Hume's Theory of Human Nature* (New York: Columbia University Press, 1991), p. x.

41 Marilyn Butler, 'Myth and Myth-Making in the Shelley Circle', in *ELH*, vol. 49 (Baltimore: Johns Hopkins University Press, 1982), pp. 50–72; Michael Rossington, '"The Voice Which is Contagion to the World": the Bacchic in Shelley', *Beyond Romanticism: New Approaches to Texts and Contexts 1780–1832* (London: Routledge, 1992), pp. 101–17.

42 Percy Bysshe Shelley, 'A Defence of Poetry', in *Selected Poetry and Prose*, ed. Alasdair D. F. Macrae (London: Routledge, 1991), p. 207, lines 97–8.

43 Ibid., lines 107–12.

Once they had been formed by poets, the metaphors were repeated ('mimickry with memory combined, / Could catch each note, and fix it in the mind', as Knight put it, in metric verse but less poetically than Shelley).[44] With repetition and mimicry by others the freshness of the original coinage is lost, and the metaphors become clichés, and inauthentic commonplaces; then, once they are utterly dead and have become ingrained in language they are seen as common sense and self-evident truth.[45] The poets in Shelley's account perform the same duties as the ancient Greeks in Knight's. They are seen as the creative individuals (Homer pre-eminent amongst them in both accounts) who, through being in touch with unformed nature can respond creatively to give voice to new concepts, which refresh not only art but the whole of civilised discourse. If the world is in a state of perpetual flux, then our ways of understanding it need constantly to be reinvented if we are to manage to keep in the swim, and even 'eternal verities' must constantly be reinterpreted if they are to be sustained. The coherence in Knight's thought comes from his ability to carry ideas from one field to another, as metaphor; so that, for example, his political thinking could become so thoroughly imbued with a sense of the landscape that it could turn into a poem about gardening. He would sense an expression of freedom in a flowing stream or in a Greek youth's sculpted head of hair. When the sun was low in the sky, and a scene gilded before dusk, paintings of a golden age would come to mind: honey oozed from the bark of oaks; gods and heroes walked the earth; and Orpheus was once more acknowledged as legislator of the world.

44 Knight, *Civil Society*, bk. I, lines 225–6, p. 12.

45 Shelley, 'A Defence of Poetry'; see also Paul Ricoeur, 'La Métaphore et le problème centrale de l'herméneutique (Résumé et summary)', *Revue philosophique de Louvain* 70 (February, 1972), pp. 93–112; 115; trans. David Pellauer as 'Metaphor and the Main Problem of Hermeneutics', *New Literary History: a Journal of Theory and Interpretation*, 6, no. 1 (1974–5), pp. 95–110.

Index